August 11-13, 2014
Glasgow, Scotland, UK

I0041869

**Association for Computing Machinery**

*Advancing Computing as a Science & Profession*

# ICER'14

Proceedings of the Tenth Annual International Conference on
**International Computing Education Research**

*Sponsored by:*
**ACM SIGCSE**

*Supported by:*
**SICSA\*, BCS, PLAN C and University of Glasgow**

**Association for Computing Machinery**

*Advancing Computing as a Science & Profession*

**The Association for Computing Machinery**
2 Penn Plaza, Suite 701
New York, New York 10121-0701

**Notice to Past Authors of ACM-Published Articles**
ACM intends to create a complete electronic archive of all articles and/or other material previously published by ACM. If you have written a work that has been previously published by ACM in any journal or conference proceedings prior to 1978, or any SIG Newsletter at any time, and you do NOT want this work to appear in the ACM Digital Library, please inform permissions@acm.org, stating the title of the work, the author(s), and where and when published.

**ISBN:** 978-1-4503-2755-8 (Digital)

**ISBN:** 978-1-4503-3258-3 (Print)

Additional copies may be ordered prepaid from:

**ACM Order Department**
PO Box 30777
New York, NY 10087-0777, USA

Phone: 1-800-342-6626 (USA and Canada)
+1-212-626-0500 (Global)
Fax: +1-212-944-1318
E-mail: acmhelp@acm.org
Hours of Operation: 8:30 am – 4:30 pm ET

Printed in the USA

# ICER 2014 Chairs' Welcome

We have great pleasure in welcoming you to the tenth annual International Computing Education Research Conference, ICER 2014, sponsored by the ACM Special Interest Group on Computer Science Education (SIGCSE). This year, our host city is Glasgow in Scotland.

This year's conference continues ICER's tradition of being the premier forum for computing education research, from discussions of preliminary ideas to presentation of contributions to the computing education research discipline. It also continues the more recent tradition of a doctoral consortium for students undertaking research in computing education. A new activity is introduced, the *critical research review*, an opportunity for researchers to bring, for example, research ideas, works-in-progress, and paper outlines to the table and receive feedback on them, as well as giving feedback to those of the other participants.

The call for papers attracted 69 submissions. All papers were double-blind peer-reviewed by members of the international program committee. After the reviewing, 17 papers were accepted (25%) for inclusion in the conference. There are also eight lightning talks, eighteen doctoral consortium abstracts and nine critical research review submissions, and we have authors and presenters from twelve countries: Australia, Brazil, Canada, Costa Rica, Finland, Germany, India, Israel, Pakistan, the United Kingdom, the United States and Uruguay.

As is traditional in ICER, the keynote speaker is from an educational background, but not a CS educational background, to spark thinking and discussion among the participants. David Nicol, Emeritus Professor of the University of Strathclyde, is in the forefront of thinking on formative assessment and peer review, topics currently very relevant in CS education.

The papers span a wide variety of topics, including the use of eye-tracking in computing education, studies investigating student behavior and success in CS1, outreach studies, a theoretical investigation of programs as dialogical entities, attitudes to academic integrity, analyzing student designs, and the development of instruments to measure self-belief and cognitive load for computing.

The chairs would like to thank the associate chairs and program committee for their work in helping us select a terrific program, as well as our supporters for their generous assistance. We are especially grateful to Simon for his excellent work in keeping us in line, once again.

**Quintin Cutts**
*ICER 2014 Chair*
*University of Glasgow*
*Glasgow, Scotland*

**Beth Simon**
*ICER 2014 Co-Chair*
*University of California,*
*San Diego*
*San Diego, USA*

**Brian Dorn**
*ICER 2014 Co-Chair*
*University of Nebraska at*
*Omaha*
*Omaha, USA*

# Table of Contents

## Session: Understanding Artifacts

## Session: Attitudes

## Session: Instruments

## Session: Doctoral Consortium

# ICER 2014 Conference Organization

**General Chairs:** Quintin Cutts *(University of Glasgow, UK)*
Beth Simon *(University of California, San Diego, USA)*
Brian Dorn *(University of Nebraska, Omaha, USA)*

**Associate Chairs:** Raymond Lister *(University of Technology, Sydney, Australia)*
Robert McCartney *(University of Connecticut, USA)*

**Submission Chair:** Simon *(University of Newcastle, Australia)*

**Lightning Talks Chair:** Colleen Lewis *(Harvey Mudd College, USA)*

**Doctoral Consortium Chairs:** Sally Fincher *(University of Kent at Canterbury, UK)*
Mark Guzdial *(Georgia Institute of Technology, USA)*

**Critical Research Review Chair:** Colleen Lewis *(Harvey Mudd College, USA)*

**Website:** Jan Erik Moström *(Umeå University, Sweden)*

**Local Arrangements Committee:** Rosanne English *(University of Glasgow, UK)*
Joseph Maguire *(University of Glasgow, UK)*

**Program Committee:** Alvarado, Christine *(University of California San Diego, USA)*
Armoni, Michal *(Weizmann Institute of Science, Rehovot, Israel)*
Astrachan, Owen *(Duke University, North Carolina, USA)*
Ben-David Kolikant, Yifat *(Hebrew University, Jerusalem, Israel)*
Boustedt, Jonas *(Hogskolan i Gavle, Sweden)*
Chen, Tzu-Yi *(Pomona College, California, USA)*
Chinn, Donald *(University of Washington, Tacoma, USA)*
Clancy, Michael *(University of California Berkeley, USA)*
Clear, Alison *(Christchurch Polytechnic Institute of Technology, New Zealand)*
Clear, Tony *(Auckland University of Technology, New Zealand)*
Cooper, Steve *(Stanford University, California, USA)*
Eckerdal, Anna *(Uppsala University, Sweden)*
Edwards, Stephen *(Virginia Tech, USA)*
Elliott Tew, Allison *(University of British Columbia, Canada)*
Fincher, Sally *(University of Kent at Canterbury, UK)*
Ginat, David *(Tel Aviv University, Israel)*
Guzdial, Mark *(Georgia Institute of Technology, USA)*
Hanks, Brian *(BFH Educational Consulting, USA)*
Hewner, Michael *(Rose-Hulman Institute of Technology, USA)*
Hundhausen, Chris *(Washington State University, USA)*
Kinnunen, Paivi *(University of Eastern Finland, Joensuu, Finland)*

**Sponsor:**

**Supporters:**

PLAN C

# Keynote Presentation

# Unlocking Learners' Evaluative Skills: A Peer Review Perspective

David J. Nicol

University of Strathclyde

Glasgow

United Kingdom

d.j.nicol@strath.ac.uk

## ABSTRACT

The recent literature on assessment and feedback in higher education emphasises the need to develop students' self-regulatory abilities. Students must be equipped with the skills to think for themselves, to set their own goals, to monitor and evaluate their own work in relation to these goals. They must also be able to carry out such regulatory activities in collaboration with others, for example, where performance goals and tasks are shared. A pivotal construct underpinning the idea of self-regulation and co-regulation is that of evaluative judgement. The capacity to regulate their own learning fundamentally depends on students having the ability to make valid and informative judgements about the quality of academic work as it is being produced. This capacity cannot be acquired through evaluative practices that are solely carried out and controlled by the teacher or where the primary conception of feedback is that of teacher transmission. In this keynote it will be argued that peer review is the most productive platform for the development of evaluative judgement and self-regulatory skills. Peer review is defined as an arrangement whereby students produce a written assignment and then review and write comments on assignments produced by peers in the same topic domain. The presentation will synthesise recent research and provide a set of research-based guiding principles for the design of peer review..

## Categories and Subject Descriptors

K.3.2 [**Computers and Education**]: Computer and Information Science Education – *self-assessment.*

## Keywords

peer review; self-regulation; evaluative judgement; feedback.

## 1. BIOGRAPHY

David Nicol is Emeritus Professor of Higher Education at the University of Strathclyde. He was previously Deputy Director of the Centre for Academic Practice and Learning Enhancement and Director of REAP, the Re-engineering Assessment Practices project (www.reap.ac.uk ), a £1m project examining how new technologies might support improved assessment and feedback practices in three Scottish Universities. David is currently an expert consultant to the JISC Assessment and Feedback programme and Visiting Professor at the University of Ulster and Swinburne University of Technology, Australia. David has published widely on assessment and feedback, on e-learning and change management in HE. He is collaborating with partners in Spain, Australia and the UK on assessment and feedback projects. Some of David's recent research on peer review can be accessed through the REAP website at http://www.reap.ac.uk/PEERToolkit.aspx

## 2. REFERENCES

[1] Nicol, D. 2014. Guiding principles of peer review: unlocking learners evaluative skills, In C. Kreber, C. Anderson, N. Entwistle and J. McArthur (eds). *Advances and Innovations in University Assessment and Feedback*, Edinburgh University Press, Chapter 10, pp197-224, ISBN 9780748694549

[2] Nicol, D., Thomson, A. and Breslin, C. 2014. Rethinking feedback practices in higher education: a peer review perspective. *Assessment & Evaluation in Higher Education*, 39(1), 102-122.

[3] Nicol, D. 2013. Resituating feedback from the reactive to the proactive, In Boud D. and Molloy E. (eds) *Feedback in Higher and Professional Education: Understanding it and doing it well*, ed.Oxon: Routledge, 34-49.

[4] Nicol, D. 2011. Developing the students' ability to construct feedback, Published by the UK QAA for Higher Education, Available here http://www.enhancementthemes.ac.uk/pages/docdetail/docs/publications/developing-students-ability-to-construct-feedback

[5] Nicol, D. 2010. The foundation of graduate attributes: developing self-regulation through self and peer assessment. Published by UK QAA for Higher Education and available at: http://tinyurl.com/ljdvy8b

ICER'14, August 11-13, 2014, Glasgow, Scotland, UK.

ACM 978-1-4503-2755-8/14/08.

http://dx.doi.org/10.1145/2632320.2632359

# Eye Tracking in Computing Education

Teresa Busjahn
Freie Universität Berlin
busjahn@inf.fu-berlin.de

Carsten Schulte
Freie Universität Berlin
schulte@inf.fu-berlin.de

Bonita Sharif
Youngstown State University
bsharif@ysu.edu

Simon
University of Newcastle
simon@newcastle.edu.au

Andrew Begel
Microsoft Research
abegel@microsoft.com

Michael Hansen
Indiana University
mihansen@indiana.edu

Roman Bednarik
University of Eastern Finland
roman.bednarik@uef.fi

Paul Orlov
University of Eastern Finland
paul.a.orlov@gmail.com

Petri Ihantola
Aalto University
petri.ihantola@aalto.fi

Galina Shchekotova
JetBrains
gshchekotova@gmail.com

Maria Antropova
JetBrains
maria.antropova@gmail.com

## ABSTRACT

The methodology of eye tracking has been gradually making its way into various fields of science, assisted by the diminishing cost of the associated technology. In an international collaboration to open up the prospect of eye movement research for programming educators, we present a case study on program comprehension and preliminary analyses together with some useful tools.

The main contributions of this paper are (1) an introduction to eye tracking to study programmers; (2) an approach that can help elucidate how novices learn to read and understand programs and to identify improvements to teaching and tools; (3) a consideration of data analysis methods and challenges, along with tools to address them; and (4) some larger computing education questions that can be addressed (or revisited) in the context of eye tracking.

## Categories and Subject Descriptors

K.3.2 [**Computers and Education**]: Computer and Information Science Education—*Computer science education*

## General Terms

Experimentation, Human Factors, Measurement

## Keywords

CS Ed Research; Code reading; Computing education; Empirical research; Eye tracking; Gaze analysis; Program comprehension; Programming education; Teaching programming

## 1. INTRODUCTION

This paper introduces eye tracking as an instrument for computer science education research. The approach builds on the outcomes of the 1st International Workshop on Eye Movements in Programming Education: Analyzing the Expert's Gaze [4], held in conjunction with the 13th Koli Calling International Conference in Computing Education Research [15]. The workshop brought together educators and practitioners to analyze how eye tracking and the rich data it affords could benefit programming education.

The observation of eye movements adds an objective source of information about programmer behavior to the collection of research methods in computing education which can be used to facilitate the teaching and learning of programming. Alternative approaches for gaining insights about learners' programming processes include analyzing the consecutive versions of assignments submitted for automated assessment [1], instrumenting student programming environments to record snapshots from compilation [18], and recording keyboard events in text editors [11]. All of these methods complement one another; augmenting them with eye tracking would provide a comprehensive view of the process of learning programming. While our focus in this paper is on programming education, eye tracking is a valuable instrument for other areas of computing education as well, *e.g.* understanding graphical data models [17].

This paper is organized as follows, the next section gives an overview of eye tracking technology, and presents previous work. In section 3, we describe our case study and the eye movement coding scheme. Finally, to address challenges we discovered in our study, we offer a set of ideas and tools to advance eye tracking in computing education. We conclude with an outline of ways in which eye tracking can help answer crucial questions in computing education.

## 2. GAZE IN COMPUTING

### 2.1 A Brief Introduction to Eye Tracking

Eye trackers are used to capture a user's eye movements when he looks at a stimulus while working on a task. In computing education, a programmer would be given a programming task to solve while looking at relevant source code. There are two important types of eye movements: the *fixation*, which is the settling of the eye gaze on an object of interest for a minimum period of time, and the *saccade*, which is a quick movement of the eyes from one location to another. Both fixations and saccades are voluntary, and indicate the location of the subject's attention. A *scan path* is a directed path formed by saccades between fixations. Processing of visual information occurs only during fixations [14], *i.e.*, as a programmer looks at programming constructs in code, various mental processes are triggered to solve the task at hand.

Eye tracking is a source of rich and valuable information which cannot be obtained by other methods. Conventional measures retrospectively record the accuracy of the subject's response and the time taken to obtain that response. For example, a programming educator will ask students to report their answers after debugging or tracing a program in a lab. This method records only the final outcome after the specific task has ended, neglecting information that might help understand how and why a student chose a particular (correct or incorrect) answer. Additionally, these measures raise a potential threat to the validity of the task, namely the difference between student responses upon completion of a task and the reality the student experienced while performing that task. In other words, a student may misreport an experience at the end of a long task, or may forget to report it altogether.

Researchers can address this issue by asking programmers to record their observations while working towards their answers. However, this has the risk of interrupting their work on the main task at hand. This same drawback exists even if explicit methods such as think-aloud are used, since they still distract the programmers from their core task. Moreover, subjects must be constantly reminded to verbalize their thoughts, since they do not often do so while they program in their natural setting. Even expert programmers find it difficult to state out loud exactly how they read a program. Many unconscious decisions go unreported, for example, encountering logical dead ends while reading a program.

Much of the critical information that is lost with traditional methods of measurement and assessment can be recovered using an eye tracker. There is nothing the programmer needs to wear in order for their eye movements to be recorded. Modern state-of-the-art eye trackers consist of a small hardware device that is placed near the programmer's monitor and can silently and unobtrusively document eye movements while the programmers looks at the screen. The additional data provides insights into the programmer's thought processes, and achieves a finer granularity of data capture across space (across the program) and time (as the task progresses) because tacit knowledge and understanding is made more explicit.

Furthermore, eye tracking makes it possible to take advantages of verbal accounts without the drawback of imposing additional cognitive load and interfering with the comprehension process at hand. Combining retrospective think-aloud with eye tracking, study participants initially work purely on their task (e.g. understanding source code). Once the task is complete, they are prompted to verbalize their thoughts, watching their recorded eye movements to aid their recollection [24, 13]. This technique makes complementary use of think-aloud and eye tracking and has been found to induce higher quality comments about cognitive processes. We strongly believe that eye tracking synergizes with other methods of assessing comprehension, and used together provides additional insights.

## 2.2 Previous Work on Eye Tracking in Computer Programming

Eye tracking has been studied in non-computer fields such as chess, reading, piloting [12], mammography [21], and surgery [25]. Here, we present an overview of work that has used eye tracking in programming research.

Crosby and Stelovsky [9] were pioneers of using eye tracking to study programmers. They found that programmers employed several distinct types of scan path patterns while they read an algorithm written in Pascal.

Uwano et al. [24] studied eye gaze patterns while five programmers detected code defects. They identified a pattern called *scan*, in which programmers appear to form an overview of the code. Approximately 70% of source code lines were viewed in the first 30% of the time spent reading the code. Sharif et al. [20] replicated this experiment with a larger sample of 15 programmers and found similar results. Programmers who spent less time to initially scan the code tended to take more time to find defects.

Fan [10] analyzed the eye gaze of programmers to learn about program ·comprehension processes used for beacons and comments in different tasks. Code scanning sequences were directly affected by comments, enabling programmers to chunk larger code blocks. Fan concluded that eye gaze data is very useful in documenting and analyzing the program comprehension processes.

Busjahn et al. [7] used eye tracking to compare natural language text reading and code reading. They found a significant increase in both fixation duration and number of backward movements when subjects read source code, indicating the different demands of these two text types and the reading patterns that they induce.

Bednarik [3] studied the differences between novices and experts during debugging using source code and graphical representations. He found that repetitive eye patterns were associated with less expertise; novices used both representations with a lot of context switching.

Turner et al. [23] conducted a preliminary study on 38 students to assess how the choice of programming language affected how programmers solve tasks. Looking at simple C++ and Python programs, they found a significant difference between the two languages for the fixation rate on buggy lines of code.

There have been a few studies using eye tracking to study programming, but none comprehensively analyze the relationship between raw eye movements and comprehension. It is extremely difficult to translate a person's eye movements into insights about his or her mental state while reading and understanding program [6]. We are confident that there will be more of these studies because of the diminishing cost of eye tracking. One of our goals is to raise awareness of the opportunities and challenges afforded by this technology in computing education research.

## 3. CASE STUDY

We conducted a case study to determine whether the use of eye tracking in computing education was feasible, could provide rich data for analysis, and could lead to novel teaching ideas. For details beyond those in this paper, please read our technical workshop report [4].

## 3.1 Experimental Setup

The eye movement data analyzed for the workshop came from a study with professional software developers reading and understanding short Java programs. We recorded them in an office at the programmers' company with an SMI RED-m 120 Hz eye tracker using the OGAMA tracking software.[1]

The recording sessions started with natural language texts followed by comprehension questions to familiarize the subjects with the instrument and the tasks. The subjects then moved on to examine Java code. After being informed that the code did not contain bugs, they were asked to read it, comprehend it, and answer a question to test their comprehension. The code segments were short enough to fit on a single screen without scrolling, to simplify the connection between gaze location on the screen and in the code.

The program read by the subjects (shown in Figure 1) calculated the area of a rectangle. Subject 1 was told to expect to answer a question about the return value of the `rect2.area()` method, while Subject 2 was told to expect a multiple-choice question about the algorithm in the code.

Each trace was given to the workshop participants as an AVI video showing the subject's current fixation location as a large red circle on top of the source code that the subject saw.[2] The prior five fixations were marked by blue circles whose size indicated the duration of the fixation. Blue lines joining the circles represented the saccades. The eye movements were quite rapid (and usually are), so the researchers could slow down the video to see all the gaze locations.

The two traces are very different. One might consider subject 1's gaze to be erratic. Viewed in real time, it flashes wildly about the code, generally spending very little time on any one point. However, when taken in total, there is a clear pattern of subject 1's eye returning to certain focal points. These points are pertinent to the question the subject was told to expect, but the fixations are so brief as to leave the analyst wondering whether if it was at all possible to gain any comprehension of the code. For example, in one 10 second span, the gaze shifts more than a dozen times between every method on the screen, typically spending less than a second on each point of interest.

By contrast, Subject 2 reads the code slowly and methodically, yet takes about 40% less time overall than Subject 1. We see evidence of linear scanning patterns, and very long gaze fixations on areas of interest. Whereas Subject 1 spent 10 seconds looking at every method on the screen, Subject 2 spent 10 seconds looking at a single variable declaration. In addition, after 1 second glances at the methods `height()` and `width()`, there was a steady 4 second gaze on `area()`, followed by another 8 seconds on the declaration of `rect2`. Our impression was that Subject 2 deliberately read through the code, understanding it the first time it was viewed.

## 3.2 The Workshop

We designed the Eye Movements in Programming workshop to bring together a number of researchers to consider various approaches of inferring cognitive processes from eye

---
[1]http://www.ogama.net
[2]These videos are available at http://www.mi.fu-berlin.de/en/inf/groups/ag-ddi/Gaze_Workshop/koli_ws_material.

```
 1 public class Rectangle {
 2       private int x1 , y1 , x2 , y2 ;
 3
 4       public Rectangle ( int x1 , int y1 , int x2 , int y2 ) {
 5           this.x1 = x1 ;
 6           this.y1 = y1 ;
 7           this.x2 = x2 ;
 8           this.y2 = y2 ;
 9       }
10
11       public int width ( ) { return this.x2 - this.x1 ; }
12
13       public int height ( ) { return this.y2 - this.y1 ; }
14
15       public double area ( ) { return this.width ( ) * this.height ( ) ; }
16
17       public static void main ( String [ ] args ) {
18           Rectangle rect1 = new Rectangle ( 0 , 0 , 10 , 10 ) ;
19           System.out.println ( rect1.area ( ) ) ;
20           Rectangle rect2 = new Rectangle ( 5 , 5 , 10 , 10 ) ;
21           System.out.println ( rect2.area ( ) ) ;
22       }
23 }
```

**Figure 1: Source code used for the workshop – overlaid with eye movements**

movements during source code reading. Prior to the workshop, the participants were given access to the two gaze traces described above. The workshop organizers developed a coding scheme for the gaze traces based specifically on the two eye gaze trace videos and the specific Java program, in order to broaden our knowledge of program comprehension strategies. We made a fundamental decision to distinguish between objective and subjective behaviors. At the most basic level, analysts using the scheme would objectively code the part of the program on which the programmer's gaze is resting. At the next level, they would use subjective codes to describe their inferences of the patterns of eye movement and the strategies being employed by the programmer to comprehend the code.

Each workshop participant individually analyzed the eye movement records (without any audio) and coded it using the ELAN video annotation software.[3] They each then wrote a position paper to describe the traces, to reflect on the validity and utility of our coding scheme, and to discuss possible applications of eye movement research for computer science education. At the full day workshop, participants explored their findings with one another, using their discussions to refine the coding scheme and plan further research.

## 3.3 Coding Scheme

The coding scheme used in the case study captures the objective eye tracking data as well as the coder's inferences about the programmer's comprehension of the source code. We present the coding scheme here to illustrate the possible outcomes of employing eye tracking in computing; it is not

---
[3]http://tla.mpi.nl/tools/tla-tools/elan

directly generalizable and should not be taken as a central contribution by itself.

We revised the coding scheme according to suggestions given by the participants in their position papers, and further refined it during the workshop (see report [4]). The scheme consists of a number of 'tiers', each of which can be coded with a choice of values. The tiers are summarized below.

**Line**: indicates the line of code the participant's gaze is on.

**Block**: indicates the block of code that the line is in. In a typical short code segment, the blocks might be the class `Attributes`, the `Constructor`, the `Main` method, or any other method.

**SubBlock**: some blocks have identifiable sub-blocks in which a reader's gaze might rest. For example, a method may contain sub-blocks of `Signature`, `Body`, `Method Call`, and `Return`. While the latter two statements are part of the method body, we code them separately because their importance makes them likely to be the focus of the reader's concentration.

**Signature**: when the gaze rests on the signature sub-block, this tier further indicates whether it dwells on the method `Name`, its `Return Type`, or its `Formal Parameter List`.

**Method Call**: when the gaze rests on a method call, this tier is used to indicate whether it focuses on the method's `Name` or its `Actual Parameter List`.

These first five tiers refer to the gaze location at a single point in time. They can be coded objectively and automatically based simply on the eye gaze location on the screen.

The next tier of the coding scheme, **Pattern**, identifies particular combinations of the observed fixations. For example, in the pattern we call `Flicking`, the gaze flicks back and forth between two (or possibly more) identified gaze points. Specific instances of this pattern may flick between the actual and formal parameter lists of a method call and its declaration, between the use and declaration of a variable, or between different locations where a variable is used. Other patterns include `Linear Scan`, in which the gaze moves linearly through some part of the code; `Jump Control`, in which gaze follows the code in execution order; and `Thrashing`, in which the gaze leaps about all over the code with no discernible intent. To date, we have identified 11 patterns. While patterns are observable in the eye gaze trace, coders must make a subjective decision about the number of fixations to combine into a single pattern; thus, these patterns cannot be automatically identified without human intervention.

The final tier of the coding scheme, **Strategy**, relies on interpretation by the coder. The analyst uses these codes to determine the cognitive actions taken by a programmer comprehending the program. Some strategies tend to be associated with particular patterns, but there is no one-to-one relation between them. For example, the `Design at Once` strategy is often associated with a linear pattern and suggests the programmer is reading sequentially through part, or all of the code, to acquire an overall understanding. `Intraprocedural` and `Interprocedural Control Flow` follow the expected control flow of the program, which implies that the programmers is simulating program execution. `Test Hypothesis` involves repetition of a gaze pattern, suggesting increased concentration is needed to better understand a particular detail of the program. `Trial and Error` is essentially a `Linear Scan` pattern with faster reading, irregular jumps, and repetition. This code is used when the programmer is searching for some part of the code that will lead to an initial understanding. So far, we have identified 14 distinct strategies.

## 3.4 Interpretation of Results

Our analyses of the two traces proved extremely interesting. Subject 1, whose gaze we described as erratic, correctly answered the study question. Subject 2, whose gaze seemed to be more methodical, chose the wrong answer to a multiple-choice question about the code. Since both of these subjects were expert programmers, we think it is unlikely that the differences in the accuracy of their answers are directly related to the differences in their gaze patterns. Indeed, we would hope that Subject 2's wrong answer indicated a simple slip, rather than a failure to comprehend the code. Perhaps Subject 1 got his answer correct because his task was more specific than Subject 2's task. Subject 2 had to memorize more of the code and remember four specific variables (`x1`, `x2`, `y1`, and `y2`) in order to choose the correct answer. Nevertheless, it is clear that different experts can display entirely different gaze patterns while reading the same code for comprehension. This diversity was apparent in the traces, even though the program was very short, simple, and bug-free.

## 3.5 Lessons Learned

As we expected, we had to revise and refine the coding scheme during the course of the case study. Participants found using ELAN to code the low-level categories (*e.g.* `Block`) to be time-consuming and inconsistent, and wished for a tool to automate this step.

The distinction between patterns as objective, observable behavior and strategies as the associated cognitive processes was valuable. However, the coding process is necessarily subjective and the coders could not be definitive about the readers' cognitive processes. Perhaps at this early stage of the research, it would be beneficial to complement the eye movement analysis with other methods, such as retrospective think-alouds.

Our aim is to correlate the subjects' cognitive strategies with observable patterns, so that we might use the pattern to identify the strategy being applied. This would make strategy coding less subjective, but is going to require a great deal more analytical work before it becomes feasible.

One threat to the validity of our coding scheme is that we based it on just two expert gaze traces of one program. However, we believe that our collaborative experiment has helped us establish a foundation that supports additional data analysis and the elaboration and development of more sophisticated analysis methods and materials. Future studies that vary programs, problem domains, and test subjects will enable the research community to refine and improve our expanded understanding of the cognitive processes involved in program comprehension.

## 4. DATA ANALYSIS - CHALLENGES AND SOLUTIONS

In this section, we discuss the challenges raised in the case study and explain how we addressed them. We present several tools to support interpretation of eye movement data and of records annotated with the coding scheme. Even though the interpretation of eye gaze data is not entirely straightforward, our workshop made it clear to us that the main challenges are already well understood.

Eye tracking videos are useful for spot-checking specific points in an experiment (e.g., did the subject look in region $X$ at time $T$), but it is not easy to get a big picture sense of the subject's behavior or to compare it with other subjects' behaviors. Static visualizations like heatmaps and fixation scatter plots can provide such global pictures, but these fail to capture the dynamics and nuances of subject behavior. Accurate eye tracking data interpretation requires additional tools and methods to combine the various views that arise during the analysis.

## 4.1 Visualizing Annotated Gaze Records

Here we present several tools to help interpret data annotated with ELAN-assigned codes. First, we present an eye movement flow chart in Figure 2, made using the D3.js library. This flow chart represents a graphical Markov chain of the elements in the coding scheme. Flow charts can help analysts find and understand eye gaze patterns, and can also be used in exploratory analysis.

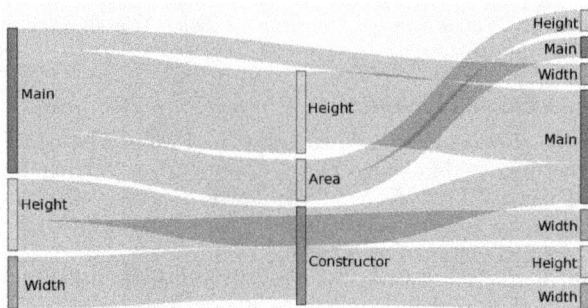

Figure 2: Gaze transition flow chart for Subject 1

The curved lines in the chart represent transitions of the subject's eye gaze from a source (left) to a target (right). The chart in Figure 2 shows two consecutive transitions. The width of the curved lines indicates the fraction of times (*i.e.*, probability) the subject transitioned from the particular source to that particular target. For example, Subject 1 looked at `Main` and then `Height` about twice as often as he did from `Main` to `Area`. However, after looking at `Area`, he switched back to `Main` and `Height` roughly the same fraction of times. We can use the flow charts to compare subjects and easily see the differences in their transition probabilities. Subject 1's flow chart shows many narrow transitions between code locations, while Subject 2's flow chart (see report [4]) shows fewer, wider lines between consecutive code locations reflecting his more methodical comprehension style.

Second, we introduce VETtool[4] which can read a file of ELAN annotations (*i.e.*, the codes from the coding scheme) and display them on a timeline based on the duration of the associated fixations. After using ELAN to assign low-level codes (*e.g.*, `Signature`), VETool's visualization can show the areas of the program that were visited during the trial.

---
[4]VETool is GPLv2 software built on the NetBeans Platform with JavaFX. The source code can be found at **https://bitbucket.org/orlovpa/visual-evaluation-tool-vetool**.

Several codes can be presented together, allowing the analyst to see the timeline of the areas of interest (AOIs) overlaid with the patterns and strategies employed to understand them.

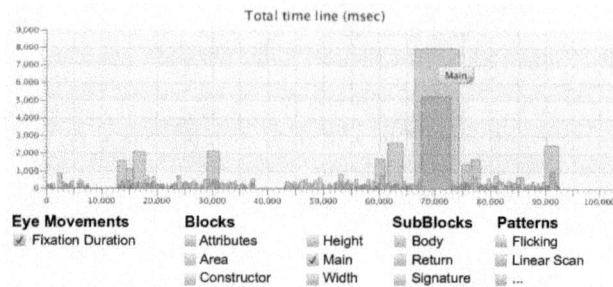

Figure 3: VETool displaying fixation durations (orange) and `Main` codes (green) for Subject 1

VETool also enables analysts to correlate fixation counts and durations with various low-level, pattern, or strategy codes, helping determine whether the subject was just briefly inspecting an area or examining it at length. Visualizing these correlations make it easier to compare two subjects by highlighting differences in their behavior. Figure 3 shows subject 1 concentrating on `Main` overlaid with fixation duration.

## 4.2 Quantizing Fixations

Next, we describe two static visualizations that we developed for understanding program comprehension. The first transforms fixations into coarse-grained areas of interest, such as single code elements, lines of code or blocks. The second plots the areas of interest (or metrics derived from them) on a timeline.

The workshop participants found coding the gaze location into code elements and blocks to be tedious and error-prone. Automatically coding these tiers would address a primary challenge of the eye tracking data analysis process [6]. So, we created a tool to draw virtual rectangles around areas of interest and assign each fixation to zero or more AOIs. Each AOI rectangle is then associated with the source code on the screen that represents each of the low-level codes in the coding scheme (*e.g.*, `Block`, `Line`, `Method Call`, etc.). For simplicity, assume that the AOI rectangles for the `Block`, `SubBlock`, `Signature`, and `Method Call` categories do not overlap, making them mutually exclusive (this is not the case for `Pattern`).

Figure 4: Sample assignment of a fixation to an AOI

To determine whether or not a fixation belongs to an AOI, the tool draws a circle around the center of the fixation point with radius $R$, and chooses the AOI rectangle with the largest area of overlap (Figure 4). The choice of the parameter $R$ influences accuracy and depends on other parameters such as the size of the computer monitor and font size used in the experiment.

Once fixations from the eye gaze record have been assigned to AOIs (and thus the low-level codes in the coding scheme),

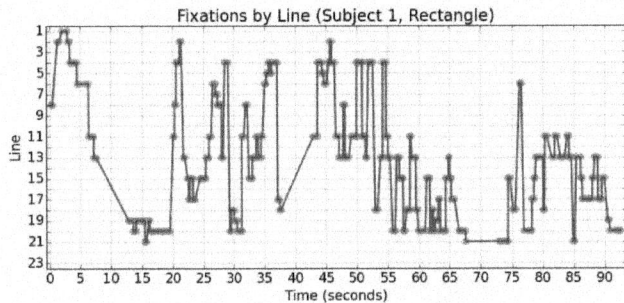

Figure 5: Fixations for Subject 1 quantized by line

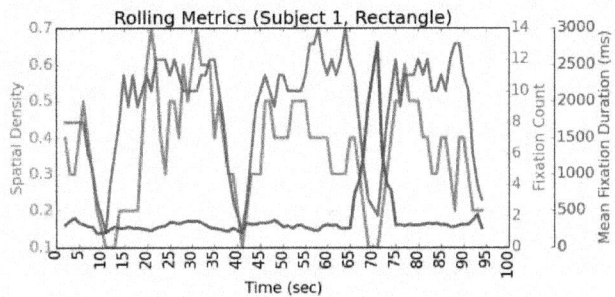

Figure 6: Fixation metrics for Subject 1

we plot them on a timeline. The timeline plot in Figure 5 shows Subject 1's fixations, quantized by `Line` using $R = 20$ pixels. These plots provide a wealth of information about a participant's behavior at a glance, enabling analysts to easily identify critical moments in the eye gaze record.

The AOI quantization tool is based on a graphical analysis of the eye gaze pixel locations on the screen. Its ability to track AOIs does not work so well on screens that contain scrolling or changing content. Applying it to IDEs in which the subject may scroll or type new code is simply infeasible for non-trivial programs and tasks [6]. Fortunately, there are IDE add-ons that can help, such as the iTrace plugin for Eclipse.[5] iTrace provides the exact source code entity a programmer looks at. Linking the eye tracker output directly to the IDE enables us to use the plugin to automatically annotate the eye gaze information with the correct program elements, solving the scrolling problem and the problem of adding or editing code.

Automatic code labeling facilitates aggregation of the data, which is valuable for group comparisons. In addition, if defined formally enough, pattern codes can be automatically derived from the low-level labels. For example, the `Linear Scan` pattern is readily apparently on a timeline plot. In Figure 5, we might say that `Linear Scan` describes the fixations between 2 and 20 seconds. We caution that someone should review the results because noise in the raw gaze data might have resulted in an incorrect classification of an AOI or low-level code, throwing off the pattern detector.

Finally, automatically labeling codes from our scheme offers a foundation for comparing results from future studies of eye tracking in computing education. We invite computing education researchers to apply our coding scheme in their own studies.

## 4.3 Strategies and Fixation Metrics

To aid in the identification and interpretation of Strategy codes, we compute three fixation metrics over the course of each trial: fixation count, mean fixation duration [19], and fixation spatial density [8]. We calculate each using a moving average of 4 second time windows, shifted by 1 second at a time. Typically, a single 4 second time window will contain about a dozen fixations.

The first metric is simply the total number of fixations in a time window. The second is the average duration of these fixations. The third metric divides the screen into a grid, and calculates the proportion of cells in the grid

that contain at least one fixation. We applied a 10-cell, vertically-divided, rectangular grid to the source code editor, so a spatial density of 1 means that each rectangle in the grid was fixated upon at least once during the 4 second time window.

Finally, we plot the metrics (after removing time windows which contain no fixations) on a timeline. Figure 6 illustrates the three metrics computed from Subject 1's trial. Dips in the spatial density (shown on the red line) correspond to time windows in which Subject 1 focused on just one or two lines of code. Sometimes this corresponds with an increase of the number of fixations (blue line), we found to be useful to distinguish between `Debugging` and `Test Hypothesis` Strategy codes.

Subject 1's erratic gaze is revealed by the very low mean fixation duration (green line), however, we see it increase sharply just after 70 seconds into the trial when Subject 1 focuses his gaze on the final line of the program: `System.out.println(rect2.area());` Recall that his task in this trial was to obtain the value of `rect2.area()`. Given the increased mean fixation duration, and the drop in fixation count and spatial density at approximately 65-75 seconds, we hypothesize that Subject 1 is performing the necessary mental calculation to compute the area of `rect2`. While it may not be possible to pinpoint changes in strategy using this kind of visualization, we can quickly identify interesting time windows that we should investigate further.

## 5. PROSPECTS FOR PROGRAMMING EDUCATION

Eye tracking offers opportunities for a great range of research questions in the areas of programming education and program comprehension. Possible research topics include

- the effects of text-based, graphical, or UML program representations [26]; syntax and language features; programming paradigms;
- the behaviors and strategies of a learner's reading, understanding, writing and debugging tasks'
- challenges for learners, *e.g.*, what makes tasks difficult for them, what obstacles impair their understanding and use of programming concepts;
- evaluation of tools for static and dynamic program visualization [5], as well as for IDEs [3]; and
- gaze-related concerns, *e.g.*, exploring the possibility of providing immediate feedback based on eye movements in programming environments [2].

---
[5]`http://www.csis.ysu.edu/~bsharif/iTrace`

These topics can lead to advances in teaching programming in the following areas.

## 5.1 Decoding the Learner

Eye tracking allows us to retrace how the novice goes about reading and understanding source code. We can obtain information about difficulties, behavior and strategies, and develop new tools to assess learners. In addition, we can describe and evaluate an individual's level of expertise on the basis of aggregated empirical studies of eye tracking that compare novice and expert programmers.

## 5.2 Advances in Teaching Material and Tools

The detailed data provided by eye trackers can also help to advance learning tools, such as IDEs for learning programming. Eye tracking is a well-established instrument in usability testing with a large corpus of analyses, metrics and examples of best practice. Applying eye tracking can help developers increase tool usability and lower the barriers to adoption. More sophisticated uses of eye tracking could provide highly-contextualized feedback to the learner, for example in an automated tutor. If an eye tracking metric moves past a particular threshold, it could indicate that the student is having difficulties with the material, and could use a hint in order to make progress. Visual cueing could be employed in an IDE, if students look too long at the wrong section of code, or thrash their gaze over the entire program without focusing on any particular part.

## 5.3 New Perspectives for Teaching Code Reading

Eye tracking studies can be used to shed light on how individuals conceptualize and discern the embedded process of computational representations. A crucial challenge yet to be solved is to explore the code reading characteristics of individuals. First a normative or generalized pattern needs to be established, e.g., a program flow gaze pattern for specific source code examples. After taking into account the learner's ability or level of understanding or the difficulty of the task, individual deviations from this normative eye gaze pattern can be used to reveal meaningful information about the concrete learning process.

These normative eye gaze patterns can help identify differences in the strategies adopted by programmers with various levels of expertise, domain knowledge, and skills. Given that the ability to read and comprehend code seems to be linked with the ability to write it, there is substantial evidence that many programming novices have not yet acquired the ability to effectively read programs [16]. As with natural language, concrete code reading skills can explicitly be taught to learners, addressing purposes like debugging code or working out why it is written that way. It is hard to do this now because reading and debugging strategies are so ingrained that people are not aware of them on a conscious level.

Eye tracking could be used to raise a novice's awareness of how they go about reading code. A novice could track himself solving a task, and later understand how what he was thinking corresponded with where he was looking. This would build a novice's self-awareness and facilitate the meta-cognition that eventually teaches a beginner to read code efficiently.

We can use eye gaze data to explore experts' strategies and develop teaching materials demonstrating their application.

Novices observing expert programmers' eye movements on a given task could get visual cues as to what is important [22]. This might lead to the creation of a tool for teaching reading skills that shows the student where to look, an approach that has proved successful in other domains [25]. If students could be taught to consciously use code reading strategies according to code size, program structure and other parameters, they could see how to make their own approach more effective. After they have been taught these reading techniques, teachers can use eye tracking to verify that students are using them, enabling better assessment of teaching interventions.

From our workshop examples, we saw that experts can read the same code using very different strategies. Therefore, the ones offered to learners should be those that were used consistently by many expert programmers. Individual students could then adopt a strategy that fits well with their own personal approach.

## 6. CONCLUSIONS AND FUTURE WORK

In this paper, we have presented eye tracking as a method to enrich computing education research. Tracking a person's gaze gives a record of their visual behavior on a super fine-grained scale in both space and time. We can build on the small, but growing, body of sound work on eye tracking in the context of programming to enhance programming education practice and research. Eye tracking has the potential to open up new methods of understanding how people program and learn to program, of corroborating existing empirical research, and of tackling currently unsolved questions. Its benefits will stretch across broad areas of research, such as program reading and comprehension, and afford new teaching material for aspects of professional expertise that have not yet been analyzed.

Gaze analysis offers intriguing prospects for further study. Eye tracking can record a person's visual behavior during reading, without interruption, adding to his cognitive load, or requiring a subjective report. Thus, this research tool provides a new quality and directness, along with a much finer data granularity, to observe cognitive processing.

Gaze analysis can also serve as an additional source of data to corroborate studies carried out with other research methods. Such study replications will help to increase our collective evidence and sharpen our theories. With more and more of the challenges associated with eye tracking being solved, with eye trackers becoming more affordable, and with relevant analytical tools becoming increasingly available, such studies might even become a standard in educational research.

Our Eye Movements in Programming workshop and this paper are a first step towards making eye tracking more accessible to computing educators. When a dozen experts in computer science education and eye tracking can agree on the potential of using eye movement data in programming education, their position must surely have some merit.

## 7. ACKNOWLEDGMENTS

We would like to thank all workshop participants for their great work.

# 8. REFERENCES

[1] A. Allevato and S. H. Edwards. Discovering patterns in student activity on programming assignments. In *ASEE Southeastern Section Annual Conference and Meeting*, 2010.

[2] V. M. G. Barrios, C. Gütl, A. M. Preis, K. Andrews, M. Pivec, F. Mödritscher, and C. Trummer. Adele: A framework for adaptive e-learning through eye tracking. In *Proc. of IKnow*, volume 4, pages 1–8. Citeseer, 2004.

[3] R. Bednarik. Expertise-dependent visual attention strategies develop over time during debugging with multiple code representations. *International J. of Human-Computer Studies*, 70(2):143–155, 2012.

[4] R. Bednarik, T. Busjahn, and C. Schulte. Eye movements in programming education: Analyzing the expert's gaze. Technical report, University of Eastern Finland, Joensuu, Finland, 2014.

[5] R. Bednarik, N. Myller, E. Sutinen, and M. Tukiainen. Effects of experience on gaze behavior during program animation. In *Proc. of 17th Annual Workshop of the Psychology of Programming Interest Group*, pages 49–61, Sussex University, 2005.

[6] R. Bednarik and M. Tukiainen. An eye-tracking methodology for characterizing program comprehension processes. In *Proc. of the Symposium on Eye Tracking Research & Applications*, pages 125–132. ACM, 2006.

[7] T. Busjahn, C. Schulte, and A. Busjahn. Analysis of code reading to gain more insight in program comprehension. In *Proc. of the 11th Koli Calling International Conference on Computing Education Research*, pages 1–9, Koli, Finland, 2011. ACM.

[8] L. Cowen, L. J. Ball, and J. Delin. An eye movement analysis of web page usability. In *People and Computers XVI-Memorable Yet Invisible*, pages 317–335. Springer, 2002.

[9] M. E. Crosby and J. Stelovsky. How do we read algorithms? A case study. *Computer*, 23(1):24–35, 1990.

[10] Q. Fan. *The effects of beacons, comments, and tasks on program comprehension process in software maintenance*. PhD thesis, University of Maryland at Baltimore County, Catonsville, MD, USA, 2010.

[11] J. Helminen, P. Ihantola, and V. Karavirta. Recording and analyzing in-browser programming sessions. In *Proc. of the 13th Koli Calling International Conference on Computing Education Research*, pages 13–22, Koli, Finland, 2013. ACM.

[12] V. A. Huemer, M. Hayashi, F. Renema, S. Elkins, J. W. McCandless, and R. S. McCann. Characterizing scan patterns in a spacecraft cockpit simulator: Expert vs. novice performance. *Proc. of the Human Factors and Ergonomics Society Annual Meeting*, 49(1):83–87, Sept. 2005.

[13] A. Hyrskykari, S. Ovaska, P. Majaranta, K.-J. Räihä, and M. Lehtinen. Gaze path stimulation in retrospective think-aloud. *J. of Eye Movement Research*, 2(4):1–18, 2008.

[14] M. Just and P. Carpenter. A theory of reading: From eye fixations to comprehension. *Psychological Review*, 87:329–354, 1980.

[15] M.-J. Laakso and Simon, editors. *Proceedings of the 13th Koli Calling International Conference on Computing Education Research*, November 2013.

[16] R. Lister, C. Fidge, and D. Teague. Further evidence of a relationship between explaining, tracing and writing skills in introductory programming. *SIGCSE Bulletin*, 41(3):161–165, 2009.

[17] J. C. Nordbotten and M. E. Crosby. The effect of graphic style on data model interpretation. *Information Systems J.*, 9(2):139–155, 1999.

[18] C. Piech, M. Sahami, D. Koller, S. Cooper, and P. Blikstein. Modeling how students learn to program. In *Proc. of the 43rd ACM Technical Symposium on Computer Science Education*, SIGCSE '12, pages 153–160, NY, USA, 2012. ACM.

[19] A. Poole and L. J. Ball. Eye tracking in human-computer interaction and usability research: Current status and future. In *Prospects, Chapter in C. Ghaoui (Ed.): Encyclopedia of Human-Computer Interaction. Pennsylvania: Idea Group, Inc*, 2005.

[20] B. Sharif, M. Falcone, and J. Maletic. An eye-tracking study on the role of scan time in finding source code defects. In *Proc. of the Symposium on Eye Tracking Research & Applications*, pages 381–384, Santa Barbara, CA, 2012. ACM.

[21] S. Sridharan, R. Bailey, A. McNamara, and C. Grimm. Subtle gaze manipulation for improved mammography training. In *Proc. of the Symposium on Eye Tracking Research & Applications*, pages 75–82, Santa Barbara, California, 2012. ACM.

[22] R. Stein and S. E. Brennan. Another person's eye gaze as a cue in solving programming problems. In *Proc. of the 6th international conference on Multimodal interfaces*, pages 9–15, PA, USA, 2004. ACM.

[23] R. Turner, M. Falcone, B. Sharif, and A. Lazar. An eye-tracking study assessing the comprehension of C++ and Python source code. In *Proc. of the Symposium on Eye Tracking Research & Applications*, pages 231–234, Safety Harbor, Florida, 2014. ACM.

[24] H. Uwano, M. Nakamura, A. Monden, and K.-i. Matsumoto. Analyzing individual performance of source code review using reviewers' eye movement. In *Proc. of the Symposium on Eye Tracking Research & Applications*, pages 133–140, San Diego, California, 2006. ACM.

[25] S. J. Vine, R. S. Masters, J. S. McGrath, E. Bright, and M. R. Wilson. Cheating experience: Guiding novices to adopt the gaze strategies of experts expedites the learning of technical laparoscopic skills. *Surgery*, 152(1):32–40, July 2012.

[26] S. Yusuf, H. Kagdi, and J. I. Maletic. Assessing the comprehension of UML class diagrams via eye tracking. In *Proc. of the 15th IEEE International Conference on Program Comprehension*, pages 113–122, 2007.

# In-Flow Peer-Review of Tests in Test-First Programming

Joe Gibbs Politz
Brown University
joe@cs.brown.edu

Shriram Krishnamurthi
Brown University
sk@cs.brown.edu

Kathi Fisler
WPI
kfisler@cs.wpi.edu

## ABSTRACT

Test-first development and peer review have been studied independently in computing courses, but their combination has not. We report on an experiment in which students in two courses conducted peer review of test suites while assignments were in progress. We find strong correlation between review ratings and staff-assessed work quality, as well as evidence that test suites improved during the review process. Student feedback suggests that reviewing had some causal impact on these improvements. We describe several lessons learned about administering and assessing peer-review within test-first development.

**Categories and Subject Descriptors:** K.3.2 [Computers and Education]: Computer and Information Science Education

**Keywords:** Peer-review, Test-first development

## 1. INTRODUCTION

In many disciplines with a craft component, apprentices learn from observing masters. Observing someone else's work and producing a critique of it helps develop critical facilities, which in turn can be applied to one's own efforts. However, programming neophytes usually lack the skills to even examine the work of a master (e.g., a beginning programming student likely has no hope of understanding the Linux kernel). What can students possibly review?

One very useful object of review is the work of fellow students. Reviewing peer work eliminates numerous variables that would otherwise make review difficult or even impossible: classmates typically use the same language, the same features, and work on the same problem. Indeed, studying the work of classmates on a problem can even help a student understand the problem better. If peer-review is then done *while* a problem is in progress, students can improve their understanding in a way that is immediately useful—this incentivizes reviewing effort. We call this *in-flow peer-review*.

One challenge with in-flow peer review lies in identifying sufficiently mature artifacts for early review. As educa-

tors who use *test-first* programming,[1] we find the point at which tests are submitted provides a natural review boundary. This moment is especially conducive for several reasons:

- Tests represent a student's understanding of a problem. Therefore, they can reveal incorrect and incomplete understanding. Reviewing at this stage therefore has the potential to set students on the right path for the remainder of the problem.

- Because tests—especially unit tests—are both (a) concrete and (b) usually understandable in isolation from one another, they can be easier to comprehend (and thus review well) than programs, which tend to be both abstract and full of subtle interdependencies.

- In some professional settings [12], tests are actually used as a means of communication. Submitting and reviewing tests reinforces this use.

- Reading others' tests might improve a student's abilities as a tester. Because testing is a vital part of modern software development,[2] and even a profession in itself, this enriches a career skill.

Our vehicle for in-flow peer-review of tests is CaptainTeach, an on-line environment designed to facilitate this process [13]. We have used CaptainTeach in two collegiate courses in the past year. Though CaptainTeach was used to provide feedback for more than test suites, including implementations, in this paper we focus on its effect on testing.

In-flow peer-review of tests raises several natural questions. Do students submit tests and reviews early enough to be of use? Do their test suites evolve during review? Are the reviews accurate and helpful? This paper explores the viability of in-flow peer review through these questions, while simultaneously reporting observations about the process. We believe this is the first study of in-flow peer-reviewing of any significant artifacts. In addition, while other projects have incorporated tests into peer-review (Section 5), we are not aware of prior work in which students review others' test suites themselves as standalone artifacts.

---

[1] We use the term test-*first* because students are asked to write tests before writing code. We do not follow the stronger test-*driven* [1] practice, which prohibits writing any code before tests have first been written and found to fail.

[2] One of the spaces at Google most likely to get an employee's attention—namely, the blank spaces that are stared at in restrooms—features a series of articles known as TotT: Testing on the Toilet (http://googletesting.blogspot.com/2007/01/introducing-testing-on-toilet.html). That is, when a major software company can best get its employees' attention, it emphasizes testing.

*ICER'14*, August 11-13, 2014, Glasgow, Scotland, UK.
Copyright 2014 ACM 978-1-4503-2755-8/14/08 ...$15.00.
http://dx.doi.org/10.1145/2632320.2632347.

## 2. ASSESSING TESTING

Traditionally, test suites are evaluated by code coverage. However, coverage is relative to a particular implementation, and is thus not meaningful for tests written before code. Instead, we must measure how well a test suite reflects the problem's intent. We use two criteria for this: *correctness* and *thoroughness*. Intuitively, correctness assesses whether tests yield answers that are consistent with the problem statement, while thoroughness assesses whether a set of tests covers the interesting inputs to a problem. In defining these criteria more rigorously, we will use two terms: a *test case* is a particular input-output pair that checks a single point in the space of a program's (or function's) behaviors; a *test suite* is a collection of test cases.

Students in our courses assessed correctness and thoroughness through peer-review; Section 3.1 explains the process. Our course staff independently assessed these criteria in assigning grades: in one course, this assessment was automated, as described in the rest of this section. (Section 4.3 compares the student- and staff-assessments.)

Course staff assess correctness using reference implementations, which we call *gold solutions*. An individual test case is correct if the gold solution returns the test case's output when given its input. Correctness is, however, insufficient to measure an entire test suite. To build intuition, suppose the programming task is to implement sorting. A weak test suite might check only a few small examples, and perhaps even only ones that are already sorted. These will all pass the gold solution, but do not represent a deep understanding of the nuances of the problem. Thoroughness fills this gap.

Staff assess thoroughness using buggy, or *coal*, solutions. Coal solutions have the same interface as the gold solution, and are usually designed to reflect a particular error. The deviation from correct behavior could be large, or it could be small and subtle. Coal solutions for sorting might include: the identity function (which "works" on already sorted lists); one that reverses its input; one that permutes the input list randomly; one that fails on empty lists; one that drops duplicate entries; one that adds arbitrary new elements (but in sorted order) to the output; and so on. A test case detects a coal solution either because (1) it expects a particular concrete answer but the coal solution yields a different answer or an exception, or (2) it expects an exception but the coal solution yields an answer or a different exception.

A test suite should act as a classifier, accurately labeling each program it is run against as gold or coal. This check can be automated, computing a test suite's grade as a function of the percentages of correct test cases and of coals detected. Section 3.3 describes the formulas used in the courses in this study. Of course, a student's test suite might also target aspects of her particular implementation: our gold/coal methodology works with any suite whose tests match the interfaces defined for the problem.

## 3. EXPERIMENTAL SETUP

We used CaptainTeach in two undergraduate courses in the fall semester of 2013 at Brown University (USA). One, which we label CS1.5, is an accelerated introduction to data structures and algorithms for first-year students that compresses the first-year curriculum into a semester, roughly like a "honors" course (though it is open to all students, and students place into it by doing extra homeworks in a regular introductory course). The other, which we dub CSPL, is an upper-level course in programming languages, attended by second-year undergraduate through graduate-level students. All programming was done in Pyret (`pyret.org`).

In CS1.5 the homeworks consisted of algorithmic tasks, often embedded in larger systems. Many assignments thus had multiple, ordered problems, each requiring both a test suite and an implementation. In CSPL, all assignments consisted of the implementation of a single significant function (interpreter, type-checker, garbage collector, etc.), and required a single test suite. Within each problem in both courses, the test suites and implementations formed distinct *steps* that had to be submitted *separately and in order* (Captain-Teach enforced this). In both courses, the staff provided the interfaces against which students wrote tests. While we *encouraged* students to write tests before implementations, we could not enforce the order in which they actually did their (offline) work. For each problem, students could submit one set of tests and one implementation for review before the deadline: we term these *initial* submissions. Subsequent submissions were recorded but not sent out for review. A student's *final* submission (for each of tests and implementation) was the last made before the deadline.

For various reasons (including the complexity of the assignments), we used gold/coal solutions in CSPL but not in CS1.5. Therefore, some of our analyses cover both courses, while others look only at CSPL. In particular, any reference to measured test-suite quality is limited to CSPL.

### 3.1 The Review Process

After submitting each step, students wrote reviews of work others did for that same step. With 50% probability, one review was of a staff-written gold or coal solution (with equal chance of being gold or coal). Other works presented for review were from classmates, chosen by picking the submissions with the fewest number of assigned reviews, breaking ties by picking earlier submissions. To have something to review for the first three students to submit, we seeded the system with three fake student submissions that were not designated as either gold or coal.

CSPL students wrote three reviews per step, while CS1.5 students typically wrote only two (they wrote three on one assignment). Each CS1.5 assignment had multiple interacting functions; students had to submit tests and bodies for each function before moving on to the next. Because these assignments had more steps, we asked for fewer reviews.

For test-suite reviews, students were asked to judge both correctness and thoroughness: each had a Likert-scale rating (required for submission) and a comment box for elaborating on their rating (not required for submission). The Likert scale had 6 ratings, from Strongly Disagree to Strongly Agree (with three positive and three negative options, and no neutral option). The two prompts were:

1. "These tests correctly reflect the desired behavior."
2. "These tests are representative of the possible inputs."

Submission for later steps was disabled while students had outstanding reviews to complete. Upon receiving a review, CaptainTeach sent email to the author of the test suite with a link a to page that displayed the review.

Despite other work that argues for detailed rubrics [10], we intentionally left ours unstructured. Because little prior work considers reviews of tests, we wanted baseline data on in-flow test reviewing that we could build on in future work.

## 3.2 Review Feedback

Students received two kinds of feedback on their reviews:

1. When students graded gold or coal solutions, Captain-Teach gave feedback on how they were doing. If their review was inappropriate (Slightly Disagree or lower for gold, Slightly Agree or higher for coal), they were informed of the discrepancy, whereas if it was appropriate (Slightly Agree or higher to gold, Slightly Disagree or lower to coal), they were informed of our agreement.

2. When reading a review, students could provide feedback to the reviewer. Submission of feedback was optional; we report on its frequency in Section 4.6. If students gave feedback, they had to fill out a Likert scale with the prompt "This review was helpful"; they could optionally also offer free-form comments.

## 3.3 Grading and Motivation

In addition to written feedback from course staff, CSPL students also received a single numeric grade for their test suite. This was computed using the gold and coals. As a baseline, we took the thoroughness (proportion of coal tests caught) of a suite. We then subtracted two percentage points for *each test case that failed* when run against the gold implementation. We did this instead of counting the number or proportion of tests that passed the gold implementation since this rewards "stuffing" the test suite with redundant or simplistic tests. Penalizing for incorrect tests while using the overall thoroughness as a baseline allowed us to avoid the most obvious ways of gaming the system.

To ensure students put a genuine effort into their initial submissions, we graded both the initial submission and the final one, and gave a weight of 75% to the initial and 25% to the final. The weights were chosen so that learning from others' work from feedback could make a qualitative difference, but would not be a substitute for students doing their own work. In particular, a student who submitted a blank test suite and copied the best of the ones given to review would be sure to get a failing grade. (Nobody tried this.)

Finally, we had repeated discussions with students about the goals and design of the peer-review process and of our system of weights. Students appeared able to articulate the benefits of peer-review, and in anonymous course evaluations found the process largely beneficial (though it was regarded much more useful for some assignments than others). Even though the workload had the potential to increase (because the assignments were largely unchanged from previous years), students did not report working significantly more time. Curiously, an independent (student-run) evaluation rated CSPL substantially easier (by one point on a four-point scale) than in previous years; though this cannot necessarily be attributed to peer-review, it does suggest that peer-review did not make the course substantially harder.

## 4. DATA ANALYSIS

Our analysis of peer-review for testing relies on a combination of data extracted from CaptainTeach and manual coding of extracted data. We extracted the contents of all review and review-feedback forms, the time of each submission (both work and reviews), and the initial access times of

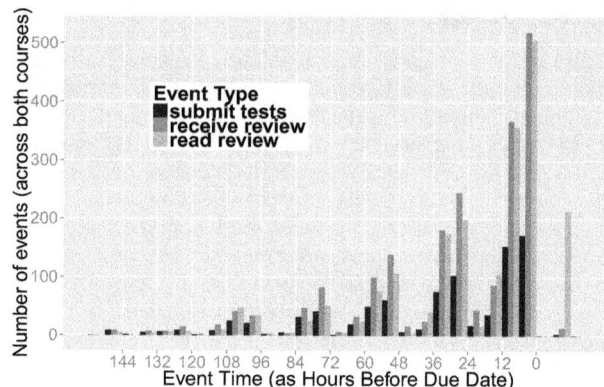

Figure 1: Timings of key events in test-suite review. Times are given as deltas from the assignment deadline, grouped in 6-hour intervals (time 0 is the deadline). Bars to the right of 0 represent late assignments. The far left bars aggregate activity earlier than 150 hours before the deadline.

each review. The course staff provided information on which submissions were seeds, to filter out in our analysis.

For analyses that looked at comment content, we developed rubrics and manually coded data. When multiple authors coded data, we coded independently only after achieving $\kappa$ of at least .75 (above .8 in most cases).

All statistical analyses were done in R version 3.0.2.[3]

*Summary of Parameters.*

Our analysis refers to key parameters of our data, as summarized in the following table. The first column is how many students completed the course (in parens is the number of those who started it and submitted *some* step for review). Next we list the number of assignments and number of actual problems (CS1.5 assignments had multiple problems with the same due date). The last two columns report the total number of test suites and reviews that were submitted in each course: the former excludes our good and bad seed solutions, but the latter includes reviews of those solutions (so the review count is not just a multiplier on the suites).

### Summary of key parameters per course

| Course | students | asgns | probs | suites | reviews |
|--------|----------|-------|-------|--------|---------|
| CS1.5  | 49 (55)  | 4     | 14    | 621    | 1565    |
| CSPL   | 37 (41)  | 8     | 8     | 288    | 863     |

## 4.1 Student Behavior in the Review Process

In-flow feedback on test suites cannot be helpful unless students engage in reviewing early enough to affect implementations. Our courses did not have a separate due date for the initial tests: students were free to submit their initial tests just before the deadline (though they had to leave at least a few minutes to submit test-suite reviews before being able to submit their implementations). Our analysis therefore begins with submission times of initial test suites and reviews, as well as access times on test-suite reviews.

Figure 1 shows distributions of when students submitted their initial test suites, received reviews, and read reviews.

---

[3]Data and scripts for this paper are available at http://cs.brown.edu/research/plt/dl/icer2014ct/.

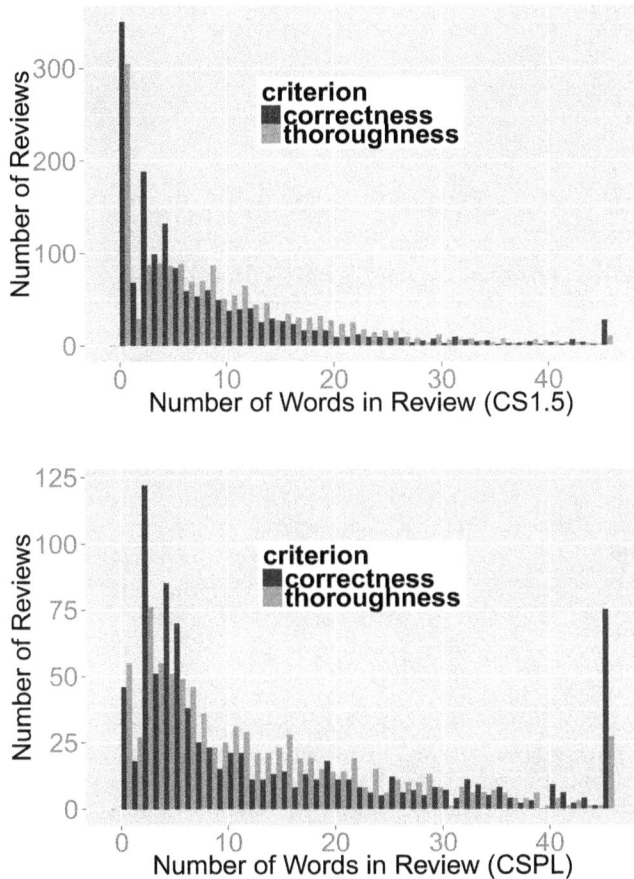

**Figure 2: Word counts of review comments. The right bar aggregates comments of 50 or more words.**

The data are clustered by 6-hour intervals leading to the deadline.[4] As each submission received 2–3 reviews, there are fewer submission events in the graph than receive-review or read-review events. We present a combined plot over both courses as their individual graphs were similar.

The graph shows that at least half of the test-suite submissions occurred at least 24 hours prior to the deadline. The bars for receive-review and read-review are fairly similar across the time intervals (though each class has a set of reviews that got read only after the assignment deadline had passed). There were only 6 instances in which students in CS1.5 didn't read their reviews for a particular assignment, and only 9 such instances in CSPL. The data suggest that most students are engaged to some extent in the review process, with some sufficiently engaged to submit work at least two days in advance. In particular, enough students took test-case reviews seriously that we can meaningfully explore the content and validity of their reviews.

## 4.2 Nature of Test-Suite Reviews

The nature of free-form review comments also reflects student engagement in reviewing. Figure 2 shows the word

---

[4]All assignments were due at midnight. The periodic dips thus correspond to the midnight–6am period, suggesting that our students might be getting some sleep!

counts of comments given on each of the thoroughness and correctness criteria. Reviews in CSPL tend to be longer than in CS1.5, as confirmed by the following summary statistics (difference in means across the courses is significant at $p=1.6e^{-11}$ for thoroughness and $p=2.2e^{-16}$ for correctness using a Mann-Whitney-Wilcox test).

| Course | thoroughness | | | correctness | | |
|--------|------|-----|------|------|-----|-------|
| | mean | med | SD | mean | med | SD |
| CS1.5 | 9.48 | 7 | 9.98 | 7.96 | 4 | 12.29 |
| CSPL | 12.85 | 9 | 12.49 | 16.01 | 7 | 21.78 |

Students often reported (anecdotally) not knowing what to say about high-quality work. We therefore expected longer comments on lower-rated work. The following plot of review rating versus word count shows the lowest Likert rating (-3) got shorter reviews than other negative or weak ratings (-2 to 1). This suggests that students reserved their writing for test suites that had some problems but did not appear hopeless. More detailed manual analysis of the review contents would be needed to confirm this interpretation.

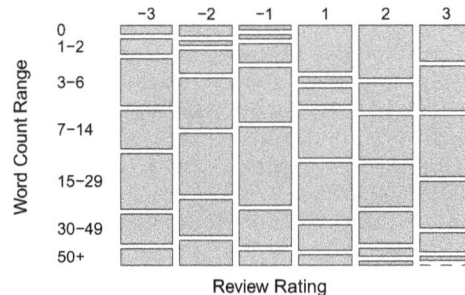

Of course, comment length matters less than content: short reviews can be useful, and reviews of the same length can differ widely in utility (e.g., "all looks good", "test nested scopes", and "missing many cases"). Therefore, one author manually coded all test-suite reviews for one assignment from each course (choosing assignments with subtleties that we hoped reviewing would uncover), looking *only* at the review text (hiding its rating). Inspired by Nelson and Schunn's rubrics for writing assignments in undergraduate humanities courses [11], we created a coarse-grained rubric with four variables: *abstract positive* (e.g., "this looks good"), *abstract negative* (e.g., "this looks bad"), *concrete but general* (e.g., "check more error cases"), and *concrete targeted* (e.g., "your third test returns the wrong answer"). A review could be marked with multiple variables. The counts of comments were as follows:

| Course | # comm | APos | ANeg | CoGen | Targeted |
|--------|--------|------|------|-------|----------|
| CS1.5-C | 96 | 64 | 3 | 4 | 20 |
| CSPL-C | 108 | 67 | 2 | 3 | 41 |
| CS1.5-T | 96 | 36 | 24 | 7 | 46 |
| CSPL-T | 108 | 57 | 6 | 27 | 34 |

Abstract positive remarks across both criteria (thoroughness and correctness) appeared almost exclusively in reviews with high Likert ratings; we believe this mirrors the anecdotal remarks about students not knowing what to say when reviewing good work. Concrete targeted comments occur fairly uniformly across the different Likert ratings. Within

14

CS1.5, abstract negative comments on thoroughness skew towards reviews with lower Likert ratings. The concrete general comments on thoroughness in CSPL have no significant relationship with review ratings.

Ideally, low-quality work would receive concrete comments that highlight its weaknesses. In CS1.5, 28 of 39 reviews that gave thoroughness ratings in the lower-half of the Likert scale included concrete targeted comments; in CSPL, 5 of 15 low-rated thoroughness reviews gave concrete targeted comments, although 9 of 15 had concrete general comments. On correctness, only 2 of 29 reviews with low ratings had no concrete targeted comments. That correctness comments are more targeted than thoroughness ones makes sense: violations of correctness would arise from individual test cases, while violations of thoroughness often arise from overlooking broad classes of program inputs.

## 4.3 Accuracy Of Test-Suite Reviews

To check whether students are effective reviewers, we compare their ratings to the gold/coal grades. Figure 3 plots the Likert review ratings against the gold (correctness) and coal (thoroughness) grades in CSPL. The plots show that initial submissions are generally strong, and that positive reviews outweigh negative ones. Thoroughness reviews are less concentrated in the upper-right quadrant than correctness ones. The horizontal bands in the thoroughness plot reflect the nature of the grading: thoroughness grades are a percentage of a single-digit number of coal solutions, so only a few grades are possible per assignment.

The interesting sections of these graphs are the lower-right and upper-left portions, which reflect reviews that were inconsistent with our grading assessment. Possible explanations in these cases include poor performance of the reviewer on that assignment, last-minute reviewing, weaknesses in our grading mechanisms (that failed to accurately assess work quality), or lack of engagement by the reviewer. For each of thoroughness and correctness, we manually inspected all data points with the top two Likert ratings and grades below 40, as well as points with the bottom two Likert ratings and grades above 60.

For the 43 cases of low thoroughness reviews with high grades, all but a couple of the free-form comments point to concrete situations or constructs that the test suite did not adequately exercise. This strongly suggests that this segment of the plot gets populated due to limitations in our suite of coal solutions.

For the 45 cases of high thoroughness reviews with low grades, just over half gave generic comments of the form "this is great", while a dozen stated specific criticisms and potential holes in the test suites that would be consistent with lower ratings. Those dozen might reflect review inflation. For the others, we looked at reviewer performance and review submission time, but found no patterns.

The comments for the 46 reviews with low correctness ratings but high grades are also detailed and concrete. These high grades could also be indicative of weaknesses in our tests. There are only 7 high-rated correctness reviews with low grades; the comments vary widely in style, and the sample is too small to draw inferences.

## 4.4 Test Suite Evolution

We are interested in how test suites evolve from the initial to the final submission, and the extent to which activities during the review process correlate with changes to the test suites. For CSPL, we can explore this by looking at the gold/coal grades on each of the initial and final submissions.

Our first question is whether test suites change, both in the number of tests and in the grade earned. Across all assignments in CSPL, the number of tests change as follows:

| fewer | same | 1-5 | 6-15 | 16+ |
|-------|------|-----|------|-----|
| 28 | 79 | 89 | 27 | 16 |

Individual test cases can change within the same number of tests. In 33 instances, grades changed within the same number of tests (each had a change in the correctness grade; 8 also had a change in thoroughness). When tests were *removed*, it was usually because the staff clarified assumptions about valid input (e.g., interpreter inputs were guaranteed to parse) after the assignment was released.

Digging deeper, we want to know how final test suites compare to initial ones relative to each of our correctness and thoroughness criteria. Understanding which errors remained and which were fixed will help us assess the effectiveness of reviews on test suites. We omit test-suites that failed to run (due to infinite loops, timeouts, etc.) in this analysis.

*Changes in Thoroughness.*

We found 155 instances of coal solutions being caught in a final test suite but not the corresponding initial one. These instances occur across 75 distinct test suites from 32 unique students (across all assignments). Only 5 of these 75 cases are from situations in which the initial test suite did not run. Thus 70 final test suites improved in thoroughness from initial to final submission.

We found only 5 instances of coal solutions being caught in an initial test suite but not in the corresponding final one (this does not count 14 students whose final suites did not run, but whose initial suites had detected some coal).

*Changes in Correctness.*

Across the course, 158 initial test suites had at least one incorrect test case; a total of 737 individual test cases failed across these 158 suites.[5] The corresponding final test suites ran for 152 of these (that is, there were 6 total cases across the course where a test suite's final submission went into an infinite loop or otherwise failed to run on the gold solution).

We are interested in incorrect test cases from the initial test suites that remain (by string equality) in the final test suites: these represent errors that "survived" any impact of seeing reviews and other students' work before final submission. Across the initial 152 test suites with corresponding final suites, there were 690 total failing test cases. Only 65 of these test cases survived, occurring across 31 final test suites. Twenty-four of the 31 test suites still had 1-2 of their original errors; the other seven retained 3-5 errors.

The 31 test suites with unfixed failures involve 6 of the 7 automatically graded assignments in CSPL, and a total of 17 students failed to remove an incorrect test case before final submission at some point in the course. The surviving 65 incorrect test cases are a majority of the 100 individual test cases that failed across all final test suites that ran. More than half of the 31 test suites were submitted at least a day before the deadline.

---

[5] Because the students were not given the output of our tests, they would not necessarily know of these failures.

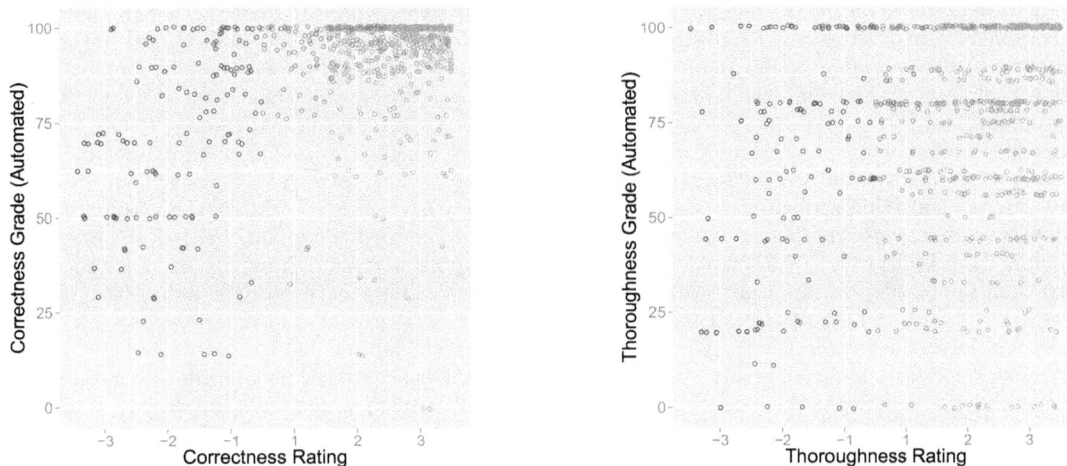

Figure 3: Review ratings versus grades on each of the correctness and thoroughness criteria (for CSPL).

## 4.5 Evolution Through Reviewing

The preceding data do not suggest the extent to which the review process either could have or did contribute to test-suite changes. Reviewing could have two impacts: students might receive reviews that pointed out problems (in their role as reviewees), or they might edit their tests after seeing others' work (in their role as reviewers). Our data allows us to explore both perspectives.

The following table summarizes how often CSPL test suites gained or lost detection of individual coals, and how often the review process had the *potential* to expose students to work that caught the corresponding coal. The dataset for this table contains one data point for the product of: students, assignments, and coals for that assignment.

|            | both | gained | lost | neither | total |
|------------|------|--------|------|---------|-------|
| # instances | 1252 | 155   | 5    | 284     | 1754  |
| as reviewer | 1209 | 138   | 4    | 183     | 1590  |
| as reviewee | 1164 | 129   | 5    | 166     | 1516  |
| neither     | 11   | 5     | 0    | 47      | 69    |

We explain the table by discussing the "gained" column. There were 155 instances of students submitting an initial test suite that failed to catch a specific coal, but a final test suite that caught the same coal. In 138 of the 155 instances, the student reviewed a test suite with a case that caught the coal. In 129 (of 155) instances, the student was reviewed by someone whose initial test suite had caught the coal. In 5 (of 155) instances, neither reviewing nor being reviewed could have exposed the student to a test that caught the coal.

We now focus on the 439 instances in which a coal was not detected initially (the "gained" and "neither" columns). We find that 89% of those who gained the coal reviewed work that caught the coal compared to 64% who did not gain the coal. This difference is significant (p=.000065, $\chi^2$=16.02), and suggests that reviewing impacts test-suite quality. It is harder to determine impacts of reviewers having caught coals without looking at the actual review contents (which we did not have the resources to do for this paper). This may be worth doing, as 84% who gained a coal were reviewed by someone who had caught the coal, compared to 61% of those who did not gain the coal (p=.00049, $\chi^2$=12.14).

These data are only suggestive of possible links, and by no means imply causation. Some causal information could have been obtained by asking the students directly, e.g., whether a reviewed test suite taught them anything new. However, in-flow reviewing already has the potential to be disruptive to workflow (though this proved to not be a major problem in practice; a paper about the tool [13] discusses this), and every extra prompt comes with a cost by increasing time and adding disruption. In addition, questions asked at the moment will not capture learning that occurs upon reflection. Nevertheless, teasing apart causes and effects in a setting where we don't wish to burden users too much remains a daunting task. We do, however, have one additional source of human input via the feedback comments.

## 4.6 Student Ratings Of Review Utility

Though providing feedback on reviews was optional, students did so more often than we expected. Out of 2428 reviews, 700 received Likert-scale feedback; 409 of the 700 also had comments (192 in CS1.5; 217 in CSPL).

Though on some social media there is a tendency to complain more than praise, Likert-ratings on reviews (when provided) were overwhelmingly positive. (This may be because students knew they were interacting with (anonymous) colleagues and friends, not unknown people on the Internet.) Across both courses, roughly 80% of feedback ratings were in the top two Likert categories; only 8% in CS1.5 and 3% in CSPL were in the lowest two Likert categories.

We manually coded all comments for indications that reviews had identified problems or led to edits in test suites (these were two of 15 categories identified during open coding of the comments). In the following table, "Ack Error" reflects feedback that acknowledged an error that was pointed out in a review, and "Will Act" captures claims that the reviewee would edit their test suite as a result of the review.

|                   | Ack Error | Will Act | Both |
|-------------------|-----------|----------|------|
| # comments CS1.5  | 40        | 27       | 2    |
| # authors CS1.5   | 20        | 13       | 2    |
| # comments CSPL   | 55        | 30       | 13   |
| # authors CSPL    | 25        | 15       | 10   |

16

For each course, the table reports on (a) the number of cases of each kind of comment across all review-feedback forms, and (b) the number of unique students who made such a comment. While a couple of students in each course made multiple such comments, most are more isolated cases.

The percentages of students who, unprompted, acknowledge errors and declare intent to act on reviews suggests that reviewing is successful at identifying problems in test suites. Of course, our data cannot tell us whether students would have found the errors discussed in these comments without the review process. An interesting question for future work is whether peer-review changes the set of errors caught and the time at which those errors are detected.

Reviewers can make mistakes, misinterpreting either the assignment or the work being reviewed. Feedback comments sometimes cited concrete errors on the part of reviewers. Comments that disputed specific parts of a review argued about the expected result of a test, whether a particular situation needed to be tested, or the reviewer's interpretation of the assignment. The following table summarizes reported instances of reviewer error, alongside data about whether the comments referenced the assignment:

|  | Dispute | Discuss Asgn | Both |
|---|---|---|---|
| # comments CS1.5 | 31 | 12 | 6 |
| # reviewers CS1.5 | 24 | 10 | 5 |
| # comments CSPL | 41 | 26 | 19 |
| # reviewers CSPL | 24 | 19 | 14 |

The large number of unique reviewers (relative to the number of disputes) suggests that reviewing errors were not due to a couple of students consistently doing a poor job. This is a positive result. Some assignments in each course had interesting subtleties (without which there would be less potential value from reviewing test cases). We expected there would be some differences in interpretation. These data suggest that some discussion of those cases occurred within the reviewing process, rather than just in office hours.

## 5. RELATED WORK

Our paper focuses on (a) in-flow (b) peer-review of (c) tests. Little prior work covers all three aspects. We focus here on projects that combine two of them.

Kulkarni, et al. study the effects of seeing examples early on in the creative process [9]. They find that early and frequent exposure to examples (in their case, artwork) leads to participants producing drawings with more unique features (a measure of creativity). One of our hopes is that seeing examples of tests early leads students to create more diverse and effective test suites for their own programs.

Buffardi and Edwards study students' testing behaviors under test-driven-development [2]. Students could submit tests and code for automated assessment multiple times before the deadline, receiving in-flow feedback. The point at which a student's tests achieve significant coverage of her code is a key parameter in their analysis. This parameter is not meaningful in our work, since students submit (and ostensibly write) tests prior to implementations. Our two groups share an interest in leveraging early testing to improve code quality; identifying appropriate roles for peer-review in that process is an interesting open question.

McCarthy [pers. comm.], after the deadline, has students answer a questionnaire with specific test-related questions.

Affirmative responses must be accompanied by references to concrete code. Other students are asked to assess these responses. All these responses are taken into account in grading. The evaluation is not in-flow. Though our gold and coal solutions simulate some of the effect of his rubrics, we may benefit from using such rubrics more directly.

Expertiza is a peer-review system with reviews of reviews, but as part of a grade rather than as helpful feedback [14]. They do not provide quantitative data on reviews of reviews. The applications of Expertiza were often on collaborative projects, where each student submitted pieces of a larger system, so students' own experience with their problem was less directly applicable to the review.

Aropä is a peer-review system that has been used in both computer science and humanities [6]. It does not support our notion of in-flow review, but it does support a review-dispute-revise loop. Since peer reviews are used as part of the grading process, accurately disputing a flawed review can lead to a better grade, so students have incentive to read their feedback with a critical eye.

Hundhausen, et al. study several variations of peer code review in their courses [7]. They do not consider testing explicitly, and do not have in-flow components. They do discuss and reflect on reviews in a group setting, as an opportunity to identify what makes for a helpful review, or what problems were seen across the class. Their work demonstrates the importance of the social aspect of peer review.

Smith, et al. have students write tests for one another as part of reviewing [16]. The tests (and any bugs found) are reported to the original authors, who evaluate the feedback, including the tests and overall testing strategy. Smith et al. do not discuss specific qualities that were evaluated of the tests and reviews, and the testing was more whole-system than in our work. When evaluating reviews, the students could also submit fixes to their program that the review identified; the authors do not provide data on how often or to what degree students exploited this.

Clark studies peer testing in larger software engineering projects across several years [3]. The testing is less automated because it involves using interactive interfaces. Afterwards, student programmers are asked to evaluate their testers with a rubric that measures helpfulness.

Søndergaard uses in-flow peer review in a course on compilers [17], though the flow is not test-first. Rather, several components of a compiler are completed in order, with review steps in between. 68% of students agreed that peer review helped them improve their work, 63% agreed it improved their ability to reflect on learning, and 89% agreed that it was useful to see other groups' solutions.

Reily, et al. have students submit test cases as part of a peer review process [15], along with Likert and open-response questions. They do not focus on reviewing test suites themselves, however, instead using tests as a kind of concrete feedback on implementations, as part of a rubric.

Gaspar, et al. surveyed students on their perceptions of Peer Testing, in which students share their test suites with classmates [5]. The time at which their students submitted tests relative to the due date is not clear, though the survey asks students about the impact of Peer Testing on their programs. Students generally perceived benefits to trading test suites. Students did not provide feedback on each others' tests, so this use of Peer Testing captures only one of the reviewing roles required of CaptainTeach students.

# 6. DISCUSSION AND FUTURE WORK

We have presented an analysis of what we believe is the first use of in-flow peer-review of tests. Both the in-flow process and the review of test suites are variables in this work, and we did not attempt to tease them apart. We also did not investigate the review of tests relative to the review of implementations, although we have analyzable data on both. We focus on review of tests here because they are a natural boundary for in-flow reviewing.

Our finding that students participate early and thoughtfully with little structure to reviews is promising. Our data on student engagement and feedback styles is thus a good candidate for comparison to students' behavior in more structured and enforced contexts. In future iterations, we wish to borrow rubrics from other authors (e.g., Kulkarni, et al. [10]). It would also be useful to directly ask students whether a review inspired them to make any changes.

Our analysis of comments on review helpfulness identifies a subtlety in rubrics for assessing reviews: prior rubrics [11] value concrete targeted comments over concrete but abstract ones on the theory that targeted comments are more actionable. While this theory holds for correctness, which focuses on individual tests, it does not apply as well to thoroughness, which is fundamentally about the overall structure of a test suite and is about material that might be *missing*.

While our data show test-suite quality improving during in-flow review, there are many possible causal explanations (besides chance). First, the process prompts students to submit material earlier, giving them more time to think about the problem and to revise work. Second, forcing the submission of tests for review emphasizes test quality. Third, students may benefit from reading the reviews that others wrote of their tests. Finally, students may benefit simply from having to read others' tests and articulate thoughts about them. Our system is not set up to discriminate across these different factors (and hence determine the impact of in-flow review). A future version of CaptainTeach that enables A/B testing may make this easier; e.g.: What if students are asked to write reviews but are not shown reviews of their own work? What if they submit tests to run against each others' code [4] but don't actually read the tests manually? These are worth exploring.

One feature we strongly considered incorporating was to give each reviewer the output of automated grading of submissions, to prompt them for things to comment on. We decided not to because we feared that if an automated system failed to find problems, human reviewers would be inclined to pass lightly over the test suite. The top-left and bottom-right of Figure 3 are especially interesting in this light: presenting this data might have helped the bottom-right group do a better job, but might it have made the top-left group complacent? Overall, our analysis of seeming inaccuracies between high-grade but low-rating reviews highlights weaknesses in relying on automated grading.

Finally, we want to consider the larger narrative around in-flow review of tests. Every test case has a lifecycle: it is created, possibly cloned and modified, fixed to reflect better understanding of a problem, modified to track a changing implementation, and sometimes even deleted. This lifecycle resembles Ko's model of software errors [8], and similarly can be affected by learning environments. CaptainTeach should help study the role of peer-review in this story.

**Acknowledgements:** Daniel Patterson helped build CaptainTeach and influenced its use. Our course staff and students engaged in this experiment with patience, humor, and insight. NSF grants and Google supported this work.

# 7. REFERENCES

[1] K. Beck. *Test-driven development by example.* Pearson Education, 2003.

[2] K. Buffardi and S. H. Edwards. Effective and ineffective software testing behaviors by novice programmers. In *International Computing Education Research Conference,* 2013.

[3] N. Clark. Peer testing in software engineering projects. In *Australasian Computing Education Conference,* 2004.

[4] S. H. Edwards, Z. Shams, M. Cogswell, and R. C. Senkbeil. Running students' software tests against each others' code: new life for an old "gimmick". In *SIGCSE Technical Symposium on Computer Science Education,* 2012.

[5] A. Gaspar, S. Langevin, N. Boyer, and R. Tindell. A preliminary review of undergraduate programming students' perspectives on writing tests, working with others, & using peer testing. In *ACM Conference on Information Technology Education,* 2013.

[6] J. Hamer, C. Kell, and F. Spence. Peer assessment using Aropä. In *Australasian Computing Education Conference,* 2007.

[7] C. D. Hundhausen, A. Agrawal, and P. Agarwal. Talking about code: Integrating pedagogical code reviews into early computing courses. *ACM Transactions on Computing Education,* 13(3), Aug. 2013.

[8] A. J. Ko and B. A. Myers. A framework and methodology for studying the causes of software errors in programming systems. *Journal of Visual Languages and Computing,* 16(1–2):41–84, 2005.

[9] C. Kulkarni, S. P. Dow, and S. R. Klemmer. Early and repeated exposure to examples improves creative work. In *Cognitive Science,* 2012.

[10] C. Kulkarni, K. P. Wei, H. Le, D. Chia, K. Papadopoulos, J. Cheng, D. Koller, and S. R. Klemmer. Peer and self assessment in massive online classes. *ACM Transactions on Computer-Human Interaction,* 2013.

[11] M. M. Nelson and C. D. Schunn. The nature of feedback: How different types of peer feedback affect writing performance. *Instructional Science,* 27(4):375–401, 2009.

[12] B. Pettichord and B. Marick. Agile acceptance testing. *Extreme Programming and Agile Methods,* 2418, 2002.

[13] J. G. Politz, D. Patterson, S. Krishnamurthi, and K. Fisler. CaptainTeach: Multi-stage, in-flow peer review for programming assignments. In *ACM SIGCSE Conference on Innovation and Technology in Computer Science Education,* 2014.

[14] L. Ramachandran and E. F. Gehringer. Reusable learning objects through peer review: The Expertiza approach. In *Innovate: Journal of Online Education,* 2007.

[15] K. Reily, P. L. Finnerty, and L. Terveen. Two peers are better than one: Aggregating peer reviews for computing assignments is surprisingly accurate. In *ACM International Conference on Supporting Group Work,* 2009.

[16] J. Smith, J. Tessler, E. Kramer, and C. Lin. Using peer review to teach software testing. In *International Computing Education Research Conference,* 2012.

[17] H. Søndergaard. Learning from and with peers: The different roles of student peer reviewing. In *ACM SIGCSE Conference on Innovation and Technology in Computer Science Education,* pages 31–35, 2009.

# A Systematic Review of Approaches for Teaching Introductory Programming and Their Influence on Success

Arto Vihavainen and Jonne Airaksinen
Department of Computer Science
University of Helsinki
Finland
{ avihavai, jonnaira }@cs.helsinki.fi

Christopher Watson
School of Engineering and Computing Sciences
University of Durham
United Kingdom
christopher.watson@dunelm.org.uk

## ABSTRACT

Decades of effort has been put into decreasing the high failure rates of introductory programming courses. Whilst numerous studies suggest approaches that provide effective means of teaching programming, to date, no study has attempted to quantitatively compare the impact that different approaches have had on the pass rates of programming courses. In this article, we report the results of a systematic review on articles describing introductory programming teaching approaches, and provide an analysis of the effect that various interventions can have on the pass rates of introductory programming courses. A total of 60 pre-intervention and post-intervention pass rates, describing thirteen different teaching approaches were extracted from relevant articles and analyzed. The results showed that on average, teaching interventions can improve programming pass rates by nearly one third when compared to a traditional lecture and lab based approach.

## Categories and Subject Descriptors

K.3.2 [**Computers and Education**]: Computer and Information Science Education—*Computer science education*

## General Terms

Human Factors

## Keywords

programming education, introductory programming, cs1, teaching interventions, analysis, systematic review

## 1. INTRODUCTION

The mean worldwide failure rates of CS1 have been suggested to be as high as one third of students failing the course [3]. A recent study showed that despite advances in pedagogy, the worldwide failure rates of CS1 have not improved over time, and that the failure rates are not substantially

influenced by aspects of the external teaching context, such as the programming language taught in the course [25].

Despite decades of research, internal factors based upon traditional learning theories have also failed to explain the CS1 failure rate phenomenon, and no factor to date has been shown to influence programming performance across a range of different teaching contexts [27]. More recently, researchers have explored the relations between desirable aspects of programming behaviour and performance [23, 26]. But despite yielded promising results there is still no overall understanding as to why many students are able to program, whilst others endlessly struggle.

Many theories have been put forward as to why learning to program is a difficult task. Some are attributed to the nature of programming itself. Programming is not a single skill, but rather a complex cognitive activity, where a student must simultaneously build and apply several higher order cognitive skills to solve a particular problem [17]. Other reasons are attributed to aspects of the students. Students may lack motivation, they may be unable to create a mental model of how programs relate to the underlying system [2], or create a clear model of program flow [10].

Further reasons are associated with the teaching methodology used. Whilst many students fail programming courses, instructors face the additional challenge of adjusting their expectations to the students' level of ability [22]. These challenges have been acknowledged, and decades of research effort has been put into creating and applying teaching interventions that facilitate students' learning [17, 13]. These interventions can include moving from a traditional lecture and lab based approach to using pair programming, game based learning, or extreme apprenticeship.

However, to date, no study has attempted to quantitatively compare the impact that these approaches can have on improving the pass rates of failing programming courses. Without any quantitative evidence on the relative strengths of different approaches, the research community as a whole will continue to lack a clear consensus of precisely which methodologies provide the most effective means of teaching programming and saving failing programming students.

## 2. RESEARCH METHOD

The purpose of this study was to explore the degree to which various approaches of teaching programming could improve pass rates. In order to gather data for use in this study, a systematic review process was adopted, in an effort to identify as many articles that provided details of pre-intervention, and post-intervention pass rates as possible.

## 2.1 Research Questions

The questions answered in this study include:

1. How do teaching interventions reported in the literature increase students' success in CS1?

2. What practices do the successful teaching interventions comprise of?

3. Do so called best practices, or practices that are significantly better than others exist?

## 2.2 Identification of Relevant Literature

To identify approaches for teaching introductory programming and their influences on course success, an initial search of articles published between the years 1980 - January 2014 was carried out. Searches were made in the ACM and IEEE databases, after which further searches were made using Google Scholar in an attempt to identify both published and unpublished work which was not indexed by ACM and IEEE. A final search was conducted by manually screening the indexes of selected conference proceedings and journals for relevant studies, including: (1) Transactions on Computing Education, (2) SIGCSE, (3) ITiCSE, (4) ICER, (5) SIGITE, (6) ICALT.

Initial articles were selected based on keywords where boolean operators AND and OR were used to refine the searches. More specifically, the search criteria used was: (Improve OR Increase OR Decrease OR Lower OR Reduce) AND (Retention OR Attrition OR Pass OR Fail OR Success) AND (Programming OR Programming Course OR Introductory Programming OR CS1). Applying the criteria resulted in over 1000 somewhat relevant articles being identified, on which two researchers performed an initial inclusion screening. After applying an inclusion screening based on title and abstract, 226 articles remained. From these, further screening was made by including full text content, excluding articles that did not describe a replicable teaching intervention or an intervention that had overall been attempted at least twice, articles that did not discuss CS1 or introductory programming courses, articles that did not include pass-rates before or after the teaching intervention, and articles that did not include the amount of students before or after the teaching intervention (or data from which the numbers could be derived from). Finally, articles that described previously reported results from another perspective and articles from which all results were included in subsequent articles were excluded. The final number of articles used for this study was 32.

## 2.3 Study Coding

From each article, the following data was extracted:

1. Article details: publication year, name, author(s).

2. Course and institution details.

3. Teaching intervention: year, semester, used practices.

4. Totals and percentages before and after teaching intervention(s): $n$, pass, fail, withdraw, fail/withdraw.

All three authors performed extraction of details, at times extracting details from the same articles more than once. When conflicts occurred, the first author did an additional review.

From the 32 articles, 60 data entries with information on the amount of students as well as pass-rates before and after the intervention were extracted. When the intervention was done on a separate section during the same semester, the non-intervention and intervention results were paired. If there were multiple sections, an average combining all sections from the same semester was used to reduce possible instructor-related impact on the results. When results were described from subsequent semesters, the pairs were formed so that the pre-pair contained an average of all reported semesters before the intervention, and each post-entry contained details from one reported semester with the intervention. If an article described combined results from multiple institutions, it was included if the totals and percentages before and after the teaching intervention were included, and that the teaching intervention was described in detail.

To utilize a comparable measure of success, the reported totals and percentages in the articles were combined to describe a WDF-rate[1], i.e. the rate of students that did not withdraw, receive a D-grade[2] and did not fail the exam. The WDF-rate is a common measure used to describe course success, and it provides a more realistic view on success due to taking into account students that are not able to continue in their studies (D-grade in some institutions), students that fail in the exam, and students that withdraw from the course before the exam. When the WDF-rate was not readily available and the calculation WDF-grade was not possible, we chose the closest possible number assuming that the metric was the same in both pre- and post-intervention details. In this article, from now on we will use the term pass rate to describe WDF-rate or the closest number available.

We acknowledge that some institutions use a grace period during which students can drop out from the course without any sanctions. Unfortunately, very few articles did report such details, and thus it cannot be taken into account. Similarly, we acknowledge that the grading schema and learning objectives vary among different universities; unless otherwise noted in the articles, our assumption was that the learning objectives and grading schema remained similar between course instances, making the pre- and post-intervention details comparable. Additionally, we did not include demographic details or gender details into the study.

## 2.4 Classifying Teaching Interventions

Extracting teaching interventions was done in three phases. In the first phase the articles were coded based on the intervention types used. As an example, the article "Combining Cooperative Learning And Peer Instruction In Introductory Computer Science" [4] was coded with tags *cooperative learning*, *student group work*, *team teaching*, and *undergraduate teaching assistants*. The coding reflects the content; the article discusses collaboration and cooperative learning as the main activities, and the peer instruction discussed in the article describes the use of peer instructors, i.e. undergraduate teaching assistants, not to be confused with Peer Instruction by Eric Mazur. To give another example, the article "Experience Report: CS1 for Majors with Media Computation" [19] was coded with tags *media computation* and *peer instruction* as the article mentions that "...*one notable difference between the courses was that the media computation course*

---

[1]The acronym DFW was also visible in the literature; we utilize the acronym WDF.

[2]Typically 40-49% of the overall course score.

*was taught using Peer Instruction in lectures, and the traditional course was not...".* Although pair programming is also used, it is not coded as it is used in both non-intervention and intervention groups.

In the second phase, articles were supplemented with additional, descriptive tags. For example, for each article that was coded with the tag *media computation*, tags *content: media, contextualization, context: media*, were added to describe that the content (material) of the course was updated to contain media-type content, the course was contextualized so that the content had more meaning to the students that participated in the course, and finally, that the context revolved around media. Similarly, for each article that was coded with the tag *peer instruction*, tags *interactive classroom, student collaboration, reading before class, quizzes in class*, and *collaboration in class* were added. No limits were set on the amount of tags that could be used as long as the tags described the intervention properly. For example, an intervention where a game-themed final project was added to the course without additional modifications, the course was not contextualized, but the content was updated to include a game-theme component (tag *content: game-theme*).

Finally, in the third phase, equivalent or closely related tags were combined, and the changes were reflected to the article coding. At the end of the extraction phase, each article had the majority of original tags as well as a set of supplement tags that provided additional information on the described teaching activities. In total, 40 different tags remained after the combination phase, and each of the 60 data entries had on average 3.5 tags.

## 3. RESULTS

The results of the survey are analyzed from three different viewpoints. First, in Section 3.1 an overview to the results is provided, then in Section 3.2, the most common activities and their effect in the data are discussed, and finally in Section 3.3, the teaching approaches are analyzed based on a primary intervention type.

The results are considered in terms of *realized improvement*, i.e. the absolute improvement divided by the potential, by which the room for improvement that varies between different institutions is taken into account. For example, if a pre-intervention pass rate were 70% and post intervention pass rate were 85%, a potential change of 100-70 = 30% is available for the intervention. Of this, 15/30 or 50% was realized as the absolute improvement, or absolute percentage, was 15%.

### 3.1 Descriptive Statistics

Table 1 contains descriptive statistics of the data. On average, the pass rates before the intervention were 61.4%, and after intervention 74.4%. Much variance in both pre- and post-passrates exists; the smallest pass rate before intervention was 22.6% and 36% after intervention, while the largest pass rate was 94.2% before intervention, and 92.5% after intervention. The studied student populations varied also a lot. The smallest pre-intervention n was 15 students, which was from a targeted intervention to at-risk students, while the smallest post-intervention n was 9 students; the intervention stragegy in the study was applied to a small summer class. The largest number of students was 2298 before intervention, where the study reported data from past 16 iterations, and 1213 after intervention, which was from a

| descriptive | min | max | median | mean | sd ($\sigma$) |
|---|---|---|---|---|---|
| pass rate pre | 22.6 | 94.2 | 63 | 61.4 | 15.5 |
| pass rate post | 36 | 92.5 | 74 | 74.4 | 11.7 |
| students pre | 15 | 2298 | 148 | 296.9 | 487.5 |
| students post | 9 | 1231 | 86 | 162.3 | 200.7 |

**Table 1: Pass rates and study sizes before and after teaching intervention.**

study that reported aggregate results from multiple institutions.

Five (8.3%) of the extracted data entries had a negative outcome (the pass rates decreased), while in 91.7% of the entries the intervention had at least a minor improvement on the overall results. On average, before the intervention, there was room for 38.4 percentage units of improvement, while after the intervention there was room for 25.6 percentage units. In other terms, the interventions improved the pass rates on average by 12.8 absolute percentage units, the realized improvement being 33.3% or nearly one third.

### 3.2 Overall Intervention Effect

Table 2 contains ten most frequent tags and the realized gains in the studies in which they appeared in. While the intervention types cannot be compared with each others due to overlapping, the table provides an overview of the realized improvements over different studies. The intervention tags encompass the following activities:

- *collaboration*: activities that encourage student collaboration either in classrooms or labs
- *content change*: at least parts of the teaching material was changed or updated
- *contextualization*: activities where course content and activities were aligned towards a specific context such as games or media
- *CS0*: the creation of a preliminary course that was to be taken before the introductory programming course; could be organized only for e.g. at-risk students
- *game-theme*: a game-themed component was introduced to the course, e.g. a game-themed project
- *grading schema*: a change in the grading schema; the most common change was to increase the amount of points rewarded from programming activities, while reducing the weight of the course exam
- *group work*: activities with increased group work commitment such as team-based learning and cooperative learning
- *media computation*: activities explicitly declaring the use of media computation (e.g. the book)
- *peer support*: support by peers in form of pairs, groups, hired peer mentors or tutors
- *support*: an umbrella term for all support activities, e.g. increased teacher hours, additional support channels etc.

When considering the median improvement, the studies that had media computation as one of the components were most successful, while studies with a game-theme were the least successful. Facilitating group work and collaboration,

| intervention tag | n | min | max | median | avg | $\sigma$ |
|---|---|---|---|---|---|---|
| collaboration | 20 | -1 | 59 | 39 | 34 | 17 |
| content change | 36 | -17 | 69 | 34 | 34 | 17 |
| contextualization | 17 | 18 | 69 | 37 | 40 | 17 |
| CS0 | 7 | 18 | 76 | 41 | 43 | 19 |
| game-theme | 9 | -39 | 42 | 21 | 18 | 23 |
| grading schema | 11 | 3 | 42 | 30 | 29 | 12 |
| group work | 7 | 36 | 59 | 44 | 45 | 7 |
| media computation | 10 | 24 | 69 | 49 | 48 | 16 |
| peer support | 23 | -1 | 59 | 36 | 34 | 16 |
| support | 9 | -29 | 67 | 36 | 33 | 19 |

Table 2: Ten most common intervention tags and the overall intervention effects of the studies in which they appeared in. Number of studies including the intervention denoted as $n$, realized pass rates reported using minimum, maximum, median, average and standard deviation ($\sigma$) in percentages.

and creating a CS0 course were also among the high-performing activities. While the effect of an intervention activity depends naturally on other activities as well, a noticeable amount of variance was observed even within similar setups. The variance can be explained with the natural variance of student populations over different semesters, student intake, teacher effect, difference in grading criteria among different institutions, and the difference with student workloads among different institutions.

## 3.3 Primary Intervention Effect

Before comparing the impact of different interventions on programming pass rates, it was first important to determine whether there existed any significant differences in the pre-intervention pass rates of each intervention category, or whether the courses which were included in this study all had a comparable pre-intervention pass rate.

Grouping the 60 pre-intervention pass rates by the five primary intervention categories, a one-way ANOVA was performed. A Shapiro Wilk test confirmed the pass rates were normally distributed for all groups ($p > .05$), with the exceptions of relatable content and contextualization ($p = .01$), and hybrid approaches ($p = .01$). However as violations from normality do not substantially affect the type I error rate, and an ANOVA is considered relatively robust against this violation, we proceeded. Homogeneity of variances was confirmed by Levene's test ($p = .298$). A one-way ANOVA showed that there were no statistically significant differences in pre-intervention pass rates for the five primary intervention categories used in this study, $F(4, 55) = 2.17$, $p = .084$. To ensure that the violation of normality had not impacted the test result, we also performed a Kruskal-Wallis test, which confirmed that there were no statistically significant differences between the pre-intervention pass rates of each group, $\chi^2(4) = 9.13$, $p = .18$.

### 3.3.1 Collaboration and Peer Support

Approaches that include collaboration and peer support include peer-led team learning activities [9], pair programming activities [28] and cooperative and collaborative practices [4, 24]. Results are shown in Table 3. A total of 14 studies were classified as having applied an intervention, which primarily consisted of moving towards a collaborative,

or peer support based approach. Three specific approaches were identified: cooperative learning (3 courses), team based learning (5 courses), and pair programming (6 courses). Out of all the interventions that were explored in this study, cooperative learning was found to yield the largest absolute improvement in CS1 pass rates (25.7% on average), and team based learning was found to yield the second largest absolute improvement (18.1% on average). Despite being frequently cited as an enabler for programming skills, the pair programming approach was only found to yield a absolute improvement of 9.6% on average, and ranked 11 out of the 13 interventions that were explored by this study. It was possible that courses to which this intervention was applied already had good pass rates, and therefore there was little scope for absolute improvement. When considering realized changes, we note that on average, pair programming yielded a realized increase of 27% in pass rates, but overall, this approach was still ranked 11th out of the 13 interventions which were explored by this study. Considering the results of all 14 courses combined, we found that instructors who applied a collaborative or peer support based intervention generally received the largest improvements in pass rates when compared to the other groups examined in this study (16.1% improvement, realized change 34.3%). A possible explanation is that the continuous feedback and cooperation from peers acts as an enabler for programming skills, supplementing feedback received from the compiler, which is not always at a sufficient level for inexperienced students to comprehend.

### 3.3.2 Bootstrapping

Bootstrapping practices either organized a course before the start of the introductory programming course [20, 7] or started the introductory programming segment using a visual programming environment such as Scratch and Alice [11]. Some of the activities were also targeted at at-risk students [16]. Results are shown in Table 4. A total of 9 studies were classified as having applied such an intervention. Two specific approaches were identified: using visual programming tools such as Scratch or Alice (5 courses), and introducing CS0 (4 courses). Out of all the interventions that were explored in this study, using visual programming tools were found to yield the fifth largest absolute improvement in pass rates (17.3% on average). A similar high ranking was found when considering realized improvement (fourth, 38.6%), which positioned using visual programming tools as the fourth overall best intervention. Whilst the absolute improvement for courses that introduced CS0 was much lower than visual programming (10.5% increase), the realized change that was yielded by this intervention was comparable (34.9% increase). Considering the results of all 9 courses combined, we found that instructors who applied a bootstrapping intervention generally received the second largest improvements in pass rates when compared to the other groups examined in this study (absolute change 14.3%, realized change 37.0%). It is possible that the initial simplification offered by these forms of intervention are able to assist students who might otherwise fail CS1, by suppressing the syntax barrier until they have gained sufficient knowledge of the underlying concepts. This also ties into research on threshold concepts, which suggested that reducing the level of complexity initially may be an effective way to assist students in overcoming thresholds.

### 3.3.3 Relatable Content and Contextualization

Approaches that introduced relateable content sought to make programming more understandable to students. These approaches include Media Computation [21], introducing real world projects [5] as well as courses that evolve around games [1]. Results are shown in Table 5. A total of 14 studies were classified as having applied an intervention, which primarily consisted of using relatable content and contextualization as a means to improve CS1 pass rates. Two specific approaches were identified: media computation (7 courses), and gamification (7 courses). Out of all the interventions that were explored in this study, using media computation was found to yield the seventh largest absolute improvement in pass rates (14.7% on average), and a comparable improvement was found for gamification (10.8% on average). However, when considering realized changes, media computation was found to yield the largest realized change across all interventions explored in this study (50.1% increase), whereas gamification was found to only yield the tenth largest (27.4% increase). Overall, and considering the results of all 14 courses combined, we found that instructors who applied a relateable content or contextualization intervention generally received the third largest improvements in pass rates when compared to the other groups examined in this study (absolute change 11.6%, realized change 38.7%). As media computation (overall rank 2) considerably outperformed gamification (overall rank 10), it could be the case that whilst games provide a useful tool to contextualize a learning task, there are still fundamental underlying programming concepts that can be better served by adopting a media computation approach.

### 3.3.4 Course Setup, Assessment, Resourcing

Approaches that modify course setup, assessment and resourcing included a broad range of practises starting from adjusting course content based on data from an assessment system [18], introducing new content, a programming tool that provides additional support and changing the grading schema assessment [15, 12]. Results are shown in Table 6. A total of 15 studies were classified as having applied an intervention which primarily consisted of changing aspects of the course setup, rather than changing elements of the teaching approach. Three specific approaches were identified: changing class size (4 courses), improving existing resources (2 courses), and changing assessment criteria (9 courses). Overall, the largest absolute improvements in pass rates were found by changing the class size (17.8% improvement) and improving existing resources (17.5%). However, when considering these improvements relatively, they were among the five worst interventions found by this study. Similarly, making changes to the assessment criteria applied in the course yielded on average an absolute improvement of 10.1% and realized improvement of 22.5%. But when considering these changes against the other 13 interventions explored by this study, changing assessment criteria ranked 12th. Considering the results from all 15 courses combined, we found that instructors who applied an intervention based on course setup generally yielded the fourth largest improvements in pass rates when compared to the other groups (absolute change 13.4%, realized change 26.8%). The findings on changing class size to improve pass rates are consistent with previous studies [3] that have suggested that smaller classes generally have lower failure rates than larger

ones. However, overall, it is possible that this group of interventions were ranked as one of the lowest because making changes to the course setup, such as the assessment criteria, do nothing to adjust the likelihood of a student overcoming thresholds understanding programming concepts.

### 3.3.5 Hybrid Approaches

Hybrid approaches are approaches that upon discussion were not included in any of the primary categories. These include combinations of different practices [19, 14, 8]. Results are shown in Table 7. A total of 8 studies were classified as having applied an intervention, which primarily consisted of combining several different teaching interventions to yield a hybrid approach. Three combinations were identified: media computation with pair programming (2 studies), extreme apprenticeship (3 courses), and collaborative learning with relateable content (e.g. games) (3 courses). Overall, combining media computation with pair programming, or adopting an extreme apprenticeship approach were found to yield mid-range improvements in pass rates, ranging from 13.5-16.5% in absolute terms, or 36.9-49.3% in realized terms. These approaches were ranked fifth and seventh among the overall 13 interventions that were explored in this study. However, combining collaborative learning with content was found to be the worst overall intervention, actually yielding a decrease in pass rates of 9.7%, or 53.7% in realized terms. However, we note that some of the courses, which switched to this approach already had a very high pass rate (> 90%), and therefore the scope for improvement was minimal.

### 3.3.6 Comparing Primary Interventions

The final question, which remained from this study, was to determine whether there were any significant differences in the post-pass rates of studies that applied different types of interventions. Grouping the 60 post-intervention pass rates by the five primary intervention categories, a one-way ANOVA was performed. A Shapiro Wilk test confirmed the pass rates were normally distributed for all intervention groups ($p > .05$) and homogeneity of variances was confirmed by Levene's test ($p = .487$). A one-way ANOVA showed no statistically significant differences in the post-intervention pass rates for the five primary intervention groups of this study, $F(4, 55) = 2.02$, $p = .105$. Similarly, a Tukey post-hoc analysis revealed no significant pairwise differences in post-intervention pass rates. This suggests that whilst substantial improvements in pass rates can be achieved by applying different interventions, the overall pass rates after applying different types of intervention are not substantially different.

## 4. DISCUSSION

The interventions reported in the literature increase introductory programming course pass rates by one third on average. A large part of the reported interventions increase student and teacher collaboration and update the teaching material and content in an attempt to make the content more relatable to the students. Support is facilitated in many ways; one approach is recruiting peer tutors that help students as they are working, while another approach is to build a CS0-course which acts as a bridge to the programming studies. Some interventions also changed the grading schema, which is known to affect students' behaviour. What may be missing however, are the reports on interventions

| Intervention | Courses | Absolute Change | | | Realized Change | | | Overall |
|---|---|---|---|---|---|---|---|---|
| | | Mean | SD | Rank | Mean | SD | Rank | |
| Cooperative | 3 | 25.7 | 3.8 | 1 / 13 | 47.7 | 10.0 | 3 / 13 | 1 / 13 |
| Team Based | 5 | 18.1 | 11.6 | 2 / 13 | 35.0 | 12.3 | 6 / 13 | 3 / 13 |
| Pair Programming | 6 | 9.6 | 10.1 | 12 / 13 | 27.0 | 23.7 | 11 / 13 | 11 / 13 |
| Overall Intervention | 14 | 16.1 | 16.1 | 1 / 5 | 34.3 | 18.6 | 3 / 5 | 1 / 5 |

**Table 3: Improvements in Pass Rates for Courses which applied Collaborative and Peer Support Interventions**

| Intervention | Courses | Absolute Change | | | Realized Change | | | Overall |
|---|---|---|---|---|---|---|---|---|
| | | Mean | SD | Rank | Mean | SD | Rank | |
| Scratch and Alice | 5 | 17.3 | 18.7 | 5 / 13 | 38.6 | 30.8 | 4 / 13 | 4 / 13 |
| CS0 | 4 | 10.5 | 4.4 | 10 / 13 | 34.9 | 9.5 | 7 / 13 | 9 / 13 |
| Overall Intervention | 9 | 14.3 | 12.9 | 2 / 5 | 37.0 | 20.3 | 2 / 5 | 2 / 5 |

**Table 4: Improvements in Pass Rates for Courses which applied Bootstrapping**

| Intervention | Courses | Absolute Change | | | Realized Change | | | Overall |
|---|---|---|---|---|---|---|---|---|
| | | Mean | SD | Rank | Mean | SD | Rank | |
| Media Computation | 7 | 14.7 | 5.4 | 7 / 13 | 50.1 | 18.9 | 1 / 13 | 2 / 13 |
| Games | 7 | 10.8 | 6.0 | 9 / 13 | 27.4 | 8.3 | 10 / 13 | 10 / 13 |
| Overall Intervention | 14 | 12.7 | 11.6 | 4 / 5 | 38.7 | 18.3 | 1 / 5 | 3 / 5 |

**Table 5: Improvements in Pass Rates for Courses which applied Relatable Content and Contextualization**

| Intervention | Courses | Absolute Change | | | Realized Change | | | Overall |
|---|---|---|---|---|---|---|---|---|
| | | Mean | SD | Rank | Mean | SD | Rank | |
| Class Size | 4 | 17.8 | 16.6 | 3 / 13 | 34.0 | 43.2 | 8 / 13 | 6 / 13 |
| Resource Improvement | 2 | 17.5 | 2.8 | 4 / 13 | 32.1 | 5.2 | 9 / 13 | 8 / 13 |
| Assessment | 9 | 10.5 | 9.9 | 11 / 13 | 22.5 | 19.4 | 12 / 13 | 12 / 13 |
| Overall Intervention | 15 | 13.4 | 18.8 | 3 / 5 | 26.8 | 27.4 | 4 / 5 | 4 / 5 |

**Table 6: Improvements in Pass Rates for Courses which applied Course Setup Interventions**

| Intervention | Courses | Absolute Change | | | Realized Change | | | Overall |
|---|---|---|---|---|---|---|---|---|
| | | Mean | SD | Rank | Mean | SD | Rank | |
| Media Computation with Pair Programming | 2 | 13.5 | 5.4 | 8 / 13 | 49.3 | 0.2 | 2 / 13 | 5 / 13 |
| Extreme Apprenticeship | 3 | 16.5 | 1.9 | 6 / 13 | 36.9 | 4.2 | 5 / 13 | 7 / 13 |
| Collaboration with Games | 3 | -9.7 | 12.2 | 13 / 13 | -53.7 | 67.9 | 13 / 13 | 13 / 13 |
| Overall Intervention | 8 | 6.0 | 13.2 | 5 / 5 | 6.0 | 61.6 | 5 / 5 | 5 / 5 |

**Table 7: Improvements in Pass Rates for Courses which applied Hybrid Learning Approaches**

that did not yield an improvement. Thus, educators that have tried an intervention but received poor results should also be encouraged and supported in reporting the results to create a more stable picture of the field.

Whilst no statistically significant differences between the effectiveness of the teaching interventions were found, marginal differences between approaches exist. The courses with relatable content (e.g. using *media computation*) with cooperative elements (e.g. pair programming) were among the top performers with CS0-courses, while courses with pair programming as the only intervention type and courses with game-theme performed more poorly when compared to others. However, these interventions were still able to improve pass rates by a minimum of 10%, suggesting that although they were not as strong as the other interventions in this study, they were still beneficial when compared to the traditional lecture and lab approach they replaced. Do note however, that many of the interventions did combine practices together, and e.g. the effect of a possible change in teaching material may be left unreported.

Nevertheless, the data confirms that educators and researchers are making a difference when trying out new teaching interventions and pedagogical approaches. One of the common denominator among all the interventions is change, while the other side of the coin – the "past situation" – may often be a state of complacency.

## 4.1 Related Work

While no such review exists from the field of introductory programming, many reviews on the influences of teaching approaches exist from other fields. The most notable one, a synthesis of 800 meta-analyses on teaching and achievement in schools by John Hattie [6], combines the results of multiple meta-analyses to form a picture of the efficiency of different teaching approaches. Although the results from Hattie's study are from schools, they provide an additional viewpoint to our findings. As an example, while collaborative and cooperative approaches were among the most effective approaches in this study, in schools the practices that require cooperation are above average in efficiency but increase in efficiency as students get older [6]. Similarly, peer tutoring in schools is not as efficient as in our study, which further provides support on the suggestion that the ability to support others and work in teams increases with age.

While many of the effects observed by Hattie were related to the teacher, such as the teacher clarity and instructional quality, little focus was on these aspects. The closest matches from our tagging are different feedback approaches and improving the course content; the first is also a part of the collaborative approaches.

## 4.2 Limitations

As the results presented in this article are derived from a synthesis of the results from other articles, a number of validity concerns, including the justification of the synthesis approach, can be raised which are discussed in this section.

Firstly, the teaching approaches that were used prior to the intervention were rarely explicitly stated in a very detailed fashion. For the most part, it was implied from the articles that the current approach was one based upon a traditional lecture and lab based approach. It is possible that in some cases important details were not reported in the articles, and thus were missed in the encoding process.

Similarly, the learning objectives of the introductory programming courses were not considered for this study.

Secondly, the soundness of the teaching intervention design and experiments were not judged, and e.g. the quality of the used teaching material was not considered. It is likely that some interventions were implemented and executed better than others, which may lead to an imbalance in the results. Thus, one should not refrain from trying out the approaches that didn't seem to work.

Thirdly, the final number of selected articles, $n = 32$ is low, especially when considering that introductory programming courses have been studied for decades. A major concern in our case is the possibility of selective reporting. As only 8.3% of the studies contained negative results, it is possible that interventions with negative results have not often been reported. To counter this, we explored sources of *gray literature* via generalized searches, but our efforts were largely unsuccessful. The tendency to only encounter results for studies where an intervention has been successful however is a common limitation of systematic reviews.

Fourthly, whilst the results suggest that almost any planned intervention improves the existing state, the results have been gathered from studies that study university-level introductory programming courses. Further analysis should be performed when applying the results in other contexts to verify whether such approaches can yield similar improvements in pass rates at all levels of education.

Fifthly, the possible teacher effect and the effect of different student populations among different institutions is not taken into account. This is a deliberate choice due to the small amount of final articles.

Sixth, the choice for primary interventions and the tagging methodology has an inherent limitation as many of the studies had more than one intervention. Thus, the results shown here depend on the used classification, and different classification approaches may yield different results.

Finally, we note the unavoidable limitation that the assessment criteria of the individual courses were not the same over all data entries. Studies within the UK generally defined 'pass rate' as consisting of those students who had scored over 40% in the course. However, other studies defined 'pass rate' as consisting of those students who had scored at least a 'C', and others defined 'pass rate' as consisting of those students who had scored anything apart from an 'F'. Other studies did not supply details at all. Therefore this study unavoidably has to assume that a consistent notion of 'pass rate' exists and holds valid across the different teaching contexts. However, we note that this is a common limitation of other studies of this nature (e.g. [3, 25]).

## 5. CONCLUSION

In this article, we performed a quantitative systematic review on articles describing introductory programming teaching approaches, and provided an analysis of the effect that various interventions can have on the pass rates of introductory programming courses. While the total amount of articles was relatively low, a total of 60 pre-intervention and post-intervention pass rates, describing thirteen different teaching approaches, were extracted and analyzed.

The results showed that on average, teaching interventions can improve programming pass rates by nearly one third when compared to a traditional lecture and lab based approach. While no statistically significant differences between the effectiveness of teaching interventions were observed, marginal differences do exist. The courses with relatable content (e.g. using *media computation*) with cooperative elements (e.g. pair programming) were among the top performers with CS0-courses, while courses with pair programming as the only intervention type and courses with game-theme performed more poorly when compared to others.

What the results of this analysis mean in practice, is that educators and researchers that are applying teaching interventions are making a difference. Whilst there is no silver bullet, no teaching approach works significantly better than others, a conscious change almost always results in an improvement in pass rates over the existing situation.

# 6. REFERENCES

[1] J. D. Bayliss. The effects of games in CS1-3. In *Microsoft Academic Days Conference on Game Development in Computer Science Education*, pages 59–63. Citeseer, 2007.

[2] M. Ben-Ari. Constructivism in computer science education. In *SIGCSE bulletin*, volume 30, pages 257–261. ACM, 1998.

[3] J. Bennedsen and M. E. Caspersen. Failure rates in introductory programming. *SIGCSE Bulletin*, 39(2):32–36, 2007.

[4] J. D. Chase and E. G. Okie. Combining cooperative learning and peer instruction in introductory computer science. *SIGCSE Bulletin*, 32(1):372–376, Mar. 2000.

[5] N. De La Mora and C. F. Reilly. The impact of real-world topic labs on student performance in CS1. In *Proc. Frontiers in Education*, pages 1–6. IEEE, 2012.

[6] J. Hattie. *Visible learning: A synthesis of over 800 meta-analyses relating to achievement*. Routledge, 2013.

[7] M. Haungs, C. Clark, J. Clements, and D. Janzen. Improving first-year success and retention through interest-based CS0 courses. In *Proc. SIGCSE*, pages 589–594. ACM, 2012.

[8] J. Kurhila and A. Vihavainen. Management, structures and tools to scale up personal advising in large programming courses. In *Proc. SIGITE*, pages 3–8. ACM, 2011.

[9] P. Lasserre and C. Szostak. Effects of team-based learning on a cs1 course. In *Proc. ITiCSE*, pages 133–137. ACM, 2011.

[10] I. Milne and G. Rowe. Difficulties in learning and teaching programming - views of students and tutors. *Educ. and Information Technologies*, 7(1):55–66, 2002.

[11] P. Mullins, D. Whitfield, and M. Conlon. Using alice 2.0 as a first language. *Journal of Computing Sciences in Colleges*, 24(3):136–143, 2009.

[12] U. Nikula, O. Gotel, and J. Kasurinen. A motivation guided holistic rehabilitation of the first programming course. *Trans. Comput. Educ.*, 11(4):24:1–24:38, Nov. 2011.

[13] A. Pears, S. Seidman, L. Malmi, L. Mannila, E. Adams, J. Bennedsen, M. Devlin, and J. Paterson. A survey of literature on the teaching of introductory programming. In *SIGCSE Bulletin*, volume 39, pages 204–223. ACM, 2007.

[14] L. Porter and B. Simon. Retaining nearly one-third more majors with a trio of instructional best practices in CS1. In *Proc. SIGCSE*, pages 165–170. ACM, 2013.

[15] D. Radošević, T. Orehovački, and A. Lovrenčić. New approaches and tools in teaching programming. In *Proc. of Central European Conference on Information and Intelligent Systems*, pages 49–57, 2009.

[16] M. Rizvi and T. Humphries. A scratch-based cs0 course for at-risk computer science majors. In *Proc. Frontiers in Education*, pages 1–5. IEEE, 2012.

[17] A. Robins, J. Rountree, and N. Rountree. Learning and teaching programming: A review and discussion. *Computer Science Education*, 13(2):137–172, 2003.

[18] S. C. Shaffer and M. B. Rosson. Increasing student success by modifying course delivery based on student submission data. *ACM Inroads*, 4(4):81–86, Dec. 2013.

[19] B. Simon, P. Kinnunen, L. Porter, and D. Zazkis. Experience report: CS1 for majors with media computation. In *Proc. ITiCSE*, pages 214–218. ACM, 2010.

[20] R. H. Sloan and P. Troy. CS 0.5: A better approach to introductory computer science for majors. *SIGCSE Bulletin*, 40(1):271–275, Mar. 2008.

[21] A. E. Tew, C. Fowler, and M. Guzdial. Tracking an innovation in introductory CS education from a research university to a two-year college. In *Proc. SIGCSE*, pages 416–420. ACM, 2005.

[22] I. Utting, A. E. Tew, M. McCracken, L. Thomas, D. Bouvier, R. Frye, J. Paterson, M. Caspersen, Y. B.-D. Kolikant, J. Sorva, and T. Wilusz. A fresh look at novice programmers' performance and their teachers' expectations. In *Proc. ITiCSE Working Group Reports*, pages 15–32. ACM, 2013.

[23] A. Vihavainen. Predicting students' performance in an introductory programming course using data from students' own programming process. In *Proc. ICALT*, pages 498–499. IEEE, 2013.

[24] H. M. Walker. Collaborative learning: a case study for CS1 at grinnell college and austin. In *SIGCSE Bulletin*, volume 29, pages 209–213. ACM, 1997.

[25] C. Watson and F. W. Li. Failure rates in introductory programming revisited. In *To appear in Proc. Innovation and Technology in Computer Science Education (ITiCSE)*. ACM, 2014.

[26] C. Watson, F. W. Li, and J. L. Godwin. Predicting performance in an introductory programming course by logging and analyzing student programming behavior. In *Proc. ICALT*, pages 319–323. IEEE, 2013.

[27] C. Watson, F. W. Li, and J. L. Godwin. No tests required: comparing traditional and dynamic predictors of programming success. In *Proc. SIGCSE*, pages 469–474. ACM, 2014.

[28] L. Williams, C. McDowell, N. Nagappan, J. Fernald, and L. Werner. Building pair programming knowledge through a family of experiments. In *Proc. Empirical Software Engineering*, pages 143–152. IEEE.

# APPENDIX

Due to space limitation and to serve as a starting point for future researchers, a list of 32 references is provided at http://bit.ly/1qkb8GI.

# Theoretical Underpinnings of Computing Education Research – What is the Evidence?

**Lauri Malmi**
Aalto University, Finland
lma@cs.hut.fi

**Judy Sheard**
Monash University, Australia
judy.sheard@monash.edu

**Simon**
University of Newcastle, Australia
simon@newcastle.edu.au

**Roman Bednarik**
University of Eastern Finland
roman.bednarik@uef.fi

**Juha Helminen**
Aalto University, Finland
juha.helminen@aalto.fi

**Päivi Kinnunen**
Aalto University, Finland
paivi.kinnunen@aalto.fi

**Ari Korhonen**
Aalto University, Finland
ari.korhonen@hut.fi

**Niko Myller**
University of Eastern Finland
nmyller@cs.joensuu.fi

**Juha Sorva**
Aalto University, Finland
juha.sorva@iki.fi

**Ahmad Taherkhani**
Aalto University, Finland
ahta47@gmail.com

## ABSTRACT

We analyze the Computing Education Research (CER) literature to discover what theories, conceptual models and frameworks recent CER builds on. This gives rise to a broad understanding of the theoretical basis of CER that is useful for researchers working in that area, and has the potential to help CER develop its own identity as an independent field of study.

Our analysis takes in seven years of publications (2005-2011, 308 papers) in three venues that publish long research papers in computing education: the journals ACM Transactions of Computing Education (TOCE) and Computer Science Education (CSEd), and the conference International Computing Education Research Workshop (ICER). We looked at the theoretical background works that are *used or extended* in the papers, not just referred to when describing related work. These background works include theories, conceptual models and frameworks. For each background work we tried to identify the discipline from which it originates, to gain an understanding of how CER relates to its neighboring fields. We also identified theoretical works originating within CER itself, showing that the field is building on its own theoretical works.

Our main findings are that there is a great richness of work on which recent CER papers build; there are no prevailing theoretical or technical works that are broadly applied across CER; about half the analyzed papers build on no previous theoretical work, but a considerable share of these are building their own theoretical constructions. We discuss the significance of these findings for the whole field and conclude with some recommendations.

## Categories and Subject Descriptors

K.3.2 [**Computers and education**]: Computer and Information Science Education – *computer science education*; A.0 [**General**]: *conference proceedings*.

## Keywords

Classifying publications, computing education, research methods.

## 1. INTRODUCTION

Computing Education Research (CER) is a relatively new field of investigation, which has emerged from the longer-standing traditions of practice reports and scholarship of learning and teaching in computing education. CER seeks to gain deep understanding of multiple aspects of the teaching and learning processes of various topics in the computing curriculum, and to build generalizable evidence about problems in students' learning and the efficacy of new teaching approaches to solve these problems.

The computing education research tradition is still young, with no firmly established ways of carrying out research. Instead it is often characterized as drawing on the approaches and methods of disciplines with more established traditions of research, such as cognitive psychology, education, and computer science. However, over the past 10 years CER has started forming its own identity as an independent field of study, as can be shown using the six structural criteria proposed by Fensham [7] for the recognition of a new research field. These criteria include, for example, research

*ICER '14*, August 11 - 13 2014, Glasgow, United Kingdom
Copyright 2014 ACM 978-1-4503-2755-8/14/08…$15.00.
http://dx.doi.org/10.1145/2632320.2632358

journals, research conferences, and research training, all of which can be found in computing education.

In examining the theories that underlie CER we are applying two of Fensham's intra-research criteria. The first is *conceptual and theoretical development*, which discusses important concepts that can be used to reduce the multiplicity of observations on a more abstract level and theoretical models that present relations between such concepts, and which have some predictive and explanatory power concerning the phenomena of interest. The second is *progression*, which discusses whether the field is using and refining previously developed concepts and theoretical models "...to expand and deepen our appreciation and understanding of ... education and its situation of occurrence" [7]. We have chosen these criteria because they are the ones that will be most readily in evidence when examining the literature.

Extensive use of existing theory is a normal part of research in the natural and human sciences, but not in computer science, where theories are few and the constructive, design and formal approaches dominate. We therefore consider it likely that for CER researchers, most of whom have computer science as their background, it is not straightforward to apply theories in the same way as in the disciplines from which CER draws.

Beyond looking for evidence that theories are being used, we are interested in whether we can find theoretical development work that originates from CER itself. CER investigates the challenges and processes in teaching and learning computing. It seems likely that this requires a theoretical understanding that is inherently related to the concepts and processes of computing itself. Neither general educational theories nor theories from neighboring fields such as Engineering Education Research can be used to explain, for example, how students understand programming concepts. Our research community needs to define its own discipline-based understanding of such issues – although of course we would expect this understanding to build where appropriate on more general theories.

The research reported here emerges from our belief that a more holistic understanding of our own field can support the whole CER community in building its identity as an independent area of research. Thus we hope to address questions such as: On what kind of work does the CER community build its current work? How can the community improve its theoretical understanding of teaching and learning processes in the computing domain? What actions could be carried out to build stronger theoretical foundations in future CER work? Addressing these questions entails an analysis of the current state of art in the field, and this research takes a step in that direction.

An overview of the theoretical foundations of CER is useful for many actors in the field, including researchers, teachers, managers, and reviewers. Revealing the richness of perspectives supports and helps the creation of new research directions and points of view, and helps to grasp the big picture of what research is being conducted in computing education. It is highly useful in research training for the field. It also helps to strengthen the identity of CER as an independent field of research by providing a picture of where we are now as a research community and where we might proceed in the future, exploiting and enhancing theoretical models that can be used for more powerful explanatory and predictive purposes. A similar argument has been presented in mathematics education research: "*One question that repeatedly confronts the field is whether or not mathematics education research is a scientific discipline akin to the hard sciences. If so, we need to consider the important role of theory building and theory usage in mathematics education research.*" [29].

In this paper we present the results of a survey of 308 research papers published in the journals Computer Science Education, and Transactions on Computing Education, and the International Computing Education Research Workshop in the seven years from 2005 to 2011. Our research questions are:

- What theoretical constructs are used in CER?

- From what disciplines do these constructs come?

- Are there indications that CER is building on its own theoretical constructs?

## 2. RELATED WORK

In recent years there have been a number of efforts to analyze the CER literature to form an overview of the research that is being conducted. This work has focused mainly on two aspects of research: the content of the research and the research process.

With regard to research content, various subareas of CER have been identified by Fincher and Petre [8] and by Pears et al. [21], using different criteria for partitioning the field. Simon et al. [25, 27] presented a more elaborate classification scheme that categorizes research by identifying the curricular context in which the research is conducted, the theme of the research within that context, the scope of the work, and the nature of the research setting. The system has been applied to nearly 600 papers from four computing education conferences and one journal over the years 2000-2007; see Simon [26] and the references in that paper. Other surveys include that of Joy et al. [13], who categorized content, considering particularly where certain kinds of work were published, and that of Kinnunen et al. [14], who looked at the pedagogical focuses of the papers published in ICER.

The second branch in the literature analysis has looked at the research process. Randolph and several other researchers critically reviewed papers in eight CS education publication forums during the years 2000-2005, focusing on the research process: whether human participants were involved, what kind of research setting was used, what data was collected, how it was analyzed, and how the research was reported. They identified many weaknesses in reported research settings [22, 23]. In our own prior work [16] we have sought to characterize research in computing education using a system that includes the theoretical basis of the research.

Sheard et al. [24] touched on both of these branches when reviewing the programming education research papers from six CER conferences from the years 2005-2008. They categorized the papers using Simon's system, but also looked at the research methods used in those papers.

However, through all of these surveys we found very little attention paid to the theoretical basis of the research being reported. We therefore broadened our scope to look at research in other areas of STEM education, to find out what it could tell us about the use of theory in those areas. Again we found many literature surveys examining various aspects of research publications, but few that analyzed the use and application of theories.

In Engineering Education Research (EER) we found only one survey addressing theories. Wankat [31] analyzed 597 papers published in the Journal of Engineering Education in the years 1993-2002. The analysis included the theoretical backgrounds to the work, noting that "a judgment was made as to whether a theory was merely being cited or it was actually being used for design or analysis". The results showed that an overwhelming majority (84%) of EER papers published during this period did not use any educational theory. The most common theories found were Kolb's experiential learning, learning styles, and the MBTI indicator, which were used in 1-3% of the papers. This survey is 10 years old, and the situation might well have changed, but we have found no more recent work on the topic.

In Physics Education Research (PER) a recent synthesis report [6] discusses the use of theoretical frameworks in different subareas of PER, and points out the need to build theoretical frameworks for PER. More than a decade earlier, a resource letter [17] presented a large list of papers in various areas of physics education research, and identified a set of example papers with theoretical development in the areas of concept development and problem solving performance.

In Mathematics Education Research (MER), theoretical foundations and the role of theory development have been discussed extensively. Sriraman and English [30] conducted a survey of the use of theories in mathematics education papers, and a Theory of Mathematics Education study group organized many international conferences on the topic in the 1980s and 1990s [29]. Work from MER is discussed in more detail in the next section.

# 3. WHY INVESTIGATE THEORY?

For the purposes of this work we define 'theory' to mean *a broad class of concepts that aim to provide a structure for conceptual explanations or established practice*, and use such terms as 'theories', 'models', and 'frameworks' to describe particular manifestations of the general concept of theory. Examples encompassed by our definition include constructivism, cognitive load theory, Bloom's taxonomy, grounded theories, phenomenographical outcome spaces, Simon's classification system [25], and established pedagogical practices such as pair programming and contributing student pedagogies. A critical reader might think it impossible to draw a line between what should be included and what should not. Our basic goal, however, is to try to establish how the field builds on existing and emerging theoretical work. From this perspective, the inclusion or exclusion of an individual theory does not have a significant effect on the whole. On the other hand, applying very strict criteria for theory would not allow us to identify and list the many interesting and relevant connections between research works.

Examining the role of theory in educational design studies, diSessa and Cobb [5] write that "the importance of theory is completely uncontested" in many fields of science (p79), but is less widely accepted in educational research. They suggest that theory development is "critical for the long-term scientific health and practical power of design-related educational research" (p101).

We have not been able to find any analysis of how theories are being used in CER. However, such analysis has been carried in

mathematics education research, which has a much longer history than CER.

Niss [19] discusses the nature, origin, and foundation of theories in mathematics education, and identifies several types of theory: 1) overarching theories giving a general framework, such as social constructivism; 2) data-driven theories such as grounded theories; 3) theories that basically provide a terminology to use, such as process-object duality; and 4) theories offering a research method, such as phenomenography. It seems reasonable to suppose that these types of theory apply equally well to computing education research. In this paper, page limits constrain us to the first three types of theory; we hope that our analysis of research methods in CER will be published separately.

Niss identifies six different roles for theories. Theories can be used to *explain* observed phenomena or to predict an occurrence of a phenomenon. For example, cognitive load theory can use the concept of working memory explain the effects on students' learning of task structure and presentation. The same theory can also provide *guidance for action or behavior* by reasoning about the principles by which learning and assessment tasks should be constructed.

Theories can provide a structured *set of lenses* to approach, observe, study or interpret the target of investigation. Good examples of this are phenomenography and variation theory, which allow us to investigate students' experiences or understandings of a specific phenomenon and present them in a consistent way. Theories can also be used as a *safeguard against unscientific approaches,* by explicating underlying assumptions and choices, thus setting the framework for research. Finally, they can be used to *protect against attacks* from sceptical colleagues from other disciplines. By demonstrating that researchers share common theoretical understandings within the research community, rather than working with *ad hoc* concepts, frameworks and procedures, members of the community are better placed to argue about the quality of their work. It is thus clearly worthwhile to strive for a good understanding of the role of theories in CER.

Taking a different perspective, Pais et al. [20] discuss the difference between 'How theories', which focus on how to solve a practical problem, and 'Why theories', which try to explain what is happening behind the observed behavior – and which they emphasize should therefore play a greater role. In CER, Hundhausen et al. [11] analyzed a number of evaluation studies in algorithm visualization and concluded that constructivism could explain the observation that better learning results can be achieved by working actively with a visualization than by following it passively. Here constructivism is used as a Why-theory. Building on this meta-study, the engagement taxonomy [18] defines six different levels of engagement for student interaction and uses these levels to suggest how visualization tools should be designed. There is some empirical evidence to support the principles, but the taxonomy itself provides no clear explanation of why each level supports better learning than the levels below it. It would thus be a How theory.

There are more advantages to using a theory. Firstly, as Niss [19] has observed, they can provide a *terminology* to be used in discussion. This supports better communication of ideas and results between researchers, as they can use a common set of concepts and terms in preference to defining their own. This does not rule out that the need to define new concepts and terms in an evolving field. Secondly, theories can suggest *hypotheses*, which can be tested empirically, such as the above-mentioned engagement taxonomy. Thirdly, they can provide better arguments for *interpreting empirical findings*, as in the case of the meta-study by Hundhausen et al [11]. Recent visualization research has therefore been investigating this complex interaction more closely, trying to either build evidence for the engagement taxonomy or refine it to better match new empirical findings.

Our current research is a first step to understanding the current role of theories in CER. In this paper, we focus on looking at how widely CER is building on existing theoretical work, where that work originates from, and to what extent CER is building on its own theoretical developments.

# 4. TMMCER CLASSIFICATION

In this work, we apply our TMMCER (Theories, Models and Methods in CER) classification system [16], which examines the theoretical/technical background and the research process evident in a paper. The system categorizes papers in seven dimensions: theoretical background, technical background, reference disciplines, research purpose, research framework, data source, and analysis method. In this paper we focus on just the two dimensions that are pertinent to the use of theories in CER.

Within the theoretical background dimension, **Theories, models, frameworks (TMF)** captures how the paper builds on previous theoretical research or established practice by *applying* or *extending* some TMF. We do not count or report methodological TMFs, such as phenomenography, as they are covered by other dimensions, and are outside the scope of this paper.

**Reference discipline** denotes the origin of a TMF by listing the field of study in which it has been developed: education, psychology, or engineering, for example. We do not list subfields, such as educational psychology. CER itself is listed if the TMF has its origin in that area. If several TMFs for a single paper build on the same discipline, we count it only once, as we are interested in finding out the share of CER papers that build on other disciplines.

# 5. RESEARCH METHOD
## 5.1 Data Pool

Our goal for this project is to build a broad view of the theoretical underpinnings of published computing education research. As the complete analysis of recent publications in all major publication venues was beyond our resources, we have had to make a pragmatic choice as to which venues to consider. We therefore chose to include Computer Science Education (CSEd) and ACM Transactions on Computing Education (TOCE), formerly published as Journal of Educational Resources in Computing (JERIC), as the most prominent journals that focus principally on computing education; and ICER, as a highly research-oriented conference [27] that accepted long papers (12 pages for most of the period we were studying, although this has now been reduced to eight pages). Long papers are important for our analysis, because they allow more discussion on theoretical issues and the research process.

There are many other journals and conferences that accept computing education research paper. But faced with a clear need to limit the scope of our research, we chose these three in the belief that they offer the greatest concentration of computing education research, as opposed, for example, to computing education practice.

Having selected these three venues, we made three further decisions regarding the inclusion or exclusion of papers. We included all special issue papers from the journals, as special issues are a frequent and focal forum for the presentation of research. We excluded editorial papers and short summaries of other papers in the issue, as they generally do not present original research. And we excluded the four discussion papers from ICER 2011, as that year's conference clearly distinguished discussion papers from research papers and imposed a lower page limit on the former. All remaining papers could be categorized as papers presenting research. This gave a data pool of 308 papers from 2005-2011: 113 from CSEd, 98 from JERIC/TOCE, and 97 from ICER. We recognized that the transition from JERIC to TOCE in 2007-2008 might influence the results for this journal, and were interested in whether we would detect such an effect.

## 5.2 Research Process

The analysis concerning TMMCER categorization was carried out by ten researchers working in pairs. The data pool for 2005-2010 was divided evenly among the pairs, who classified the papers independently and then came to a consensus. The papers from 2011 were subsequently classified by the two first authors. While this paper reports only on TMFs and reference disciplines, we did classify the papers along all of the TMMCER dimensions.

In research of this nature, the inter-rater reliability of classifications results must always be established. We have addressed this matter in the following way. First, satisfactory inter-rater reliability between the same pairs of classifiers was established earlier in the project; full details of the reliability process and results are reported in an earlier paper [16]. Second, the one new project member, who had considerable experience in classifying papers using other schemes, was paired with one of the principal developers of our classification scheme to ensure optimal support for learning the new system. The leader in this pair took care that the interpretation of categories did not change from that used earlier in the project.

The process of identifying TMFs in the papers is not clear-cut, because we want to identify TMFs that are clearly used or extended in a paper, rather than just referred to as related work. For example, a paper might mention grounded theory in its literature review, but not apply grounded theory in the actual research. Such a paper cannot be said to be using grounded theory. We look for evidence that the theoretical constructs are used, for example, to guide research design, to formulate hypotheses, or to interpret previous or new results. Therefore we read the papers carefully to decide whether a TMF that was mentioned should be included or not. The main indicators for including a TMF were: 1) the paper had a (sub)section which presented its theoretical framework; 2) in the abstract, introduction or description of research design it was explained that the research was based on some specific theoretical framework; and 3) in the discussion section(s) it was explained that the results were interpreted using some theoretical framework. Investigation of the last two indicators included looking for citations and theory names in the text and whether the context of citations informed us that the work was using some theory. Citations that focused on building motivation for the research or presenting parallel independent work were not counted. In many cases the analysis required negotiation between the classifiers to reach a consensus. Therefore the method of working in pairs turned out to be a clear advantage, despite the fact that the classification took a long time, several months, before all pairs had completed their efforts. There are definitely cases where the decision to include/exclude some TMF could easily have gone the other way. However, we are confident that the big picture is reasonably accurate, and that counts far more in this kind of research than whether there were 64, 65, or 66 papers in a particular category.

There were also occasional problems in determining reference disciplines. These were typically deduced from the forum in which the TMF was originally published, which in most cases provided a clear indication. However, we also had to make judgments between fields, as for reasons of clarity we listed only the principal fields. Thus, for example, TMFs in educational psychology may have been classified either in education or in psychology, as our expertise did not allow us to make a clear decision. Moreover, some TMFs might have clear origins that span multiple disciplines. Once again, however, the effect on the big picture is small.

# 6. RESULTS

## 6.1 Theories, Models and Frameworks
In 157 papers (51%) we identified at least one theory, model or framework (TMF) that had been used. We identified 314 instances of work based on TMFs, and 226 of these were *distinct* TMFs. The most common TMF was constructivism or some of its sub-theories (communal constructivism, constructionism, social constructivism, situated learning) (15 mentions), followed by some curricular framework (10 mentions, mostly different versions of ACM/IEEE Curriculum), the pair programming model (10), Bloom's taxonomy (7), and pedagogical patterns (6). Among other theories of learning and psychological theories, the most common were Bandura's self-efficacy theory (5), cognitive load theory (4), and schema theory (4). Among the 226 distinct TMFs, more than 150 could be identified with a designated name (such as Bloom's taxonomy or Kolb's experiential cycle), while the rest were generally references to individual papers. Almost 200 TMFs were identified only once in the whole data pool.

When considering the publication venues, a small majority of papers in both ICER (57%) and CSEd (57%) were based on some TMF, while the number for JERIC/TOCE was somewhat smaller (39%). This difference between the venues is significant (Pearson $\chi^2$, p = 0.014). We also looked at whether there were trends in the use of TMFs during the analysis period. Figure 1 shows the average share of papers that build on some TMF during the period. The total number of papers per year in all forums is fairly small (typically 20) and there is considerable yearly fluctuation in the results. We have tried to smooth this fluctuation by combining the results into three groups: the years 2005-2007 (135 papers), 2008-2009 (88 papers), and 2010-2011 (85 papers). The numbers of papers in these groups are far from equal, but they do serve to give a broad picture of possible trends. It seems that papers in JERIC/TOCE have increased their use of TMFs, suggesting that the transition from JERIC to TOCE had an effect on the characteristics of the papers, while there is no clear trend in the other venues.

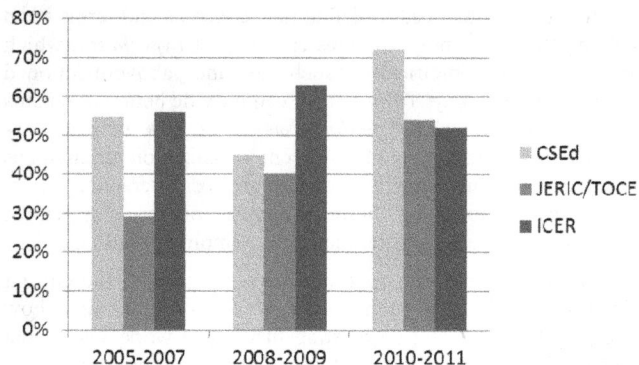

**Figure 1: Proportions of papers at each venue that build on some TMF**

Almost half of the papers do not appear to be based on any TMFs. This concurs with Wankat's findings from EER [31], although the numbers themselves cannot be directly compared, as Wankat's exact criteria for including TMFs were not given in his paper. Examining the 43% of the CSEd papers and the 43% of the ICER papers in which we had failed to find TMFs, we identified three types of paper. First, there were papers that formed new theories. These included various categorizations of data (e.g. phenomenographical outcome spaces), hypotheses that were formulated and possibly tested with the collected data, and new explanatory theories such as models or grounded theories. A second group of papers analyzed and discussed their data, perhaps presenting a new method of analysis, but did not present a finding with enough structure to be considered a theory in the sense being used in our analysis. Finally, there were papers including literature surveys, reports of technical contributions such as novel educational software or hardware, and reports of novel instructional methods. The first group of papers, those presenting new theories, formed a considerable share of the CSEd papers and a majority of the ICER papers, demonstrating that many new TMFs are being formulated within CER itself.

## 6.2 Reference Disciplines
For each paper with TMFs, we identified the reference disciplines from which those TMFs originated, counting only the *distinct* disciplines from each paper. This decision is based on the observation that only a very small share of the papers had more than one TMF from the same discipline, but these papers often had many of them. We decided that to reveal the general picture of how CER papers link to work in other disciplines, we should not give undue weight to such 'theory-rich' papers.

Although all of the analyzed papers are in computing education research, we listed CER as a reference discipline only where the identified TMF had been developed within CER; an example is contributing student pedagogy [9].

Narrowing the focus to papers that build on TMFs from other fields, we see that 20% (63) of these papers use some TMF from education, 13% (41) from psychology, and only 6% (20) from both. These are not large numbers. Almost half of the papers examined do not build on any theory, model, or framework, and 80% of the computing education papers in in our data pool do not build on theoretical research from education. When interpreting these numbers it is worthwhile to recall that we deliberately adopted a loose definition of theory, and even then our findings indicate low numbers of papers building on previous theoretical work.

Table 1 presents the percentages of reference disciplines for TMFs in each venue. The three disciplines of computing, education and psychology were referenced rather more than CER. The 'others' category includes medicine, philosophy, linguistics, management, and systems theory. Many papers had two or more reference disciplines, as they used TMFs from different areas. There are no significant differences between the venues (Pearson $\chi2$, p = 0.833).

**Table 1: Reference disciplines of TMFs as a percentage of the total reference disciplines from each venue**

|  | CSEd | JERIC/TOCE | ICER | Total |
|---|---|---|---|---|
| Count | 91 | 53 | 75 | 219 |
| CER | 15 % | 17 % | 17 % | 16 % |
| Computing | 27 % | 25 % | 20 % | 24 % |
| Education | 31 % | 26 % | 28 % | 29 % |
| Psychology | 18 % | 15 % | 23 % | 19 % |
| Others | 9 % | 17 % | 12 % | 12 % |

As we identified very few theories originating in CER (23 in all), we chose to look more closely at these. About half of them were categorization schemes or taxonomies, such as Simon's system [25] or the engagement taxonomy for algorithm visualization [18]. The remainder included questionnaires, pedagogical practices such as contributing student pedagogy [9], and theoretical constructions such as Jadud's EQ [12] and Hazzan's 'reducing abstraction' framework [10]. While we have been using the word 'theory' more or less interchangeably with TMF, it is perhaps timely to recall that the full phrase is Theories, Models, and Frameworks; some of the TMFs mentioned above clearly fall into the second or third group rather than the first.. The most common single TMF was the engagement taxonomy, used in three papers. As a whole, although the numbers are small, we conclude that there is some theoretical work in CER itself on which the field is building, and not just referencing as related work. As we noted in the previous section, there appears to be considerable new theoretical work in our data pool. This suggests that future research will have a wider pool of TMFs from CER on which to build. However, within our limited seven-year data pool, with such a small number of TMFs from CER, we are not yet able to identify such an increasing trend. We hope to see it in the future.

# 7. DISCUSSION

We have found clear evidence that the field of CER draws extensively on work from other disciplines. Over half of the TMFs originate in fields outside CER and computing, mostly in education and psychology. This is not a bad thing, but we do expect in the future to see more use of TMFs originating in CER.

We were surprised at the vast number of distinct TMFs that we identified, especially as we were counting only those that are really used or extended in the paper, not those that are just mentioned. However, it is in accord with Wankat's findings in EER [31]. What might explain the large number? One obvious factor is simply the richness of the CER field: people are investigating so many different things that many different TMFs need to be used. Moreover, different theories provide different points of view and can thus shed more light on the complex phenomena we are investigating. Another possible explanation could be pragmatic: because CER has created only few TMFs of its own, researchers must look elsewhere when seeking a solid foundation for their work. Most researchers in CER will be familiar with TMFs from the discipline of computing itself, but when those are not appropriate, they are left to study the broader literature on their own. The range of TMFs in the social sciences is large, so it is easy to imagine that researchers will adopt whatever TMFs they find that seem reasonably pertinent to their work. Moreover, many CER papers do not build clearly on any TMF. Thus it may be difficult to find work that is closely related to one's own research topic and has a strong theoretical background, which would make it easier to use the same TMFs. Having read all of the papers in this data pool, we believe that if researchers were to explicit list the theories and frameworks that they use, this would help other researchers to find work related to their own research, leading in turn to higher citation counts.

The richness brings advantages and disadvantages. It is a good sign that work from other research disciplines is widely used, and provides evidence that CER is truly cross-disciplinary and is actively adding to its theory base. Also the wealth of different theories provides more versatile views for the phenomena being investigated. On the other hand, this may also be a hindrance, as CER is building not on a small and stable theoretical base but on a large and dispersed one. There are mixed terminologies and ways of building arguments, as there will always be in cross-disciplinary work. Comparing one's own results to those of others may not be easy when the results are interpreted according to different theoretical arguments. This may lead to a situation where knowledge in the field accumulates only in small isolated areas, which may be referenced as related work but which are not used as a foundation for new research.

This challenge has certainly been grasped as an opportunity in mathematics education research, as research combining different theoretical views may reveal novel understandings that are unlikely to emerge from single approaches [4]. Bikner-Ahsbahs and Prediger [3] discuss four different strategies for coping with the challenge. It is possible to *unify* theories that are developed locally to address similar phenomena or *integrate* theories by combining different approaches. Treating the same data set with different theories (*comparing and contrasting*) can reveal interesting differences and similarities in the theories while respecting the diversity. Finally, *networking* of theories is used when the previous strategies are systematically applied by first comparing and contrasting and then integrating new perspectives giving a progressively deeper understanding of the phenomenon. Research using any of these strategies is currently scarce in CER, but examples can be found [15, 28]. Of course this is not to diminish the value of papers that discuss the role of single theory in the CER context, such as those of Ben-Ari [1, 2]

A further finding of our analysis is that in nearly half of the papers we found no TMF. Our analysis cannot reveal why their authors have not based their work on any TMF, but as we have explained in the previous section, there can be some very good reasons. Therefore we are not concerned about each individual paper that uses no TMF: our concern is more with the sheer proportion of such papers.

It must be noted that our analysis says nothing about how the TMFs are used in the papers we have examined, nor about the intrinsic worth of the TMFs we have found. These are highly important considerations, but are clearly well beyond the scope of this analysis. The merit of a simple count of TMFs lies not in what it says about any individual paper or the TMFs that it uses, but in the big picture that it presents of computing education research.

# 8. CONCLUSION AND IMPLICATIONS

We have carried out a comprehensive analysis of the papers published in two leading journals and the leading research-oriented conference. We have surveyed 308 publications from the seven years to 2011 to examine their theoretical underpinnings. The analysis has given us a deep look at CER, helping us to understand the many facets of the published research. Here we comment briefly on some of the main findings and present some recommendations for the whole field.

One of the goals of the work was to discover to what extent research in computing education is building on previous work, particularly theoretical work from other fields, because wide use of theoretical frameworks is one aspect of a maturing discipline. In mathematics education research this issue was widely discussed more than 20 years ago [29], and we hope that CER will consider it equally important.

Computing education research has been considered as a multi-disciplinary research field that combines computing with the human sciences, particularly education and psychology. We found clear support for this claim, as more than half of the papers in our data pool were based on one or more TMFs, more than half of those originating in disciplines outside CER and computing.

We also found TMFs from CER itself being used in other papers. These were mainly categorization schemes and taxonomies. Although they are not Why-theories [20] that can be used to explain observed phenomena from empirical work, they form a basis on which other research can better build. We hope to see more such work.

While much of the research in the field is somewhat insular, there is also a great and perhaps even excessive richness of the application of work from other fields. We suggest that the whole community of CER should emphasize building a better understanding of the role of TMFs in its research, not simply to learn more about specific theories but to discuss how the field can benefit from a broader use of theoretical work.

In order to address the challenge and opportunity of theory-richness within CER we propose the following.

- Some of the computing education conferences could host one- or two-day theoretical workshops in which a few carefully selected TMFs are discussed in some detail with invited experts in those theories, and a critical comparison is carried out of the literature and the findings from these approaches.

- Another way of organizing theoretical workshops could be that they solicit papers with a strong focus on applying different theories to bring about more visibility for the role of theory.

- We recommend the establishment of new research that purposefully combines different theoretical approaches. Journals in the field could solicit papers that compare, contrast or combine different theories in CER to be included in a special issue.

- When specifying review criteria in conferences and journals, the role of theory could be elaborated to clarify what expressions such as 'solid theoretical framework' actually imply. This includes giving some guidelines as to how the use of theoretical frameworks should be reported in the paper.

- As a community we should actively look at the achievements in our neighboring disciplines of mathematics, physics, science and engineering education research to learn about how theories are used in those contexts.

Through this work we have tried to capture the scope of theoretical underpinnings in work carried out in computing education research. This has increased our own understanding of the field as a whole, allowing us to make a number of observations and suggestions as to how the research tradition in the field could improve and mature. We hope that computing education research will continue to develop its own identifiable research tradition, shared methodologies, and some theories of its own, placing it on a more even footing with longer-established education research fields.

We have only skimmed the questions of the role and impact of theories in CER. Many questions remain to be addressed in our future work. What are the 'homegrown' TMFs in the field? How can they be characterized? Have they been validated in any way? How widely are they used in the CER literature outside our data pool? How and for what purposes are homegrown theories and borrowed theories from other disciplines used to support research (with reference to some of the theory-usage classifications from mathematics education research [3, 19, 20])? How are theories developed within CER? How is the acquired theoretical knowledge transferred into practical pedagogical content knowledge for computer science teachers? It is clear that much yet remains to be done.

## References

[1] Ben-Ari, M. (2001). Constructivism in computer science education. *Journal of Computers in Mathematics and Science Teaching, 20*(1), 45-73.

[2] Ben-Ari, M. (2004). Situated learning in computer science education. *Computer Science Education, 14*(2), 85-100.

[3] Bikner-Ahsbahs, A., Prediger, S. (2006). Diversity of theories in mathematics education – how can we deal with it? ZDM, 38(1), 52-57.

[4] Bikner-Ahsbahs, A., and Prediger, S. (2010). Networking of theories—an approach for exploiting the diversity of theoretical approaches. *Theories of Mathematics Education* (pp. 483-506), Springer.

[5] diSessa, A., and Cobb, P. (2004) Ontological innovation and the role of theory in design experiments. Journal of the Learning Sciences, 13(1), 77-103.

[6] Docktor J. L., and Mestre J. P. (2011). A synthesis of discipline-based education research in physics. In Board of Science Education (Eds), *Commissioned Papers, Status,*

*Contributions, and Future Direction of Discipline-Based Education Research (DBER)*: National Academies, USA. URL: http://sites.nationalacademies.org/DBASSE/BOSE/ DBASSE_080124#.UdHKAuuae3h

[7] Fensham, Peter F. (2004). Defining an Identity - The evolution of Science Education as a Field of Research, Springer.

[8] Fincher, S., and Petre, M. (Eds.) (2004). *Computer Science Education Research*. Netherlands: Taylor & Francis.

[9] Hamer, J., Cutts, Q., Jackova, J., Luxton-Reilly, A., McCartney, R., Purchase, H., Riedesel, C., Saeli, M., Sanders, K., and Sheard, J. (2008). Contributing student pedagogy. *Inroads – SIGCSE Bulletin, 40*(4), 194-212.

[10] Hazzan, O. (2003). How students attempt to reduce abstraction in the learning of mathematics and in the learning of computer science. *Computer Science Education, 13*(2), 95-122.

[11] Hundhausen, C., Douglas, S., Stasko, J. (2002). A meta-study of algorithm visualization effectiveness. *Journal of Visual Languages & Computing, 13*(3), 259-290.

[12] Jadud, M. (2006). Methods and tools for exploring novice compilation behavior. Proceedings of the 2nd International Computing Education Research Workshop, 73-84.

[13] Joy, M., Sinclair, J., Sun, S., Sitthiworachart, J., and López-González, J. (2009). Categorising computer science education research. *Education and Information Technologies, 14*, 105-126.

[14] Kinnunen, P., Meisalo, V., and Malmi, L. (2010). Have we missed something? Identifying missing types of research in computing education. Proceedings of the 6th International Computing Education Research Workshop, 13-22.

[15] Koski, M.-I., Kurhila, J., and Pasanen, T. (2008). Why using robots to teach computer science can be successful: Theoretical reflection to andragogy and minimalism. Proceedings of the 8th Koli Calling International Conference on Computing Education Research, Koli, Finland.

[16] Malmi, L., Sheard, J., Simon, Bednarik, R., Helminen, J., Korhonen, A., Myller, N., Sorva, J., and Taherkhani, A. (2010). Characterizing research in computing education: a preliminary analysis of the literature. Proceedings of the 6th International Computing Education Research Workshop, 3-12.

[17] McDermott, L., and Redish, E. (1999). Resource letter: PER-1: Physics education research. *American Journal of Physics, 67*(9), 755-767.

[18] Naps, T., Roessling G., Almstrum, V., Dann, W., Fleischer, R., Hundhausen, C., Korhonen, A., Malmi, L., McNally, M., Rodger, S., and Velázquez-Iturbide A. (2002). Exploring the role of visualization and engagement in computer science education. *SIGCSE Bulletin, 35*(2), 131-152.

[19] Niss, M. (2007). The concept and role of theory in mathematics education. In C. Bergsten et al. (Eds.), Relating practice and research in mathematics education. Proceedings of Norma 05 (pp. 97-110) Trondheim: Tapir Academic Press.

[20] Pais, A., Stentoft, D., and Valero, P. (2010). From questions of how to questions of why in mathematics education research. In Proceedings of the Third International Mathematics Education Society Conference (Vol. 2, pp. 369–378). Berlin: Freie Universität Berlin.

[21] Pears, A., Seidman, S., Eney, C., Kinnunen, P., and Malmi, L. (2005). Constructing a core literature for computing education research. *SIGCSE Bulletin, 37*(4), 152-161.

[22] Randolph, J. (2007). *Computer Science at the Crossroads: A Methodological Review of the Computer Science Education Research: 2000-2005*. Doctoral dissertation, Utah State University. http://archive.org/details/randolph_dissertation

[23] Randolph, J. J., Julnes, G., Bednarik, R., and Sutinen, E. (2007). A comparison of the methodological quality of articles in computer science education journals and conference proceedings. *Computer Science Education, 17*(4), 263-274.

[24] Sheard, J., Simon, Hamilton, M., and Lönnberg, J. (2009). Analysis of research into the teaching and learning of programming. Proceedings of the 5th International Workshop on Computing Education Research. 93-104.

[25] Simon (2007). A classification of recent Australasian computing education publications. *Computer Science Education, 17*(3), 155-170.

[26] Simon (2009). Informatics in Education and Koli Calling: A comparative analysis. *Informatics in Education, 8*(1), 101-114.

[27] Simon, Carbone, A., de Raadt, M. , Lister, R., Hamilton, M., and Sheard, J. (2008). Classifying computing education papers: Process and results. Proceedings of the 4th International Workshop on Computing Education Research, 161-172.

[28] Sorva, J. (2013). Notional machines and introductory programming education. *ACM Transactions on Computing Education, 13*(2), Article 8.

[29] Sriraman, B., and English, L. (2005). Theories of mathematics education: a global survey of theoretical frameworks/trends in mathematics education research. *ZDM, 37*(6).

[30] Sriraman, B., and English, L. (2010). Surveying theories and philosophies of mathematics education. *Theories of Mathematics Education* (pp. 7-32): Springer.

[31] Wankat, P. (2004). Analysis of the first ten years of the Journal of Engineering Education. *Journal of Engineering Education, 93*(1), 13-21.

# The Recurring Rainfall Problem

Kathi Fisler
WPI Dept of Computer Science
kfisler@cs.wpi.edu

## ABSTRACT

Many studies have used Soloway's Rainfall problem to explore plan composition and programming errors by novice programmers. Few of these have explored students from CS1 courses that use functional programming. The concepts and programming styles commonly taught in such courses give CS1 students more viable plan-composition options than in traditional imperative CS1 courses. Using data from five functional-language CS1 courses at four schools, we show that our students choose different high-level structures and make fewer low-level errors compared to results of other Rainfall studies. We discuss the potential role of language in these results and raise various questions that could further explore these effects.

**Categories and Subject Descriptors:** K.3.2 [Computers and Education]: Computer and Information Science Education

**Keywords:** Plan composition, novice programmers, functional programming

## 1. INTRODUCTION

Soloway's Rainfall problem [10] has been used in several studies to assess students' progress in learning to construct programs. Rainfall is interesting because it is conceptually straightforward (a variation on averaging a collection of numbers), yet with enough components to raise subtleties in code. Soloway proposed the problem in the context of exploring *plan composition*: how students weave together the different components of a problem into a single program.

Over the years, multiple papers have reported on student performance on Rainfall, sometimes categorizing the errors that students make. Across prior studies, students typically solved Rainfall under three common constraints: they (nearly always) programmed imperatively, they (usually) obtained the numeric data through keyboard input, and they (often) had limited prior exposure to data structures, with the possible exception of arrays. These constraints don't arise in CS1 courses based on functional programming. Such courses emphasize different linguistic constructs (e.g., recursion instead of loops), rarely cover interactive I/O, and have students work extensively with lists from the early weeks of a course. This naturally raises a question: what do students from functional-first CS1 courses do with Rainfall?

Both facility with lists and limited use of I/O are interesting parameters. Because lists are easy to construct dynamically (unlike many array implementations), they enable a variety of viable high-level structures for Rainfall programs; some of these are harder or inaccessible with other or no data structures. Earlier Rainfall studies have shown that I/O patterns are difficult to get right, especially when data can be noisy. Avoiding I/O frees students to focus on computational tasks that arise across devices and platforms. Studying Rainfall on functional-first CS1 students could change how we view this classic question.

This paper makes three contributions. First, we propose a two-level analysis methodology for plan composition that looks at (a) the high-level structure of a solution, and (b) low-level errors when implementing tasks within that structure. While our coding rubric draws heavily on those from prior Rainfall studies, we found existing rubrics too coarse-grained for important nuances that arise in our dataset. Second, we apply our methodology to over 200 Rainfall samples across five functional-first CS1 courses at four schools (three universities and one high school) in the USA; we partly explore an additional dataset from a traditional Java-based CS1. Our functional-first participants produce solutions with rather different structures than in earlier studies, and seem to make fewer low-level errors. Our third contribution reflects the formative nature of this study: we identify several open research questions inspired by our observations.

## 2. THE RAINFALL PROBLEM

Soloway proposed the Rainfall problem in the 1980s [10]. The original wording was simply about computing averages:

> Write a program that will read in integers and output their average. Stop reading when the value 99999 is input.

Soloway identified four key goals within this problem: taking in input, summing the inputs, computing the average (which involves counting the inputs), and outputting the average. Programs that solve this problem must compose fragments of code that achieve each of these goals. Soloway proposed this problem in part to study approaches to plan composition, particularly in novices.

The "Rainfall" context has inspired many variations on the problem: some versions [1, 9] added negative numbers that the programmer should treat as input errors; some added output requirements [1], such as reporting the count of days with non-zero rainfall or the maximum daily rainfall in addition to the average. All variations shared common core goals of summing, counting, averaging, input and output.

In this study, we include negative numbers in the input, but only require producing the average as output. We also provide the inputs in a data structure (as our students had not learned I/O). Our specific wording is as follows:

> Design a program called rainfall that consumes a list of numbers representing daily rainfall amounts as entered by a user. The list may contain the number -999 indicating the end of the data of interest. Produce the average of the non-negative values in the list up to the first -999 (if it shows up). There may be negative numbers other than -999 in the list.

## 3. A FUNCTIONAL-FIRST CS1

Functional programming has many broad characteristics, including using recursion over unbounded-depth data structures (such as lists and trees), using few (if any) side-effects, and parameterizing functions over other functions. Functional languages and their corresponding programming styles vary widely (e.g., contrast LISP, Haskell, and Erlang).

This study focuses on a particular functional-first CS1 curriculum, *How to Design Programs* (henceforth HTDP) [2]. HTDP teaches a data- and test-driven approach to program design. While HTDP can be (and has been) used with non-functional languages, the textbook and accompanying software use Racket (a variant of Scheme).

The first part of HTDP teaches a bottom-up method for designing programs: given a problem, students define required datatypes, make concrete instances of the data, write concrete test cases (both inputs and expected outputs), write a code skeleton that traverses the input structurally (but does no problem-specific computation), then complete the skeleton with problem-specific code. Each step typically counts in grading: functions that produce correct answers but whose code structure deviates from the shape of the input data, for example, lose significant points (in Soloway's terms [10], HTDP requires code to have an *explanation*). HTDP takes students through this same core method multiple times on increasingly rich data structures: atomic values, structures, nested structures, lists, and (in most college-level courses for CS majors) trees. Later parts cover top-down design and problems requiring more than structural recursion.

HTDP teaches a limited set of language constructs: function definition, function invocation, conditionals, user-defined structures, lists (built-in), and perhaps naming intermediate computations. Roughly 5 weeks into a college-level CS1 for majors, students learn higher-order functions (such as `filter` and `map`) that implement common iteration patterns over lists, taking a function over individual list elements as input. In contrast to most non-functional CS1 courses, students do *not* learn standard `for/while` loops, arrays, or I/O; assignment operators, if covered at all, come towards the end of the course, and then only for use in contexts that require memory across calls to the same function.

HTDP's emphasis on a structured recipe for design makes it a particularly interesting context in which to study plan composition. Two aspects of this recipe—writing tests first and writing code against skeletons that traverse data—are particularly relevant. The testing emphasis means that students should have thought out (and written down!) the space of program inputs before writing even a single line of code. A good set of test cases would capture many common troublespots (such as the possibility of an empty list of inputs). The emphasis on skeletons that match the shape of data (identical to the Interpreter pattern in Object-Oriented design [3]) prescribes a default plan. As such, these skeletons are schemas in Soloway's sense, but aligned to data rather than control. HTDP seeks to have students master this bottom-up approach before tackling problems that require top-down planning. As a result, problems (like Rainfall) that require at least some top-down planning are fascinating testbeds for HTDP.

## 4. PLAN COMPOSITIONS

Rainfall requires students to compose code implementing multiple tasks. Our version (in Section 2) requires six tasks:

- Sentinel: Ignore inputs after the sentinel value
- Negative: Ignore negative inputs
- Sum: Total the non-negative inputs
- Count: Count the non-negative inputs
- DivZero: Guard against division by zero
- Average: Average the non-negative inputs

Our version omits I/O tasks common to earlier formalizations of Rainfall (as our students had not studied it). Of course, this omission changes the problem and some of its standard plan-composition nuances (such as where a student should re-query a user for an invalid input). Although Simon [9] questions whether such changes alter the problem too much, we believe the fundamental questions about plan composition remain unchanged.

Conceptually, these tasks can be executed and combined in various ways. Figure 1 shows three (of many) examples:

- "Single Loop" (left) iteratively consumes inputs, increments sum and count on each non-negative input, then checks for division by zero and computes the average upon reaching the sentinel.
- "Clean First" (middle) iteratively adds non-negative inputs to a data structure until the sentinel is reached. It then counts and sums the cleaned data, checks for division by zero, and computes the average.
- "Clean Multiple" (right) traverses the input twice, once to count non-negative inputs and once to sum them. Each traversal terminates at the sentinel. It then checks for division by zero and computes the average.

The data structures that students know affect which options are feasible for them. A student who has learned no data structures (an apparent constraint in early plan-composition papers) has only the "Single Loop" option, as the other two require building intermediate data structures. A student who has learned only arrays could implement one of "Clean First" or "Clean Multiple", but probably would not because a typical array declaration expects the programmer to provide a size, which is unknown (the technique of creating a larger-than-needed array is not typically covered in

```
     ** SINGLE LOOP **              ** CLEAN FIRST **              ** CLEAN MULTIPLE **
repeat until find sentinel {    repeat until find sentinel {   repeat until find sentinel {
  if next input is non-negative    if next input is non-negative    if next input is non-negative
    increment count                  add to set of clean data         increment count
    add it to the running sum    }                               }
}                               if at least one clean datum     repeat until find sentinel {
if count is at least 1            count the clean data            if next input is non-negative
  compute the average as sum/count sum the clean data                add it to the running sum
else report ''no data''           compute average as sum/count  }
                                else report ''no data''         if count is at least 1
                                                                  compute average as sum/count
                                                                else report ''no data''
```

**Figure 1: Three high-level structures for Rainfall. We present these in imperative pseudocode for the benefit of readers who are less familiar with functional programming.**

CS1). A student who has worked with lists, however, has all three options readily at her disposal.

Going into this study, we hypothesized that many students trained in list-based functional programming would use a high-level structure that traversed the inputs more than once. HTDP drills students on the idea of "one task per function", emphasizing correctness over performance; this might dispose students to one of the multi-traversal plans.

# 5. METHODOLOGY

## 5.1 Data Collection

We collected data in the Fall of 2013. We contacted colleagues teaching HTDP-based CS1 courses at two institutions, then mentioned the study on a mailing list for users of HTDP. Three additional faculty (two university, one high school) offered to participate.[1]

All sites used the problem wording given in Section 2. The logistics of assigning the problem differed across the courses: some included the problem on exams, others used supervised lab time, and others used out-of-class time (but still required the assignment). Table 1 summarizes the nature of the courses, sample sizes, and the conditions under which students completed the problem in each course.

The solutions were passed along to the author either electronically or on paper via postal mail, as appropriate. Solutions were stripped of identifying information before being supplied to the author. Resource constraints led us to code only a subset of the solutions from some courses. We coded a higher percentage of the T3Non samples since their students were both non-majors and had the least experience with HTDP. We coded all HS and T1Acc samples since their populations were smaller. We used the sample command in R (ver 2.15.2) to randomly choose which samples to code. In hindsight, this method did not guarantee that each sample was representative within the course. The author did all of the coding, so there was no need to assess inter-coder reliability. All statistical analysis was done in R (ver 3.0.3).

## 5.2 Coding Composition Structures

We coded composition structures by reducing each student's program to a regular-expression-like summary. We used a single-letter token for each of the six tasks (S for sum,

T for sentinel, etc), combined with operators indicating interleaved (&), parallel (|), sequential (;), or guarded (→) composition. As examples, the following two codes capture the "Clean First" and "Single Loop" programs from Figure 1:

```
Clean First: T&N ; D -> (S|C); A
Single Loop: (T & N & S & C) ; D -> A
```

These expressions capture the structural essence of each solution. They do not capture details such as how many functions students wrote, whether sequential tasks were in the same or different functions, or whether students used higher-order functions. Additional coding captured some of this information. For each task within each solution, we recorded when the task was implemented (a) within the main Rainfall function, (b) within a helper function, (c) across multiple functions, or (d) missing entirely. We also recorded whether the task was implemented using a built-in operation or higher-order function (e.g., length or filter).

Some solutions were sufficiently mangled that we could not construct meaningful summaries for them. In such cases, our code either captured which tasks were represented at all, or recorded "None" if no tasks were evident.

Overall, our dataset included 32 different high-level structures that included all six required tasks. For analysis, we grouped these into six clusters, as discussed in Section 6.1.

## 5.3 Coding Task Errors

When a student implemented a task incorrectly, we used separate codes to record the errors. Our error codes derive (with minimal changes) from Ebrahimi's [1] Rainfall codes, which in turn built on Ostrand and Weyuker's error-coding system [8]. An error code is a sequence of 2 or 3 letters: a category of difference, a component of difference, and (optionally) the extent of difference (which defaulted to Full if omitted). Each piece had the following options (normal-face items are from Ebrahimi; italics mark our additions):

**Categories of Difference**: Missing (X), Misplaced (P), Malformed (F), Spurious (S), *Inconsistent with Tests* (I)

**Component of Difference**: Initialize (I), *Base Case* (B), Update (U), Guard (G), *Input* (P), *Header* (H)

***Extent of Difference*** [optional]: Partial (P), Full (F)

Thus, an error code of F-B means "malformed base case" (which might arise if the base case of a recursive function

---

[1]None of the data were collected in the author's own school. The author is, however, a long-time HTDP instructor.

| Label | Course Type | School Type | Samples | # Coded | Conditions | Language |
|-------|-------------|-------------|---------|---------|------------|----------|
| T2 | CS1 | 2nd Tier | 224 | 63 | Exam, 20-30 mins, 10 weeks in | Racket |
| T1 | CS1 | 1st Tier | 154 | 61 | Home, no limit, 13 weeks in | Racket, OCaml |
| HS | CS1 | High School | 7 | 7 | Lab, 20 min, 18 weeks in | Racket |
| T3Non | Non-majors Intro | 3rd Tier | 65 | 43 | Lab, 10 mins, 10 weeks in | Racket |
| T1Acc | Accelerated CS1 | 1st Tier | 44 | 44 | Home, no limit, 13 weeks in | Racket, Pyret |

Table 1: Summary of participating courses (all in the USA). "Tier" in the School Type column reflects competitiveness of admission (lower numbers are more competitive); this approximates general academic ability. The two 1st-Tier courses are from the same university, with T1Acc being an accelerated course that students tested into after a month in T1 (most in T1Acc had prior programming experience from high-school). For the two populations that worked at home, nearly all students self-reported spending no more than 30 minutes on the problem.)

did the wrong test or had a serious syntax error), while X-G-P means "missing guard partially" (which might arise if a student guarded against division-by-zero on only some control-flow paths through a program).[2]

Three of Ebrahimi's original components of difference—input, output, and loop—can not arise in our programs. We folded his "syntax concept" errors into "malformed", as both manifest similarly in Racket.

Nuances in our data required options (italicized) beyond Ebrahimi's. *Inconsistent with Tests* applies when a student's test case expected a different result than his program produced. *Base Case* captures errors in setting up the base case for a recursive function; if the base case has the right guard but the wrong return value, we use the (existing) Initialize code. *Header* captures problems in the name or parameter list in a function definition. *Input* captures problems in the actual parameters passed to functions (such as a task being correct relative to its formal parameter, but receiving an incorrect actual parameter). *Extent of difference* captures cases in which a task was implemented correctly on some control-flow paths but not others (e.g., forgetting to check for division-by-zero after cleaning negatives from the input).

In contrast to earlier studies, we recorded errors at the level of individual tasks (Sum, Average, etc), rather than for the entire program. This granularity seems important: students might make some errors (such as forgetting guards) more frequently in some tasks. In functional languages, where students might write separate functions for individual tasks, per-task coding helps cluster errors that occurred in the same function. The downside is that the same source-code error may affect (and thus count towards) multiple tasks, thus inflating sums of errors across tasks.

## 6. DATA ANALYSIS

We first analyze high-level program structure (methodology from Section 5.2), which reflects the essence of plan composition. We then explore low-level errors within those structures (methodology from Section 5.3). Finally, we contrast our results to those of prior Rainfall studies as best as we can around our subtle differences in methodology.

### 6.1 High-Level Composition Structure

Table 2 summarizes the high-level structures that students used, broken out by course. We have six clusters of

---

[2]The full coding manual is available at www.cs.wpi.edu/~kfisler/Pubs/icer14-rainfall/.

|  | T2 | T1 | HS | T3Non | T1Acc | total |
|--|----|----|----|-------|-------|-------|
| Single Loop | 1 | 23 | 0 | 1 | 13 | 38 |
| Clean First | 40 | 25 | 1 | 1 | 20 | 87 |
| Clean Multiple | 12 | 13 | 3 | 15 | 9 | 43 |
| Clean After | 1 | 0 | 1 | 1 | 0 | 3 |
| No Cleaning | 1 | 0 | 1 | 5 | 0 | 7 |
| Unclear | 8 | 0 | 0 | 19 | 2 | 29 |

Table 2: Number of students implementing each high-level structure within each course.

high-level structure: the three from Figure 1 ("Single Loop", "Clean First", and "Clean Multiple"), "Clean After" (attempt to adjust the results of sum and count to handle negative and sentinel), "No Cleaning" (omitted negative and sentinel, but included sum/count/average), and "Unclear" (generally mangled code with no clear structure).

Two observations stand out from this table: the distribution of solutions across different high-level structures, and the low percentage but skewed distribution of students producing "Unclear" solutions. We discuss each in turn.

*Diverse Composition Structures.*

Table 2 shows that the single-loop structure of traditional for/while loop solutions was not dominant in our data. This is partly due to course organization: neither T3Non nor HS had covered recursive functions that accumulate answers in parameters (an advanced topic in HTDP, coming after trees and higher-order functions); T2 started the topic just before the exam that included Rainfall, but most sections were told not to use it on the exam. Even in courses where students had either seen this material (T1) or learned for/while loops in high-school (most students in T1Acc), other structures are more common than "Single Loop".

What drives students towards "Clean First" or "Clean Multiple" instead of "Single Loop"? Spohrer and Soloway's model of plan composition in MARCEL [11] suggested that novices start from an initial plan, refining it as needed to add tasks and handle errors. If this theory holds, we should consider how different initial plan choices might lead to different structures. For example, students might:

- Start with the overall problem (average), which most students know is computed from the sum and length of a list. Sum and length are common exercises in functional courses: students could either augment their existing plans for these to also clean input ("Clean Multiple") or clean data before using their existing plans ("Clean First").

- Start by asking which tasks higher-order functions could capture succinctly. Sum, Count, and Negative are often used to illustrate higher-order functions. Students could clean input ("Clean First") to provide data to their existing higher-order plans for these tasks.

- Start by traversing the inputs, expecting to process each as they go ("Single Loop").

We are not claiming that our students did follow these thought processes (our data cannot indicate this). Rather, we are claiming that these are initial plans that (a) are accessible to our students and (b) have plausible paths to each of the common structures.

The idea of built-in or higher-order functions as initial plans warrants more discussion. Soloway described plans as "template-like structures" for common problems [10]; higher-order functions merely turn these templates into functions that are parameterized over other computation. For example, `filter` takes a list and a predicate over individual list elements, returning the sublist of elements that satisfy the predicate. The names of higher-order functions indicate their effects on the input: a programmer who sees (`filter <Foo> numList`) knows immediately that the result is a subset of `numList` chosen by `Foo`. Conventional loops lack this feature. Seeing `for` simply says that something will be traversed, but nothing about what will happen during that traversal. In this sense, higher-order functions may provide more concise and targeted plans than conventional loops. This echoes Miller's proposal for looping "macros" whose names align with functionality, which arose after studying program plan composition through natural-language [6].

Students in T2, T1, and T1Acc had seen higher-order functions prior to this study; all students had seen `length` (of a list). The following table summarizes how many students in each high-level structure category used higher-order or built-in functions for each task. It shows that students with "Clean First" solutions use these features heavily.

| | N | Sum | Count | Neg | Sentl |
|---|---|---|---|---|---|
| Single Loop | 38 | 1 | 1 | 0 | 1 |
| Clean First | 87 | 72 | 83 | 24 | 3 |
| Clean Multiple | 43 | 4 | 2 | 2 | 3 |
| Other | 39 | 1 | 12 | 0 | 1 |

**# of students using built-in functions, by structure**

Count was nearly always implemented with the `length` function (built-in) on lists (a few students used a higher-order function called `fold`). Even in T3Non, which had a high rate of "Unclear" structures, 11 students used `length`. Within "Clean First", all but two of the Sum cases used `fold`; all but three of the Negative cases used `filter`. The "Single Loop" entries came from one student who wrote all of Rainfall via a single use of `fold`.

TAKE AWAY: The overwhelming correlation between high-level structure and using built-in and higher-order functions in "Clean First" suggests that knowing these functions significantly influences how students structure Rainfall solutions.

OPEN QUESTIONS: Do students who know higher-order functions use them as initial plans? Are looping constructs whose names describe impacts on data more useful as initial plans than those named more for control-flow?

*Unclear Composition Structures.*

Only 14% of students (31 out of 218) had "Unclear" composition structures. This includes 7 students with no relevant code, and another 5 who had a function for average but did not integrate it with the other tasks. Thus, only 5% of students (12 of 218) had no evident plan for solving Rainfall.

All but one of the remaining 19 students (8% of total) used the HTDP design recipe to write Rainfall: they wrote a recursive function with a single parameter (for the list), and attempted to compute the average piecewise as they encountered each element. These solutions had the following structure, with some mix of the Sentinel, Negative, Sum, and Count tasks intermingled in place of the ellipses:

```
(define (rainfall alon)
  (cond [(empty? alon) 0]
        [(cons? alon) ... (first alon)
                      ... (rainfall (rest alon))]))
```

These students' main failing lay in using the default HTDP list skeleton as their overall plan; this plan was not suitable for Rainfall. This is not an indictment of HTDP per se: these students may perform well on writing straightforward traversals. In addition, the parts of HTDP that address accumulating data and problem decomposition occur later in the course, beyond what some of our participating courses had covered. The distribution of "Unclear" solutions across courses is therefore relevant.

Ten of the 18 students who naively followed HTDP were in course T3Non, which had three potentially-confounding variables: these students had been given only 10 minutes to work on the problem, they had covered less material than those in other courses, and they were non-majors. If a T3Non student had tried the default and realized another approach was needed, she would not have had time to implement it. We therefore interpret the T3Non data as indicating students initial plan choices (ala Spohrer and Soloway): that many of the "Unclear" structure students at least ended up in the HTDP default suggests that HTDP students are learning techniques for getting started on programs.

TAKE AWAY: HTDP students absorb techniques for writing list traversals, but likely need later parts of the course to handle situations when structural recursion does not apply.

OPEN QUESTIONS: What is the relationship between extent of coverage of HTDP and performance on Rainfall?

*Which High-Level Structure is Preferable?.*

Are certain high-level Rainfall structures preferable for students coming out of CS1? "Single Loop" appears most efficient (traversing the input only once and not building intermediate data);[3] "Clean First" separates the concerns (tasks) of the problem, which simplifies maintenance (and arguably human comprehension).

We informally polled long-standing HTDP instructors for their preference among "Clean First", "Clean Multiple", and "Single Loop". We gave them a canonical solution in each structure (all written in Racket), and asked which they preferred and why. We got 8 responses, 3 from instructors who had provided data for this study. Uniformly, they preferred

---

[3] The efficiency argument is not valid in light of long-standing compilation techniques that interweave nested list traversals (e.g., [13]), though belief in it persists.

either "Clean First" or "Clean Multiple" to "Single Loop", with justifications referring to separation of concerns, ease of testing individual tasks, and overall cleanliness.[4] Half preferred "Single Loop" to "Clean Multiple" on grounds of efficiency (with both behind "Clean First").

OPEN QUESTIONS: What design principles (e.g., clean data first, reduce traversals, etc) should students prioritize coming out of CS1? Which principles should be reflected as plans that students choose instinctively? Which should students treat as optimizations to apply once programs are working?

## 6.2 What Errors Do Students Make?

Low-level programming errors occur both within implementations of specific tasks and in the glue that composes them. Arguably, many student errors in previous plan-composition studies have been in the glue: for example, students might know how to increment a counter, but perform the increment in the wrong location. In functional programming, individual functions tend to align with individual or a few thematically-related tasks. Some mistakes are also harder to make in functional languages: when variables are parameters to recursive functions, it is harder to miss updating them. We might expect this isolation of task to lead to fewer low-level implementation errors, both within and across functions. This section explores low-level errors.

### 6.2.1 Error Rates Per Task

The most frequent error in our data, by far, was omitting a task entirely. The *percentage* of students omitting each task within each high-level structure category is as follows:

|  | Sum | Count | Neg | Sentl | DivZ | Avg |
|---|---|---|---|---|---|---|
| Single Loop | 0 | 0 | 16 | 0 | 16 | 0 |
| Clean First | 0 | 1 | 18 | 3 | 36 | 0 |
| Clean Mult | 0 | 0 | 58 | 0 | 52 | 0 |
| Clean After | 0 | 0 | 100 | 0 | 33 | 0 |
| No Cleaning | 14 | 14 | 100 | 100 | 43 | 0 |
| Unclear | 24 | 66 | 97 | 41 | 59 | 38 |

**% of students within category who omitted task**

"No Cleaning" is defined by omitting both Negative and Sentinel, so their 100% omission rate is not surprising. Students with a clear structure rarely omitted Sum, Count, Sentinel, or Average. Many omitted Negative and DivZero, though these are rather different omissions: failure to include Negative means that students *missed part of the overall problem statement*, whereas failure to include DivZero means that students *failed to consider a subset of possible inputs to the problem*. Different techniques are likely needed to mitigate each problem, which raises another question:

OPEN QUESTIONS: Would asking students to provide test cases as part of plan-composition studies help identify the source of certain classes of errors?

The relative rates of omission of Negative and DivZero across "Single Loop", "Clean First", and "Clean Multiple" suggests that perhaps students in one of the first two categories are simply stronger programmers. This is plausible, as we have already argued that "Single Loop" is an advanced approach under HTDP. Course-level data does not, however, support this hypothesis: students in (the accelerated) T1Acc

make significantly more errors of omission than their fellow students in T1 on many cells of this table.

Setting aside missing tasks, we now explore the low-level errors that students made within (at least partially) implemented tasks. Our error-coding method (Section 5.3) has 30 possible error categories (setting aside the "partial" modifier), of which 21 appear in our data. For sake of space, here we report in detail only on errors in solutions with a clear high-level structure (N=187) that occurred in more than 5% (10) of the solutions across all tasks. The following table lists the number of occurrences of each error code within each task. Since the same error in source code could affect multiple tasks, the total within each row may be larger than the number of students who made the corresponding error.

|  | Sum | Count | Neg | Sentl | DivZero | Avg |
|---|---|---|---|---|---|---|
| X-G-P | 0 | 0 | 1 | 0 | 33 | 0 |
| X-B | 12 | 6 | 2 | 6 | 0 | 0 |
| F-U | 7 | 5 | 4 | 6 | 1 | 3 |
| F-G | 2 | 2 | 11 | 5 | 1 | 0 |

**Error count per task, clear structure only (N=187)**

The 33 X-G-P (missing guard partial) DivZero errors reflect a student checking emptiness of the original input list but forgetting this check *after* handling negatives and the sentinel. Half of these cases were in "Clean First"; the other half split between "Clean Multiple" and "Single Loop".

Of the 26 X-B (missing base case) errors, 19 occur with "Clean Multiple". By definition, such solutions implement multiple tasks in one function, so a missing base case might affect more than one task. A total of 10 students made the 19 X-B errors within "Clean Multiple" solutions. On the one hand, these errors are surprising within HTDP, as students who start from the list skeleton would automatically (and instinctively) include the base case. However, the low rate of this problem (under 2% of students) suggests that perhaps the HTDP list skeleton is doing its job.[5]

The F-G (malformed guard) errors in Negative often reflect treating 0 as negative (e.g., using < instead of ≤).

Overall, our data show fairly low error rates once students have a clear high-level structure. Setting aside missing tasks and solutions with "Unclear" structures, we found a total of 153 coded errors, some of which are over-counted (as discussed in Section 5.3). A total of 98 students had at least one error (other than "missing"). Thus, our data set has between 98 and 153 unique error locations within 187 solutions with clear high-level structures. An error rate below one per solution is quite low relative to other Rainfall studies. Including missing tasks as errors yields 296 errors within clear structures, for a maximum error rate of 1.58 per student.

Low-level error counts varied only slightly with high-level structure. The following table summarizes the total number of errors per student within the three major high-level structures. Each cell indicates the percentage of students with the given structure (row) and error count (column). Some errors are over-counted in "Clean Multiple". Since X-G-P errors in DivZero were the most common overall, the last column reports the percentage of students who made that error. The differences between "Single Loop" and "Clean Multiple" are not significant, though they become so (p =.002) without X-G-P. We do not compare significance of these

---

[4]A couple of T1Acc students left apology-like comments in their code for choosing "Single Loop" for efficiency reasons.

[5]We cannot compare data on this error to previous studies, as no prior studies included the X-B code.

against "Clean Multiple" given its over-counting. This table supports our claim that "Single Loop" solutions came from stronger programmers.

| | 0 errors | 1 | 2 | 3-6 | 9 | X-G-P |
|---|---|---|---|---|---|---|
| Single Loop | 74 | 21 | 5 | 0 | 0 | 18 |
| Clean First | 66 | 22 | 7 | 6 | 0 | 18 |
| Clean Multiple | 46 | 23 | 13 | 15 | 2 | 21 |

**% of students with each error count, by structure**

Finally, our error codes distinguish within-task errors from between-task errors: the latter correspond to mistakes in composing functions for separate tasks. We find only 25 instances of between-task error codes (F-P, X-P, and P-P) in the entire data set. Of these, 23 were malformed actual parameters (F-P), 18 of which occurred in solutions with "Unclear" structure. We had only 3 instances of between-task composition errors in solutions with clear structure.

TAKE AWAY: HTDP solutions with clear high-level structure have low error rates and few composition errors.

OPEN QUESTIONS: Can HTDP and top-down planning curricula (such as Pattern-Oriented Instruction [7]) complement one other to improve performance on Rainfall?

## 6.3 Comparison to Other Rainfall Studies

Two prior Rainfall studies had conditions that overlap our own: Ebrahimi [1] included some functional programming, while Simon [9] provided the input in a data structure rather than require I/O. This section relates our findings to theirs, as best we can within the limits of differing methodologies.

### *Comparison to Ebrahimi.*

Ebrahimi [1] studied student performance on Rainfall in four languages (C, FORTRAN, Pascal, and LISP). It is tempting to compare our error rates to those of his LISP and non-LISP students. Unfortunately, such comparison would be imprecise at best. Although our error codes are derived from his, our two-level methodology captures missing tasks outside of error codes, while he captured them within. Unlike Ebrahimi, we did not record low-level error codes for students whose solutions had no relevant code. Both of these undercount certain errors, while our per-task error-coding method overcounts others. Although these differences prevent direct comparison, differences in magnitude of our error rates suggest that our students did better. The most frequent errors among Ebrahimi's 20 LISP students were missing if-guards (50%; includes DivZero), misplaced updates (40%, includes computing average in loop and sum/count outside of loop), malformed updates (40%), and spurious output (40%, not relevant for our data). These rates are noticeably higher than for any of our error codes.

Differing course styles also hinder meaningful comparison of our data with Ebrahimi's. His students were in a position to write imperative LISP code: they had seen assignment operators, I/O, and iteration, and had previously used Pascal. They had been "encouraged" to use recursion and functions for each task when writing Rainfall.[6] We do not, however, know whether students heeded these instructions. Code written in functional languages is not necessarily "functional" (e.g., it might use side-effects): this is an important caveat for any study that crosses linguistic paradigms.

[6]Email communication with Ebrahimi, April 2014.

### *Comparison to Simon.*

Simon [9] reported broad categories of mistakes and implementation choices across 149 students in a C#-based CS1. Four of his categories do not apply to us: using a `while` loop, using a `for` loop, initializing sum, and avoiding integer division.[7] The rest reflect at least partial implementation of specific tasks. In the following comparison, we report ranges that cover best- and worst-case interpretations of Simon's grading in our context. Ideally, percentages should be low in the first row and high in the others.

| Simon Issue | Simon % | Our % range |
|---|---|---|
| No (pertinent) code | 36 | 3 – 6 |
| Loop terminated by sentinel | 22 | 81 – 90 |
| Days counted within loop | 21 | 85 – 89 |
| Negative values ignored | 40 | 57 |
| Guarded division for average | 0 | 55 – 61 |

For "no (pertinent) code", we report a range from students with no discernible plan (low) to students with either no plan or one marked as "Far Off" (high). For the remaining rows, we report the range of students who included each task at least partially (high) or did so within a clear high-level structure (low; guarantees that a student had a recursive function—a.k.a. loop—covering that task).

Our students are clearly performing better than Simon's. Given that he also avoided I/O, this comparison suggests that that the difficulties with Rainfall go beyond I/O plans. Our requirements on negative numbers were slightly different (ours dropped them while his treated them as zero), but this seems insignificant as both versions require checking the sign of each input. Thus, we have to wonder whether the style of programming taught in our respective versions explains the large differences in performance. Additional studies would be required to explore this further.

### *Comparison to a Java-based CS1.*

One university instructor on the HTDP listserv collected data in his (non-HTDP) Java-based CS1 course (which had covered arrays, but not lists). He used our problem wording, substituting "array of integers" for "list of numbers". We did not code his data (N=51) for low-level errors. Coding for high-level structure showed 50 "Single Loop" solutions: 28 used `for`, 12 used `while`, and 8 nested a `while` directly within a `for`. Only 1 student had two loops in sequence (`while` to clean the data then `for` to compute the average); only 2 students (including this one) used a second array. This supports our claim that something about either functional programming or HTDP steers students towards non-"Single Loop" solutions with auxiliary data structures.

## 7. DISCUSSION

In 2010, Mark Guzdial [5] challenged computing education researchers to make progress on Rainfall, mentioning HTDP as worthy of studying. Inspired by Mark's question, this paper reports on student performance on Rainfall from an HTDP perspective. Our participants made fewer errors than in prior Rainfall studies and used a diverse set of high-level composition structures; one high-level structure correlated strongly with use of higher-order and built-in functions. Our current hypothesis is that some combination of

[7]Except for OCaml, the languages used in this study all return exact answers to division, regardless of input type.

using lightweight data structures (in our case, lists), avoiding I/O, teaching data-oriented iterators, and emphasizing a single, widely reusable design method (as in HTDP) underlie these results.

We are not attempting to launch another grenade in the CS1 language-paradigm wars. The ideas in our hypothesis, while hallmarks of functional programming, are hardly unique to it: even Java 8 recently announced the addition of `lambda`, which simplifies writing and using data-oriented iterators. That said, traditional linguistic choices and constraints may well have made Rainfall harder than it needs to be. If students internalize "traverse arrays with `for` loops" and "only create an array if you know the size", they inevitably end up having to interleave multiple tasks in one loop to implement Rainfall. Code that interleaves concerns is arguably harder to implement, harder to test, and ultimately more error-prone than code which keeps them separate. Ginat *et al.* [4] document novices' difficulties interleaving algorithmic plans (though we disagree with their preference for interleaved solutions in CS1).

Whether students learn to separate concerns is a likely a function of how we teach them to program. We suspect that including I/O discourages novices from separating concerns, especially when students are taught to think about programming top-down. Getting input is usually the first step to be executed in a computation. If Spohrer and Soloway's initial-plan model is correct, that input must occur first could well bias students towards picking an input plan first, then adapting it to accommodate other tasks. In contrast, a bottom-up approach that starts with a more behavioral task (such as "find the sentinel") should guide students to first write focused individual functions for other tasks. The influence of I/O on plan selection remains an interesting open question.

This study leaves us thinking about the design principles that students should learn from CS1. We see many students taking CS1 to learn to write small scripts for use in other subjects. They want to grab (noisy) data from the web or write small apps that work on various devices with different input mechanisms. For this environment, students arguably should internalize principles such as "clean your data first", and "separate I/O from core processing". The "Clean First" students in this study landed in this space, but we don't know why. The time appears right to articulate the principles, not just the basic concepts, that our students need, and to reopen studies of planning and plan composition with these principles in mind.

This study leaves us curious about which plans students carry into new languages. We strongly suspect that our same participants would produce solutions with very different structures after learning conventional loops and I/O in CS2 (in Java for most of our participants). New constructs obviously should change how students work, but not at the cost of using solid design principles.

Including students' testing behavior also stands to contribute significantly to plan-composition studies. Test cases can reveal sources of errors: did a student misunderstand the problem, overlook a possible input, or incorrectly implement a correct model of the problem? Prior studies correlated Rainfall performance with language or code comprehension [1, 12]; this makes sense for control-flow errors (i.e., misplaced statements), but less for problem-comprehension ones (i.e., handling division by zero). Testing is lightweight and thus easy to require (as HTDP does) in many functional languages. Indeed, the vast majority of our participants included test cases. We should study whether test cases influence which tasks (and their nuances) students handle.

Going forward, we need data from HTDP students that explores what drives them towards particular high-level structures. We are also extending our project to include other classic CS1 benchmarks (e.g., McCracken). One could argue that Rainfall is biased in favor of functional programming because average has a well-known algorithm (divide sum by count), and both sum and count are standard, heavily-exercised problems in functional CS1 courses. Other classic problems whose algorithms are less evident should prove useful in further understanding the impact of functional programming and HTDP on learning design in CS1.

**Acknowledgements:** Mark Guzdial encouraged this study during a research visit in Fall 2013. The instructors who contributed data made it happen on short notice. Shriram Krishnamurthi and Matthias Felleisen engaged in helpful discussion of the results. NSF funds supported this work.

## 8. REFERENCES

[1] A. Ebrahimi. Novice programmer errors: language constructs and plan composition. *International Journal of Human-Computer Studies*, 41:457–480, 1994.

[2] M. Felleisen, R. B. Findler, M. Flatt, and S. Krishnamurthi. *How to Design Programs*. MIT Press, 2001.

[3] E. Gamma, R. Helm, R. Johnson, and J. Vlissides. *Design Patterns : Elements of Reusable Object-Oriented Software*. Addison-Wesley, 1995.

[4] D. Ginat, E. Menashe, and A. Taya. Novice difficulties with interleaved pattern composition. In *International Conference on Informatics in Schools: Situation, Evolution, and Perspectives*, ISSEP'13, pages 57–67, 2013.

[5] M. Guzdial. A challenge to computing education research: Make measurable progress. https://computinged.wordpress.com/2010/08/16/a-challenge-to-computing-education-research-make-measurable-progress/, Aug. 2010. Accessed April 18, 2014.

[6] L. A. Miller. Natural language programming: Styles, strategies, and contrasts. *IBM Systems Journal*, 20(2):184–215, June 1981.

[7] O. Muller, B. Haberman, and D. Ginat. Pattern-oriented instruction and its influence on problem decomposition and solution construction. In *Proceedings of ITiCSE*, 2007.

[8] T. Ostrand and E. Weyuker. Collecting and categorizing software error data in an industrial environment. *Journal of Science and Software*, 4:289–300, 1984.

[9] Simon. Soloway's Rainfall problem has become harder. *Learning and Teaching in Computing and Enginering*, pages 130–135, 2013.

[10] E. Soloway. Learning to program = learning to construct mechanisms and explanations. *Communications of the ACM*, 29(9):850–858, Sept. 1986.

[11] J. C. Spohrer and E. Soloway. Simulating student programmers. In *International Joint Conference on Artificial Intelligence*, pages 543–549, 1989.

[12] A. Venables, G. Tan, and R. Lister. A closer look at tracing, explaining and code writing skills in the novice programmer. In *Computing Education Research Workshop (ICER)*, pages 117–128, 2009.

[13] P. Wadler. Listlessness is better than laziness: Lazy evaluation and garbage collection at compile-time. In *ACM Symposium on LISP and Functional Programming*, pages 45–52, 1984.

# Investigating Novice Programming Mistakes: Educator Beliefs vs Student Data

Neil C. C. Brown and Amjad Altadmri
School of Computing
University of Kent
Canterbury, Kent, UK
{nccb,aa803}@kent.ac.uk

## ABSTRACT

Educators often form opinions on which programming mistakes novices make most often – for example, in Java: "they always confuse equality with assignment", or "they always call methods with the wrong types". These opinions are generally based solely on personal experience. We report a study to determine if programming educators form a consensus about which Java programming mistakes are the most common. We used the Blackbox data set to check whether the educators' opinions matched data from over 100,000 students – and checked whether this agreement was mediated by educators' experience. We found that educators formed only a weak consensus about which mistakes are most frequent, that their rankings bore only a moderate correspondence to the students in the Blackbox data, and that educators' experience had *no* effect on this level of agreement. These results raise questions about claims educators make regarding which errors students are most likely to commit.

## Categories and Subject Descriptors

K.3.2 [**Computers And Education**]: Computer and Information Science Education

## General Terms

Experimentation, Human Factors

## Keywords

Programming Mistakes; Educators

## 1. INTRODUCTION

Educators naturally form opinions on common mistakes that their students make when learning to program. Such opinions are reflected in textbooks – for example, in Java: "Failing to use equals() to compare two strings is probably the most common single mistake made by Java novices" [22], "The most common mistake made with an if statement is the use of a single equal sign to compare equality" [7], "A common mistake in for loops is to accidentally put a semicolon at the end of the line that includes the for statement" [4]. In this paper, we set out to determine: are such observations accurate in general? This matters for several reasons. Firstly, recent research by Sadler et al [15] suggests that knowledge of student misconceptions is important to educator efficacy, and thus it is of interest whether educators' impressions about student mistakes are correct. Secondly, when educators communicate with each other (face-to-face or online), it matters whether their opinions on common student mistakes are accurate and generalise to each other's students. Knowing which mistakes are common also informs the writing of instructional materials such as textbooks.

Previous studies that have investigated student errors during [Java] programming have focused on cohorts of up to 600 students at a single institution [1, 5, 6, 10, 11, 19]. However, the recently launched Blackbox data collection project [3] affords an opportunity to observe the mistakes of a large number of students at a variety of institutions – for example, from September to December 2013, the project collected error messages and Java code from around 110,000 users.

In this paper we describe a study to check if educators' opinions on beginners' mistakes in Java form a consensus, and whether they generalise to all students. We combine a survey of educators with data from the Blackbox project to answer the following research questions:

- Do educators' views form a consensus about the frequency of specified student Java mistakes?

- Do educators' views of mistake frequency match the observed behaviour of students in a large-scale multi-institution data set?

- Are more experienced educators' views more likely to match the students' data than novice educators?

## 2. RELATED WORK

### 2.1 Observing Student Errors

The concept of monitoring student behaviour and mistakes while programming has a long history in computing education research. The Empirical Studies of Programming [16] workshops in the 1980s had several papers making use of this technique for Pascal and other languages. More recently, there have been many such studies specifically focused on Java, which is also the topic of this study.

*ICER'14*, August 11-13, 2014, Glasgow, Scotland, UK.
Copyright is held by the owner/author(s). Publication rights licensed to ACM.
ACM 978-1-4503-2755-8/14/08 ...$15.00.
http://dx.doi.org/10.1145/2632320.2632343.

Many of these studies used compiler error messages to classify mistakes. Jadud [11] looked in detail at student mistakes in Java and how students went about solving them. Tabanao et al. [19] investigated the assocation between errors and student course performance. Denny et al. [5] looked at how long students take to solve different errors, Dy and Rodrigo [6] looked at improving the error messages given to students, and Ahmadzadeh et al. [1] looked at student error frequencies and debugging behaviour. Jackson et al. [10] identified the most frequent errors among their novice programming students. All six of these studies used compiler error messages to classify errors. However, early results from McCall [14] suggest that compiler error messages have an imperfect (many-to-many) mapping to student misconceptions. Additionally, all six studies looked at cohorts of (up to 600) students from a single institution.

Our study is novel in that it looks at student mistakes from a much larger number of students (over 100,000) from a large number of institutions[1], thus providing more robust data about error frequencies. An earlier paper about Blackbox gave a brief list of the most frequent compiler error messages [3], but in this study we do not simply use compiler error messages to classify errors. Instead, we borrow error classifications from Hristova et al. [9], which are based on surveying educators to ask for the most common Java mistakes they saw among their students.

## 2.2 Educators' Opinions

Spohrer and Soloway [17] proposed in 1986 to examine the accuracy of educator folk wisdom. However, they did not survey educators, and instead took two anecdotal folk wisdoms about learning to program and then compared them to actual data from students (in Pascal). Ben-David Kolikant [2] interviewed some educators about students' approaches to programming, but at a higher level, without reference to a specific language. Hristova et al. [9] surveyed a combination of local teaching assistants and students, as well as educators from 58 universities, asking about common Java mistakes. This data was combined to form a list of 20 Java mistakes that were detectable at compile-time. We base our classification of mistakes on this work, but Hristova et al. did not test these predictions themselves against actual student data. As far as we are aware, our study is the first to survey educators about Java programming mistakes and compare their opinions to actual data.

## 3. METHOD

### 3.1 Student Mistakes

We used Hristova et al's [9] twenty student mistakes as a basis for our analysis. We removed two mistakes: firstly, "leaving a space after a period when calling a method", which is a style issue not a programming mistake, and secondly, "improper casting" which was not described clearly enough for us to operationalise. We also altered one further question "invoking a class method on an object" after several of our pilot testers remarked that this was not a mistake, but the reverse (invoking an instance method on a class) was, and they had seen the latter much more often. This left eighteen misconceptions, which we labelled A through R:

[1]We have no way of measuring the number of institutions in the Blackbox data, but simply: the 100,000 students must be split over at least several hundred institutions.

**A**: Confusing the assignment operator (=) with the comparison operator (==).
For example: `if (a = b) ...`

**B**: Use of == instead of `.equals` to compare strings.
For example: `if (a == "start") ...`

**C**: Unbalanced parentheses, curly brackets, square brackets and quotation marks, or using these different symbols interchangeably.
For example: `while (a == 0]`

**D**: Confusing "short-circuit" evaluators (&& and ||) with conventional logical operators (& and |).
For example: `if ((a == 0) & (b == 0)) ...`

**E**: Incorrect semi-colon after an if selection structure before the if statement or after the for or while repetition structure before the respective for or while loop.
For example:
```
if (a == b);
    return 6;
```

**F**: Wrong separators in for loops (using commas instead of semi-colons)
For example: `for (int i = 0, i < 6, i++) ...`

**G**: Inserting the condition of an if statement within curly brackets instead of parentheses.
For example: `if {a == b} ...`

**H**: Using keywords as method names or variable names.
For example: `int new;`

**I**: Invoking methods with wrong arguments (e.g. wrong types).
For example: `list.get("abc")`

**J**: Forgetting parentheses after a method call.
For example: `myObject.toString;`

**K**: Incorrect semicolon at the end of a method header.
For example:
```
public void foo();
{
    ...
}
```

**L**: Getting greater than or equal/less than or equal wrong, i.e. using => or =< instead of >= and <=.
For example: `if (a =< b) ...`

**M**: Trying to invoke a non-static method as if it was static.
For example: `MyClass.toString();`

**N**: A method that has a non-void return type is called and its return value ignored/discarded.
For example: `myObject.toString();`

**O**: Control flow can reach end of non-void method without returning.
For example:
```
public int foo(int x)
{
    if (x < 0)
        return 0;
    x += 1;
}
```

**P**: Including the types of parameters when invoking a method.
For example: `myObject.foo(int x, String s);`

**Q**: Incompatible types between method return and type of variable that the value is assigned to.
For example: `int x = myObject.toString();`

**R**: Class claims to implement an interface, but does not implement all the required methods.
For example: `class Foo implements ActionListener { }`

## 3.2 Educators' Survey

We prepared a questionnaire that listed our eighteen student mistakes and asked respondents to rate each mistake on a scale of infrequent to frequent, by making a mark along a visual analogue scale (a straight line with endpoints, like so: ├───┤ ). These scales were measured to the nearest $\frac{1}{100}$ of their length and recorded as a number from 0 to 100.

This paper questionnaire was given out to attendees of the ICER 2013 conference. An equivalent online electronic version of the questionnaire was also later developed, and was advertised via the SIGCSE mailing list, the UK Computing At School forum and through Twitter. (Those who had responded to the paper version were instructed not to complete the online version.)

29 participants returned a paper questionnaire and 191 started filling out the online questionnaire (although many did not complete). Only 76 participants filled in all scales for all questions (20 paper and 56 online), and this formed the sample set for all analyses. Participants were also asked about their educational experience in different sectors. 56 had experience only in the tertiary sector (age 18+), 3 only in secondary (ages 11–18), 14 in secondary and tertiary, and the remaining 3 in tertiary, secondary and primary (ages 4–11). The educators' experience is detailed and analysed in the results in section 4.1.

### 3.2.1 Inter-Educator Agreement

To measure agreement among educators we used Kendall's coefficient of concordance (aka Kendall's $W$) [12]. This statistic can be used to assess the agreement among ranks assigned by a group of raters to a set of items, by looking at the variance among the ranks of the different mistakes.

## 3.3 Student data

Data about student mistakes was taken from the Blackbox data set [3], which collects Java code written by users of BlueJ, the Java beginners' IDE. We used data from the period $1^{\text{st}}$ Sep. 2013 to $31^{\text{st}}$ Dec. 2013 (inclusive), as representing the autumn/winter term in the northern hemisphere.

We had three methods of detecting mistakes. For four of the student mistakes, $I, M, O, R$, we were able to use the compiler error message directly to detect the mistake. However, this was not possible for the other errors, as some of them are logical errors that do not cause a compiler error or warning, while in other cases the error messages do not have a one-to-one mapping to our mistakes of interest. Thus for one of the other mistakes ($C$) we performed a post-lexing analysis (matching brackets) and for the final thirteen we used a customised permissive parser to parse the source code and look for the errors. The source code of all the tools used will be available shortly.

We took each source file in the data set, and tracked the file over time. At each compilation we checked the source file for the eighteen mistakes. If the mistake was present, we then looked forward in time to find the next compilation where the mistake was no longer present (or until we had no further data for that source file). When the mistake was no longer found – which could have been because the mistake was corrected or because the offending code was removed or commented out – we counted this as one instance of the mistake. Further occurrences in the same source file were treated as further instances.

## 3.4 Educator and Student Agreement

To measure agreement between educators' ratings and the Blackbox frequencies, we used the average Spearman's $\rho$ (rho) for pairwise comparisons between each educator and the Blackbox data (thus: one correlation per rater)[2]. (We term these pairwise correlations between educators and the Blackbox data: educator *accord*.) This use of the average was originally recommended by Lyerly [13], then explained and generalised by Taylor and Fong [21, 20] to add a significance test. In our example, Taylor's $\bar{\rho}_{t,c}$ is the average of the pairwise correlations between the Blackbox data and each educator, corrected for continuity.

## 3.5 Educator and Student Agreement – Effect of Experience

To check if this accord was affected by educators' experience, we used the following procedure. As described in the previous section, we first calculated educator accord, using Spearman's $\rho$ as a measure of agreement between each educator's rankings and the Blackbox rankings (one correlation per rater). This accord was then correlated (again with Spearman's $\rho$) with the educators' total years of experience[3]. A significant correlation would indicate an effect of experience on educators' agreement with the Blackbox data.

## 4. RESULTS

### 4.1 Educators

Our analysis used responses from the 76 educators who gave rankings to all of the eighteen student mistakes. Educators were also asked how many years they had been an educator, to the nearest year[4]. Educators were also asked for the number of years spent teaching introductory programming, in any language or in Java, to three different age groups (4–11, 11–18, and 18+), so 6 numbers in all. We wished to combine these into a measurement of years spent teaching introductory programming in any language or in Java (i.e. collapsing across age group)[5]. Examination of the data suggested that some educators had taught some age groups simultaneously, so rather than summing across the age groups, we used the maximum figure from the three age groups. (Only 17 of the 76 had taught more than one age group.) We also capped the years spent teaching Java at 19, the language's current age, which affected two educators who claimed to have been teaching Java for more than 19 years. Frequencies for the years of experience are given in Figure 1.

### 4.2 Agreement Among Educators

Our analysis of Kendall's coefficient of concordance among the educators produced the result $W = 0.408$. For aid in

---

[2]Spearman's $\rho$ is a correlation between the ranks of the two different variables, and thus looks only at the *ordering* of mistake frequency, not the exact frequencies nor the educator's 0–100 ratings.

[3]Our use of $\rho$ here means that we do not look for a linear effect of experience (e.g. accuracy increasing linearly from 5 to 10 to 15 years), but rather: when educators are ordered by experience, does this match their ordering by accuracy?

[4]Since most educators begin their career in September, asking for a more precise measurement than the nearest year would not provide greater fidelity.

[5]In hindsight, we should have asked for these figures directly.

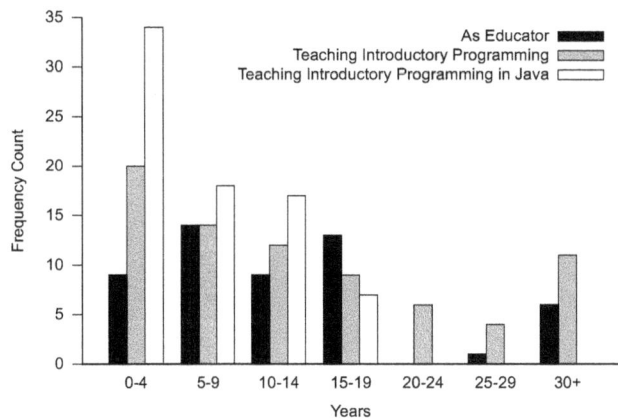

Figure 1: The distribution of years for surveyed educators: how long they have been an educator (solid black bar, $N = 56$), how many years they have spent teaching introductory programming (grey bar, $N = 76$) and how many years they have spent teaching introductory programming in Java (hollow bar, $N = 76$). Note that due to the different number of total responses, comparisons between the black bar and other bars are problematic.

| Mistake | Frequency | Error Type |
|---|---|---|
| C | 404560 | Syntax |
| I | 165832 | Type |
| O | 137230 | Semantic |
| N | 86107 | Semantic |
| A | 68254 | Syntax |
| B | 45012 | Semantic |
| M | 30754 | Semantic |
| R | 24846 | Semantic |
| P | 21694 | Syntax |
| E | 20264 | Syntax |
| K | 16156 | Syntax |
| Q | 14371 | Type |
| D | 11212 | Syntax |
| J | 8332 | Syntax |
| L | 1916 | Syntax |
| F | 1171 | Syntax |
| H | 415 | Syntax |
| G | 63 | Syntax |

Table 1: Frequency of mistakes committed by students from 1st Sep. 2013 to 31st Dec. 2013 (incl.).

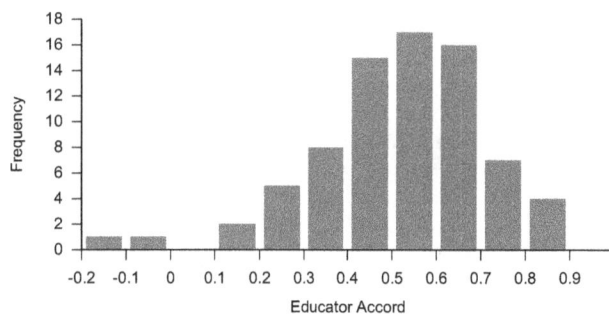

Figure 2: The distribution of accord scores. Picking ranks randomly would give an educator an average accord of 0, while 1 would indicate perfect agreement (and -1 perfect disagreement). Inspection of Q-Q plots confirms data is normal, as expected [21], with two notable outliers (visible above, far left).

interpretation, we use a conversion to Spearman's $\rho$ correlation for ranked data [8, p313], which gives $\rho = 0.400$. Informally, this means that the educators are closer to chance agreement than they are to complete agreement. The educators we surveyed form a very weak consensus about which errors are most frequently made by students.

## 4.3 Student Mistakes

We used our detector to look for the number of instances of mistakes, as described in the method section. The data set featured 14,235,239 compilation events, of which 7,333,201 were successful and 6,902,038 were unsuccessful. Each compilation may include multiple source files – the total number of source files considered was 17,144,721 files, of which 8,787,189 were compiled successfully and 8,357,532 were not.

We can informally categorise the mistakes as follows:

**Misunderstanding (or forgetting) syntax:**

- $A$ (confusing = with ==),
- $C$ (mismatched parentheses),
- $D$ (confusing & with &&),
- $E$ (spurious semi-colon after if, for, while),
- $F$ (wrong separator in for),
- $G$ (wrong brackets in if),
- $H$ (keyword as variable or method name),
- $J$ (forgetting parentheses when calling methods),
- $K$ (spurious semi-colon after method header),
- $L$ (less-than/greater-than operators wrong),
- $P$ (including types in actual method arguments).

**Type errors:**

- $I$ (calling method with wrong types),
- $Q$ (type mismatch assigning method result).

**Other semantic errors:**

- $B$ (using == to compare strings),

- $M$ (invoking instance method as static),
- $N$ (discarding method return),
- $O$ (missing return statement),
- $R$ (missing methods when implementing interface).

Note that mistake $N$ (ignoring the non-void result of a method) is not a compile error, and is not always an error (e.g. when you call a remove method that returns the item removed, you may not need to do anything with the return).

The frequencies of the number of instances of the different mistakes are shown in table 1, along with our informal classification of the error message. It can be seen that the type and semantic errors generally occur more frequently than the syntax errors.

## 4.4 Educator and Student Agreement

The average $\rho$ for correlations between each educator and the Blackbox data was 0.514 (3 s.f.). Corrected for continuity [20], this gives a $\bar{\rho}_{t,c} = 0.514$, so $z = 18.5$ (3 s.f.) and thus $p < 0.001$. Since the standard deviation of $\bar{\rho}_{t}, c$ is 0.028 [21]

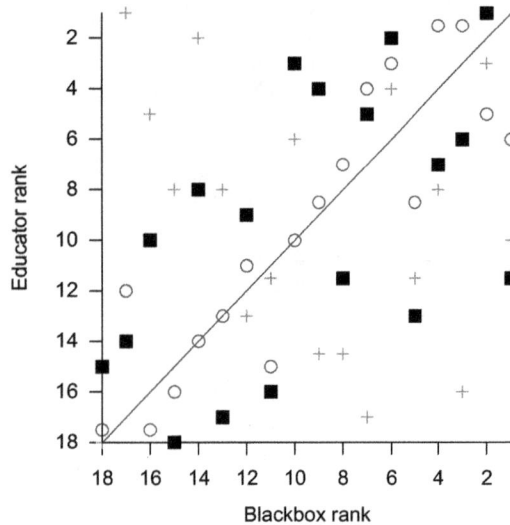

Figure 3: Examples of different accord scores. Perfect agreement is shown by the solid line, and accord is proportional to the square of the vertical distance of each point from the line. The empty circles are the ranks assigned by the educator with highest accord (0.876). The solid squares are the ranks assigned by one of the two educators surrounding the median accord (0.537). The pluses are the ranks assigned by the educator with lowest accord (-0.137).

and normality is assumed, the 95% confidence interval is [0.460, 0.569] (3 s.f.). Therefore, there was a statistically significant overall agreement, termed accord, between educators and the Blackbox data, with an average correlation of 0.514. The distribution of accord scores is shown in Figure 2. An example of accord is shown in Figure 3. The latter figure shows that while the educator with highest accord was reasonably close to the correct answer, the median educator in our sample (the solid squares) had only a moderate level of agreement, ranking the most popular Blackbox mistake as joint eleventh, and getting most other errors wrong by around four ranks. This level of agreement between educators and the student data was thus in general quite low.

## 4.5 Educator and Student Agreement – Effect of Experience

The relationship between educator accord (i.e. agreement with the Blackbox data) and years of being an educator is shown in Figure 4. The Spearman's $\rho$ correlation was not significant at the 5% level, $\rho = -0.180, p = 0.202$. As a follow up analysis, we also examined whether years of experience teaching introductory programming or teaching introductory programming in Java had an effect (alpha corrected to 0.025 for multiple comparisons). The result for correlating years spent teaching introductory programming in any language with accord was not significant, $\rho = -0.151, p = 0.192$, and neither was the result correlating years spent teaching introductory Java programming with accord: $\rho = 0.04, p = 0.972$. Thus, there was no effect of educator experience (in any measure we tried) on an educator's level of agreement with the Blackbox data.

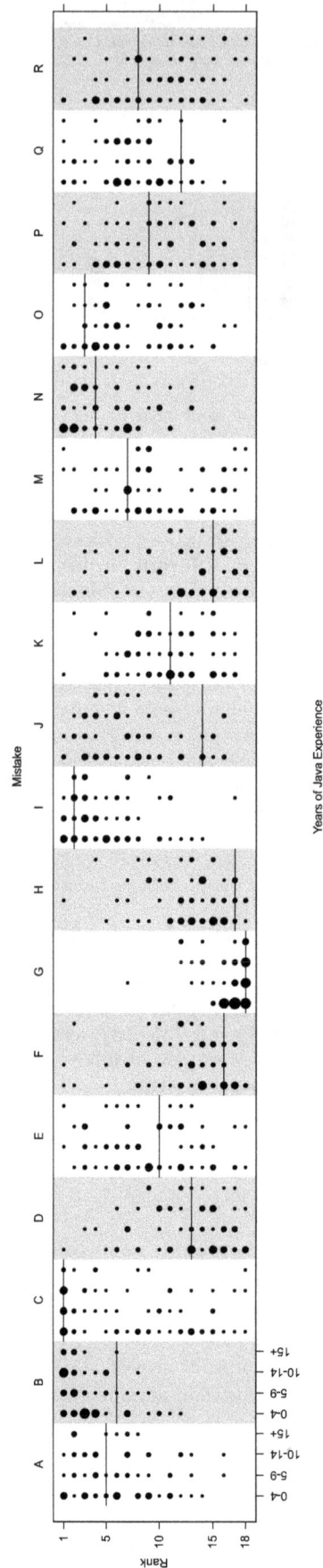

Figure 5: Graphic illustrating the effect of years spent teaching introductory programming in Java on mistake frequency rating. Each vertical band (alternately shaded for presentation) is a separate mistake and effectively a separate graph, with years plotted along the X axis, grouped into 4 groups, versus ranking (Y axis). The area of each circle is proportional to frequency (number of educators). If there was agreement among all raters, we would expect to see horizontal grouping around a common rating within each band. Alternatively, if the amount of experience had an effect on rating, we would expect to see a non-horizontal diagonal trend within each band. In this diagram, it can be seen that agreement of either kind is generally weak. For information, the rank derived from the Blackbox data is drawn on to each band as a horizontal line, and thus accord is (informally) the vertical distance of the circles from these horizontal lines. If experience had an effect on accord, we would see that the righthand points within each band were closer to the horizontal line than the lefthand points, but this is not the case.

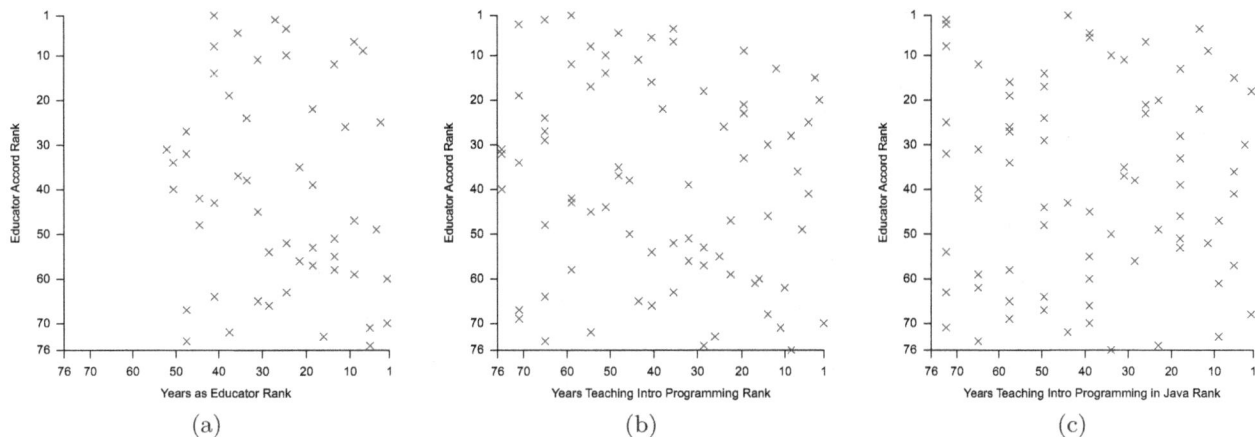

Figure 4: Graphs showing ranks for educator accord (i.e. their agreement with the Blackbox data) against ranks for (a) the years they have been an educator, (b) the years they have taught introductory programming and (c) the years they have taught introductory programming in Java. Ranks are plotted such that the highest values (and thus lowest ranks) are towards the top or right of the graph. Perfect agreement would be a diagonal line from bottom-left to top-right; perfect disagreement would be a diagonal line from top-left to bottom-right. Note that for (a), only 52 of the 76 educators in our sample answered this question (whereas all answered for (b) and (c)). Rank correlations were insignificant in all three cases.

# 5. DISCUSSION

The answers to our research questions from section 1 are:

- Educators' views form only a weak consensus about the frequency of the specified student Java mistakes.

- Educators' views of mistake frequency have only a moderate match ("accord") with the observed behaviour of students in a large-scale multi-institution data set.

- This accord has no association with educator experience.

A graphic displaying most of the study results together can be found in Figure 5.

## 5.1 Inter-Educator Agreement

Our implicit expectation when beginning this research was that there would be a reasonably strong consensus among educators as to the frequency of Java mistakes. The low level of agreement between educators was a surprise – and even more so because years of experience (generally, or within Java) made no apparent difference to the ratings assigned by the educators (see Figure 5 for a visualisation of these results). This result colours some of the interpretation of the results regarding agreement between the educators and Blackbox: if educators don't agree among each other, it is unlikely that there would be very strong agreement between the educators and the Blackbox data.

Our results show that educator opinions about student mistakes are not very consistent across educators. There are several possible explanations for this. One explanation is that the educators are all correct, in their own context: each educator may be correct about their own classroom, but their opinions do not generalise to other classrooms. Further work would be needed to investigate this, either directly by getting educators to tag their own students in the data set, or indirectly by breaking down the mistakes by student and comparing the variance between students to the variance between educator ratings.

Another explanation for the lack of generalisability is that looking at frequencies of Java mistakes is the wrong level of abstraction to find common ground among educators. If educators talked about programming features at a higher level (e.g. the conceptual difficulties that students have with looping, or variables) then we might find much more agreement and consensus that looking at the lower level aspects of the frequency of specific syntax and semantic mistakes. There is a reasonable argument to be made that educators' knowledge of mistake frequencies is not important in understanding student difficulties. However, it remains the case that educators do not form a consensus. This may be because educators do not form a consistent memory of mistake frequency, or generalise inaccurately from their own experience to larger bodies of students.

## 5.2 Student Mistakes

Our results from the Blackbox data provide a large sample-size result for the frequency of different Java errors, distinct from compiler error messages (shown in Table 1). Mismatched brackets – a syntax error – was the most frequent type of error, but otherwise the semantic errors tended to appear higher than the syntax errors. We should not over-interpret this result, as it is greatly affected by which mistakes we included in the study – but we wonder if this hints that semantic errors are a more serious challenge than syntax errors. Recent research has suggested that Java has syntax which is not much better than an arbitrary choice of syntax for learning [18], but perhaps the syntax of a language does not matter as much as semantics. Further work could investigate whether the frequency of these mistakes change over time (i.e. do students make fewer syntactic mistakes over time?), but that is beyond the scope of this paper. We also note that some of the errors which we took from Hristova et al. [9] are very infrequent, so their list of mistakes may not be suitable when considering just the most frequent Java mistakes.

## 5.3 Educator-Student Accord

Our examination of educators' frequency rankings against frequency rankings from the Blackbox data set (termed *accord*) showed a significant but moderate correlation of $\rho = 0.514$. As previously mentioned, given the weak levels of consensus among educators, it would not have been possible to achieve very high levels of correlation[6]. Still, it means that for any given educator from our sample, the expected correlation to the real data would be 0.514, which is lower than we had expected. If an educator states that from their experience, students always make a certain mistake in Java, our results must suggest to be wary of such a claim.

A visual inspection of figure 5 shows the big "hits and misses" from the educators. Mistake $B$, the use of == to compare strings, was clearly overrated by most, as was mistake $E$ (spurious semi-colons after if, for and while). Mistakes $J$ (forgetting parentheses for a method call) and $Q$ (incompatible types when assigning a method call result) were also overrated in terms of frequency. Of course, some of these mistakes are relative to the use of the underlying constructs: if students wrote fewer method calls than educators expected, this would explain the lower frequency of mistakes in making method calls. Similarly, the frequency of mistake R (not implementing all methods from an interface) will depend heavily on the frequency with which the sampled students implement interfaces (a relatively advanced feature for novices).

The mistakes in this study were automatically detected using a set of tools. If the tools were not sufficiently accurate in picking up mistakes, this could have affected our measure of educator accord. To this end, we have made the source code available (see section 3.3) in case further investigation is warranted. As well as the tool, the choice of mistakes has an effect on educator accord. Looking at Table 1, it is clear that some of the mistakes (especially $L$, $F$, $H$ and $G$) are particularly low frequency, in contrast to Hristova et al.'s [9] aim to find the most common errors. Figure 5 confirms that, especially for $G$, educators predicted these low frequency items consistently – if $G$ were excluded from the analysis, educator accord would reduce. As an illustration, if mistakes $L$, $F$, $H$ and $G$ are removed from the analysis, the average educator accord would drop from 0.514 to 0.311 – a much weaker level of accord. A more principled search for the top mistakes, and accurate classifiers for these, may provide a better picture of educator accord, but this may decrease educator accord rather than increase it. Educators seem to be accurate at identifying rare mistakes as rare but not at comparing higher frequency mistakes.

## 5.4 Affect of Experience on Educator-Student Accord

Our analysis, depicted visually in Figure 4, found that there was no effect of educator experience (as measured by years as an educator, years teaching introductory programming in any language, or years teaching introductory programming in Java) on educator accord. That is: no matter how many years the educator had been teaching, it made no

---

[6]As an illustration, if the Blackbox data had had frequencies ranked in order of the average ranks assigned by the educators, the average accord would have been 0.692. Although this is not necessarily the mathematical maximum of the average correlation, it can be used as an informal indicator of the highest levels of accord that could have been achieved.

effect on their accuracy in predicting the frequencies from the Blackbox student data. This is a very surprising result. Our expectation had been that experience would surely provide some sort of increase to accuracy.

The results show that experience has no effect on the task of rating mistakes by frequency. Further work could investigate more closely: for example, some tertiary educators lecture but do not supervise programming classes directly, so this could have an effect on accuracy. However, an initial analysis of our results suggests this may not be the issue: the average accord of educators who had taught in secondary education was 0.509, while the average accord of educators who had taught only in tertiary education was 0.516.

If one assumes that educator experience must make a difference to educator efficacy, then this would imply that ranking student mistakes is therefore unrelated to educator efficacy. However, work from Sadler et al. [15] in physics found that "a teacher's ability to identify students' most common wrong answer on multiple-choice items... is an additional measure of science teacher competence." While picking answers to a multiple choice question is not exactly the same as programming mistakes, there is a conflict here – either the Sadler et al. result does not transfer and ranking common student mistakes is not a measure of programming teacher competenece, or experience has no effect on teacher competence. The first option seems more likely.

## 6. CONCLUSIONS

Our study investigated educators' opinions about the frequency of eighteen mistakes in Java among programming novices. Our first finding was that educators have only a weak consensus about these frequencies. It remains possible that these frequencies are contextual, and thus each educator is correct for their own students. Regardless, this suggests that in cases where educators communicate with each other (e.g. via online communities), talking about which mistakes student make will not provide much agreement. Our further result that educators are not very accurate compared to a large data set of students suggests that educators are also not accurate about the frequencies of these mistakes, so any claims that "students always make mistake X" are unlikely to be accurate. Of course, this may just require that a different level of discourse is required: educators may still be accurate about the cause of mistakes and student's conceptions of the mistakes, but just not about the frequency of such mistakes.

Our most surprising result was that an educator's level of experience (as measured by years as an educator, years teaching introductory programming in any language, or years teaching introductory programming in Java) had no effect on how closely the educator's frequency rankings agreed with those from the Blackbox data. A strong interpretation of this result would be that experience has little effect on educator efficacy. However, it must be remembered that this task (ranking mistakes by frequency) is not necessarily aligned with educator efficacy – this result only shows that experience has no effect on ranking mistake frequency. Instead, this result may indicate that such a task is therefore not representative of educator efficacy (which we would expect to increase with experience).

Our data also provides frequencies from a large data set (over 100,000 students) for our chosen eighteen novice mistakes. Given the lack of agreement between educators and this data (see figure 5), we can therefore state that the results will be surprising to most (and that any educators who claim they are "exactly as expected" were not participants in our study!). Mismatched brackets – a syntax error – were the most frequent type of mistake, and otherwise many of the top mistakes were not syntactic. Notable mistakes that were mispredicted by our sample of educators (and thus probably the most surprising results) were as follows. Mistake $B$, the use of == to compare strings, was clearly overrated by most, as was mistake $E$ (spurious semi-colons after if, for and while). Mistakes $J$ (forgetting parentheses for a method call) and $Q$ (incompatible types when assigning a method call result) were also overrated in terms of frequency. One hypothesis is that educators overrated in terms of frequency those mistakes which students have most trouble with understanding, or were likely to spend most time on fixing. We aim to investigate this possibility in future work.

## Acknowledgements

The authors are grateful to Kristina Dietz for her help with the statistical analysis methodology, to Sally Fincher for her advice on the research design, to Davin McCall for his knowledge of the area, and to Michael Kölling and Ian Utting for their observations about untested educator folk wisdom that inspired the research.

## 7. REFERENCES

[1] M. Ahmadzadeh, D. Elliman, and C. Higgins. An analysis of patterns of debugging among novice computer science students. In *Proceedings of the 10th Annual SIGCSE Conference on Innovation and Technology in Computer Science Education*, ITiCSE '05, pages 84–88, New York, NY, USA, 2005. ACM.

[2] Y. Ben-David Kolikant. Computer science education as a cultural encounter: a socio-cultural framework for articulating teaching difficulties. *Instructional Science*, 39(4):543–559, 2011.

[3] N. C. C. Brown, M. Kölling, D. McCall, and I. Utting. Blackbox: A large scale repository of novice programmers' activity. In *Proceedings of the 45th ACM Technical Symposium on Computer Science Education*, SIGCSE '14, pages 223–228, New York, NY, USA, 2014. ACM.

[4] R. Cadenhead. *Sams Teach Yourself Java in 21 Days*. Pearson Education, 2012.

[5] P. Denny, A. Luxton-Reilly, and E. Tempero. All syntax errors are not equal. In *Proceedings of the 17th ACM Annual Conference on Innovation and Technology in Computer Science Education*, ITiCSE '12, pages 75–80, New York, NY, USA, 2012. ACM.

[6] T. Dy and M. M. Rodrigo. A detector for non-literal Java errors. In *Proceedings of the 10th Koli Calling International Conference on Computing Education Research*, Koli Calling '10, pages 118–122, New York, NY, USA, 2010. ACM.

[7] C. Hoisington. *Android Boot Camp for Developers using Java*. Cengage Learning, 2012.

[8] D. C. Howell. *Statistical Methods for Psychology*. Duxbury, fifth edition, 2002.

[9] M. Hristova, A. Misra, M. Rutter, and R. Mercuri. Identifying and correcting Java programming errors for introductory computer science students. In *Proceedings of the 34th SIGCSE Technical Symposium on Computer Science Education*, SIGCSE '03, pages 153–156, New York, NY, USA, 2003. ACM.

[10] J. Jackson, M. Cobb, and C. Carver. Identifying top Java errors for novice programmers. In *Frontiers in Education, 2005. FIE '05. Proceedings 35th Annual Conference*, Oct 2005.

[11] M. C. Jadud. Methods and tools for exploring novice compilation behaviour. In *Proceedings of the Second International Workshop on Computing Education Research*, ICER '06, pages 73–84, New York, NY, USA, 2006. ACM.

[12] M. Kendall. *Rank Correlation Methods*. Edward Arnold, fifth edition, 1990.

[13] S. B. Lyerly. The average spearman rank correlation coefficient. *Psykometrika*, 17:421–428, 1952.

[14] D. McCall. Improving the experience of novice programmers – language and tools. Technical report, University of Kent, 2013.

[15] P. M. Sadler, G. Sonnert, H. P. Coyle, N. Cook-Smith, and J. L. Miller. The influence of teachers' knowledge on student learning in middle school physical science classrooms. *American Educational Research Journal*, 50(5):1020–1049, 2013.

[16] E. Soloway and S. Iyengar, editors. *Empirical Studies of Programmers: Papers Presented at the First Workshop on Empirical Studies of Programmers*. Intellect Books, 1986.

[17] J. C. Spohrer and E. Soloway. Novice mistakes: Are the folk wisdoms correct? *Commun. ACM*, 29(7):624–632, July 1986.

[18] A. Stefik and S. Siebert. An empirical investigation into programming language syntax. *Trans. Comput. Educ.*, 13(4):19:1–19:40, Nov. 2013.

[19] E. S. Tabanao, M. M. T. Rodrigo, and M. C. Jadud. Predicting at-risk novice Java programmers through the analysis of online protocols. In *Proceedings of the Seventh International Workshop on Computing Education Research*, ICER '11, pages 85–92, New York, NY, USA, 2011. ACM.

[20] W. L. Taylor. Correcting the average rank correlation coefficient for ties in rankings. *Journal of the American Statistical Association*, 59(307):872–876, 1964.

[21] W. L. Taylor and C. Fong. Some contributions to average rank correlation methods and to the distribution of the average rank correlation coefficient. *Journal of the American Statistical Association*, 58(303):756–769, 1963.

[22] P. van der Linden. *Just Java 2*. Pearson Education, 2004.

# Predicting Student Success using Fine Grain Clicker Data

Leo Porter
Department of Math and
Computer Science
Skidmore College
Saratoga Springs, NY, USA

Daniel Zingaro
Mathematical and
Computational Sciences
Univ. of Toronto Mississauga
Toronto, ON, Canada

Raymond Lister
School of Software
Univ. of Technology, Sydney
Sydney, Australia

## ABSTRACT

Recent research suggests that the first weeks of a CS1 course have a strong influence on end-of-course student performance. The present work aims to refine the understanding of this phenomenon by using in-class clicker questions as a source of student performance. Clicker questions generate per-lecture and per-question data with which to assess student understanding. This work demonstrates that clicker question performance early in the term predicts student outcomes at the end of the term. The predictive nature of these questions applies to code-writing questions, multiple choice questions, and the final exam as a whole. The most predictive clicker questions are identified and the relationships between these questions and final exam performance are examined.

## Categories and Subject Descriptors

K.3.2 [**Computer Science Education**]: Computer and Information Science Education

## Keywords

CS1; clickers; assessment

## 1. INTRODUCTION

The first computer science course (CS1) is of utmost importance to computer science educators as it is the gateway for the major. Unfortunately, researchers have repeatedly recognized that CS1 has high failure and drop rates [3] causing many students' first exposure to the field to also be their last. This is of paramount importance for those wishing to both grow our field and increase its diversity.

Computer science education researchers have studied various elements of CS1 courses and reliable pedagogical best-practices are emerging. However, even in classes employing these instructional practices, there appears to be a vast divide among the students who succeed and those who fail. For example, researchers have shown independent of pedagogical style that students with prior experience in programming fare much better than those without prior experience [17].

*ICER '14*, August 11–13, 2014, Glasgow, United Kingdom
Copyright 2014 ACM 978-1-4503-2755-8/14/08 ...$15.00.
http://dx.doi.org/10.1145/2632320.2632354

Perhaps more concerning is a trend reported in recent research that suggests strong links between early tests and overall course performance [1, 2, 11]. The existence of such a relationship has implications for both researchers and teachers. Researchers may be interested in the mechanisms underlying this relationship; already there are a number of competing theories attempting to explain how and why students differentiate so quickly [1]. Instructors will be interested in early identification and intervention possibilities, especially if such early performance sets students on paths from which it is difficult to recover.

In this work, we examine student performance on clicker questions from lectures in a CS1 class taught in python. We bring clicker data to bear on our research questions because it is naturalistic data produced in the context of a real course, its generation begins immediately (in week 1), it represents responses to targeted conceptual questions, and it provides a mechanism to track students through the term.

The contributions of this work include:

- We find that student performance on clicker questions correlates with outcomes on the final exam (similar to findings reported in [10]) and this predictive value applies to code-writing questions, multiple choice questions, and the final exam as a whole.

- Tracking students throughout the term suggests that by binning students into quartiles based on their week 1-3 performance, instructors may be able to identify struggling students who are likely to perform poorly on key final exam questions.

- We identify specific clicker questions (and their associated concepts) that are most predictive of student success on final exam questions.

## 2. BACKGROUND

It is widely believed that many students in CS1 courses receive extreme grades: very high or (more concerningly) very low. Whether or not this is evidence of a bimodal distribution [1], the fact remains that many students do poorly in CS1 [3]. Further, it seems that the students that will ultimately fail a CS1 can with some accuracy be identified early in the term. Research shows, for example, that those with previous experience or those who can think in abstract ways are more likely to succeed in CS1 [17, 5].

Rather than examine particulars of students, other research offers that CS is qualitatively different from other learning domains, so that the material itself is implicated in high failure rates. Robins, for example, suggests that topics are so tightly interconnected that faltering on one topic can set off a chain of more and more likely failures [11]. On the other hand, students who successfully learn one topic are well-positioned to understand a follow-on topic, because the interconnected nature of CS concepts constrains the ways in which the new concept can be understood. Others note that being able to write code requires mastery of other preliminary skills such as code-tracing and code-reading, and that failure to acquire these underlying skills is common among poor performers [14].

A convenient research artifact for investigating student learning is the final exam written by students at the end of a CS1. For example, Venables et al. [14] studied student scores on explaining, tracing, and code-writing questions on a final exam and found significant relationships between these skills. Students who cannot accurately trace or explain code can usually not write code [6].

Other work has considered multiple time points in an attempt to acquire more fine-grained assessments of student learning. For example, Ahadi and Lister [1] provide data on several quizzes, showing that even the earliest quizzes suggest large separation between what appear to be different types of students. These authors also find wide variation in scores on a quiz as early as week 3, suggesting the importance of early data in understanding the progression of our students. It is within this context of improved temporal understanding that we aim to provide insight into when students begin to fall behind and the topics/questions that best predict these struggles.

To visualize temporal understanding, we evaluate data from Peer Instruction (PI) multiple-choice clicker questions. PI is a pedagogy that engages students in conceptual discussions with their peers. Recent research suggests that PI is advantageous for CS majors [12] and weak students [16], decreases failure rates [8] and contributes to increased retention [9]. More important for the present work is the use of clickers in the implementation of PI. Clicker software automatically categorizes responses as correct or incorrect, and we use this data as fine-grained assessments of what students understand as they proceed through the term.

## 3. METHOD

We report on data collected from a 12-week CS1 offered in 2013 at a large research-intensive university. The instructor is the second author of this paper. He has taught CS1 many times in both PI and non-PI offerings and has implemented best-practices such as pair programming and contextual assignments in addition to PI. Students participated in 34 PI class meetings and 8 practical labs, completed two assignments, and took one midterm and one final exam. Students also completed pre-lecture reading quizzes.

The class meetings largely centered around multiple choice questions, with instructor live-programming to supplement student discussion and argumentation. Each "PI cycle" occurred 2-3 times per class. The following steps summarize a PI cycle; we use these names later in the paper when focused on particular parts of the process:

**Individual Vote.** The instructor poses a conceptual question on which students vote individually.

**Group Vote.** Students then discuss the question with their seatmates for 2-3 minutes and vote again.

**Classwide Discussion.** The instructor leads a classwide discussion of relevant concepts and misconceptions.

For one PI cycle in each class, we appended an **isomorphic vote**. This vote was taken on a similar, isomorphic question, and students answered this new question individually (see [7] for rationale and examples of using isomorphic votes in CS courses; we closely adopted their method). We added these isomorphic questions because we are interested in separating the effects of knowledge that students have at the start of class (Individual Vote) from the knowledge acquired during class. The instructor chose the concept in each class that he thought was most important, and wrote an isomorphic question to accompany the initial PI question. The placement of isomorphic questions is such that they measure learning from the full PI cycle (including group discussion and classwide discussion).

### 3.1 Data Analysis

Given the small number of clicker questions per class, we combine questions across three-week intervals to reduce noise in the dataset (e.g. Weeks 1, 2, and 3 were combined, and so forth). Student absences are particularly problematic in producing noise and potentially polluting the dataset. We handle absences for each student by dividing correct responses by total responses submitted (effectively not penalizing absences; see Section 4.1). For each tri-weekly period, we omit a student's data if they do not answer at least 25% of the questions for that period.

### 3.2 Final Exam

In addition to clicker correctness, we analyze scores on the final exam given at the completion of the course. The final exam consisted of a variety of question types, as follows: multiple choice (30 points), code-explaining (9 points), code-writing (38 points), code-tracing (8 points), testing (3 points), complexity (11 points), and terminology (6 points). We focus in particular on two questions, both code-writing questions: FQ1 and FQ2. Final exam question content varies widely, so we chose FQ1 as it is well-known in the literature. We selected FQ2 to be of the same style (code-writing), because it addressed later term content.

**FQ1**: FQ1 asks students to solve two problems from the CS1 research literature: the speed limit problem and a version of the rainfall problem [14, 13]. Each problem was worth 5 points. The Speed Limit Problem and associated solution with rubric can be found in Figure 1. The Rainfall Problem and associated solution with rubric can be found in Figure 2. FQ1 requires concepts from the first four weeks of the term: conditionals, booleans, and loops.

**FQ2**: FQ2 asks students to parse a file and produce an appropriate data structure based on the contents of the file. FQ2 and its associated solution and grading rubric appear in Figure 3. This question requires concepts through Week 8 in the term, including files and lists (or another data structure of the students' choosing).

## 4. RESULTS

### 4.1 Managing Absences

As mentioned in Section 3.1, student class absences are problematic as each absence leads to missing data. We considered three options for handling these absences. We could (1) credit students for clicking-in on questions (i.e., measuring attendance), (2) credit students for the number of questions answered correctly (i.e., count unanswered questions as incorrect), or (3) credit students for the number of questions correctly answered divided by the total number of questions answered.

After a brief analysis of the data, we believe that option (3) is most meaningful for our analysis. One reason is that some strong students chose not to attend frequently but,

The speed limit on a highway is 100 km/h. Drivers exceeding the speed limit are issued a ticket. The amount of the ticket charge depends on two things: whether it is their first offense, and the amount over the speed limit at which they were driving:

| Speed (km/h) | First Offense? | Charge ($) |
|---|---|---|
| ≤ 100 | not applicable | 0 |
| 101-120 | yes | 105 |
| ≥ 121 | yes | 160 |
| ≥ 101 | no | 200 |

Write the body for the following function. You **are required to** use nested if-statements to solve this question.

```
def ticket_cost(speed, first_offense):
    '''(int, bool) -> int
    Return the charge according to the above table
    for a speed of speed and whether
    this is the first_offense.
    '''
```

(a) Question

```
if speed <= 100:
    return 0
else:
    if first_offense:
        if speed <= 120:
            return 105
        else:
            return 160
    else:
        return 200
```

The following grading scheme was used, out of 5 points:

```
+1 for the no-fine logic
+1 for the else associated with the first if
+1 for an if that uses first_offense
+1 for correct code for prior offense
+1 for correct code for no prior offense
```

(b) Solution and Rubric

Figure 1: FQ1 Part A - Speed Limit Problem.

Write a program (not a function!) that asks the user for positive integers. When the user is finished entering their integers, they enter a negative integer to tell the program to stop asking them for more integers. Once input is complete, the program prints "No integers to average" if the user provided no positive integers, and the average of the positive integers otherwise. You **must not** use lists, tuples, or dictionaries in your response.

Here is a sample program run where the user enters 4 and then 8 and then -1:

```
Integer: 4
Integer: 8
Integer: -1
Average: 6.0
```

Here is another run where the user types -3 to the first prompt:

```
Integer: -3
No integers to average
```

(a) Question

```
n = 0
total = 0
num = int(input('Integer: '))
while num >= 0:
    n = n + 1
    total = total + num
    num = int(input('Integer: '))
if n > 0:
    print('Average:', total / n)
else:
    print('no integers to average')
```
The following grading scheme was used, out of 5 points:
```
+1 for initializing variables
+1 for input prompt(s)
+1 for correct while-condition
+1 for adding to the variables inside the loop
+1 for if-statement below the loop
-1 for writing a function (it should be a program)
```

(b) Solution and Rubric

Figure 2: FQ1 Part B - Rainfall Problem.

Each line of a **hockey file** contains a four-digit year, a team name, and a two-digit number of wins. Here is one such file, hockey.txt:
```
2003maple leafs45
2005maple leafs41
1996maple leafs30
1995senators18
2000senators48
2012canadiens48
```
The first line of the file, for example, says that in 2003 (year), the maple leafs (team name) had 45 wins.

Write a function that takes an **open** hockey file and returns a list of lists, where each inner list refers to a team name and that team's maximum number of wins.

Here is a sample call of the function on hockey.txt:
```
>>> teams_and_most_wins(open('hockey.txt'))
[['maple leafs', 45], ['senators', 48],
['canadiens', 48]]

def teams_and_most_wins(f):
    '''(file) -> list of list of [str, int]
    f is a hockey file. Return a list where each inner list
    refers to a team name and that team's maximum wins.
    '''
```

(a) Question

```
lst = []
for line in f:
    line = line.strip()
    team = line[4:-2]
    wins = int(line[-2:])
    i = 0
    while i < len(lst) and lst[i][0] != team:
        i = i + 1
    if i == len(lst):
        lst.append([team, 0])
    lst[i][1] = max(wins, lst[i][1])
return lst
```

The following grading scheme was used (a similar rubric was applied for students using a dictionary rather than a list):

```
+1 for creating an empty list
+1 for looping through each line of the file
+2 for extracting team name and wins
+1 for searching the list for the team
+1 for adding new team sublist if the team does not exist
+1 for updating maximum wins
+1 for returning the list
```

(b) Solution and Rubric

Figure 3: FQ2 - Hockey Problem.

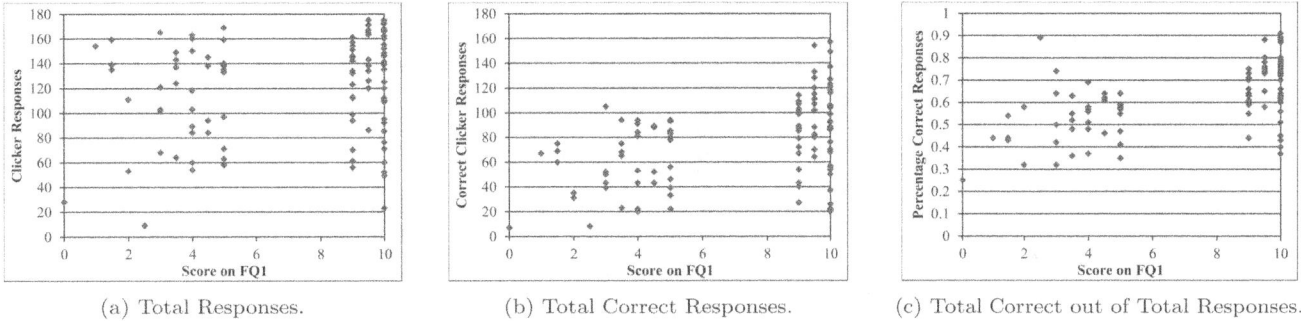

(a) Total Responses.

(b) Total Correct Responses.

(c) Total Correct out of Total Responses.

Figure 4: Relationship of total clicker responses, total correct clicker responses, and correctness of clicker responses among those answered, to the score on FQ1 among top ($\geq 9$) and bottom ($\leq 5$) performers.

Table 1: Correlations between Clicker Correctness and Final Exam Performance. All values are significant ($\alpha < 0.05$).

| Clicker | Final Exam | | | |
|---|---|---|---|---|
| Weeks | FQ1 | FQ2 | MCQs | Overall |
| 1,2,3 | 0.56 | 0.42 | 0.49 | 0.61 |
| 4,5,6 | 0.41 | 0.39 | 0.27 | 0.43 |
| 7,8,9 | 0.40 | 0.36 | 0.45 | 0.49 |
| 10,11,12 | 0.27 | 0.32 | 0.36 | 0.40 |
| All Questions | 0.53 | 0.50 | 0.53 | 0.64 |

Table 2: Course Content by Tri-Weekly Period.

| Weeks | Content |
|---|---|
| 1,2,3 | variables, types, functions, conditionals |
| 4,5,6 | loops, strings, lists, tuples, files |
| 7,8,9 | dictionaries, testing, classes |
| 10,11,12 | classes, complexity, sorting |

when they did attend, were able to answer many questions correctly. For these students, option (2) would reflect poor performance whereas option (3) would more-accurately reflect their strong performance.

Figure 4 provides a comparison of the three approaches for managing absences through a plot of student performance on clicker responses versus FQ1. To best illustrate this relationship, we focus here only on the students in the top ($\geq 9$ out of 10) and bottom ($\leq 5$ out of 10) quartiles on FQ1. The relationship between attendance and performance on FQ1 is surprisingly weak, showing that attending class is not a strong predictor for success (Figure 4a; $r = 0.17$). The relationship improves substantially when scoring based on total correct responses (Figure 4b; $r = 0.43$). This relationship improves again when scoring by the percentage correct among questions answered (Figure 4c; $r = 0.59$).

## 4.2 Clickers-Exam Correlation

To further investigate the relationship between term and exam performance, we study correlations between clicker responses and components of the final exam. For clicker responses, we examine tri-weekly periods (i.e. weeks {1,2,3}, ..., {10,11,12}) of student correctness along with clicker responses over the entire term (All Questions). For the final exam, we evaluate student performance on FQ1 and FQ2, multiple choice questions (MCQs), and the entire exam (Overall).

These correlations appear in Table 1. Overall clicker performance correlates highly with overall final exam performance ($r = 0.64$). Examining weekly correlations, we find

that the first three weeks are more predictive of student outcomes on FQ1, FQ2, the MCQs, and the final exam overall than any other tri-weekly period. The concepts covered in the first three weeks are certainly critical for the entire class (see Table 2), but other tri-weekly periods seem critical as well (e.g., Weeks 4-6).

We have anecdotally observed teachers wondering whether PI MCQ performance will lead to code-writing performance, or whether these skills are just "too different". Do scores on MCQs simply predict scores on later MCQs, or do such scores tell us something useful about programming ability? While we cannot make causal claims, we do observe that clicker questions explain MCQs no more strongly than they explain the other exam questions, suggesting interesting links between MCQs and programming-related skills.

## 4.3 Student Tracking

Correlations provided in the previous section offer insight into the high-level relationship between weekly performance and student outcomes. To gain a more fine-grained view of student performance, we gathered clicker responses from the individual votes of the PI process and graphed that data against final exam questions. As mentioned in prior sections, the noisiness of these data obscures useful trends on a per-student level. However, when we grouped students by end-of-term performance, a trend emerged.

Figures 5 and 6 graph each student's performance throughout the term; we include performance on clicker questions (averaged tri-weekly) and FQ1. Figure 5 contains the students who achieve > 90% on FQ1 (roughly the top performance quartile on that question). Figure 6 contains the students who achieve $\leq 50\%$ on FQ1 (roughly the bottom quartile). Despite the noise among individual students, the difference between these two groups is readily apparent: students in the top quartile on FQ1 generally do better throughout the term than students in the bottom quartile on FQ1.

To follow the quartiles through the term as in Figures 5 and 6, we consolidate per-student data into average performance for each quartile (and for students who drop) in Figure 7. The differences between these groups are evident in the first weeks of the term and persist throughout the term. A notably odd feature of this graph is that students who drop the class before the exam do slightly better than those in the bottom quartile.

Clearly, early term performance is important for FQ1, but FQ1 focuses on loops and conditionals which are covered early in the term. To see whether this trend persists on topics from later in the term, we provide similar results for FQ2 in Figure 8. Again, the groups of students (nearly quartiles) are established early in the term, and strong performance

54

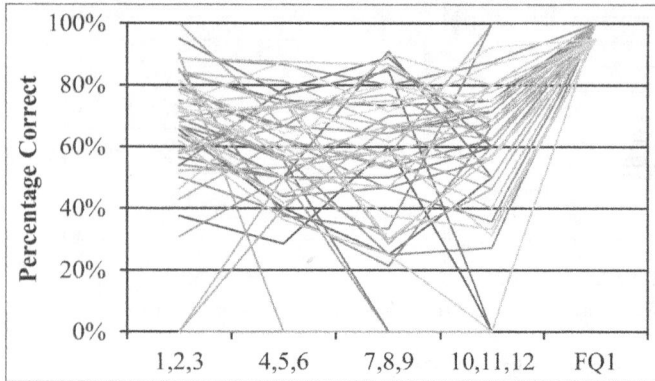

Figure 5: Individual student performance on clicker questions (individual vote) in tri-weekly periods for students who achieve a score > 90% on FQ1.

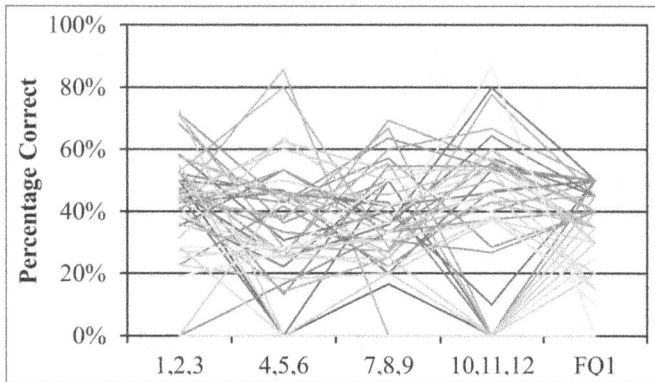

Figure 6: Individual student performance on clicker questions (individual vote) in tri-weekly periods for students who achieve a score ≤ 50% on FQ1.

on FQ2 is associated with strong term performance. This shows the importance of early term performance even on material taught later in the term.

These results for FQ1 and FQ2 suggest that early term performance can be used to group students for purposes of predicting their performance on the exam. Rather than grouping by various measures of student performance at the end of the term (as done in prior graphs), perhaps a more meaningful grouping would be to group students by their performance early in the term, specifically on Weeks 1,2,3, to examine how those groups progress.

Figure 9 groups students by their performance on clicker questions (again, individual vote) in Weeks 1-3 and compares their performance on FQ1 and FQ2. Specifically, we are examining whether a student in a particular quartile in early weeks ultimately achieves a score above or below the median. Focusing first on FQ1, for students in the top half of the class in Weeks 1-3 (top two quartiles), students are quite likely to achieve a grade above or equal to the median score. As the median on FQ1 is 8 out of 10, this is encouraging as this represents good performance on the question. Most discouraging here are the results for the bottom quartile, whose students are almost certain to fall below the median on FQ1. FQ2 was a more difficult question, with the median being 3 out of 8. A similar trend to FQ1 manifests for FQ2.

Using the median is useful for identifying relationships between early student quartiles and final exam placement (e.g., that bottom-quartile students are highly likely to appear in the bottom half on the exam). However, binning

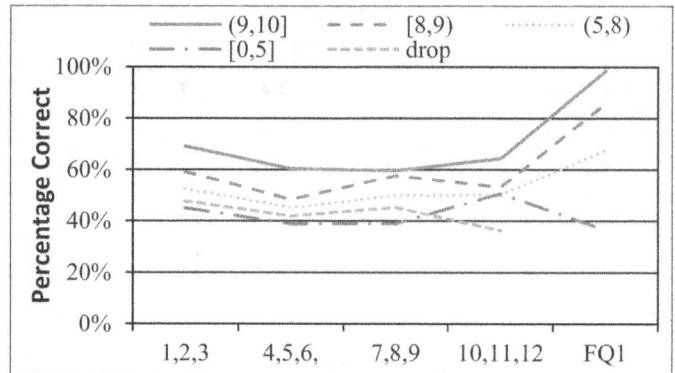

Figure 7: Average performance among students grouped by scores on FQ1 and among students who drop the class.

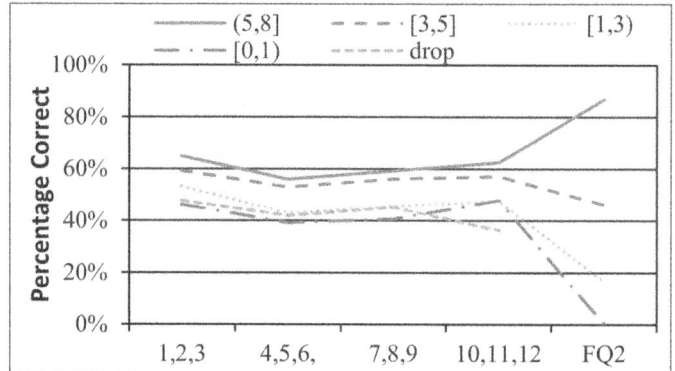

Figure 8: Average performance among students grouped by scores on FQ2 and among students who drop the class.

students at the end of term based on this median-split loses important pedagogical information. For example, if most students fail a question, being above or below the median is relatively unimportant in terms of learning. To gain insight into the relationship between scores and meaningful student outcomes, the course instructor binned student performance on each question, based on the rubric, as doing well ("good"), passing ("acceptable"), or below passing standards ("poor"). Figure 10 provides the percentage of students who fall into these categories (good, acceptable, and poor) from each of the Week 1-3 quartiles. For example, we see that > 70% of the students in the top quartile from Week 1-3 achieve "good" scores on FQ1. Of the students in the bottom quartile from Week 1-3, over 50% do poorly on FQ1. These results show that students who are in the bottom quartile in the first three weeks are very likely to do poorly (below passing standards) on key final exam questions.

## 4.4 Most Predictive Clicker Questions

In this section, we present the specific clicker questions that are most predictive of student performance on FQ1 and FQ2. For each of those two final exam questions, three highly predictive clicker questions are presented, one question for each of three criteria:

**Sufficiency:** This is the increase in the probability that the student was in the upper 50% on a particular final exam question when it is known that the student answered the clicker question correctly. A clicker question with a high degree of sufficiency is a hard question that only strong students tend to get right; getting it wrong is not a strong indication that a student will be in the lower 50% of the final exam question.

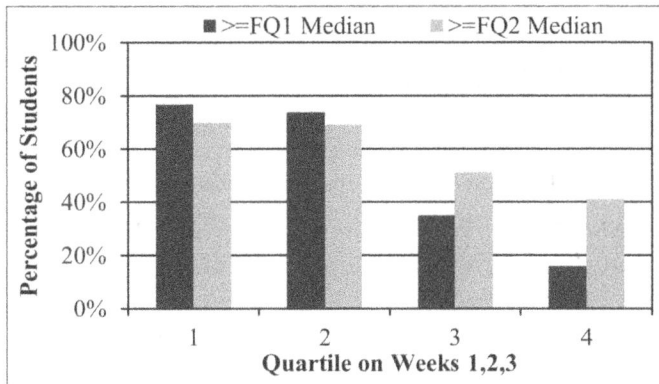

Figure 9: Grouped by performance in Week 1-3, the percentage of students who achieve a score $\geq$ the median score on FQ1 and FQ2.

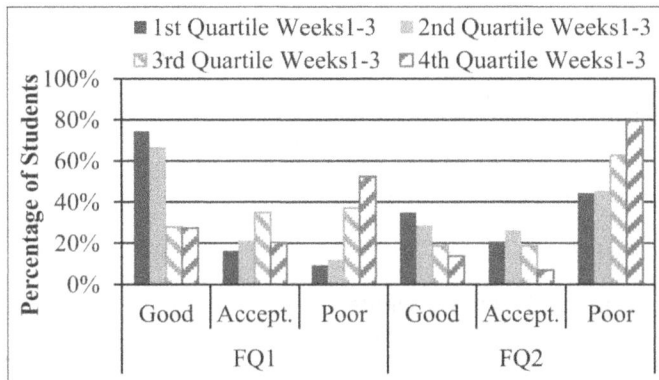

Figure 10: Grouped by performance in Week 1-3, the percentage of students who achieve "good", "acceptable" and "poor" scores on FQ1 and FQ2.

**Necessity:** This is the decrease in the probability that the student was in the upper 50% on a particular final exam question when it is known that the student answered the clicker question incorrectly. A clicker question with a substantial degree of necessity is not an especially difficult question; answering the question correctly, therefore, is not a strong indicator that the student will be in the upper 50% on the exam question.

**Accuracy:** This is a combination of sufficiency and necessity. It characterizes the increase in probability of being in the top 50% on a final exam question for those answering the clicker question correctly and the decrease in probability for those answering the clicker question incorrectly.

These concepts are more fully described in Bayesian statistics and Expert Systems literature [4].

### 4.4.1 Most Predictive Questions for FQ1

The most accurate predictor for FQ1 was a question asked in the third week of the term. This question appears in Figure 11 (for this and the remaining questions, the correct response is bolded). This question had an accuracy of 73%. It is an isomorphic question testing if-statements on which students voted alone after having just worked through a similar question in a PI cycle. How is it that a question as early as week 3 has such predictive value? We can only surmise here, but perhaps the ability to trace and understand if-statements is a predictor of one's capacity to understand and work with other constructs too, such as functions and loops. Note that, by virtue of being an isomorphic question,

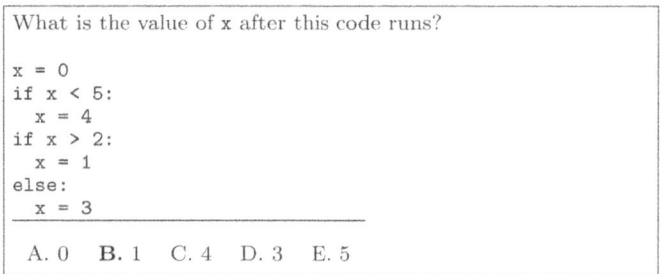

What is the value of x after this code runs?

```
x = 0
if x < 5:
  x = 4
if x > 2:
  x = 1
else:
  x = 3
```

A. 0   **B.** 1   C. 4   D. 3   E. 5

Figure 11: Question of highest accuracy for FQ1.

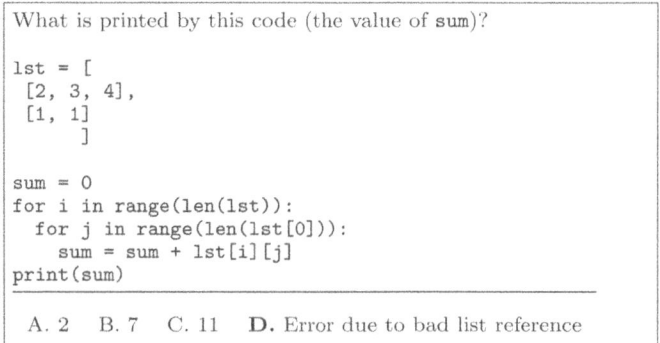

What is printed by this code (the value of sum)?

```
lst = [
[2, 3, 4],
[1, 1]
]

sum = 0
for i in range(len(lst)):
  for j in range(len(lst[0])):
    sum = sum + lst[i][j]
print(sum)
```

A. 2   B. 7   C. 11   **D.** Error due to bad list reference

Figure 12: Question of Highest Sufficiency for FQ1.

it reflects student understanding at the end of presenting the material in lecture (we address this further in Section 5)

The question with the highest degree of sufficiency was posed to students in the sixth week. This question (Figure 12) was an isomorphic question on which students voted alone after answering and discussing a similar question on accessing a nested list. Getting this question right increased the probability that a student would be in the top 50% of FQ1 from 0.50 to 0.78. However, getting this question wrong only decreased that probability to 0.38. Thus, this difficult question identified stronger students.

The question with the most substantial degree of necessity was posed to students extremely early: in the third class of the first week (Figure 13). The individual vote for this question was most predictive. Answering correctly only marginally increased the probability that a student would be in the top 50% of FQ1, but answering incorrectly decreased that probability from 0.5 to 0.07. Thus, this was an easy code-tracing question that identified students who almost-immediately began to struggle.

### 4.4.2 Most Predictive Questions for FQ2

Two clicker questions were equally the most accurate predictors for FQ2. These questions had an accuracy of 69%. One of those clicker questions was posed to students in week 9. In Figure 14, we present the other question, which was posed to students in week 2. It is another isomorphic question on which students voted alone after answering and discussing a similar question on argument passing and variable scope. In our experience, introductory students often struggle with the lifetime of variables, believing a variable declared anywhere can be referenced anywhere. Correctly answering this question demonstrates a lack of this common, and problematic, misunderstanding.

The question with the highest degree of sufficiency increased the probability that a student would be in the top 50% of FQ2 from 0.50 to 0.83. This isomorphic question was posed to students in the sixth week of the term. In fact, it

```
What is the output of this code?

def calculate(w, x, y):
    a = x
    b = w + 1
    return a + b + 3

print(calculate(3, 2, 0))
```

A. 5    **B.** 9    C. 0    D. 3

Figure 13: Question of highest Necessity for FQ1.

```
What is the output of this code?

def a(num):
    return val + num + 3

def b(val):
    return a(1)

print(b(2))
```

A. 6    B. 7    C. 4    D. 5
**E.** Error because of an undefined variable

Figure 14: Question of Highest Accuracy for FQ2.

```
if temperature > 0:
    print("above freezing")
elif temperature == 0:
    print("at freezing")
else:
    print("below freezing")
```

Does the code below do exactly the same thing as the code above?

```
if temperature > 0:
    print("above freezing")
elif temperature == 0:
    print("at freezing")
print("below freezing")
```

A. Yes                **B.** No

Figure 15: Question of highest Necessity for FQ2.

is the same clicker question which had the highest degree of sufficiency for FQ1 (see preceding section and Figure 12).

The question with the highest necessity for FQ2 appears in Figure 15 and was posed to students in only the third week of term. This is a code-tracing question aimed at tracing through conditionals, on which students voted after group discussion. Correctly answering this question only marginally increased the probability that a student would be in the top 50% of FQ2, but incorrectly answering decreased that probability from 0.5 to 0.2. Thus, this easy question identified struggling students.

## 4.5    Data Sensitivity and Bootstrapping

If we taught this course again, to a different student cohort, but with the same clicker questions and the same final exam, would we see similar results? We used the well-established bootstrap technique [15] to offer confidence that our results would be replicable. Bootstrapping involves generating a large number of "bootstrap samples" from the original data. Each of these new bootstrap samples is the same size as the original sample, and is constructed by selecting data points (here, students) at random from the original sample. The random selection of data is done with replacement. That is, within a single bootstrap sample, some students from the original data may be selected more than once, and some students may not be selected at all.

We constructed 100 bootstrap samples. We then used each of these 100 bootstrap samples to calculate the accuracy of each clicker question (as defined in Section 4.4) for both FQ1 and FQ2. For each clicker question, on each of the two final exam questions, the mean of the 100 "bootstrap accuracies" was the same, to two significant figures, as the accuracy for the original sample. Of greater interest is the standard deviation of these bootstrap accuracies, which was around 5% for almost all the clicker questions on both FQ1 and FQ2. Such a modest standard deviation indicates that our broad finding—that the early weeks of term are highly predictive of performance on the final exam—should generalize to other student cohorts.

The greatest variation in the bootstrap samples concerned exactly which clicker questions were highly predictive (as

presented in Section 4.4). For FQ1, the clicker question which was most accurate with the original data (as presented in Section 4.4.1) was also the most accurate in 50 of our 100 bootstrap runs. That same clicker question was in the top 2 in 75 bootstrap runs, and the top 5 in 90 bootstrap runs.

For FQ2, the bootstrap results were more mixed. The clicker question which was most accurate with the original data was the most accurate in only 17 of our 100 bootstrap runs. That clicker question was in the top 3 in 25 bootstrap runs and the top 7 in half the bootstrap runs. These mixed results for FQ2 are a result of the original data having 27 clicker questions within 5% accuracy (i.e. one standard deviation) of the most accurate clicker question. However, in 38 of the 100 bootstrap runs, the most accurate clicker question was from the first 3 weeks of lectures. In 56 bootstrap runs, a clicker question from weeks 1-3 was in the top 2, and in 90 of the runs a clicker question from weeks 1-3 was in the top 7. Thus, while the most accurate clicker question varied considerably over the 100 bootstrap samples for FQ2, clicker questions from weeks 1-3 remained prominent.

## 5.    DISCUSSION

In this work, we explored whether and how clicker question performance during the term relates to performance on the final exam. We find that clicker question performance, particularly in the early weeks of the term, is highly correlated with performance on code-writing questions, multiple choice questions, and the final exam overall. Using the per-class clicker data, we were then able to track students as they progress through the term, finding that students are effectively binned by quartiles in the first weeks of the term and that those bins remain consistent relative to one another throughout the term and, ultimately, on the exam. To clarify these findings, we examined student clicker question performance in the first three weeks of the term and found that students in the top quartile at the start of the term are highly likely to do well on final exam questions whereas those in the bottom quartile are highly likely to achieve scores below a "passing standard" set by the instructor. Lastly, we investigated the individual clicker questions that are most predictive of final exam performance. Many of these questions target concepts taught early in the term. We now elaborate on several aspects of our findings.

**Peer Instruction:** The importance of early term performance has been hypothesized in standard lecture classes [11]. Given the positive evidence in support of PI, one might suspect that changing the pedagogical practice might temper this effect. However, the effect is still present in the PI class in this study. As a result, we know that student relative rankings continue to be set heavily by those first few weeks of class, but it remains possible that all students (or a subset of students) learned more (or less) using PI. Moreover, it is difficult to say whether using PI for this study may have changed the trends described here. Further study is necessary to determine whether similar results would be found in a standard lecture class. The difficulty in replicating this study in a standard lecture class is that fine-grained data is typically not available, and adding collection of that data may in turn change the course. We see this as an interesting research puzzle going forward.

**In-Class Learning:** One encouraging result from our analysis was that the isomorphic questions were often the top predictors of student outcomes. Although isomorphic questions are intended to target key concepts, the corresponding question used for individual and group votes was rarely among the top predictors. This suggests that student understanding is better reflected *after* group and classwide discussion; hence, learning in the classroom may persist and is certainly visible in final exam performance.

**Instructor Implications:** These results suggest that students in jeopardy of doing poorly in the class can be identified early in the term (at least as early as week 3). Armed with evidence that students in the bottom quartile at week 3 do much worse than students in the top two quartiles at week 3 on final exam questions, instructors can reach out to this group of students for a possible intervention. It is likely that a portion of that group of students is doing poorly due to a lack of commitment, but for those desiring to learn, an early intervention may be helpful.

# 6. CONCLUSION

In this paper, we have shown that naturally-occurring PI data can be used to predict student performance in CS1. We see that those in the bottom quartile early in the term are very unlikely to do well on final exam questions compared to those in the top quartile early in the term. This pattern holds for a code-writing question that targets early concepts as well as a code-writing question that tests material from later in the term. Multiple choice clicker questions are qualitatively different from code-writing exam questions, yet our findings suggest that some common set of skills may underlie performance on both types of questions. We have further identified the clicker questions most predictive of final exam performance, finding that many of those questions were administered in the first three weeks of term.

Clicker data is generated automatically as part of teaching PI, and has diagnostic utility as demonstrated here. We encourage instructors to use such data to identify struggling students as early as possible. Our data suggest that crucial learning occurs in the first few weeks and that this learning strongly impacts the remainder of the course. PI data may provide instructors with the data granularity necessary to intervene before it is too late.

# 7. ACKNOWLEDGMENTS

Thank you to Quintin Cutts for his helpful feedback on early versions of this work and to the anonymous reviewers. This work was supported by NSF grant 1140731.

# 8. REFERENCES

[1] A. Ahadi and R. Lister. Geek genes, prior knowledge, stumbling points and learning edge momentum: parts of the one elephant? In *ICER*, pages 123–128, 2013.

[2] A. Ahadi, R. Lister, and D. Teague. Falling behind early and staying behind when learning to program. In *25th Anniversary Psychology of Programming Annual Conference*, 2014.

[3] J. Bennedsen and M. E. Caspersen. Failure rates in introductory programming. *SIGCSE Bulletin*, 39:32–36, 2007.

[4] R. Duda, J. Gaschnig, and P. Hart. Model design in the PROSPECTOR consultant system for mineral exploration. In *Expert systems in the micro- electronic age*, pages 153–167. 1979.

[5] M. A. Hudak and D. E. Anderson. Formal operations and learning style predict success in statistics and computer science courses. *Teaching of Psychology*, 17(4):231–234, 1990.

[6] R. Lister, C. Fidge, and D. Teague. Further evidence of a relationship between explaining, tracing and writing skills in introductory programming. In *ITiCSE*, pages 161–165, 2009.

[7] L. Porter, C. Bailey-Lee, B. Simon, and D. Zingaro. Peer instruction: Do students really learn from peer discussion in computing? In *ICER*, 2011.

[8] L. Porter, C. B. Lee, and B. Simon. Halving fail rates using peer instruction: A study of four computer science courses. In *SIGCSE*, pages 177–182, 2013.

[9] L. Porter and B. Simon. Retaining nearly one-third more majors with a trio of instructional best practices in cs1. In *SIGCSE*, pages 165–170, 2013.

[10] L. Porter and D. Zingaro. Importance of early performance in cs1: Two conflicting assessment stories. In *SIGCSE*, pages 295–300, 2014.

[11] A. Robins. Learning edge momentum: A new account of outcomes. *Computer Science Education*, 20(1):37–71, 2010.

[12] B. Simon, M. Kohanfars, J. Lee, K. Tamayo, and Q. Cutts. Experience report: Peer instruction in introductory computing. In *SIGCSE*, pages 341–345, 2010.

[13] E. Soloway. Cognitive strategies and looping constructs: An empirical study. *Communications of the ACM*, 26(11):853–860, 1983.

[14] A. Venables, G. Tan, and R. Lister. A closer look at tracing, explaining and code writing skills in the novice programmer. In *ICER*, pages 117–128, 2009.

[15] D. Wright, K. London, and A. Field. Using bootstrap estimation and the plug-in principle for clinical psychology data. *Journal of Experimental Psychopathology*, 2(2):252–270, 2011.

[16] D. Zingaro. Experience report: Peer instruction in remedial computer science. In *Ed-Media*, pages 5030–5035, 2010.

[17] D. Zingaro. Peer instruction contributes to self-efficacy in CS1. In *SIGCSE*, pages 373–378, 2014.

# A Structured Approach to Teaching Recursion Using Cargo-Bot

Elynn Lee    Victoria Shan    Bradley Beth    Calvin Lin
The University of Texas at Austin
Department of Computer Science
2317 Speedway, Stop D9500
Austin, TX 78712
{elynnlee, vshan, bbeth, lin}@cs.utexas.edu

## ABSTRACT

Recursion is a notoriously difficult concept to learn. This paper presents a structured approach to teaching recursion that combines classroom lectures and self-paced interaction with Cargo-Bot, a video game in which users solve puzzles using a simple visual programming language. After mapping Cargo-Bot games to a set of learning goals, we devise a lesson plan that uses Cargo-Bot game playing to scaffold key concepts used in writing recursive Java programs. We empirically evaluate our approach using 204 undergraduates enrolled in a CS2 course, and we show strong statistical evidence that our approach improves student learning of recursion over traditional lecture-based instruction alone.

## Categories and Subject Descriptors

D.3.3 [**Language Constructs and Features**]: Recursion; K.3.2 [**Computer and Information Science Education**]: Computer Science Education

## Keywords

Education; recursion; video games

## 1.  INTRODUCTION

Recursion is a fundamental concept in computer science that novices often struggle to understand [14, 15, 22]. In particular, students often fail to understand the *passive flow* of recursion [22], which is the backward flow of control that can take place after reaching the base case. While there is considerable prior work in teaching recursion [1, 3, 6–12, 16–21, 23–25, 27–29], there exist few controlled empirical studies. Chaffin et al. [2] and Hulsizer [13] demonstrate statistically significant results in experiments with fewer than 17 students, but neither compares the results against a controlled baseline.

To date, the largest controlled empirical study [26] leverages a video game, Cargo-Bot, in which players write vi-

sual programs to solve puzzles involving cranes and boxes; procedure calls are the only construct for repetition, so the authors posit that this game can contextualize the learning of recursion. In their study involving 47 magnet school students taking AP Computer Science A, the authors find that an experimental group—which first plays Cargo-Bot for 70 minutes and then receives 50 minutes of direct instruction—sees a statistically significant improvement in assessment scores when compared against a control group—which first receives 50 minutes of direct instruction and then plays Cargo-Bot for 70 minutes. Interestingly, both groups experience the greatest learning gains directly after playing the video game. Thus, we observe that the game appears to have some educational benefit beyond simply contextualizing recursion.

Unfortunately, our attempt to repeat the experiment at a larger scale at a major university failed to produce statistically significant findings, and we conjecture that the approach was too unstructured. The game offers many puzzles of widely varying difficulty, and the unstructured approach does not tell students where they should focus their efforts, so it is unclear if students ever progress to the puzzles that involve more difficult recursive concepts such as passive flow.

In this paper, we hypothesize that a structured use of Cargo-Bot can improve students' ability to learn recursion. In particular, we propose a structure that (1) defines a set of learning goals with respect to recursion, (2) maps these learning goals to Cargo-Bot puzzles, (3) prescribes a minimal set of puzzles for students to solve, and (4) follows this gameplay with direct classroom instruction. We test this hypothesis by conducting an experiment with 204 students spread across two classes of CS2 at The University of Texas at Austin. One class serves as a control group: They receive four 50 minute lectures of direct instruction. The other class serves as the experimental group: They spend two class periods playing nine games of Cargo-Bot in a self-paced manner; they then receive two 50 minute class periods of direct instruction. We assess student learning by administering tests before and after the experiment.

We find with statistical significance that on calibrated assessments, the experimental group is better at writing recursive Java code than the control group ($p \leq 0.04612$). When we only consider the experimental students who complete the nine Cargo-Bot puzzles, the $p$-value falls below 0.0018.

This paper makes the following contributions:

- We define a set of learning goals related to recursive Java programming, and we map these learning goals to nine Cargo-Bot puzzles.

- We design two condensed lectures that integrate examples from Cargo-Bot into the discussion and that replace an existing four lecture sequence.

- Using a study of 204 college students, we confirm our hypothesis that structured use of Cargo-Bot improves student learning of recursion.

## 2. RELATED WORK

Our work is informed by previous studies outlining best practices in teaching recursion [1, 6, 9–11, 18, 20, 23] and identifying common misconceptions of recursion. Students often create incorrect models of recursion [14, 29]. Most commonly they mistakenly model recursion as a loop structure and view recursion as iteration [6, 15, 24]. Moreover, students often struggle to understand the passive flow of recursion and the use of the stack for backtracking [22].

Our work is part of a growing effort to use visualizations and games to teach recursion [8, 25, 28]. For example, Alice is a 3D visual programming language that is useful for teaching basic recursion, but it is insufficient for teaching the more sophisticated details of recursion [4] because the state-less nature of Alice prevents the platform from visually representing recursion at a low level.

Two studies empirically study the use of games on student understanding of recursion. Chaffin, et al [2] use a game in which 16 students (including 14 upperclassmen) write depth-first search programs to visualize the traversal of a binary tree. Hulsizer [13] describes a similar experiment, reporting statistically significant results for a pool of 10 participants. Our work differs in two ways: We integrate gameplay with classroom instruction, and we use larger populations in our study.

As mentioned in the previous section, our work builds directly on that of Tessler et al. [26], who combine the unstructured use of Cargo-Bot and classroom instruction.

## 3. BACKGROUND: CARGO-BOT

Cargo-Bot is a game originally created for the Apple iPad by Two Lives Left[1]. Gameplay centers on a crane that moves and stacks a set of colored crates. Players write small visual programs to move the crates from an initial configuration to a goal configuration. The set of available instructions is quite small. The crane can be directed to (1) move left; (2) move right; or (3) move down and then up, in which case it attempts to pick up a crate if it is empty, or it drops its crate if it is not empty. Conditionals and procedure calls are also provided. Significantly, recursion is the only mechanism for repetition.

## 4. STRUCTURED LEARNING

To support structured learning, we first identify general subtopics within recursion, leveraging numerous resources such as existing course lecture materials, recursive problems on past course assessments, and online instructional tools such as CodingBat[2]. Our analysis reveals a few notable content clusters, and we give these clusters the following names to summarize their commonalities: recursion with conditionals, mutual recursion, recursive backtracking, and recursion with accumulators.

These clusters are mapped to the following learning goals:

1. Write recursive methods to progress toward some set of base cases.

2. Write code that conditionally selects one of multiple paths to make progress toward the base cases.

3. Trace a recursive call by visualizing the program stack.

4. Write code that uses passive flow to maintain state.

5. Utilize mutual recursion.

6. Utilize recursive calls as accumulators.

To scaffold student learning, we then align gameplay with instruction by mapping a set of Cargo-Bot puzzles to each learning goal. We find that Cargo-Bot puzzles bifurcate into two classes: (1) counting problems and (2) divide and conquer problems. This phenomenon is reflected in the initial branching in the tree of Cargo-Bot puzzles depicted in Figure 1. The tree is rooted with three basic puzzles that introduce students to the mechanics of Cargo-Bot and basic gameplay. From there, each of the two main branches moves through different recursive topics, roughly in order of increasing complexity, progressing from recursion using conditionals, to mutual recursion, to recursive backtracking, and finally to recursion with accumulators.

Puzzles in the left branch are solved by using the stack to count the number of times to execute a series of instructions. Puzzles in the right branch are solved using divide and conquer algorithms, focusing on conditioning recursion on the colors of crates. In our study, we prescribe a series of nine puzzles through the left, or counting, branch that strikes a balance between content coverage and brevity. These puzzles align with the learning goals #1–4 above and are shown connected by the red arcs (light grey arcs) in Figure 1. They are: Cargo-Bot 101, Transporter, Recurses, Go Left, Go Left 2, The Stacker, Clarify, Up the Greens, and Come Together.

### 4.1 Recursion in Cargo-Bot

Solutions to the easier puzzles utilize tail recursion, which is indistinguishable from GOTO-style control flow. Later puzzles require students to use recursive backtracking to maintain a counter that is implicitly stored as state on the program stack.

To illustrate this complexity, consider the puzzle "Come Together," the final puzzle in our set of prescribed puzzles. Figure 2 depicts the puzzle's goal state and its corresponding recursive solution. The execution of a Cargo-Bot program starts with the left-most instruction in the $F0$ function. From there, each subsequent instruction is executed left-to-right. We see that the $F1$ function is recursive: It calls itself whenever it encounters an empty column, and it effectively remembers the number of times that the crane has moved right, because the function moves left once for each time that it moves right.

### 4.2 Modifications to Cargo-Bot

Beyond identifying and establishing a prescribed course of Cargo-Bot content, we improve upon the game to support accompanying instruction and to improve students' experience with the game.

[1] http://twolivesleft.com/CargoBot/
[2] http://www.codingbat.com/

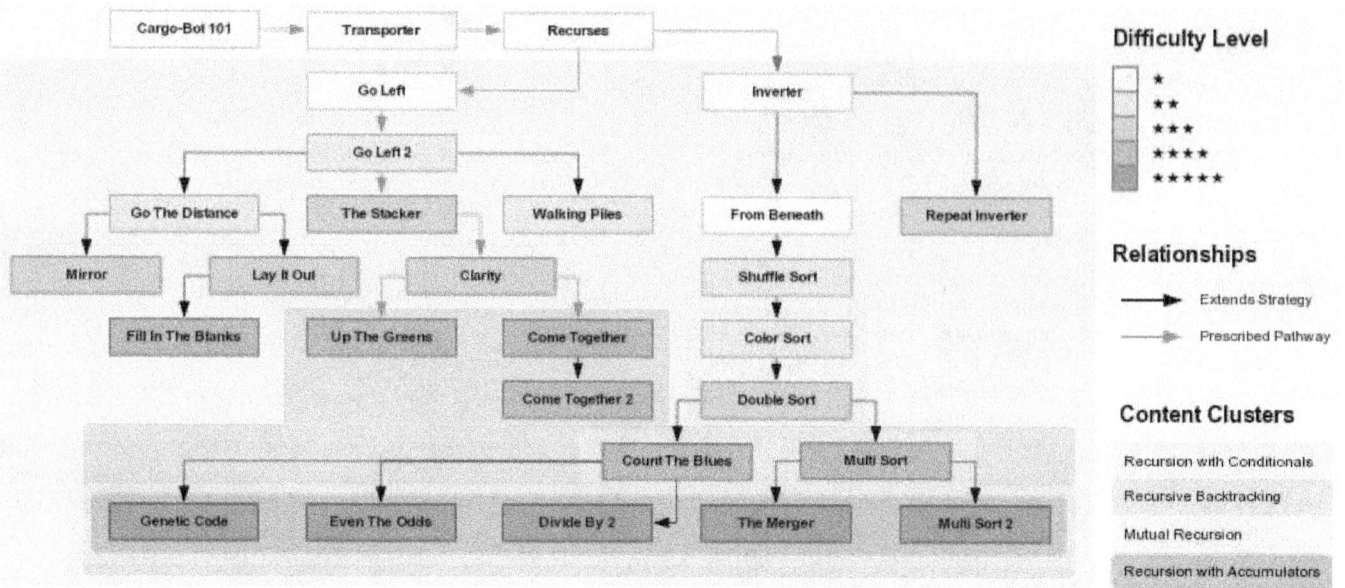

Figure 1: Taxonomy of Cargo-Bot puzzles.

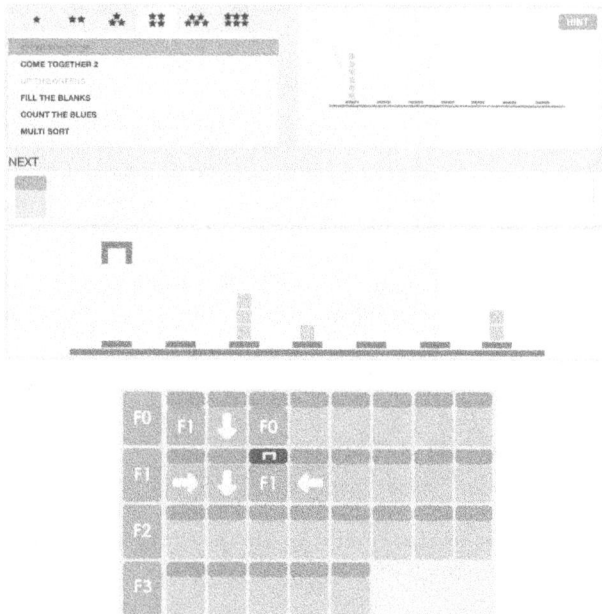

Figure 2: Cargo-Bot puzzle "Come Together".

### 4.2.1 Visualizing the Stack

Since an understanding of recursive solutions often requires an understanding of the program stack, we modify the game to include a visualization of the program stack, which is particularly helpful in counting and backtracking puzzles. These visual representations align with demonstrations of the program stack in the companion classroom lectures.

### 4.2.2 Improving Game Feedback

In the original game, players are rewarded with up to three stars depending on the length of their solution, but this metric often rewards complex, inelegant solutions, so we adjust the rating system to reward what we believe are the cleanest, most elegant solutions.

### 4.2.3 Instrumentation

To facilitate data collection, users enter a unique university ID when loading the initial page. All clickable actions are logged and tagged with the associated university ID and IP address. The log files can then be analyzed both at the individual level and in aggregate. Collected data include the number of attempts per puzzle, the ratings of correct solutions, the time spent on each puzzle, and the number of incorrect attempts at a solution.

## 5. EXPERIMENTAL DESIGN

Our experiment follows students in two sections of CS2 that are taught by the same instructor. One section of 136 students serves as the experimental group, while the other section of 187 students serves as the control group. Only those students consenting to the research study and completing all of the required parts of the experiment are included in our results, resulting in 88 students in the experimental group and 116 in the control group. These numbers are nearly equally proportional to their corresponding section total enrollments (65% *vs.* 62%, respectively), and there are no statistically significant differences in student population samples between the two groups.

## 5.1 Instruction and Gameplay

The existing CS2 course scope and sequence allots four 50 minute lectures to cover recursion: two on basic recursion and two on recursive backtracking. To compare our intervention to the *status quo*, the control group receives the four lectures as they are traditionally given, while students in the experimental group spend the first two lecture periods playing Cargo-Bot and the last two lecture periods receiving condensed lectures on recursion, one on basic recursion and the other on recursive backtracking. These two experimental lectures are given by one of the co-authors; for the control group, the four lectures are given by the course instructor.

Students in the experimental group are given five days to complete the nine prescribed Cargo-Bot puzzles. They are allowed to play the game during class with guidance from the instructors and are encouraged to play on their own outside of class. During these first two lecture periods, the experimental group does not receive any formal instruction outside of the Cargo-Bot gameplay mechanics. The two condensed lectures cover the same content as the four lectures given to the control group, and they reference Cargo-Bot through worked examples. These lectures are condensed by omitting several worked examples of recursive Java code.

## 5.2 Evaluation

Each participating student takes a pre-test and a post-test, and each test evaluates student understanding of recursion by asking them to complete two tasks: (1) trace and explain the outcome of a recursive function and (2) write a recursive function to accomplish a given task. Each test also contains a survey that gauges student motivation and self-awareness: Students rate their abilities on a scale from "Strongly Agree" to "Strongly Disagree" regarding their understanding of recursion, their ability to follow the execution of a recursive function, and their ability to write a recursive function. The experimental group also rates their enjoyment of Cargo-Bot, rates their ability to play Cargo-Bot, and indicates whether they recognize that their Cargo-Bot solutions use recursion. All students take the pre-test prior to any instruction or formal discussion of recursion. Likewise, the post-test is given only after students complete the four 50 minute class meetings appropriate to their group.

### 5.2.1 Designing the Evaluations

To measure student understanding of recursion, the pre- and post-tests use performance tasks aligned with our descriptive taxonomy (see Figure 1). Each assessment is designed to be completed within the 10 minutes allotted for daily quizzes and to be structured similarly to previous daily quizzes. Our quizzes are constructed to reflect the following learning objectives:

- When **tracing** recursive functions, students will be able to (1) track function calls on the program stack and (2) explain the purpose of a given recursive function.

- When **writing** recursive functions, students will be able to use Java to (1) identify and construct appropriate base cases, (2) divide a problem into suitable subproblems, and (3) return values appropriately through both active and passive control flow.

Table 1 summarizes each of the tests' contents (Section 5.2.3 explains why there are four test forms). Figures 3 shows an example of a tracing problem that assesses students' ability to trace and understand recursive functions. In this example, an ideal answer to the second question is "the function counts the number of digits in the positive integer $n$".

Figures 4–7 show the writing problems for Forms A-D, respectively. For example, in Figure 7, the solution requires the programmer to maintain a counter, and an elegant recursive solution uses backtracking. Students must break the problem into subproblems, identify the base cases, and return the proper values up the stack.

|  | Form | Tracing | Writing |
|---|---|---|---|
| Pre-Test | A | Decimal-to-binary conversion | Greatest Common Denominator |
|  | B | Count number of digits | Flood Fill |
| Post-Test | C | Modulus | Count subset sums |
|  | D | Duplicate removal | Stairway |

Table 1: Summary of test items. Forms A and B are pre-tests, while Forms C and D are post-tests.

```
public int foo(int n) {
    if (n == 0)
        return 0;
    return 1 + foo(n / 10);
}

What is the value of foo(12346)?

What do you think this function does?
```

Figure 3: A recursive tracing problem.

### 5.2.2 Grading Rubric

The grading rubric outlined in Table 2 is applied to all test forms to evaluate students' final test scores. The tracing problem is worth 6 points, and the writing problem is worth 14 points, for a total of 20 possible points.

| Tracing Problem | 6 |
|---|---|
| Correct return value | 3 |
| Correct function description | 3 |

| Writing Problem | 14 |
|---|---|
| Non-recursive solution | 0 |
| Recursive solution, non-terminating | 3 |
| Recursive solution, terminating | 6 |
| Recursive solution, terminates w/progress | 9 |
| Recursive solution, correct, with: | 14 |
| — *Invalid Java syntax* | -1 |
| — *Unnecessary base cases* | -1 |
| — *Unnecessary function calls* | -1 |
| — *Extra return values* | -1 |

Table 2: Grading Rubric for pre- and post-tests.

### 5.2.3 Test Validation

To strengthen the reliability of our assessments, each of the pre- and post-tests has two versions: Students in both groups randomly take either Form A or Form B as a pre-test and either Form C or Form D as a post-test. Because each test is open-ended, we assume that the tests may be uneven in difficulty. To accurately evaluate students across all combinations of test forms, we take a two-pronged approach:

1. Each of the open-ended responses is graded by the same grader using a common rubric (see Table 2).

```
Given two numbers, write a recursive
function that returns their greatest
common divisor (the largest number
that is a factor of both numbers).

Examples:
   gcd(12, 36) returns 12
   gcd(14, 10) returns 2

Please implement your method in proper Java
syntax and use the following method signature:

public int gcd(int a, int b)
{
   // ...
}
```

Figure 4: The recursive writing problem for Form A.

2. We create a baseline set of scores by asking 36 current computer science majors who have already completed CS2 to take one or two of the four tests. Their raw scores are used to provide summary statistics for each test form, which allow us to establish a mapping from raw scores to standard $z$-scores. The summary statistics of the baseline group are shown in Table 3.

| | Tracing | | Writing | | Total | |
|---|---|---|---|---|---|---|
| | *mean* | *stdev* | *mean* | *stdev* | *mean* | *stdev* |
| Form A | 5.12 | 1.76 | 7.11 | 6.92 | 12.11 | 6.88 |
| Form B | 4.58 | 2.32 | 11.14 | 3.98 | 15.43 | 4.59 |
| Form C | 5.81 | 0.75 | 7.75 | 5.14 | 13.56 | 5.38 |
| Form D | 4.06 | 2.84 | 10.44 | 4.95 | 14.50 | 6.48 |

Table 3: Baseline Scores from Upperclassmen. Forms A and B are pre-tests, while Forms C and D are post-tests.

## 5.3 Student Diversity

To minimize bias and priming effects on survey and performance data, the gender and race/ethnicity data associated with each ID are retrieved from institutional data records only after the student assessments are collected (see Table 4). Here, the ethnic label "Hispanic" supersedes the race label "White"; university institutional data equate the label "White" with "Non-Hispanic White". The "Other" category encapsulates students who identify as races other than those listed, as multiracial, or who choose to withhold this information from public records.

## 6. RESULTS

By examining the performance gains from the pre-test to post-test scores, we show by a statistically significant margin that students who play our prescribed pathway through Cargo-Bot score higher than those who do not.

## 6.1 Statistical Tools

To account for variation in the two different forms of the pre- and post-tests, we calculate the standard $z$-score for each student. A $z$-score gives the relationship of a given raw score to the mean score and standard deviation of the

```
In any modern image editor, you have
access to the "fill" or paint bucket tool,
which fills all instances of a target
color with a given replacement color
at some given location in the image.
Your task is to implement this algorithm
recursively.

Example:
   If fill is called on a pixel in the middle
   area in the image on the left below,
   fill should return the image on the right.

   Assume you have access to the Image
   class with the following methods:

      Color getColor(int x, int y) -
      returns the color at (x,y) or null if
      the given (x,y) is outside of the image.

      void setColor(int x, int y, Color c) -
      sets the color at (x,y) or throws an
      error if (x,y) is outside of the image.

   Also, you can easily compare two colors
   using the equals method, e.g.,

      color1.equals(color2).

Please implement your method in proper Java
syntax and use the following method signature:

public void fill(Image img, Color targetColor,
                 Color replaceColor, int x, int y)
{
   // ...
}
```

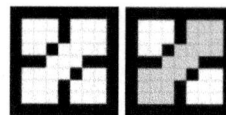

Figure 5: The recursive writing problem for Form B.

population as a whole,

$$z = \frac{score - \mu}{\sigma}$$

Here, the population as a whole is defined by the baseline scores, as explained in Section 5.2.3.

By using $z$-scores instead of raw test scores, we account for the variance in difficulty among tests when comparing the pre-test scores to the post-test scores. Negative $z$-scores in our study are to be expected, since the baseline represents students who have completed the course. The difference between the post-test and pre-test $z$-scores measures a student's performance gains. A positive difference indicates that a student has improved over time, while a negative difference means that they have regressed over time.

We use a one-way Type-III ANCOVA (Analysis of Covariance) model to minimize the variance in error of our results. We use four possible combinations of pre-tests and post-tests in our experiment. By randomly assigning each student a pre-test and a post-test, we mitigate the potential for systemic bias among particular test forms. We must, however, account for potential sources of variance, such as the pre-test scores, that could affect the outcome of the study. Following

| | Female | Male | Asian | Black | Hispanic | White | Other |
|---|---|---|---|---|---|---|---|
| Control | 21.3% | 78.7% | 29.31% | 2.59% | 28.45% | 37.07% | 2.59% |
| Experimental | 22.3% | 77.7% | 29.55% | 4.55% | 17.05% | 46.59% | 2.27% |
| **Total** | **21.7%** | **78.3%** | **29.41%** | **3.43%** | **23.53%** | **41.18%** | **2.45%** |

Table 4: Demographic breakdown of student groups.

```
Given an array of integers, arr, and a
target sum, sum, write a recursive
function that returns the number of
subsets in arr that contain elements
that add up to sum.

Example:
    given arr = [1,2,3,2] and sum = 4, there
    are 2 subsets, [1,3] and [2,2] that sum
    to 4, so countSubsets(arr, sum) returns 2.

Please implement your method in proper Java
syntax and use the following method signature:

public int countSubsets(int[] arr, int sum) {
{
    // ...
}
```

Figure 6: The recursive writing problem for Form C.

```
A child can climb stairs 1, 2, or 3
steps at a time. Write a recursive
function that returns the number
of distinct ways the child can
climb n stairs.

Please implement your method in proper Java
syntax and use the following method signature:

public int stairways(int n)
{
    // ...
}
```

Figure 7: The recursive writing problem for Form D.

the practices established by Dimitrov and Rumrill, Jr. [5] to evaluate improvement between pre-tests and post-tests, we use the ANCOVA model with the pre-test scores serving as a covariate. This model allows us to measure the post-test score as it relates to a given independent variable such as group (control or experimental) or gender, using the pre-test as a covariate. To extend our analysis, we use a Tukey test to determine the differences among categories, such as gender or group.

## 6.2 Analysis of Student Performance Gains

Figure 8 shows the increase from the average pre-test $z$-score to average post-test $z$-score for the control and experimental groups. While the experimental group clearly improves more than the control group, we find that the increase in scores is not statistically significant. When we run the ANCOVA model for each group with the pre-test as a covariate, we see statistically significant results for the writing score ($p \leq 0.04612$) but not for the tracing or total score.

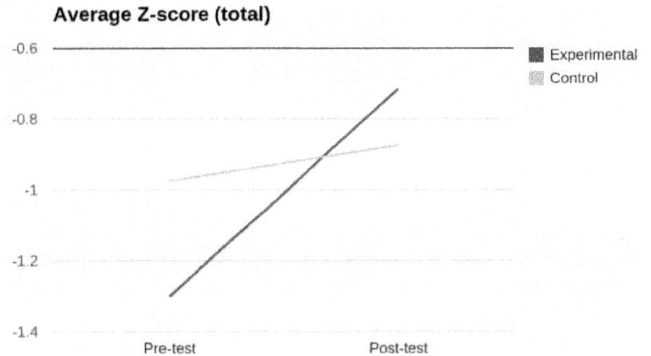

Figure 8: Improvement in terms of $z$-scores from the pre-test to the post-test.

The results of the tracing scores are consistent with those of Tessler et al.'s experiment [26]. When we use ANCOVA to model gains by gender and race/ethnicity with pre-test as a covariate, we find that gender and race/ethnicity are not significant factors for gains in total, tracing, or writing scores across the entire group.

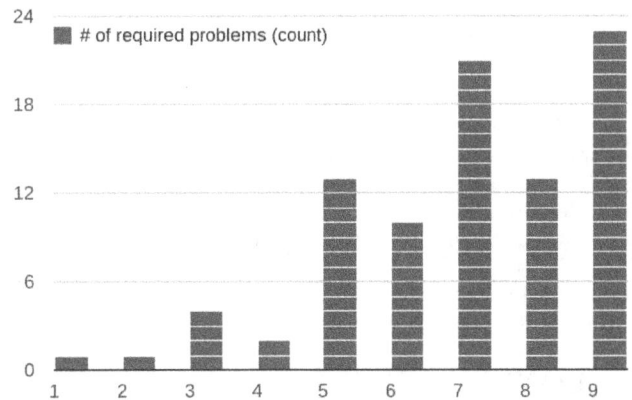

Figure 9: Number of puzzles completed by students in the experimental group.

Figure 9 shows the number of prescribed Cargo-Bot puzzles completed by the students in the experimental group. Only 26.14% percent of students completed all nine assigned puzzles. 40.9% completed at least eight and 64.77% completed at least seven of the prescribed puzzles. On average, students completed seven of the nine required puzzles and a total of eight puzzles on average. We see in Table 5 that those students who complete eight or nine puzzles score higher than the control group by a statistically significant margin. By contrast, students who complete seven or fewer

| Exp *vs* Control | Total Score ($p$) | Writing Score ($p$) |
|---|---|---|
| 6 puzzles | 0.8701 | 0.8391 |
| 7 puzzles | 0.8706 | 0.9812 |
| 8 puzzles | 0.0439 | 0.0746 |
| 9 puzzles | 0.0043 | 0.0018 |

Table 5: Results of experimental group performance against the control sorted by number of puzzles completed. The completion of eight or nine puzzles correlates to a statistically significant difference in group performance ($\alpha < 0.05$).

puzzles do not score significantly higher than the control group.

Finally, we explore the effect of our intervention on final exam performance, which takes place after students have submitted a significant recursive programming assignment. We find that the experimental group retains some of their advantage on the final exam's recursion-related questions, which are created and graded by the course's instructional staff. Those who complete at least 8 prescribed puzzles perform better than the control group in both tracing ($p \leq 0.03997$) and writing ($p \leq 0.08867$), though the latter is not statistically significant. The advantage is also not statistically significant for those who complete just 7 of the puzzles ($p \leq 0.3851$ for tracing, $p \leq 0.3469$ for writing).

## 6.3 Survey Results

Our assessments ask students to rate their attitudes and abilities in relation to recursion. Students are shown the following three statements and are asked to choose "Strongly Agree", "Agree", "Neither Agree nor Disagree", "Disagree", or "Strongly Disagree" in response:

- I understand recursion.
- I can follow the execution of a recursive function.
- I can write a recursive function.

In comparing the experimental and control groups, we find no statistically significant results from the surveys. We do, however, see a few interesting points. We find that student attitudes do not always match student performance. We see that most students enjoy playing Cargo-Bot, but less than 36% of the students are confident in their Cargo-Bot abilities, while over 62% of these same students are confident in their ability to write a recursive function (see Figure 10).

## 7. CONCLUSIONS

In this paper, we have proposed a new method of teaching recursion that uses Cargo-Bot in conjunction with classroom instruction. Our results are encouraging both because of the strong statistical evidence of the approach's effectiveness and because of the fairly large number of students—204—involved.

While these results are encouraging, empirical educational studies are clearly methodologically difficult, so we plan to conduct additional studies that refine the methodology and that explore other related questions. For example, direct instruction might be considered the most passive of educational methods, so it would be interesting to compare self-guided game playing with self-guided problem solving using instruments similar to CodingBat.

*Acknowledgments.*
We thank Mike Scott, Lara Schmidt, and Zhao Song for their help in conducting our experiment on their class. We thank the students who participated in our study and Alex Suchman for his guidance on statistical analysis. Our work is partially supported by the National Science Foundation under grant #CNS-1138506 and by OnRamps coordinated by The University of Texas at Austin. Any opinions, findings, and conclusions or recommendations expressed in this material are those of the authors and do not necessarily reflect the views of its funding sources.

## References

[1] Alan C. Benander and Barbara A. Benander. Student monks—teaching recursion in an IS or CS programming course using the Towers of Hanoi. *Journal of Information Systems Education*, 19(4):455–467, 2008.

[2] Amanda Chaffin, Katelyn Doran, Drew Hicks, and Tiffany Barnes. Experimental evaluation of teaching recursion in a video game. In *Proceedings of the 2009 ACM SIGGRAPH Symposium on Video Games*, Sandbox '09, pages 79–86, New York, NY, USA, 2009. ACM.

[3] Diana I. Cordova and Mark R. Lepper. Intrinsic motivation and the process of learning: Beneficial effects of contextualization, personalization, and choice. *Journal of Educational Psychology*, 88(4):715–730, 1996.

[4] Wanda Dann, Stephen Cooper, and Randy Pausch. Using visualization to teach novices recursion. In *Proceedings of the 6th Annual Conference on Innovation and Technology in Computer Science Education*, ITiCSE '01, pages 109–112, New York, NY, USA, 2001. ACM.

[5] Dimiter M Dimitrov and Phillip D Rumrill, Jr. Pretest-posttest designs and measurement of change. *Work: A Journal of Prevention, Assessment and Rehabilitation*, 20(2):159–165, 2003.

[6] Jeffrey Edgington. Teaching and viewing recursion as delegation. *J. Computing Sciences in Colleges*, 23(1):241–246, October 2007.

[7] Gary Ford. A framework for teaching recursion. *SIGCSE Bulletin*, 14(2):32–39, June 1982.

[8] Carlisle E. George. EROSI—visualising recursion and discovering new errors. *SIGCSE Bulletin*, 32(1):305–309, March 2000.

[9] David Ginat and Eyal Shifroni. Teaching recursion in a procedural environment—how much should we emphasize the computing model? *SIGCSE Bulletin*, 31(1):127–131, March 1999.

[10] James Eugene Greer. *An empirical comparison of techniques for teaching recursion in introductory computer sciences*. Ph.D. dissertation, The University of Texas at Austin, May 1987.

[11] Katherine Gunion, Todd Milford, and Ulrike Stege. Curing recursion aversion. *SIGCSE Bulletin*, 41(3):124–128, July 2009.

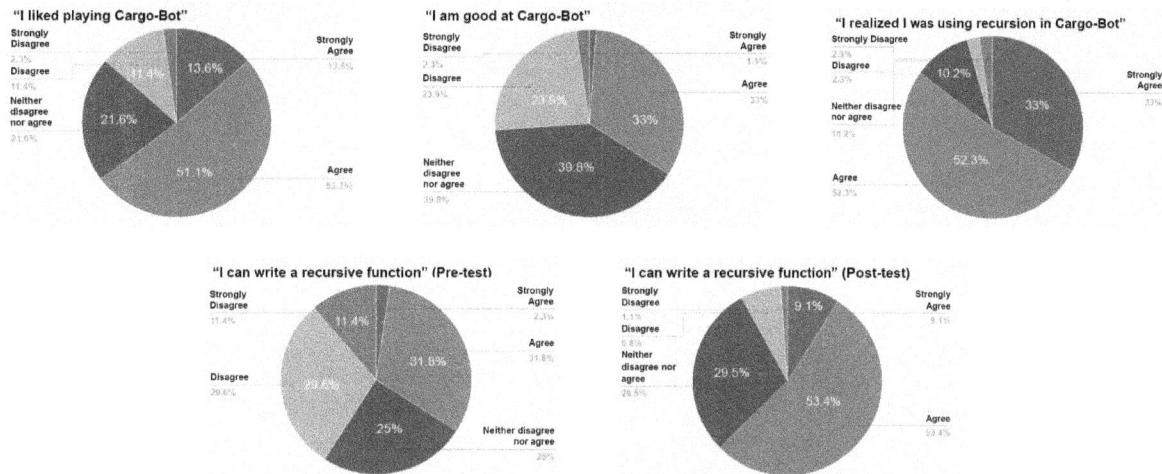

Figure 10: Post-test (except where noted) survey results for experimental group.

[12] WenJung Hsin. Teaching recursion using recursion graphs. *Journal of Computing Sciences in Colleges*, 23(4):217–222, April 2008.

[13] Andrew Hulsizer. *Teaching Recursion Through Interactive Media*. Masters thesis, The University of Texas at Austin, 2011.

[14] Hank Kahney. What do novice programmers know about recursion? In Elliot Soloway and James C. Spohrer, editors, *Studying the Novice Programmer*. Lawrence Erlbaum Associates, Hillsdale, New Jersey, 1989.

[15] Claudius M. Kessler and John R. Anderson. Learning control flow: Recursive and iterative procedures. In Elliot Soloway and James C. Spohrer, editors, *Studying the Novice Programmer*. Lawrence Erlbaum Associates, Hillsdale, New Jersey, 1989.

[16] Robert L. Kruse. On teaching recursion. *SIGCSE Bulletin*, 14(1):92–96, February 1982.

[17] Dalit Levy and Tami Lapidot. Recursively speaking: analyzing students' discourse of recursive phenomena. *SIGCSE Bulletin*, 32(1):315–319, March 2000.

[18] Peter L. Pirolli and John R. Anderson. The role of learning from examples in the acquisition of recursive programming skills. *Canadian Journal of Psychology*, 39(2):240–272, June 1985.

[19] Irene Polycarpou, Ana Pasztor, and Malek Adjouadi. A conceptual approach to teaching induction for computer science. *SIGCSE Bulletin*, 40(1):9–13, March 2008.

[20] Anthony Robins, Nathan Rountree, and Janet Rountree. My program is correct but it doesn't run: a review of novice programming and a study of an introductory programming paper. *Technical Report*, OUCS-2001-06, 2001. University of Otago.

[21] Manuel Rubio-Sánchez and Isidoro Hernán-Losada. Exploring recursion with Fibonacci numbers. *SIGCSE Bulletin*, 39(3):359–359, June 2007.

[22] Tamarisk Lurlyn Scholtz and Ian Sanders. Mental models of recursion: Investigating students' understanding of recursion. In *Proceedings of the Fifteenth Annual Conference on Innovation and Technology in Computer Science Education*, ITiCSE '10, pages 103–107, New York, NY, USA, 2010. ACM.

[23] Amber Settle. What's motivation got to do with it? A survey of recursion in the computing education literature. *Technical Reports*, Paper 23, 2014. DePaul University. http://via.library.depaul.edu/tr/23.

[24] Raja Sooriamurthi. Problems in comprehending recursion and suggested solutions. *SIGCSE Bulletin*, 33(3):25–28, June 2001.

[25] John Stasko, Albert Badre, and Clayton Lewis. Do algorithm animations assist learning?: an empirical study and analysis. In *Proceedings of the INTERACT '93 and CHI '93 Conference on Human Factors in Computing Systems*, CHI '93, pages 61–66, New York, NY, USA, 1993. ACM.

[26] Joe Tessler, Bradley Beth, and Calvin Lin. Using Cargo-Bot to provide contextualized learning of recursion. In *Proceedings of the Ninth Annual International ACM Conference on International Computing Education Research*, ICER '13, pages 161–168, New York, NY, USA, August 2013. ACM.

[27] Susan Wiedenbeck. Learning recursion as a concept and as a programming technique. *SIGCSE Bulletin*, 20(1):275–278, February 1988.

[28] Derek Wilcocks and Ian Sanders. Animating recursion as an aid to instruction. *Computers & Education*, 23(3):221–226, 1994.

[29] Michael Wirth. Introducing recursion by parking cars. *SIGCSE Bulletin*, 40(4):52–55, November 2008.

# Exploring Variation in Students' Correct Traces of Linear Recursion

Colleen M. Lewis
Harvey Mudd College
301 Platt Blvd, Claremont, CA 91711
lewis@cs.hmc.edu

## ABSTRACT

There has been a wealth of education research focused on recursion. This research has documented students' persistent difficulties with recursion, a variety of pedagogical approaches, and students' correct and incorrect mental models of recursion. This paper explores the variation in students' successful attempts to trace linear recursion. The findings go beyond correct and incorrect mental models to show how each of four modes of tracing linear recursion may require or facilitate a particular understanding of recursion. Additionally, the current study shows how knowledge of algebraic substitution can be applied to tracing linear recursion, and identifies a potential difficulty in students transferring this knowledge.

## Categories and Subject Descriptors

K.3.2 [**Computers and Education**]: Computer and Information Science Education – *computer science education.*

## Keywords

Recursion; mental models; transfer; representations.

## 1. INTRODUCTION

Rather than testing a hypothesis with quantitative methods, this study used a grounded approach [1] to identify examples in which students appear to use out-of-domain knowledge to reason about computer programs [8]. The data considered came from clinical interviews [2] with thirty college students who were enrolled in an introductory computer science (CS) course. During the clinical interviews, students did a think aloud while solving problems.

The connection between algebraic substitution and tracing recursive functions became a central focus when the participant Emily (all names pseudonyms) explicitly connected a technique she used to trace a recursive function with algebraic substitution.

Inspired by Emily's statements, I looked to see if I could identify times when other participants may have been building upon knowledge from algebraic substitution. I do not assume these students consciously used this out-of-domain knowledge.

This article describes connections between algebraic substitution and four effective techniques for tracing recursive functions. To contribute a clear model of each substitution technique, I provide

a description of each substitution technique using a factorial function. To demonstrate the empirical validity of the research, I provide excerpts from clinical interviews in which a participant appeared to use each substitution technique. The data and analysis presented make the following contributions:

**Theoretical Contributions:**

- While no assessment of prior knowledge correlates with success learning to program [10], the current study shows how knowledge of algebraic substitution can be transferred to CS, and identifies a potential difficulty in students transferring this knowledge.
- While correct and incorrect mental models of recursion have been identified [6][12], this research shows a more granular subdivision of correct mental models of recursion. The techniques presented in this article may be used as an initial taxonomy for researchers investigating students' mental models of linear recursion.

**Pedagogical Contributions:**

- These substitution techniques highlight an opportunity to build students' understanding of the difficult topic of recursion upon their knowledge of algebraic substitution.

## 2. PREVIOUS RESEARCH

This research contributes to CS pedagogical content knowledge (PCK), which is knowledge about how to teach CS and is distinct from CS content knowledge or domain-general pedagogical knowledge [4]. CS PCK research is sparse [4] and I focus on a subset of PCK seeking to understand how educators can build upon students' out-of-domain knowledge. For example, Seymour Papert recommends that students "play turtle" when programming the movement of a turtle in the programming language Logo [9]. He claims that this technique encourages students to use their "well-established knowledge of 'body-geometry'" (p. 58, [9], *i.e.* out-of-domain knowledge).

Students' understanding of recursion has been extensively studied (*e.g.,* [3][4][6][7][12]) and two mental models of recursion have been identified [6]: the copies model, a correct model of recursion, and the looping model, which incorrectly assumes that recursion is equivalent to looping. While previous research has presented a more granular taxonomy for students' incorrect attempts to trace recursive functions [12], little attention has been paid to variations within students' effective techniques for tracing recursion.

This paper builds upon the work of Leron and Zazkis [7] who described different orderings in which execution of recursive functions could be considered and described how recursion could build upon students' understanding of induction.

Leron and Zazkis [7] generalized that mathematicians and computer scientists discuss recursive process as progressing in different directions. They claimed that "mathematicians think of the first part of the definition as a 'start rule', whereas computer scientists refer to it as a 'stop rule'." (p. 25, [7]) They provided a "likely" description of the factorial function from the perspective of both a mathematician and computer scientist. They claimed that a mathematician would justify that the "definition enables us to compute 1!, then 2!, then 3! And so on to any desired n" (p. 25, [7]) whereas a computer scientist would justify that "we can compute n! as soon as we know (n-1)!, which in turn can be computed if we know (n-2)! , and so on until we reach 1!" (p. 26, [7]).

Leron and Zazkis [7] noted the similarity between recursion and mathematical induction, which is another connection between mathematics and CS. However, induction may be no less difficult for students than recursion. This is in stark contrast to the pedagogical recommendation of this paper to build upon students' competence with algebraic substitution, which I expect is an unproblematic technique for many students.

# 3. METHODS

## 3.1 Theoretical Framework

The following four goals, which fall within the Knowledge in Pieces theoretical framework [15], encapsulate the theoretical and practical commitments that have guided the research. Each method of data collection, data analysis, and presentation of results have been shaped by these goals as referenced within sections 3.2, 3.3, and 3.4.

- **Goal #1:** Focus on individuals' understandings rather than testing hypotheses or determining the reliability of patterns.
- **Goal #2:** Focus on pedagogically relevant insights and students' correct reasoning rather than their wrong answers.
- **Goal #3:** Focus on representations created by students.
- **Goal #4:** Focus on connection between CS and out-of-domain knowledge.

Goal #1 was informed by Grounded Theory [1] and emulates methods used extensively within physics [15] and mathematics education research. Goal #2 is based upon the assumption that what some students can do, or do with help [14], is relevant PCK [4], because it is relevant for designing instruction and instructional goals. Goal #3 was inspired by research within physics [15] and mathematics [11] education about the ways representations scaffold and document students' understandings. Goal #4 was inspired by the hypothesis that college-level CS instruction could be improved if we built explicitly on students' pre-college out-of-domain knowledge [8].

## 3.2 Study Design & Data Collection

Aspects of the study design and data collection are listed below. Each was informed by one of the goals described above.

- **Participant Recruitment:**
  - Collecting data from a small set of students (N=30) rather than a large sample with which to test a hypothesis or reliably demonstrate a pattern (Goal #1).
  - Interviewing students during their first CS course (Goal #4).
  - Selecting interview participants who were academically successful and therefore likely to have a wealth of out-of-domain knowledge (Goal #4).

- **Data Collection:**
  - Conducting videotaped, one-on-one interviews to be able to watch and re-watch students solving problems (Goal #1).
  - Capturing video of students' hands and inscriptions rather than their faces (Goal #3).
  - Saving and scanning inscriptions students made (Goal #3).

- **Interview content and interaction:**
  - Encouraging interview participants to talk aloud to capture more of students' thought processes than whether they answered correctly or incorrectly (Goal #1).
  - Asking students a guiding question and encouraging them to retry the problem if they answered incorrectly (Goal #2).
  - Using interview questions that were found to be highly correlated with success on the 1988 AP CS exam [10] (Goal #2).
  - Asking interview participants about how things they learned outside of a CS class were helpful to them in their CS class (analysis not presented here) (Goal #4).

### 3.2.1 Interview Problems

The interview questions were questions from the 1988 Advanced Placement Computer Science A (AP CS A) exam that were highly correlated with success [10]. This article narrates participants' solutions from two of the interview problems. These problems involve the WhatIsIt and Mult recursive functions that are shown in Figure 1 and Figure 2 respectively. These questions are shown in the programming language Scheme, which was used by the majority of the interview participants.

The WhatIsIt function calculates the exponent $x^n$ by multiplying x by itself n times. Therefore the correct answer for what WhatIsIt(4, 4) returns is answer option E, 256 or $4^4$. The correct answer for the mult question is answer option D: Statement 1, which executes if x is equal to one, should be y because if x is one, x times y is simply y. Statement 2 must add y to the result of multiplying y by one less than x, which corresponds to answer option D. Notably, answer option E produces code equivalent to the WhatIstIt code and the two methods, WhatIstIt and mult, differ only in the names of the function and variables and the operation * in WhatIsIt versus + in mult.

```
What value is returned by WhatIsIt(4, 4)?
 (define (WhatIsIt x n)
      (if (= n 1)
           x
           (* x (WhatIsIt x (- n 1)))))
a) 8    b) 16    c) 24    d) 64    e) 256
```

**Figure 1. The WhatIsIt Question, a replication of a question from the 1988 APCS exam, translated to Scheme.**

```
Consider the following function where

• x is an integer and x > 0
• It should calculate x * y

(define (mult x y)
   (if (= x 1)
        ;; statement 1
        ;; statement 2
   ))


Which of the following statement pairs properly completes the function?
        <Statement 1>              <Statement 2>
   A.   (* x y)                    ;; none
   B.   y                          (mult (- x 1) (+ y 1))
   C.   y                          (mult (- x 1) (+ y y))
   D.   y                          (+ y (mult (- x 1) y))
   E.   y                          (* y (mult (- x 1) y))
```

**Figure 2. The mult question, a replication of a question from the 1988 APCS exam, translated to Scheme.**

In my explanations of the substitution techniques I will use the factorial function shown in Figure 3, which calculates the factorial of an input x in the programming language Scheme.

```
(define (fact x)
      (if (<= x 1)
            1
            (* x (fact (- x 1))))))
```

**Figure 3. Example factorial function written in Scheme.**

## 3.3 Data Analysis

The data analysis was grounded [1] and required the following activities:

- Watching, transcribing, and re-watching video to ground the analysis in data (Goal #1).
- Looking for variation between individuals and for patterns across individuals (Goal #1).
- Identifying patterns and subtlety in students' reasoning rather than coding or counting data (Goal #1).
- Analyzing students' correct inferences and answers rather than their incorrect inferences and answers (Goal #2).
- Decomposing students' correct answers to explore the variation in ways students may successfully reason (Goal #2).
- Organizing and analyzing scanned copies of students' inscriptions by question to highlight variation and themes within the representations students used (Goal #3).
- Pursuing one students' claim that she used algebraic substitution when tracing recursion to see how other students might be tacitly building upon their competence with algebraic substitution (Goal #4).

## 3.4 Presentation of Results

The selection and presentation of data is guided by the same four goals described in Section 3.1.

- Providing excerpts of students' solutions to show variation (Goal #1).
- Presenting hypotheses about students' ways of understanding, rather than presenting claims about generalizability (Goal #1).
- Presenting idealized substitution technique before students' data to make the techniques as clear as possible (Goal #2).
- Presenting students' correct answers, but not assuming that students have a perfect understanding (Goal #2).

- Presenting representations students made (Goal #3).
- Highlighting how algebraic substitution may be used to support each technique (Goal #4).

## 4. OVERVIEW OF TECHNIQUES

Table 1 shows diagrams of the four substitution techniques. To aid in my description of these substitution techniques I use "recursive call" to refer to a function call that is within the body of a function that calls the same function. The initial function call, which does not originate from within that function, will not be referred to as a recursive call; instead, I will refer to that as the "initial function call." I will refer to both initial functions and recursive calls as "function calls."

The top rectangle in each diagram in Table 1 represents the initial function call that is being traced by the person using this technique. The other rectangles represent recursive calls and, in some of the diagrams, include calculations that are generated during execution of that recursive call. The arrows indicate the order in which the technique requires the individual to reason about each recursive call. Each of these techniques and accompanying diagrams will be described in detail, but even without these details it is possible to observe differences between the techniques in the relative order of execution.

- *simulating execution* begins at the initial function call and then progresses down to the base case and back up.
- *accumulating pending calculations* progresses only from the initial function call down to the base case.
- *dynamic programming* starts from the base case to build up to the initial function call.
- *predicting the result* includes only the initial function call and the first recursive call, but does not consider other recursive calls or the base case.

**Table 1. Table of all substitution techniques**

| #1: Simulating Execution 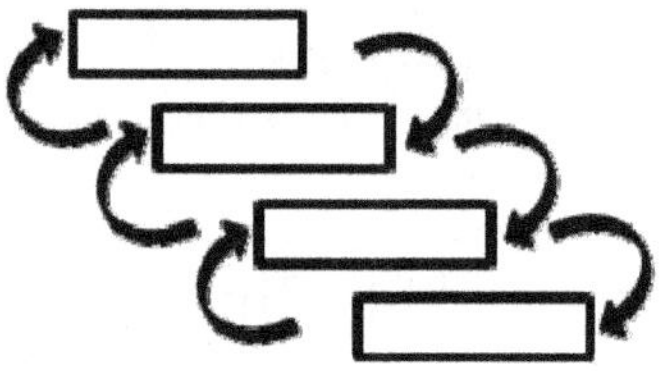 | #3: Dynamic Programming 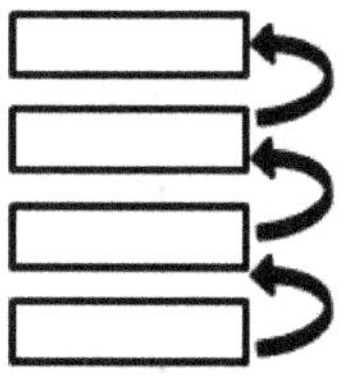 |
|---|---|
| #2: Accumulating Pending Calculations 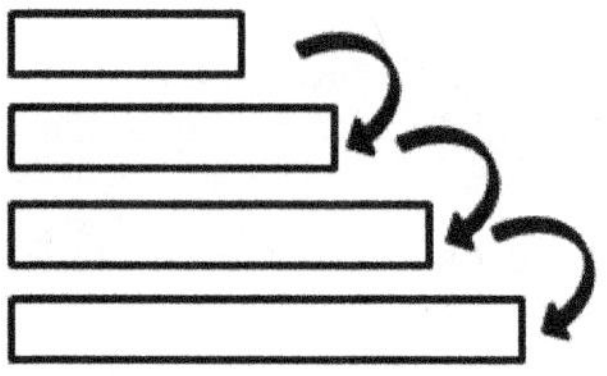 | #4: Predicting the Result 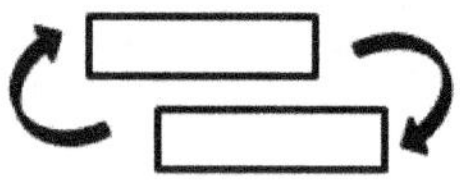 |

# 5. SUBSTITUTION TECHNIQUES

## 5.1 Technique #1: Simulating Execution

### 5.1.1 Description

I refer to the first substitution technique as *simulating execution*. This is the traditional method of tracing recursive functions whereby the recursive calls are traced in the order they would be executed by a computer. The output from each recursive call can be conceived of as being substituted into the expression that generated that recursive call.

For example, using the substitution technique of *simulating execution* to trace the function `fact` with the argument 4 would generate the recursive calls shown in Figure 4.

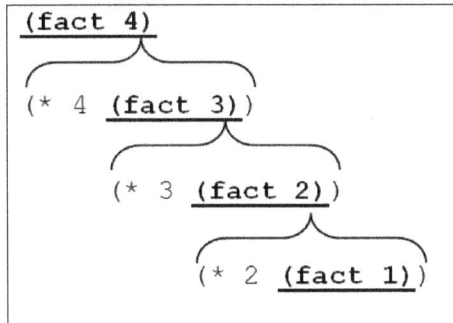

**Figure 4. Recursive calls generated by a call to (fact 4).**

The underlined calls in Figure 4 are expanded from the top to the bottom. When the base case is reached, the value of 1 is substituted for the call (`fact 1`). This is multiplied by 2 and the resulting value of 2 is substituted for the call (`fact 2`). This is multiplied by 3 and the resulting value of 6 is substituted for the call (`fact 3`). This is multiplied by 4 and the resulting value of 24 is substituted for the call (`fact 4`).

Figure 5 shows my schematization of this technique. Each rectangle represents a function call. The rectangle shown on the top is the initial function call. The arrows to the right of these rectangles represent the instantiation of a recursive call. These arrows show the flow of control in a recursive function, which pauses execution within a particular function call when a recursive call is made. In a final recursive call, corresponding to the base case, in which no additional recursive calls are made, the value returned by this recursive call is provided to the calling function that had paused execution. The substitution of this return value at each step is shown with the arrows on the left of the rectangles. This also represents a change in what code is being executed. Therefore the flow of control begins at the initial function call and then proceeds to each subsequent recursive call before eventually returning from each recursive call in sequence. Each arrow is essentially an instance of substitution; the downward arrows are substitutions that work as an expansion of a particular recursive call, and the upward arrows are substitutions of return values from a recursive call. This representation is the most accurate in simulating the flow of control in a recursive function. Arrows on the right correspond to the generation of a new stack frame and each time a value is substituted, which corresponds to the arrows on the left, it returns the flow of control to the stack frame for that previous call.

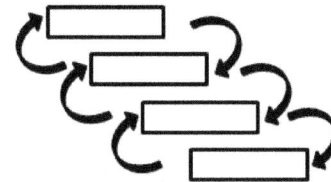

**Figure 5. Diagram of the *simulating execution* substitution technique**

### 5.1.2 Example

Figure 6 shows a representation created by Kate when tracing the call (`WhatIsIt 4 4`). This example was selected from the apparent instances of simulating execution because it showed the most legible and most easily interpreted representation. Each line in her representation shows the expression that would be generated by the recursive call on the previous line. However, she did not show the initial function call (`WhatIsIt 4 4`). When the return value for each line is identified, starting from the bottom, this value can be substituted in the previous line. The participant did not identify each substitution, but summarized "and then you multiply all the fours," which is consistent with the implied substitution in the representation.

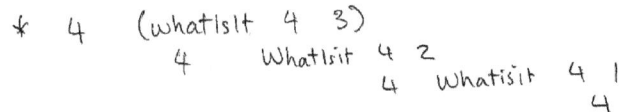

**Figure 6. Written work on the WhatIsIt question by Kate**

### 5.1.3 Implications

The substitution technique of *simulating execution* requires a relatively complete model of how a computer executes recursive functions. Connecting this technique to the next substitution technique of *accumulating pending calculations* may help students reason about the fact that the flow of control returns to the previous recursive calls. This feature of how a computer executes recursive calls is important for reasoning about non-linear recursion and recursion in an imperative programming environment, which both require returning to the previous recursive call to execute any remaining commands.

## 5.2 Technique #2: Accumulating Pending Calculations

### 5.2.1 Description

This technique contrasts with *simulating execution* in that the calculations that are performed when returning control to a paused recursive function call are accumulated in a single expression that contains all pending calculations.

For example, using the substitution technique of *accumulating pending calculations* to trace the function `fact` with the argument 4 would generate the recursive calls and calculations shown in Figure 7.

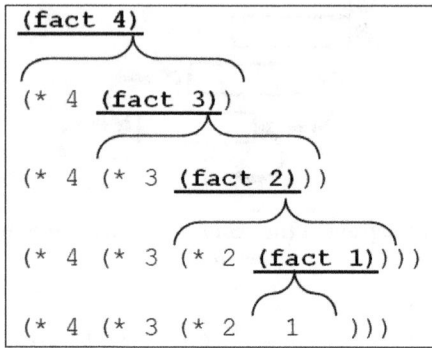

```
(fact 4)

(* 4 (fact 3))

(* 4 (* 3 (fact 2)))

(* 4 (* 3 (* 2 (fact 1))))

(* 4 (* 3 (* 2   1   )))
```

**Figure 7. Recursive calls generated by a call to (fact 4).**

Again the underlined calls to fact in Figure 7 are expanded from the top to the bottom. However, each line includes all pending calculations. For example, the expanded version of (fact 3) is substituted in to the expression (* 4 (fact 3)) to produce (* 4 (*3 (fact 2))), which is shown on the third line in Figure 7. The same process generates the fourth line. Between the fourth and fifth lines the value returned by the call (fact 1) is substituted into the expression to produce the final expression (* 4 (* 3 (* 2 1))). With this substitution technique consideration never returns to previous lines because the final expression contains all necessary calculations.

Figure 8 shows my schematization of this technique, which unlike the diagram of *simulating execution* in Figure 5 does not include an arrow indicating the flow of control returning to the calling recursive function. Each rectangle still includes a function call, but each rectangle also includes all pending calculations. In the subsequent line, the recursive call from the previous line is replaced with the equivalent, expanded, recursive relationship. Instead of representing the flow of control, each downward arrow signifies a substitution in which the recursive call is expanded and substituted in to the expression.

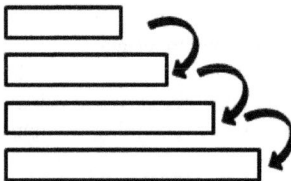

**Figure 8. Schematization of the *Accumulating Pending Calculations* substitution technique**

The *accumulating pending calculations* technique does not involve retracing through the previous recursive calls like the substitution technique of *simulating execution* because all pending calculations are accumulated in the final expression.

### 5.2.2 Example

In the next case, Jim copied the full expression each time that he substituted in an expanded expression generated by a recursive call. For example, between the first and second line he appeared to substitute "(* 4 (WhatIsIt 4 2))" in for the expression "(WhatIsIt 4 3)." He was not explicit about this process of substitution, but he arrived at the correct answer and I infer from the representation in Figure 9 that he substituted in the expanded expression from each recursive call.

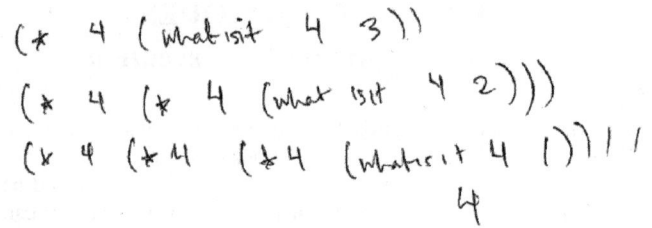

**Figure 9. Written work on the WhatIsIt question by Jim**

Like the *simulating execution* representation shown in Figure 6, he did not write the initial call of "(WhatIsIt 4 4)." In the final line in Figure 9, he wrote the number 4, which he said (WhatIsIt 4 1) will "return." Writing only 4 on the last line instead of the full set of pending calculations, (* 4 (* 4 (* 4 4 ) ) ) is also a departure from this technique. Despite these subtle departures, this was the most legible and most easily interpreted use of this technique.

### 5.2.3 Implications

The substitution technique of *accumulating pending calculations* does not require reasoning about the execution of multiple recursive calls at a time, but requires considering each recursive call in an uninterrupted sequence. This uninterrupted sequence of recursive calls is identical to the sequence of recursive calls executed by a computer. Transitioning from the use of *dynamic programming* to the use of *accumulating pending calculations* could potentially focus students on this sequence of recursive calls.

## 5.3 Technique #3: Dynamic Programming

### 5.3.1 Description

The third abstraction technique relies on calculating and storing the values of particular functions calls that build up to the initial function call. This is similar to dynamic programming, which is a technique to avoid redundant function calls.

Although the technique relies on previously calculated values, this substitution technique can be used to calculate the value for an arbitrary function call. To do this you begin by calculating the value of the recursive function for an input that does not require any recursive calls. In the case of the fact function, shown in Figure 3, this would be evaluating the fact function with an x value of 1. A call to fact with an x value of 1 results in evaluating the true case of the "if" statement and returns the value 1. Now we know that (fact 1) returns 1. Next, you evaluate the function call of fact with an x value of 2 or (fact 2). This calculation results in multiplying the x value, 2, by (fact 1). We know that (fact 1) returns 1 and can substitute in that value for (fact 1). It would not be an example of the substitution technique if an individual instead traced the function again for the x value of 1. If we now know that (fact 2) returns 2, this resulting value from (fact 2) can be used when evaluating the fact function for the value 3. This pattern can be continued to identify the result of an arbitrary recursive call.

This process can be seen as starting at the base case and working toward the desired recursive call. Figure 10 shows a schematization of this substitution technique. For consistency with my diagrams of the other substitution techniques, I have shown the base case at the bottom of this diagram, but this diagram is not representative of the diagrams I would expect individuals to generate. In this substitution technique, the individuals' consideration of the function begins with the base case. If this was written at the top of the individuals' representation, it would generate a diagram that is an inverted version of the one shown in Figure 10.

In Figure 10 the bottom rectangle is a statement of the output of the function at the base case. For an instance of the `mult` function this would be "(mult 1 5) = 5." All other rectangles include an expansion of the recursive relationship, such as "(mult 2 5) = (+ 5 (mult 1 5))." The arrows show the process of substituting in a previously calculated value such as "(mult 1 5) = 5" into the expression above. After this substitution, the full contents of the rectangle would be "(mult 2 5) = (+ 5 (mult 1 5)) = (+ 5 5) = 10." Again, the arrows do not show the flow of control, but they show the steps of substitution of previously calculated values such as "(mult 1 5) = 5" or "(mult 2 5) = 10" into a recursive call that is farther from the base case.

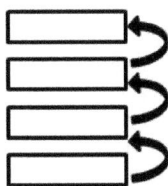

**Figure 10. Schematization of the *dynamic programming* substitution technique**

### 5.3.2 Example
Emily, who was quoted as connecting her technique to algebraic substitution, used the substitution technique of *dynamic programming* on the `WhatIsIt` problem. I will narrate a single step in her use of the strategy.

Emily was reasoning about the expression she had written that is shown in Figure 11. She had already calculated the result of (`WhatIsIt` 4 1) to be 4. In the following transcript, Emily was able to articulate how you could use the result from (`WhatIsIt` 4 1) when calculating (`WhatIsIt` 4 2). *"I'm thinking that because we found that it was a 4 here, that it would be 4 times 4. And that would be 16."* She then paused and said *"But I think I'm over simplifying things."* I asked her to clarify and she said:

> *"Um because like when it was 4 and 1, like okay, so that was straight forward, but for when it was 4 and 2, what I was doing was like okay, If you have, when you start here. It becomes 4 and 2 minus 1, so then it's 1. So then uh oh well so we know what that is, and that was [4], so then you take it times 4."*

**Figure 11. Previously generated tracing of (WhatIsIt 4 2)**

A key element in Emily's explanation of this process is her statement *"we know what this is."* This is the central idea in the substitution technique of *dynamic programming*. Her statement *"that was 4"* stands in place of where she otherwise would have needed to explicitly trace the value of (`WhatIsIt` 4 1). Emily proceeded to use the same technique to determine the return value of (`WhatIsIt` 4 4).

### 5.3.3 Implications
The substitution technique of *dynamic programming* may be the most accessible to a novice student because the student only

needs to consider a single execution of the recursive function at a time. Even without reasoning about an uninterrupted sequence of recursive calls, the student still has the opportunity to reason about the base case as producing a known value and the recursive expression producing a value that depends upon another execution of the recursive function.

## 5.4 Technique #4: Predicting the Result
### 5.4.1 Description
In the substitution technique of *predicting the result* the individual predicts the output of the first recursive call made in the body of the initial call to the function. I define "predicting the output of the first recursive call" as using a method that is independent of the recursive function to predict the output of the function. I refer to this substitution technique as *predicting the result* because the output of the first recursive call is determined "by hand" and not by using the recursive function.

If we were executing the correct version of the function `mult` with the arguments 5 and 3, the first recursive call made would be (mult 4 3). This substitution technique involves predicting the output of (mult 4 3). The function `mult` is supposed to multiply its arguments. Therefore *predicting the result* is trivial and (mult 4 3) is expected to output the value 12, 4x3. This expected output can be substituted into the expression in place of the first recursive call.

This requires that the individual is able to predict the output of the function and therefore requires that the specification of the function is well understood. The `WhatIsIt` function, for which the behavior of the function is not provided, is not a candidate for the use of this technique. In the example that follows, the student reasoned about the `mult` function where the expected output for various inputs could easily be identified.

This technique does not require tracing each recursive call. The initial function call is traced; however, the next recursive call is replaced with a value calculated by hand. This single step of execution is shown in Figure 12, where each rectangle represents a recursive call. The right arrow shows the flow of control that causes the first expansion of the recursive call, but the flow of control to subsequent recursive calls is not shown or considered by the individual using this technique. In the second rectangle, the value that is calculated by hand is substituted into the recursive expression. The left arrow shows the resulting value from this expression returned as the output of the function.

**Figure 12. Schematization of the *predicting the result* substitution technique**

This is a normative technique to evaluate the correctness of a recursive call, which is parallel to checking one case of an inductive chain. However, this technique does not guarantee that the recursive function is correct; the base case also needs to be correct and the recursive relationship needs to be consistent throughout the execution of the recursive function.

### 5.4.2 Example
In the following examples, the participant Tim used this technique twice when reasoning about the recursive function `mult` as

specified by two answer options. Tim had already used the substitution technique of *simulating execution* to trace the function, but because of a systematic error in his tracing of answer option C, he could not distinguish the behavior of the functions specified by answer options C and D. The recursive relationships for these answer options are shown in Equation 1 and Equation 2 respectively. Answer option D is correct and answer option C is incorrect, but he believed them to both be correct. In the transcript below, Tim attempted a new technique, which I classify as *predicting the result* to identify whether answer option C or D was correct.

$$(\text{mult } x \; y) = (+ \; y \; (\text{mult} \; (- \; x \; 1) \; y))$$

**Equation 1. Correct recurrence relationship specified by answer option D.**

Tim created the representation shown in Figure 13 and did so without tracing individual recursive calls. There are a number of aspects of his representation that are not explicit. He created the representation shown in Figure 13 during the following interview transcript where he was tracing the correct answer, option D.

> *"Well if we look at it this way. This one's going to be y plus (wrote 'y+'), and assuming this works (pointing to answer option D) it's going to be x minus 1 times y. So it'll be like 4 y (wrote '4 y') so that'll be 5 y (wrote '= 5 y' on the second line), if we start with 5 y (wrote '5 y' on the first line). So like that should definitely work."*

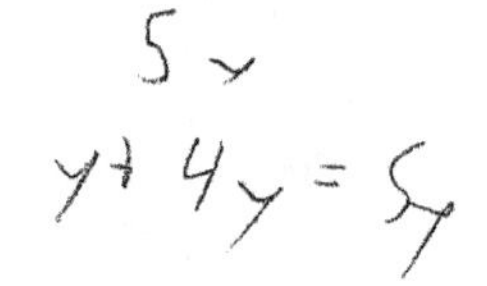

**Figure 13 Inscriptions created by Tim to trace through answer option D**

This technique can be used to evaluate the correctness of the recursive call as I described, but it is uncertain whether or not Tim used this technique. I interpret Tim's statements and inscriptions as indicating that he used the technique that I refer to as *predicting the result*, but continue my narration of this case by discussing some of the assumptions in my interpretation of his solution.

Tim used the inscription of "5 y" in both the first and second lines of Figure 13 and I interpret the meaning of them differently. In the first line I interpret "5 y" as representing the initial function call to `mult` with the arguments 5 and y, which is typically written as (mult 5 y). The "5 y" from the second line I interpret as representing the desired output of the function call (mult 5 y). It is ambiguous if his inscription of "4 y" should be interpreted as mathematical notation for 4 times y or as shorthand for the recursive call (mult 4 y). However, regardless of the interpretation of this inscription his statement "assuming this works" is consistent with the use of this technique and he did not show any indication of tracing a recursive call or referring to a previously calculated value.

At this point he became *"pretty confident"* that answer option D was correct. He said: *"So I'm thinking it is more likely to be this one, and I'm just not thinking this one (answer option C) through. I think it's D. I think it's D. I'm pretty confident."* Despite his confidence, he was still unable to use *simulating execution* to show that answer option C does not also produce the correct

result. After two additional attempts to trace answer option C, I encouraged him to try to see if answer option C was correct using the technique he used when creating Figure 13. The recurrence relationship from answer option C is shown in Equation 2. Using this method he convinced himself that answer option C is incorrect in the following interview transcript.

$$(\text{mult } x \; y) = (\text{mult} \; (- \; x \; 1) \; (+ \; y \; y))$$

**Equation 2. Incorrect recurrence relationship specified by answer option C.**

**Figure 14 Inscriptions created by Tim to trace through answer option C**

> *"Alright, well that reasoning is – that in theory multiply works. And does what we want. So if we start with four and um. Four y (wrote '4y'). When you run this, it's going to give us multiply (wrote 'mult') three times y plus y (wrote '(3 y + y)'). And three times y plus y. Three times two y is six y (wrote '6 y' and drew a box around it). So that's not right. And that would convince me I'm wrong (referring to his conclusion that answer option C was correct)."*

Like the first example where he proceeded by "assuming this works," here he explained his reasoning as "that in theory multiply works and does what you want." Using answer option C, Tim again traced a single execution of the recursive call specified by answer option C and substituted in the expected output of the `mult` function. Again he appeared to represent the initial function call of (mult 4 y) as "4 y." He was explicit about the recursive call to `mult` that would result. Applying the recurrence relationship from answer option C shown in Equation 2 and wrote "mult (3 y+y)."

### 5.4.3 Implications

The substitution technique of *predicting the result* builds upon students' experience reasoning about algorithms, which may be another connection to students' out-of-domain knowledge. A barrier to reasoning using the other techniques is the layering of multiple steps. This technique requires considering only two function calls and therefore may be less overwhelming to a student.

## 6. DISCUSSION

The techniques identified in this article are not intended to be comprehensive of all possible techniques for reasoning about recursive functions. As a counter example, one technique, instead of using substitution, involves seeing that the algorithm is the same as the algorithm known by the individual to perform the same calculation. This mapping allows an individual to conclude that the recursive function works as expected, but does not involve tracing specific values. This technique was used by only a single participant on the `mult` problem, despite participants' likely familiarity with the algorithm for multiplication.

When reasoning about the `mult` problem, Peter describes "x*y" as *"really saying x plus x plus x, y times."* He observed that answer option D "looks like it might do that" and came to the correct conclusion that answer option D was the correct answer without ever tracing the function. During the segment documented in the following interview transcript, Peter created the representation shown in Figure 15.

*"Umm, I can't really explain it, but this seems reasonable as an answer. (Interviewer: OK, Why?) Umm, because I kind of think of multiplication as if we have x times y (wrote 'x\*y' shown in Figure 15) that's really saying x plus x plus x, y times (completed inscriptions in Figure 15). So, and this looks like. Looks like it might do that, but I'm not sure (pause). So statement 1, umm. I guess that would imply this (points to answer option D), so I guess I'll try D out first."*

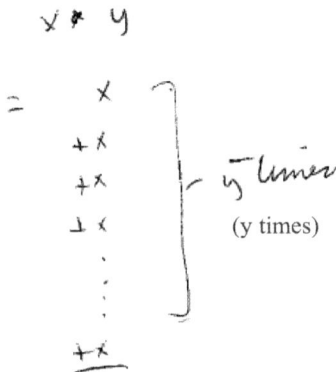

**Figure 15. Peter's notes when explaining why answer option D was correct**

After making the conclusion that answer option D "seems reasonable as an answer" Peter used *simulating execution* to trace through each of the answer options with sample input. Although Peter did not use the technique to determine his final answer, this is a valid technique with which to reason about the function and does not involve substitution.

# 7. CONCLUSIONS

This article includes descriptions and empirical examples of four kinds of substitution techniques that I refer to as *simulating execution*, *accumulating pending calculations*, *dynamic programming*, and *predicting the result*.

The diversity of these techniques may be a tool to make CS more accessible. Students may find various techniques more or less intuitive and may be able to use a single technique as an intuitive foothold to build toward a rich understanding of recursion.

The substitution techniques of *simulating execution*, *accumulating pending calculations*, and *dynamic programming* all trace each recursive call, but do so in different orders. I hypothesize that the differences between these three techniques may provide the opportunity to scaffold students' understanding of how recursive functions are executed by computers and may provide the opportunity to highlight relevant features of the execution of recursive functions. For example, these substitution techniques and the corresponding representations for tracking execution could be taught to students, which may support students in more accurately tracing execution.

# 8. ACKNOWLEDGEMENTS

This work was partially funded by NSF grants #1044106 and #1339404. The paper also benefitted from feedback provided by anonymous reviewers, Michael Clancy, Andrea diSessa, Katherine Lewis, and Arielle Schlesinger.

# 9. REFERENCES

[1] Corbin, J. M., & Strauss, A. C. (2008). Basics of Qualitative Research. Thousand Oaks, CA: SAGE Publications.

[2] diSessa, A. A. (2007). An interactional analysis of clinical interviewing. *Cognition and Instruction. 25(4)*, 523-565.

[3] George, C. E. (2000) Experiences with Novices: The Importance of Graphical Representation in Supporting Mental Models. In A. F. Blackwell & E. Bilotta (Eds). Proc. PPIG 12

[4] Hubwieser, Magenheim, Muhling, & Ruf (2013). Towards a Conceptualization of Pedagogical Content Knowledge for Computer Science. *ICER.* 1-8.

[5] Kahney, H. (1989) What do novice programmers know about recursion? *Studying the Novice Programmer* (E. Soloway & J.C. Spohrer, Eds.) Hillsdale, New Jersey: Lawrence Erlbaum Associates Inc., 209-228.

[6] Kurland, D. M., & Pea, R. D., (1989). Children's mental models of recursive logo programs. *Studying the Novice Programmer (E. Soloway & J.C. Spohrer, Eds.)* Hillsdale, New Jersey: Lawrence Erlbaum Associates Inc., 315-323.

[7] Leron, U. & Zazkis, R. (1986). Computational Recursion and Mathematical Induction. *For the Learning of Mathematics, 6(2)*. 25–28.

[8] Lewis, C. M. (2012). *Applications of Out-of-Domain Knowledge in Students' Reasoning about Computer Program State.* (Doctoral dissertation). Retrieved from ProQuest Dissertations and Theses. (Accession Order No. 12710).

[9] Papert, S. (1980). Mindstorms: Children, Computers, and Powerful Ideas. New York: Basic Books, Inc.

[10] Reges, S. (2008) They mystery of b := (b = false). *ACM SIGCSE*, 39, 21-25.

[11] Schoenfeld, A. H. (2007). Reflections on an assessment interview: What a close look at student understanding can reveal. In A. H. Schoenfeld (Eds.) *Assessing Mathematical Proficiency* (pp. 267-280). Cambridge: Cambridge University Press.

[12] Scholtz & Sanders (2010). Mental Models of Recursion: Investigating Students' Understanding of Recursion. *ITiCSE*, 103-107.

[13] Simon *et al.* (2006). The ability to articulate strategy as a predictor of programming skill. *Proc Eighth Australasian Computing Education Conference*, Hobart, Australia.

[14] Vygotsky, L.S. (1978). Mind in society: The development of higher psychological processes.

[15] Wagner, J. F. (2006). Transfer in Pieces. Cognition and Instruction, 24(1), 1-71.

# Diversifying High School Students' Views About Computing with Electronic Textiles

Kristin A. Searle, Deborah A. Fields*, Debora A. Lui, & Yasmin B. Kafai

University of Pennsylvania
Graduate School of Education
3700 Walnut St.
Philadelphia, PA 19104
searle@gse.upenn.edu, dlui@asc.upenn.edu,
kafai@upenn.edu

*Utah State University
College of Education
2830 Old Main Hill
Logan, UT 84322
deborah.fields@usu.edu

## ABSTRACT

More than twenty years ago, Turkle and Papert wrote about the lack of epistemological pluralism in computing and the resulting exclusivity in the field. Although research on what constitutes a personal epistemology has expanded since then, students continue to hold narrow views of computing that are disconnected from the field at large. To align with current research, we use the term "views" to encompass students' expectations of, attitudes towards, and beliefs about computing. We took a crafts-oriented approach to expanding students' views of computing and broadening participation in computer science by engaging high school students in a 10-week electronic textiles unit. Students were introduced to computational concepts and practices as they designed and programmed electronic artifacts. We found their views shifted from pre- to post-interviews in ways that allowed them to see computing as accessible, transparent, personal, and creative. We discuss how e-textiles materials and the design of classroom activities brought back a diversity of ways thinking about who can do computing, how to do it, and what computing can be.

## Categories and Subject Descriptors

K.3.0 [**Computers and Education**]: General

## Keywords

Electronic textiles, education, K-12, broadening participation, attitude, novice programmers

## 1. INTRODUCTION

More than twenty years ago, Sherry Turkle and Seymour Papert [33] wrote an article about the lack of diversity in approaches to computing, where abstract, rule-driven "hard" styles were seen as more valid approaches to problem solving than negotiated, tinkering "soft" styles. In privileging "hard" approaches, the field at-large pushed forward a particular kind of pedagogy, which promoted a "top-down," "divide-and-conquer" approach over a more "bricoleur" perspective, which relied on constant rearrangement and negotiation of materials. Because certain

groups were shown to prefer this "bricoleur" approach (particularly girls), Turkle and Papert [33] argued for the need to diversify approaches for thinking about and teaching computing, thus promoting what they called "epistemological pluralism". In this way, educators could work to broaden engagement in computing. Throughout the years these insights fueled many shifts in pedagogy, including changing learning and teaching cultures around computer science in schools [22], providing appealing programming activities [16, 19, 24], and developing programming tools [18] to make technology cultures more inclusive to girls and students from underrepresented backgrounds. Research on college-level introductory programming courses has also attempted broaden participation in computing by addressing factors influencing student success [2], examining students' perceptions of computing [31], and developing interventions like pair programming or giving students a meaningful context for doing computing [14, 26] Nonetheless, several studies have documented students' continued disinterest in computer science and the ways these relate to students' stereotypical perceptions of the field at-large [8, 12, 35]. In this paper, we return to the question of epistemological pluralism and its potential to broaden participation in computing through a new intervention in computer science: the tangible and expressive use of electronic textiles.

While there have been many efforts to change perceptions and broaden participation to unlock the existing clubhouses of computing [21, 22], a very different approach has been to build new clubhouses of computing [4]. By clubhouses, we refer to the exclusive, club-like atmosphere of many computing spaces. In their work, Margolis & Fisher [21] focused on the gender gap in computing and unlocking "boys only" clubhouses to include female participants. We extend the metaphor to include how additional ways of thinking about and doing computing can also be valued. We envision these new clubhouses as not only more inclusive but also as more culturally distinct spaces where multiple ways of knowing about and doing computing are valued.

One approach to building new clubhouses of computing has been to employ computational construction kits, such as the LilyPad Arduino Construction Kit for making electronic textiles [3, 5], that challenge conventional conceptions of computing. Electronic textiles are made by stitching together sewable microcontrollers (e.g., the LilyPad Arduino), different actuators (LEDs, speakers), and sensors with conductive thread on a fabric backing (perhaps a sweatshirt or bag) and programming them to execute particular behaviors, such as causing a series of LEDs to blink faster or slower depending on the values read from a light sensor (i.e. how light or dark a given environment is) (see Figure

1). By design, electronic textiles (e-textiles hereafter) combine practices such as engineering and computing, which have historically have been viewed as masculine activities, with sewing and crafting, which have been viewed as feminine activities [30]. E-textiles also add a tangible dimension to computing that so far has mostly been experienced in the virtual realm with the exception of robotics (generally a male-dominated activity). Finally, e-textiles move computing from stationary machines into the wearable domain. By their very design, e-textiles challenge norms by engaging with ideas about what computing can be (tangible, wearable), who can do it (women, men), how it can be done (crafting, sewing), and why and where it matters.

**Figure 1: The LilyPad Arduino construction kit.**

Prior research with electronic textiles in high school classes [17] became the starting point for this investigation into how students conceptualized computing culture and their places within such a culture before and after engaging with e-textiles. We wanted to revisit epistemological pluralism in computing culture [33] in light of the relevance that students' views of learning have shown in other fields [1, 13, 28]. To this end, we focus on extensive debriefing interviews with high school participants in a 10-week e-textile unit as part of an elective computer science class at their high school. Within these interviews, we focused on students' perceptions of the computational process and computer science as a field. Our research addresses the following questions: How does taking a hands-on, crafts-oriented approach to computing in an elective computer science course influence how students engage with learning computational concepts and practices? How might this shift their conceptions about computing culture at-large and their place within it? In the discussion, we review how the physicality of e-textiles materials themselves and the design of classroom activities can foster a diversity of ways of thinking about computing and contribute to broadening participation within the field of computer science.

## 2. BACKGROUND

Recent work by educational psychologists has defined an epistemological standpoint to a discipline as having at least two components, (1) an individual's views/attitudes about the discipline and (2) an individual's conceptualization of the nature of knowledge production within the discipline [1, 13]. Students and professionals within a given discipline are likely to have vastly different epistemological standpoints, and these standpoints may influence how successful an individual is within a discipline. In this paper we focus primarily on the first component of an epistemological standpoint. We explore how students' attitudes towards computing are shaped by engagement with e-textiles materials and how these relate (or fail to relate) to computational thinking.

As a starting point for our investigation into student views about computing, we draw upon the multiple approaches to computing identified by Turkle and Papert [33]. Based on interviews with elementary school students working with the Logo programming environment and college students enrolled in an introductory computer science course, Turkle and Papert [33] found that numerous students employed a bricolage approach to computing that valued more concrete rather than abstract approaches to engaging with computer code. This "soft" approach valued "mid-course corrections" and "negotiations" of material for the purposes of problem solving (p. 136). While such a perspective ran counter to the usual approach to computing favored by the computer science community, students using these strategies were shown to be equally successful in arriving at viable solutions. Despite this finding, computer science pedagogies have continued to favor the "top-down, divide-and-conquer [...] 'planner's'" approach to coding (p. 136), thus continuing to alienate those who thrived using the more expressive, "conversational" styles of the bricoleur. This divide in computing has deepened over the years rather than dissipated, even as digital technologies have moved out of the computer laboratories and workplaces and infiltrated our everyday lives.

In addition to the preferred approaches to computing outlined by Turkle and Papert [33], there are numerous studies that illustrate that teenagers' thinking about computing is fairly stereotypical, describing it as "tedious", "boring" and just "sitting in front a screen all day… working in solitude" [35, see also 8, 12]. Students additionally viewed the field as not creative, despite the fact that they were often enthusiastically involved in the products of computation (blogs, social networking services, etc.). Even younger students, when asked to draw a computer scientist, mirror these sentiments by drawing a white male with a beard, crazy hair, and pocket protector [23; see also 6]. These views of computing and computer scientists reflect students' perspectives.

Within the discipline the nature of computing is seen as capturing "aspects of designing systems, solving problems, and understanding human behaviors" [34, p.6], otherwise referred to as computational thinking. Computational thinking—while often strictly associated with computer science—applies computer science principles to other disciplines in order to help break down the constituent elements of any problem, determine their relationship to each other and the greater whole, and then devise algorithms to arrive at an automated solution. While this view on the nature of computing is not uncontested, it does present a professional view that understanding the world computationally gives a particular lens to understanding problems and contributing to their solutions. Today, numerous efforts are underway to promote computational thinking in K-12 [25] but much has focused on developing activities that engage students in computing, leaving aside the thorny issues of how students think about computing. In this paper we seek to connect these two issues by addressing the relationship between activities used to teach computational concepts and practices and students' perceptions of the computation process before and after participating in those activities. In this paper, we argue that by engaging students in activities rooted in a variety of approaches to computing—particularly the more bricoleur-friendly approach of e-textiles—we are able to expand not only their knowledge base but also their ideas about what computing is.

## 3. PARTICIPANTS, RESEARCH METHODS, DATA SOURCES & ANALYSIS

Participants were 27 high school juniors and seniors, 16-18 years old, from a public magnet high school focused on science and technology in a large urban school district. The demographic composition of our group of participants mirrored the overall demographics of the school: 46% African American, 10% Latino, 9% Asian/Pacific Islander, 33% White, and 2% other. Forty-nine percent of students received free or reduced lunch. Students' experiences with computing varied widely prior to their freshman year of high school when each student was issued a laptop for academic and personal use during the school year. All participants were enrolled in an elective computer science course that met for an hour twice per week. Prior to engaging with e-textiles, they had spent a semester learning to program in Alice [www.Alice.org], an environment for programming 3D animations. Many participants had also taken a physics course during which they programmed robots. We implemented two 10-week e-textiles units in which students, split into two groups, were introduced to the basics of e-textiles through building and debugging simple circuits, writing code for LilyPad ProtoSnap boards, and finally engaging in the process of designing, making, and programming their own e-textile artifacts. Students were tasked with making an e-textile artifact using the LilyPad Arduino, 2–4 LEDs, and two conductive fabric patches that acted as touch sensors (see Figure 2) [for more details on the curriculum see, 17].

We conducted and recorded pre- and post-project interviews with 24 of the 27 students based on their willingness to participate and availability during the school day. Each interview was semi-structured in nature and lasted for approximately 30 minutes. In both interviews, we asked students about their experiences with computing to-date and whether or not they had career aspirations related to computing. In the post-interviews, we asked additional questions about what they learned, how they saw themselves in relation to computing, and whether or not they found the assignment creative. All interviews were logged, which involves a close but not word-for-word transcription [9, 10]. Any segments directly quoted in this paper were fully transcribed at a later date. We then conducted a thematic analysis using a grounded theory approach [7] choosing to focus on the accessibility of computing via e-textiles, the transparency and functionality in learning computing using e-textiles, the positionality of participants' and their e-textile artifacts in relation to computing and to other audiences, such as parents or siblings, and the creativity of the assignment. In this paper we focus primarily on findings from the post-project interviews because they illustrate the impact of a 10-week engagement with e-textiles on students' attitudes towards and perceptions of computing.

## 4. FINDINGS

We begin by providing an overview of students' perceptions as they were expressed in pre-interviews. One overarching theme that arose from analyzing the pre-interviews was the understanding of computer science as narrow and limited (limited to the screen, a solitary activity) versus a broader sense of its relevance in everyday contexts. In pre-interviews, students were very vague about computing and said things like, "I knew that it is dealing with programs and computers" (Giuliana, pre-interview, 12/08/11) or "I knew it had something to do with computers...So I thought maybe like computers and test tubes...computer science!" (Marsha, pre-interview, 12/07/11). For other (mostly male) students, computing was linked to game play and wanting to know what went on "behind the scenes." These conceptions of computing expressed in the pre-interviews illustrate the narrow view of the field often found in others studies [35, 8, 12].

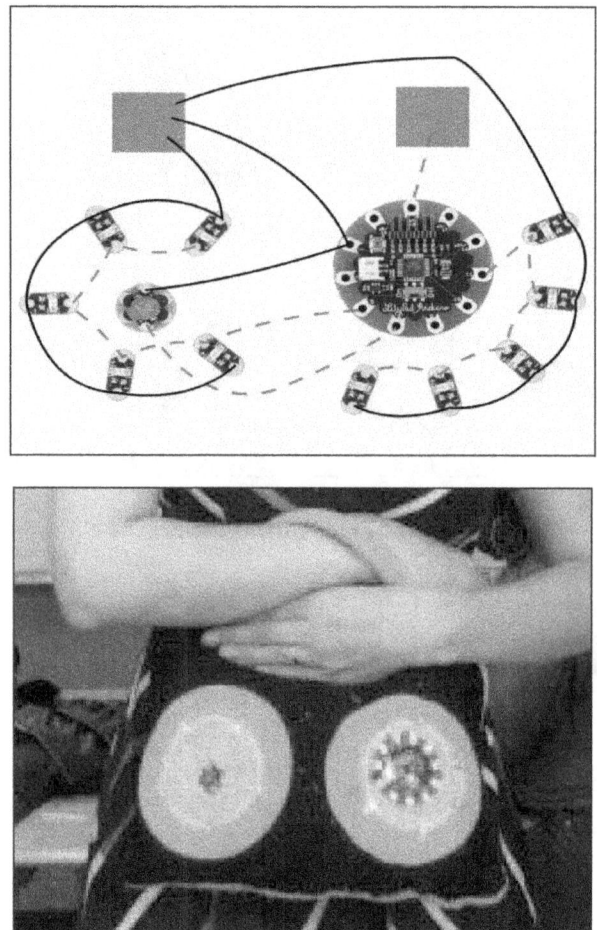

**Figure 2: E-Textile Boombox by Lloyd: The circuitry diagram (upper) and completed artifact (lower design).**

In addition to thinking about computing in narrow ways, students had difficulties connecting what they did in school with what computing professionals do. Specifically, they saw a disconnect between the highly constrained "drag and drop" programming environment they were working with in Alice and the kinds of scenarios they were asked to create ("learning how to make a fish swim around an island") and "real programming" as done by professionals. Out of 24 students who participated in these interviews, only four students made comments about the logic of computer programming or the importance of planning and sequencing which we might associate with the more prevalent, top-down approach to computing.

In post-interviews, students more clearly articulated a range of perspectives on computing, which could be linked to professional practice. This could be viewed as a first step in developing students' epistemological stances towards computing as a discipline. Of the twenty-four students who completed post-interviews, 23 students noted that the initial hands-on, low tech nature of making an e-textile artifact and the ability to literally see one's progress (e.g., number of stitches sewn, number of lights), made it more *accessible*. All twenty-four students also commented that the ability to make code visible by watching one's lights go on, and tracing connections between components by looking at the stitching made e-textiles more *transparent* than other computing activities. These students (24/24) also noted that that e-textiles projects highlighted issues of *positionality and audience* in ways that other computing assignments did not because they could choose to emphasize particular personal interests in what they made, and they could also more easily show the project off to parents and friends because of the physical, portable nature of e-textiles. Finally, a smaller (18/24) but still significant number of students appreciated the *creativity* and *variability* in learning computing using e-textiles. In spite of the fact that all students were given the same assignment with the noted constraints, many enjoyed the process and observed that all of the class projects looked distinct (see Figure 3). To expand on these themes, we provide vignettes of individual students' perspectives. These vignettes provide more detail on each theme as they played out in students' reflections on their learning with e-textiles.

Figure 3: E-textile Artifacts, belonging to (clockwise from top left) Megan, Bridget, Eldore, and Carlton.

## 4.1 Accessibility: Moving Computing Beyond the Screen

Like many of the other students, Carlton entered the semester course without much previous experience with programming. Even though he had seen e-textiles style products for children in the real world, he did not originally think about those in terms of computer science. The e-textiles unit expanded

his understanding of the general applicability of computation. As Carlton described, "e-textiles kind of widened the possibility of what Computer Science can do or what... how it can be applied to one's life.... it kind of opens up the possibilities to what it can do and how it can serve a purpose in our day-to-day lives" (post-interview, 6/1/12). While Carlton viewed the previous work he had done on Alice as entirely contained within the computer, for e-textiles, he described how the computation could be tangibly appreciated: "with this... you create something on the computer and it can... you know, breathe life in a t-shirt." Like other students, working with e-textiles allowed Carlton to connect the work he did for a school assignment with the work of professional computer scientists who tackle real-world problems and program objects used in our everyday lives.

Carlton was also able to access computing in the e-textiles unit because of its connection to craft. Whether or not students had experience with sewing or coding (Carlton had neither), all the students were able to "set the bar [appropriately] low" to where they were comfortable (post-interview, 6/1/12). The existence of these multiple access points (whether through sewing or through coding) promoted the feeling that e-textiles construction was available to all, thus challenging existing stereotypes about the high barrier to entry into computer science. Overall, students' familiarity with e-textiles artifacts in the world, the varieties of hands-on skills required for e-textiles crafting, and their sense of accomplishment derived from tangibly being able to see one's progress, created a sense of greater accessibility to computing than might have been afforded through traditional, formal approaches to teaching computer science.

## 4.2 Transparency and Functionality: Seeing and Feeling Computing in Action

In her pre-interview, Megan described herself as being "really comfortable with a computer" and various software programs but not the coding behind it, in spite of using Scratch in engineering class and "messing around" with some online design tools. She did not choose to take computer science as an elective but was placed into it because the course worked in her schedule. She tried to withdraw from the course and, when that failed, resigned herself to taking computer science because at least it was "better than drama." Given her less than enthusiastic response to the class before the e-textiles unit and initial difficulties with threading needles for conductive sewing, we were not surprised when Megan set out to make the ugliest, creepiest e-textile project she could manage. A family member had given her what she described as an "ugly monkey t-shirt" and she decided that adding lights could only improve upon the design [see Figure 3].

Over time, as Megan added lights and other conductive elements to her shirt and learned more about programming, Megan began to like programming. In her post-interview she said, "I loved programming... we worked with the [LilyPad ProtoSnap boards]...and, um, it was fun seeing how like, if I made this do something, it's gonna vibrate and if I add in this port, it's going to you know, light up here." (post-interview, 5/21/12). The process Megan described—one of being able to build code on a computer and immediately see its impact in the behavior of lights and other actuators—was a central theme in many students' reflections on computing with e-textiles.

When asked to compare e-textiles to other things she had done in computer science, Megan said:

Well, there's a lot more hands-on stuff, there's a lot of what we did before with Alice and, like, making a program happen. But now, it's like, now we have to sew, we have to figure out how the circuits work, and then we can go onto the computer and make stuff happen. But it's a lot more like -- we can touch it, we can feel it, we know what's going on with our hands and not just with looking at it and hoping that it works (post-interview, 5/21/12).

For novices, this ability to connect code to a physical artifact and "know that it works" is highly motivating. As Megan noted, she still had to use the kinds of computational concepts and practices taught in other introductory computer science classes, but she had to link the pieces to a more complex whole and was able to derive instant, incredibly satisfying feedback when testing code. In this sense, the tangibility of making e-textiles made the process of computing more transparent to students.

## 4.3 Positionality and Audience: Using Code to Tell a Story

Eldore also lacked prior computer science experience, but was enamored with code from the beginning of the class. In his pre-interview, he emphasized the progression in his learning about programming and made connections to his love of video games. Eldore decided to make a shirt emphasizing his pride in being Jamaican, with an outline of the island, a smiley face, and "Cool JAM" spelled out. JAM was used not only as short form for Jamaica, but also because of Jamaica's world renown for reggae music. As Eldore described:

> So you can see there's a lot of story behind my shirt... and also, I added a speaker to make it play a Bob Marley song and also I added a LED to show where I was from in Jamaica on the map and... my negative patch was my smiley face and the J-A-M were all my positive patches. And I had it programmed to when you press the negative patch and a letter, it can do a chase effect or it lights up or it just blinks (post-interview, 5/25/12).

What is notable here is the way in which Eldore combines craft and technical elements to tell a story utilizing a coded e-textile artifact, from using an LED to spotlight where he was from in Jamaica to playing reggae music. Furthermore, Eldore's desire for these personal connections pushed him to work through a potential circuitry problem when he had no digital ports remaining for his speaker and to learn more advanced programming skills. The reggae song he chose, Bob Marley's "One Love" is a rhythmically complex song and it took many tries to code the speaker to play something that began to resemble "One Love." As Eldore reflected when asked about challenges he had faced in coding his project:

> Coding challenges... Getting the hertz and everything for the song, the chorus that I'm using... It's very complicated because you have to have the perfect delay in between each note and you have to... sometimes you have to increase the octave and you have to put in another delay after the delay to make it

delay some more. So it's very complicated just to get the sound to do what you want it to do. So... I'm currently working on perfecting that.

Importantly, the speaker wasn't part of Eldore's initial idea but evolved over time as he worked on the project, something that more than likely would have been excluded in more top-down approaches to programming.

Eldore was also excited about showing off his shirt to an audience. Many students reflected similar sentiments in their post-interviews, wanting to show it off to friends and family and then placing it in their rooms as a trophy of sorts. What stood out for us was not only that making an e-textile artifact was seen as a tremendous personal accomplishment (in a way that making a fish swim around an island in Alice was not), but also that parents and friends could understand and share in the accomplishment. The desire of Eldore and other students to use their e-textile artifacts to "say something" to a particular audience highlights the ways in which e-textiles provide a meaningful context for learning computing.

## 4.4 Creativity and Variability: Taking Ownership of Computing

Both Charles and Will enjoyed the greater level of innovation and creativity afforded to them through the e-textiles course. Students were all free to choose the aesthetic design of their projects even though there were a number of technical limitations on all projects (number of LEDs and conductive patches). Charles, in particular, described this as freedom to "create our own thing" for his project. He spoke about the diversity of projects found within the class and how it motivated people:

> So I've seen a whole bunch of different projects like recycling, shamrocks, names, stuff like that. And I think people wanted to complete that, because instead of just having something that someone assigned, you don't really want to complete that because it's not your own, and you know everybody's going to have that (post-interview, 5/15/12).

In his own work, he created a shirt with an icon of an eagle along with letters spelling out the word 'Eagles' in honor of his love of Philadelphia's NFL team, the Eagles (see Figure 4).

While Charles focused on the diversity of project designs, Will focused on the expansive possibilities of coding. In particular, he liked the way that he could code and recode his Scooby-Doo themed t-shirt (see Figure 4): "It's a lot easier to change what you want the shirt to do... [in order to] give the shirt a different look even though it's the exact same thing". Will contrasted this with the "repetitive[ness]" of formal approaches to computer science (i.e., Alice) he was previously exposed to, which he describes as follows: "although we were making different programs, nothing was different. We were programming something to do something and then we would watch it." Within the shared constraints of the e-textile project then, students had what Will called "a bigger realm of creativity" that allowed for greater autonomy and personal expression. Overall, rather than making identical projects, students were motivated by the multiple possibilities of e-textiles to take ownership of the computing process by making something unique to them.

**Figure 4: In-progress e-textiles t-shirts designed by Charles (top) and Will (bottom).**

## 5. DISCUSSION

E-textiles are purposefully designed as a hybrid technology that combines elements of craft and circuitry with computer programming [5]. Our findings suggest that students learning with e-textiles created a link between coding and making that opened up their views of computer science. Across the interviews, we saw students' engagement with bricoleur approaches to computing through the themes of *transparency and functionality* and *creativity and variability*. Rather than being hidden from view in a series of procedures, code is made highly visible through the stitching and the lights turning on and off as part of the design. As Megan described when she talked about coming to love programming, students could trace the circuits they had sewn with their fingers and *feel* their impact, just as they could *see* the code they had written play out in the behavior of the conductive patches, lights, and speakers that were components of their e-textile artifacts. Megan's approach to coding was based more on expressivity and improvisation, rather than abstract, top-down planning. In Will's description of coding and recoding his shirt, he similarly articulates this 'softer' approach to computation, which depends more on constant rearrangement rather than predetermined plans. Other elements of the class, such as external reflections allowed students to see and translate their own and others' work, essentially contributing to an open horizon of observation [13]. These qualities of e-textiles initiated a shift in students' thinking about code, highlighting how a crafts-centered perspective to computation, as opposed to a "black box" perspective [27] can promote shifts in students' epistemological stances.

E-textiles also allowed students to more easily make connections between practical, classroom computing activities and the work done by 'real world' computer scientists.. This became most apparent when looking at the themes of *accessibility* and *positionality/audience*. By making an e-textile t-shirt, Carlton was able to connect what he did in class with what's done by professional computer scientists on commercially available products such as light up sneakers for children or the costumes worn by rock stars and other kinds of performers. Eldore likewise emphasized his ability to show off his Jamaica themed shirt to friends, family, and even strangers on public transportation. He appreciated that others could value his computational handiwork, which was much more difficult in an environment like Alice where student-made games and animations fell short of others' expectations. Most students made these kinds of connections; they saw themselves not only as learners within the classroom, but also as designers making products that had value in the real world. Many students additionally shifted from seeing themselves as inexperienced novices in pre-interviews to individuals with enough experience to help others design and program an e-textile artifact. In these ways our findings suggest that working with e-textiles can help students feel more connected to the work of computer scientists at large.

We would be amiss, however, if we didn't take into account other factors that might explain students' broadened perspectives on computing. While e-textiles could be taught in a very traditional, abstracted way, the design challenge and the social structure of this class loosely followed a studio model of design [26]. Rather than being forced to create identical projects (as occurred in the Alice curriculum), students were given a few constraints (use of the Lilypad, number of LEDs and sensing patches) within which they could create individualized projects. The tangibility of e-textiles in terms of the materials themselves coupled with the studio atmosphere of the class allowed students to observe and constructively critique each others' work, promoting transparency in the process of coding. In other words, beyond the technology itself, the class environment also became a model for transparency. Students could easily share ideas and provide support and critique since the artifacts visibly displayed their work, and could garner attention not only from peers in class but also others outside of the classroom space. This ability to 'show off' one's work suggests a provocative idea about the role of audience in the nature of computing. As highlighted above, students considered their peers and family members as an audience for their computational products; computational work was therefore done not only for themselves or for an assignment but for a personally and culturally relevant audience [9]. Indeed, we could argue that considerations of audience shaped the students' programming and design. The concept of audience, long an important concept in literacy studies [32], may thus have an important role in shaping students' understanding of computing. Key questions that expert writers ask—"What is the purpose of the writing? What form should it take? Who is the audience?" [20 p. 180]—suggest key questions that programmers should also ask: What is the purpose of this code? What form should it take? Who is (or are) the audience(s)? Current standards of computing touch ever so lightly on the need to understand the specifications and requirements for a computer program. We suggest taking this a step further to examine the role of authorship of code, attending to the cognitive and sociocultural conditions of its production and reception by authentic audiences. Might such a connection provide students with critical ways of thinking about various approaches to computation, and their differential values within the field at large? We hope that future research will examine these connections.

E-textiles are part of a broader movement that brings a new layer of concreteness and tangibility to earlier progressive approaches to programming education. Turkle and Papert [33] argued that tinkerers viewed virtual objects on the computer as dabs of paint rather than as abstractions as the planners viewed them. Types of programming software that allow students to program visual objects, such as Scratch, lend themselves to a more artistic, expressive form of computing. Taking this a step further, we suggest that with e-textiles the programmable objects are dabs of light—light controlled by programming LEDs on and off or by altering their levels of brightness. These new computational objects take the artistic expression allowed in progressive programming platforms a step further, especially when combined with the mobility and aesthetics of crafts. They connect computing into multiple domains: personal and playful, artistic and creative, as well as geeky and algorithmic. Students' programming illustrated in this paper has less to do with the efficiency of code (fewer lines of code and more "elegant" solutions) and more to do with enacting their visions of what they want to accomplish. Moving away from the traditional aesthetic of abstract, 'black-boxed' computing than is currently dominant in formal computer science education, this work instead illustrates a personal, functional aesthetic of computing [11] that involves individual expression, practical functionality, and attunement to potential viewers and wearers of the computational object. This is much closer to a vision that computing is a human invention, and that what determines the elegance or beauty of code is a social construct rather than an absolute.

# 6. ACKNOWLEDGMENTS

This work was supported by a collaborative grant (0855868) from the National Science Foundation to Yasmin Kafai, Leah Buechley and Kylie Peppler. Any opinions, findings, and conclusions or recommendations expressed in this chapter are those of the authors and do not necessarily reflect the views of the National Science Foundation the University of Pennsylvania, or Utah State University.

# 7. REFERENCES

[1] Bates, S.P., Galloway, R.K., Loptson, C., & Slaughter, K.A. 2011. How attitudes and beliefs about physics change from high school to faculty. *Physics Education Research, 7*(2), 1-8.

[2] Bennedssen, J. & Caspersen, M.E. 2008. Abstraction ability as an indicator of success for learning computer science? In *ICER '08: Proceeding of the Fourth International Workshop on Computing Education Research* (pp. 15-26). Sydney, Australia: ACM.

[3] Buechley, L. 2006. A construction kit for electronic textiles. In Proceedings of *IEEE International Symposium on Wearable Computers* (ISWC) (pp. 83-92). Montreux, Switzerland.

[4] Buechley, L. & Hill, B. M. 2010. LilyPad in the Wild: How Hardware's Long Tail is Supporting New Engineering and Design Communities. *Proceedings of Designing Interactive systems (DIS)*, 199-207. Aarhus, Denmark: ACM.

[5] Buechley, L., Peppler, K., Eisenberg, M. & Kafai, Y. Eds. 2013. *Textile messages: Dispatches from the world of e-textiles and education.* New York: Peter Lang.

[6] Chambers, D. W. 1983. Stereotypic images of the scientist: The draw-a-scientist test. *Science Education, 67*(2), 255-265.

[7] Charmaz, K. 2003. Grounded Theory. Objectivist and constructionist methods. In N. K. Denzinger and Y. S. Lincoln (Eds.), *Strategies for qualitative inquiry* (2nd edition, pp. 249-291). Thousand Oaks, CA: Sage.

[8] DiSalvo, B. & Bruckman, A. 2011. From Interests To Values: Computer science is not that difficult but wanting to learn it is. *Communications of the ACM*, 27-29.

[9] Enyedy, N., Danish, J. & Fields, D. A. 2011. Negotiating the "relevant" in culturally relevant mathematics. *Canadian Journal of Mathematics,* 11(3), 273-291.

[10] Erickson, F. 2006. Definition and analysis of data from videotape: Some research procedures and their rationales. In J. Green, Camilli, G., & Elmore, P. (Eds.), *Handbook of complementary research methods in education research* (3rd ed.). American Educational Research Association.

[11] Fields, D.A., Kafai, Y.B., & Searle, K.A. 2012. Functional aesthetics for learning: Creative tensions in youth e-textiles designs. In van Aalst, J., Thompson, K., Jacobson, M.J., & Reimann, P. (Eds.), *The Future of Learning: Proceedings of the 10th International Conference of the Learning Sciences (ICLS 2012), Volume 1, Full Papers.* International Society of the Learning Sciences: Sydney, NSW, Australia, 196-203.

[12] Forte, A. & Guzdial, M. 2004. Motivation and nonmajors in computer science: Identifying discrete audiences from introductory courses. *IEEE Transactions on Education,* 48 (2), 248-253.

[13] Greene, J.A., Torney-Purta, J., & Azevedo, R. 2010. Empirical evidence regarding relations among a model of epistemic and ontological cognition, academic performance, and educational level. *Journal of Educational Psychology, 102(1), 234-255.*

[14] Guzdial, M. 2013. Exploring hypotheses about media computation. In *ICER '13: Proceeding of the Ninth International Workshop on Computing Education Research* (pp. 19-26). San Diego, CA: ACM

[15] Hutchins, E. 1995. *Cognition in the Wild.* Cambridge, MA: MIT Press.

[16] Kafai, Y. B. 1995. *Minds in Play.* Hillsdale, NJ: Lawrence Erlbaum Associates.

[17] Kafai, Y., Lee, E., Searle, K., Kaplan, E., Fields, D., & Lui, D. 2014. A Crafts-Oriented Approach to Computing in High School: Introducing Computational Concepts, Practices, and Perspectives with Electronic Textiles. *ACM Transactions on Computing Education,* 14(1), 1-20.

[18] Kelleher, C., Pausch, R., and Kiesler, S. 2007. Storytelling Alice Motivates Middle School Girls to Learn Computer Programming. In Proceedings of the SIGCHI Conference on Human Factors in Computing Systems (pp. 1455-1464). San Jose, CA.

[19] Lee, M.J. 2013. How can a social debugging game effectively teach computer programming concepts? In *ICER'13: Proceeding of the Ninth International Workshop on Computing Education Research* (pp. 181-182). San Diego, CA: ACM.

[20] Magnifico, A.M. 2010. Writing for Whom? Cognition, motivation, and a writer's audience. *Educational Psychologist, 45*(3), 167-184.

[21] Margolis, J. & Fisher, A. 2002. *Unlocking the clubhouse.* Cambridge, MA: The MIT Press.

[22] Margolis, J.. Estella, R., Goode, J., Holme, J., & Nao, K. 2008. *Stuck in the shallow end: Education, race, and computing.* Cambridge, MA: MIT Press.

[23] Martin, C. 2004. Draw a computer scientist. ITiCSE-WGR '04 Working group reports from ITiCSE on Innovation and technology in computer science education (pp. 11-12). New York, NY: ACM.

[24] Meerbaum-Salant, O., Armoni, M. & Ben-Ari, M. 2010. Learning Computer Science Concepts with Scratch. In *ICER '10: Proceeding of the Sixth International Workshop on Computing Education Research* (pp. 69-76). Aarhus, Denmark: ACM.

[25] National Research Council. 2011. *Successful K-12 STEM Education.* Washington, DC: The National Academies Press.

[26] Porter, L., Guzdial, M., McDowell, C., & Simon, B. 2013. Success in introductory programming: What works? *Communications of the ACM, 56*(8), 34-36.

[27] Resnick, M., Berg, R., & Eisenberg, M. 2000. Beyond Black Boxes: Bringing Transparency and Aesthetics Back to Scientific Investigation. *Journal of the Learning Sciences, 9*(1), 7-30.

[28] Sandoval, W.A. 2005. Understanding students' practical epistemologies and their influence on learning through inquiry. *Science Education, 89*, 634-656.

[29] Sawyer, K. 2012. Learning how to create: Toward a learning sciences of art and design. In *Proceedings of the 10th International Conference of the Learning Sciences (ICLS 2012)* (pp. 33-39). Sydney, Australia: International Society of the Learning Sciences.

[30] Searle, K., Kafai, Y., & Fields, D.A. 2013. Building New Clubhouses of Computing with Electronic Textiles: Reshaping Gendered Histories of Computing for High School Youth. Paper presented at the American Educational Research Association Annual Meeting. San Francisco, CA.

[31] Simon, B., Hanks, B., Murphy, L., Fitzgerald, S., McCauley, R., Thomas, L., & Zander, C. 2008. Saying isn't necessarily believing: Influencing self-theories in computing. In *ICER '08: Proceeding of the Fourth International Workshop on Computing Education Research* (pp. 173-184). Sydney, Australia: ACM

[32] Thesen, L. 2001. Modes, literacies, and power: A university case study. *Language and Education, 15*(2 & 3), 132-145.

[33] Turkle, S. & Papert, S. 1990. Epistemological pluralism and the reevaluation of the concrete. *SIGNS: Journal of Women in Culture and Society, 16*(1), 128-157. Retrieved on October 13, 2013 from http://papert.org/articles/EpistemologicalPluralism.html.

[34] Wing, J. M. 2006. Computational thinking. *Communications of the ACM, 49*, 33-35.

[35] Yardi, S. & Bruckman, A. 2007. What is computing? Bridging the gap between teenagers' perceptions and graduate students' experiences. In *Proceedings of the 3rd International Workshop on Computing Education Research* (pp. 39-50), Atlanta, GA.

# New Enactments of Mentoring and Activism

## U.S. Women of Color in Computing Education and Careers

Apriel K. Hodari
Eureka Scientific, Inc
2452 Delmer Street Suite 100
Oakland, CA 94602-3017
00 1 510 530 1688
AKHodari@EurekaSci.com

Maria Ong
TERC
2067 Massachusetts Avenue
Cambridge, MA 02140
00 1 617 873 9600
Maria_Ong@terc.edu

Lily T. Ko
TERC
2067 Massachusetts Avenue
Cambridge, MA 02140
00 1 617 873 9600
Lily_Ko@terc.edu

Rachel R. Kachchaf
TERC
2067 Massachusetts Avenue
Cambridge, MA 02140
00 1 617 873 9600
Rachel_Kachchaf@terc.edu

## ABSTRACT

In this paper we present themes from our National Science Foundation-funded projects, *Beyond the Double Bind: Women of Color in STEM* and *Computing Beyond the Double Bind: Women of Color in Computing Education and Careers*. The findings come from 14 interviews and 85 extant texts about 40 women of color. Our study contributes an analysis of how the intersection of gender and race affects career and education experiences in computing. We ask, *What strategies work to enable U.S. women of color to achieve higher levels of advancement in computing education and careers?* The findings bring to light new, emergent enactments of support, mentoring, and activism. This research will increase knowledge about success strategies to retain U.S. women of color, a population widely considered an untapped source of talent to fill the country's and the world's scientific workforce needs. The research may also provide other countries with new strategies to explore to retain and promote their underrepresented groups in computing.

## Categories and Subject Descriptors

K.3.2 [**Computers and Education**]: Computer and Information Science Education – *computer science education*; K.7.4 [**The Computing Profession**]: Professional Ethics – *codes of ethics, codes of good practice;* A.0 [**General**]: *conference proceedings.*

**Keywords:** computing; race; gender; women of color; mentoring; success; support; activism

## 1. INTRODUCTION

Research has shown that diverse groups' unique backgrounds, cultural traditions, perspectives, and experiences could bring dramatically new approaches to discovery and innovation within science, technology, engineering and mathematics (STEM) fields [1,2]. Thus, to remain globally competitive, all nations would

benefit from increasing the size and diversity of their computing workforce.

In the U.S., as in other parts of the world (e.g., [3-5]), women, and especially women of color (African American or Black, Latina, Native American, Asian American, Arab American, or mixed race women), are a promising, underutilized resource that could contribute innovative approaches to fields such as computing. As U.S. colleges are already majority female (57%) and are increasingly enrolling more minority students (44%), women of color represent a growing source of untapped talent to help meet the nation's and the world's computing needs. However, the trends of women of color earning degrees and entering careers in computing fields runs counter to what one should expect. From 2001 to 2010, the percent of women of color receiving a bachelor's degree in computer science declined from 12.2% to 6.8% (see Figure 1) [6,7].

**Figure 1. Percent of U.S. Women of Color Receiving Bachelor's Degrees in Computer Science: 2001-2010[1] [6,7]**

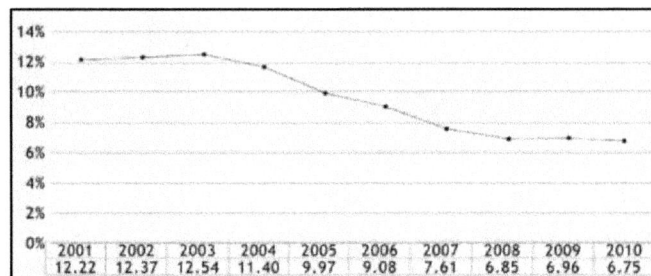

| | 2001 | 2002 | 2003 | 2004 | 2005 | 2006 | 2007 | 2008 | 2009 | 2010 |
|---|---|---|---|---|---|---|---|---|---|---|
| | 12.22 | 12.37 | 12.54 | 11.40 | 9.97 | 9.08 | 7.61 | 6.85 | 6.96 | 6.75 |

An education in computing offers great employment opportunities. In 2009, individuals with degrees in computer sciences and mathematics (CSM) held 21% of all jobs in the science and engineering (S&E) fields and 17% of research and development jobs [8]. Unfortunately, the representation of U.S. women of color in computing has been decreasing [6,7], even as national job prospects in technology fields increase [9]—the U.S. Bureau of Labor projects a 64% increase in CSM occupations by 2016—and as the representation of women of color is increasing in nearly every other STEM field [10].

---

[1] This data includes only U.S. citizens and permanent residents.

The low representation of U.S. women of color in computing also raises an important social justice issue: schools and workplaces must make greater efforts to address social and cultural inequities and to achieve environments that support broadened participation in STEM. While many institutions have attempted such efforts, the statistics show that too few are succeeding.

While our study is focused on American women of color, the findings may be relevant to many countries where the computing fields have little diversity in terms of race and gender. The large declines in computing education and careers for women of color may appear to be insoluble, but they are, in fact, a great opportunity. Through the voices of the 40 women of color from our study, we uncover and make explicit the assumptions, attitudes, beliefs, and practices that enable, or impose limitations on, these women. We ask:

*What strategies work to enable U.S. women of color to achieve higher levels of advancement in computing education and careers?*

Our analysis reveals a range of supportive people, policies and practices, and new findings and activism that push computing education towards increased inclusion and productivity.

## 2. CONCEPTUAL FRAMEWORK

U.S. women of color are severely underrepresented in STEM fields, and little research exists to examine the experiences of these women. Because of their race and gender, women of color are caught in a double bind, an idea first advanced by Shirley Malcom, Paula Hall, and Janet Brown, in their 1976 AAAS report, *The Double Bind: The Price of Being a Minority Woman in Science* [11]. The authors argue that the struggles to be scientists are greater for women of color than for white women or for men of any color. A comment by Tiffani Bell, an African American early career computing entrepreneur, illustrates the situation for many women of color in computing when she describes the difficulty of breaking into a computing community [12]:

*Coming in as a double minority—a black woman—has been tough in the tech space. It's also hard being located in North Carolina... there's a pretty healthy VC [venture capital] community. But the tech scene there is just as homogenous in some respects, plus you just don't have the access to people like you do in Silicon Valley. It's been great to talk to these big names—and to show that a lot of us in the tech space might not fit the image of what you'd expect.*

Research suggests that women who dually occupy the particularly undervalued identities of femaleness and non-whiteness [13,14] often experience challenges to a degree that white women and men of color do not [15-17]. Thus, intersectionality theory allows for a deeper understanding of the experiences of women of color in computer science by describing how their race and gender function simultaneously [18]. Empirical research on women of color in computer science (e.g., [19-22]) and personal narratives (e.g., [23,24]) illustrate how the intersection of race and gender can cause women to feel as though they are "being divided between two groups by society" ([23], p. 22). Taylor [24] further explains that, "women of color usually participate in both women's organizations in computing as well as ethnic organizations; yet, any one group meets only part of their needs." Women of color often do not have their needs fully met and are usually "the only one" in their computing department, resulting in isolation [19,25,24]. Research also suggests that this "sense of isolation is often heightened by what they perceive as an unwelcoming environment and others' lowered expectations of them." [26]

A comment by Serena[2], an Asian American postdoctoral scholar in computing education research, provides a vivid illustration of the abilities of women of color to rise above their isolation and succeed where so many around them do not [26].

*In my computer science class, a lot of the projects were group [work] and so I found two... [minority] groupmates, who were heaven-sent. And we stuck by each other and actually, after we found each other, planned all of our schedules in sync with each other, so we took the same classes in order to get through the undergraduate experience together. Because a part of being a minority is that people don't want to work with you. They don't look at you and sense that you are a smart person they want to work with. So finding people who believe in you and you believe in, and then sticking together, was really important.* [Originally cited in 26.]

Research has shown that the isolation Serena described is frequently compounded by a lack of access to mentors and role models who look like them and understand their experiences [27,25]. Yet, mentoring and a sense of community are repeatedly cited as essential in promoting young women of color in computing [19,28,29]. Researchers have suggested that mentoring is a critical factor to promote women of color in nontraditional fields, and that women of color seek out academic and personal support from a host of networks, including family, faculty, and peers inside and outside of STEM [19]. Others have found that women of color who experience isolation often become mentors later in their careers [30-32,29], providing invaluable resources for future women of color computing professionals.

Another method that women of color use to combat isolation is to enact activism—which we define as "STEM-related volunteer work"—to improve their own environments and create opportunities for women who follow them. While existing literature (e.g., [19]) mentions examples of activism, very few have examined it in detail, including various meanings it holds for women of color. In our previous work (e.g., [33,34]), we found that activism was often catalyzed by experiences related to race, gender or both. For instance, Chloe, then a physics graduate student and now a cosmologist, talked about a program she volunteered for, at her school, in which her groups had mostly non-white females. She recalled:

*[B]ecause I'm always either one of only two female mentors that they can choose from... I had two students from [where] my family's from... So for me, it was really, really exciting to have these young women of Caribbean origin in my group.* [Originally cited in 34.]

Our previous studies have described motivations, tactics, self-sacrifice, and doubts about activism for these women of color in physics, astrophysics and astronomy. In analyzing our data on women of color in computing, we found new enactments of activism that build on computing technology's inherent accessibility and amenability for promoting social justice aims. In an interview for PBS, Shaundra Daily, an African American computing professional, describes how an experience teaching children how to program "lights," music, and animations that were controlled through sensors attached to their bodies" while she was a graduate student at MIT [35]. From this experience, she

---

[2] All first-names-only are pseudonyms for people we interviewed.

and her husband started a company that helps African American students incorporate performance arts and technology, such as learning swing dance or hip hop, then learning to program a virtual dance partner. In doing this, Daily used technology for her teaching and helped students *create* technology to increase participation of under-served youth in computing.

Mentoring and activism are examples of what we describe as a range of support successful women of color experience in computing. Following an explanation of our data and methods, we will use this range to contextualize our findings. We present detailed insight into women of color's experiences pursuing computing, focusing on experiences of being mentored and the activism women enact to prevent others from experiencing isolation. We ask: What aspects did women of color in computing note as helpful or lacking from their educational and career experiences? We discuss the implications of these findings and develop recommendations for policies and practices that support the success of women of color in computing.

## 3. DATA AND METHODS

Our data come from two National Science Foundation (NSF)-funded research studies: *Beyond the Double Bind: Women of Color in STEM* (BDB) and *Computing Beyond the Double Bind: Women of Color in Computing Education and Careers* (CBDB). Both studies are empirical research studies with goals of advancing knowledge about women of color in STEM by analyzing the educational and career navigation strategies of women of color. CBDB has additional goals of studying programs that have successfully served women of color in computing and creating a mentoring intervention for young women of color in computing based on our findings.

Data for this paper are a subset from the larger studies described above; they comprise interviews, extant texts and program analyses that reflect the lived experiences of successful women of color in computing education and careers.

### 3.1 Data Sources

We gathered data on 40 women of color in computing through three sources in our studies.

#### 3.1.1 Case Study Data: A National Computing Community

Our analysis includes case study data from one national student support community, Coalition[3]. This community serves a diverse population (by race, gender, class, immigrant status, physical ability and family educational background). Students come from many different educational and geographic settings. The programs, events, and other opportunities provided within this community promote computing excellence for their students and increase participation of underrepresented students in cutting edge computing organizations. We conducted a three-day site visit of Coalition in 2013. Our data collection methodology included ethnographic field notes in various contexts (e.g., community spaces, meetings, conferences, classrooms, collaborative spaces) and interviews with staff, affiliated faculty, and students. For this paper, the ethnographic fieldnotes helped to contextualize the lived experiences of some of the women of color in our study. For this analysis, we included eight interviews with computing students and three interviews with computing professionals from Coalition (see section 3.1.3 for interview methods).

*3.1.2 Extant Texts*

Our sources also included 85 extant texts—publicly available documents that we had no hand in shaping and were not written for research purposes, but were treated as data [36]—that were written between 1996 and 2013. The texts were autobiographies, biographies, interviews, news articles, journal articles or personal essays. They were located by conducting online searches of key terms related to women of color and computing. Our project's selection criteria required the texts to include full descriptions or stories of personal successes, challenges, and sources of inspiration or support in STEM.

*3.1.3 Interviews*

We conducted 15 interviews to gather a limited but in-depth set of contemporary, discipline-specific experiences and viewpoints that may not have been represented in the public extant texts. The majority of interviews were conducted in person during a Coalition event, though four were conducted by phone. Coalition participants were voluntary. We selected the four participants from a pool of candidates who were recommended to us through broad personal and professional networks, and via email solicitations to professional organizations for women or minorities in STEM. Interviews were semi-structured, open-ended, lasted between 1 to 1.5 hours, audio-recorded and transcribed. Participants were asked a broad set of questions about their academic background and interests, a challenging time and how they overcame it, factors that promote their success, mentoring and role models, and advice for institutions and individuals like themselves. Interviewees from Coalition were asked a set of questions regarding their experiences as part of the community and at community events.

*3.1.4 Data Demographics*

**Table 1. Career stage of participants**

| Career stage | Number |
|---|---|
| Undergraduate student | 4 |
| Graduate student | 5 |
| Postdoctoral fellow | 2 |
| Early Career | 6 |
| Mid Career | 11 |
| Late Career | 12 |

**Table 2. Career stage of participants**

| Race / Ethnicity[4] | Number |
|---|---|
| Black | 16 |
| Arab American | 2 |
| Asian American | 3 |
| Latina | 14 |
| Native American | 2 |
| Mixed race[5] | 2 |
| Unknown woman of color[6] | 1 |

---

[3] A pseudonym.

[4] Our sample includes three international students who came to the U.S. for undergraduate or graduate education in computing.

[5] This is one African American/Asian American woman, and one Latina/White woman.

[6] From an extant text in which the woman was identified as a woman of color, but the specific race was not published.

## 3.2 Data Analysis

Riessman [37] states that *narrative analysis*, a method of seeing beyond individual life stories to broader patterns, is especially effective for understanding the experiences of those who are traditionally marginalized. For our studies, narrative analysis required transparent processes of laying out stories, identifying codes, entering codes into a matrix, then inductively creating conceptual groupings and orderings from the data. Building categories of themes from the bottom up (see [38]), we coded and discussed until we established a comprehensive set of themes. The data coding process included individual coding, paired consensus, and routine team calibrations to ensure that all members were applying emergent codes in similar manners. We were then individually assigned a set of related codes to detect emerging themes. Team members exchanged their work with one another, and everyone then analyzed the themes to affirm or re-construct the themes. By combining these systematic methods and utilizing multiple researchers, the researchers created a form of triangulation to develop their understanding of the experiences of women of color.

## 4. FINDINGS

U.S. women of color face complex challenges in computing, and in doing so, they experience a range of supportive and unsupportive people, policies and practices. For this paper, we are presenting findings, which focus on success factors for women of color in two areas: supportive practices and activism. In presenting supportive practices, we describe a broad range of institutional and organizational structures and individual mentoring behaviors that support women of color, followed by a detailed account of activism activities in computing. Across these findings, we seek to understand policies and practices enacted by institutions, individuals, and the women themselves, all of which promote their success in computing. These findings point to clear opportunities for both organizations and individuals to increase the success of *everyone* in computing, but they have been found to be particularly helpful for women of color.

## 4.1 Supportive Practices

We found that among supportive experiences, women of color reported a range. We identified six themes to describe this range. The first theme reflects actions taken at the institutional or organizational level to provide a supportive environment to women of color. The next five themes are mentoring actions taken at the individual level that encourage and promote women of color to persist and excel in computing. The six themes follow:

- Some institutions, departments, and groups were active in **Creating Warm Environments In and Out of STEM** to promote women of color's success.
- Individuals who practiced **Verbalizing Faith and Encouraging the Pursuit of STEM** helped women of color overcome lack of confidence.
- Those who were in the position of **Serving as a Role Model** helped women of color connect to disciplinary communities and empowered success.
- Faculty and other mentors who were **Being Generous with their Time and were Helping with STEM Content** demonstrated that women of color were worthy of investments of time and effort.
- Those who were helping women of color in **Navigating the Science Environment** often helped to provide them with missing resources and social capital.

- Individuals who were **Demonstrating a Caring Attitude** provided women with a strong sense of social support, which was found to be as essential as support with technical content or with building professional networks.

### 4.1.1 Creating Warm Environments In and Out of STEM

Our participants described some aspects of how they benefited from institutions' and groups' efforts of creating warm environments in and out of STEM. Maddie, an Asian American computational scientist, described how the environment of her all-female undergraduate institution supported her intellectual and emotional development:

*If I had to do it over again, I would definitely go back to a women's college. I think it was really, really worth it because it gave me a nice time to kind of develop. Undergraduate, you know, you have to kind of develop your foundation… kind of intellectually, emotionally, if that makes sense. You know? I mean, kind of like you have to develop a certain confidence for yourself intellectually that I think a same-sex environment really helps with.*

Corinda, an African graduate student in computer science, served as a leader of a group for women faculty, graduate students and undergraduates, where they discussed computing content, professionalism and leadership skills, but they also could relied on each other as a community. She said:

*We have a lot of social events… I feel, as a woman, it's always good to have a group of women where we, we call it like an ice cream event where we say we're not discussing academics today, let's be women and just enjoy ourselves. We tend to have like things like that. To me, I feel that has helped us to have like a small community where you see them outside and you're like, oh hi.*

As a student who grew up outside the U.S., Corinda found that this kind of socializing helped her feel at home within the institution, and thereby promoted her ability to succeed in computing.

### 4.1.2 Verbalizing Faith and Encouraging the Pursuit of STEM

Family members often provided crucial support to women of color in computing even when their support was not directly related to STEM content. Although this phenomenon is not unique to women of color, the cultural contexts from which many women of color come often provide different types of encouragement and support from those experienced by men and white women [26]. Sometimes, this support must counter inter-generational beliefs about what girls and women can or should do. Miranda, a Latina undergraduate in computer science, described how her father instilled confidence in her by articulating his faith in her to do whatever she wanted:

*I remember when I was little I wanted to learn how to ride a horse because my grandpa was teaching my little brother. I got on the horse and my grandpa tried to take me off. My dad grabbed me and put me back on the horse and said, "She can do anything she wants." Ever since that moment he's been one of the driving forces… he's one of the people who encourages me more and he still tells me I can do anything that I want to. He's helped me get the competitive trait; he's helped me develop that. I'm just as hard headed as he can be.*

Miranda indicated that the confidence and "competitive trait" that she developed as a result of her father's expressed faith in her helped her to persist and excel in her computing studies.

Unfortunately, not all participants felt supported, and when others doubted the women, it affected their science careers. We present a counterexample to Verbalizing Faith. After Maddie, an Asian American Ph.D. student in computational science, had an unsuccessful presentation, her advisor expressed extreme disappointment in her, saying he had "serious doubts about [her] scientific abilities." Furthermore, rather than discuss Maddie's performance, he stopped communicating with her for months. Maddie explained the harmful effect this had on her motivation to pursue computing:

*It was kind of, unfortunately, a defining moment which probably pushed me away from science... I eventually got a thesis and defended* [but] *we never really spoke about that again... He said he was relieved to know that I wasn't completely clueless, but it was really upsetting, because his first assumption was that I was clueless.*

The short narratives of Miranda and Maddie illustrate the importance of strong and consistent expressions of faith in the abilities of women of color to retain them in computing.

## 4.1.3 Serving as a Role Model

Role models served as a critical source of support for many women, as examples of what success looks like. For some women, role models need only be people who look like them attending a computing event. Amanda, an African American postdoctoral scholar in information science, said:

*Well first of all, it's a beautiful* [event]. *I can tell you that I've never gone to a*[n event] *and said, "These people look like me." I mean literally, people look like me. We could be cousins. I love that about the* [event].

When we asked women what the social environment at a Coalition event felt like, they gave us several examples of the importance of role models. Francesa, an Asian American computer science undergraduate, said:

*I feel somewhat empowered because like I said earlier, there are a lot of women who are really successful, and I guess they've been through a lot of some like hurdles along their way that they needed to overcome, and they overcame them successfully. And I can learn from their experiences as well.*

Role models also helped women of color connect to disciplinary communities and thereby empowered success. In the words of Hailey, an Arab American graduate student:

*I love the social aspect of* [Coalition]. *I love how amazingly easy to talk to everybody is, and the ones who are high up understand that these students are in need to network and need to be pushed up and stuff. So they don't have a lot of expectations as to like... it's not like an expectation. It's more like, "I'm here to help you so just let me know how I can do that" sort of attitude.*

Further, Amanda, a Black postdoctoral scholar, describes the accessibility of several different mentors:

*I talk to* [Woman's Full Name] *here. I've seen her. I was talking to her earlier, maybe two years ago and I just walked up to her. "How's it going?" She was in...we talked. She was like, "Look. You just asked me questions. I'm good at answering." She was mentoring me. I would call her a mentor.* [Woman's First Name], *I talk to her.* [Man's First Name], *I've talked to him. Some random guy that I met and like he was giving me...* [laughs] *And*

[Man's First Name], *that was his assigned role. But at this point, I know I have mentors all over the place if I need something. If I need support, I know where to go. And I think it's partly because of this* [Coalition event]. *I don't know if I could say that if we didn't have these* [Coalition events].

## 4.1.4 Being Generous with Time and Helping with Computing Content and Skills

Many participants described needing support to master aspects of learning computing content, including: technical skills, research skills, and presenting skills. Francesa, an Asian American undergraduate in computer science, described how one of her professors supported her and her peers' development by being generous with his time, and thereby creating space for them to learn. He did so without relaxing his expectation of excellence:

*He actually pushes you to your limit until you get the answer. Even though it'll take you days to figure out, he tries to guide you step by step, unlike some of my teachers back in high school. He has the patience, and he will just wait and wait, and not let you get discouraged.*

While this professor held high expectations, his patience created a comfortable and exciting environment for student learning. Similarly, Lexie described how having an advisor support her to learn the content helped her overcome challenging times:

*My adviser is really helpful, because he has been doing database research for a really long time, and he's seen a lot of what there is to see. So, I could pretty much ask him anything... he'll know the answer... When I'm stuck, he's really good about putting me back on track.*

These interactions took place at the professional level, too. For example, Cindy Vasquez, a Latina professional in industry, received leadership skills training from an internal mentoring relationship that she sought out. Because of the time the mentor took in this relationship, Cindy "advanced from being an individual contributor learning her job to training new team members." Georgette, a Latina professor, also describes how the continuing generosity of a long-time mentor is helpful to her. She says:

*I pick up the phone and I call them when I have...like with* [Man's first name]...*I spent three hours yesterday with* [Man's First name]. *I left right after the second plenary in the afternoon. I spent all afternoon talking with him in his office for three hours and then we went and had dinner with his wife. It's that asking advice..."Here's the situations I'm facing. This is how I've been dealing with it. What do you think?"...getting that kind of feedback. And there are other times when I really need to make a quick decision, I call them.*

Having support to tackle difficult facets of computing, including technical and interpersonal skills, were key elements of support that helped participants advance in the field.

## 4.1.5 Navigating the Science Environment

Previous research [34] found that women of color dedicate large amounts of energy to navigating a science environment in which they greatly differ from their peers. A few women in our study noted that, unlike the majority of their white male peers, they were the first in their families to attend college and/or pursue computing and therefore needed support to navigate the environment. Serena, an Asian American educational researcher with degrees in computer science and educational technology, described the challenges of growing up as the first in her family and first among her close friends to be on the path to pursue higher education and computing:

*One component, out of many, of being an immigrant—in particular, an immigrant whose parents don't have access to a lot of resources—is that you don't come with a lot of social capital... You're really, from the ground up, building a set of networks and you don't have a lot of mentors... whether it's the time you go in high school taking SATs because your parents have no clue and have never even heard of it, don't know anything about what college applications should look like, don't really know friends or have other people that they know at their companies that are in positions where they could write you letters of recommendation... And so, I didn't have, kind of access to this whole set of social capital at that time that made it make a difference.*

As Serena's comment illustrates, social capital can be decisive. In a counterexample regarding the having and sharing of social capital, Lexie, an African American and Asian American graduate student in computer science, explained how her mentors formed a powerful network of support and assisted her in locating proper resources to succeed in her field. Lexie's advisor, who had many connections with companies in the area, helped Lexie get an internship after her first year of graduate school, and encouraged her to network with important people who could further her career. Furthermore, Lexie benefited from having older graduate student peers who helped her find new opportunities in the field:

*They sort of know the ropes as far as what you want, when you want to get things done in the building or good resources for whatever project I'm working on. And lots of times, they'll forward me things that sound relevant to me, if they see them on the web... They might mention a project that they worked on or someone else worked on that sounds like I might be interested in it for my work. So, they'll tell me what paper to read or what project to find.*

Here, Lexie's peers served not only as role models, but as also as strategic resources to help her advance in her classes. While Lexie interacted with these peers on a regular basis, Serena described how a simple, yet significant, piece of advice helped her advance. While Serena was working in industry, a colleague advised her to write down her accomplishments weekly—even if they felt minor—rather than waiting until right before her review for promotions and raises. Serena acknowledged the significance of this advice saying, "If I didn't do that, there were so many…little things that I had done that would have kind of fallen by the wayside if I had waited until the end of the year." By recording her contributions, Serena kept detailed evidence of her professional worth, not only for the sake of her company, but for herself as well.

### 4.1.6 Demonstrating a Caring Attitude

Our participants noted that it was not enough for someone to provide support to learn content and build a strong network, but having a mentor care for the woman was just as critical. Types of caring attitudes included being approachable, expressing belief in the woman, and demonstrating interest in her personal life. This support often came from individuals in positions of authority, such as advisors and supervisors. Vallerie Parrish-Porter, a black computing professional, tried to model her own behavior after her approachable supervisor, whom she considered her mentor and "a true leader." His impact on her was notable, as her colleagues said, "Parrish-Porter's most endearing trait is her personal touch." Similarly, Lexie explained how her advisor encouraged her by being "really good about driving [her] to get stuff done without making [her] feel bad," and allowing her to ask "dumb questions"

without making her feel uncomfortable. As a result, Lexie gained confidence in her own abilities.

Supporters also exhibited moral support by demonstrating interest in participants' personal lives. Cosette, a Black computing professional in industry, said of her boss, "he definitely cares about me and my family life and what's going on with me," something Cossette greatly appreciated, as family was a top priority for her. Furthermore, her boss understood the work-life balance issues that Cosette navigated as she pursued a graduate degree and worked full-time:

*I [could say], "Hey, I stayed up really late last night writing a paper. Do you mind if I come in late?" at the last minute or such like that... They're definitely very understanding and they definitely want you to succeed.*

Clearly, our participants felt that good supportive practices went beyond teaching technical skills and supporters cared about the women on a deeper level, something that helped them be successful in the field.

## 4.2 Computing Technology *for* Activism

Our analysis also revealed a specific form of activism enacted by women of color in computing. We have previously reported on how women of color in physics, astrophysics and astronomy enact activism, which we define as "STEM-focused volunteer work" [39]. In our data on women of color in computing, we find a very particular kind of activism, one in which women use disciplinary knowledge itself to enact their activism.

Current computing technology is a particularly accessible and amenable medium for promoting social justice aims. Not only is computing technology used as a communication medium for activism, but many computing activists also create technology as part of their activism. As the story of Shaundra Daily illustrates (see Conceptual Framework), computing technology can be used both for teaching content and to increase participation of underserved youth.

Serena, an Asian American postdoctoral scholar in computing education research, told us:

*I'm really interested in issues of power and empowerment in the classroom—specifically among marginalized youth. And my own background's in computer science and I'm really excited about and interested in getting young people excited about technology. But not just technology from a consumption standpoint, but technology from a production standpoint. So really, what does it look like to get young people to not just use the internet or surf the web or look at movies or clips on YouTube, but really be kind of powerful producers, in a computational, media environment where they are expressive, they are creative, they are the ones in the position of power to make choices that will constrain and guide how other people use their technology?*

Serena enacted this by teaching lessons to students expelled from a mainstream high school on construction projects in a virtual space. She explicitly taught the technology content in a context where marginalized students could recognized "themes of relevance in their lives and in their communities as the launching point for their work in developing computational literacy." Thus, Serena taught students to create technology that empowers them, a social justice goal. Although their forms of activism could have been undertaken by others, these women's gendered and raced identities served as both personal motivation and points of connection to the populations they served.

Similar to our previous findings in other STEM fields, activism in computing instills confidence in undergraduate students; provides safe spaces where students can talk about their experiences; and provides information about career opportunities in the field.

Unlike other disciplines, computing technology is often central to the activism itself. This provides the additional opportunity for women who participate in activism, particularly students, to increase their computing skills while promoting the success of their peers and those that follow them. Activism often extends beyond the original scope of the project, as Francesa, an Asian computer science undergraduate student, articulates:

*So basically these games actually helped beginning algebra students to learn math, which is really, really cool. And we've been trying to continue it as much as we can until today. We're still trying to code up our games, and I think the plan would be that we're going to upload it to our school website and then other people can use it for free.*

This additional plan to make the games they developed available to a broader audience is a unique feature of computing due to the ease and relatively low cost of making products like this accessible.

## 4.3 Limitations of the Study

The numbers of participants in our study are not meant to be a racial representation amongst the current representation among computer science. We aimed to have a purposive sample that included women of various races and ethnicities, as well as women in differing career stages. Individuals and programs self-selected into the study and may differ from those who did not volunteer to participate.

## 5. CONCLUSIONS & IMPLICATIONS

Our findings inform an analysis of the ways in which the experiences of U.S. women of color are shaped by the intersection of race and gender, and how this intersection influences persistence in computing. We described a range of positive support women received, and highlighted two themes in the lives of women of color as they navigate computing education and careers: technology for activism and being mentored in computing. These are only two salient themes that have surfaced from the many we have discovered, and we look forward to discussing more in the future. By producing an expanded knowledge base about success factors for retaining women of color, we aim to enhance efforts of the STEM education research community to broaden overall participation rates of women of color in computing professions and transform understanding of the challenges they face as they work towards their educational and career objectives. Some notable insights into and implications for teaching and learning follow:

- Create and nurture school and work environments that are welcoming and supportive of all of its participants, as well as sensitive to those who are non-traditional in the field;
- Strictly enforce a zero-tolerance policy for racial or gender discrimination;
- Verbalize your faith in women of color to succeed in computing to them;
- Provide women of color and other marginalized groups with formal mentoring;
- Create opportunities, such as departmental social events, for informal mentoring and networking to take place;
- Be generous with your time in helping students learn STEM content and skills, including research and professional skills;

- Invite open dialogue, through formal events and informal conversations, on racial- or gender-related issues in computing;
- Support women of color in their efforts to diversify computing; identify opportunities in which they may participate.

## 6. ACKNOWLEDGMENTS
We are grateful to Jodut Hashmi and Irene Liefshitz, for their dedication and help in coding and organizing the data. This material is based upon work supported by the National Science Foundation under Grant Nos. CNS-1240768 and DRL-0909762. Any opinions, findings, and conclusions or recommendations expressed in this material are those of the authors and do not necessarily reflect the views of the National Science Foundation.

## 7. REFERENCES
[1] Page, S. 2007. *The Difference: How the Power of Diversity Creates Better Groups, Firms, Schools, and Societies.* Princeton, NJ: Princeton University Press.

[2] Spencer, D. B. and Dawes, S. 2009. *Report of the Advisory Committee for GPRA Performance Assessment: FY 2009* (NSF Report 09-68). Arlington, VA: National Science Foundation.

[3] Adams, E. S., Hazzan, O., Loftsson, H., and Young, A. 2003. International perspective of women and computer science. *ACM SIGCSE Bulletin, 35*(1), 45-46.

[4] Craig, A., Fisher, J., Forgasz, H., and Lang, C. 2011. Evaluation framework underpinning the digital divas programme. In *Proceedings of the 16th Annual Joint Conference on Innovation and Technology in Computer Science Education* (Darmstadt, Germany, 2011). ACM, New York, NY, 313-317. DOI= 10.1145/1999747.1999835

[5] Tupu, J., Ngatuere, J., and A. Young. 2004. Te Korowai Hou. In *Proceedings of the 17th Annual Conference of the NACCQ* (Tauranga, 2004). 191-200. Retrieved from http://www.citrenz.ac.nz/conferences/2004/tupu.pdf

[6] National Science Foundation. 2013. *Table 5-3. Bachelor's degrees awarded, by field, citizenship, and race/ethnicity: 2001–10.* [Data table]. Retrieved from http://nsf.gov/statistics/wmpd/2013/tables.cfm

[7] National Science Foundation. 2013. *Table 5-4. Bachelor's degrees awarded to women, by field, citizenship, and race/ethnicity: 2001–10.* [Data table]. Retrieved from http://nsf.gov/statistics/wmpd/2013/tables.cfm

[8] Bureau of Labor Statistics. 2010. Office of Occupational Statistics and Employment Projections. *Science and Engineering Indicators 2010, 3-32.*

[9] Thibodeau, P. 2012. IT jobs will grow 22% through 2020, says U.S. *Computerworld*. Retrieved from http://www.computerworld.com/s/article/9225673/IT_jobs_will_grow_22_through_2020_says_U.S.

[10] National Science Foundation, Division of Science Resources Statistics. 2011. *Women, Minorities, and Persons with Disabilities in Science and Engineering: 2011.* Special Report NSF 11-309. Arlington, VA. Retrieved from http://www.nsf.gov/statistics/wmpd/

[11] Malcom, S., Hall, P., and Brown, J. 1976. *The Double Bind: The Price of Being a Minority Woman in Science.* American Association for the Advancement of Science. Washington, DC.

[12] Bell, T. 2011. *8 entrepreneurs diversifying the tech scene.* CNN Money. Retrieved from http://money.cnn.com/galleries/2011/technology/1107/gallery.newme_accelerator/5.html; retrieved 30 August 2011.

[13] Ong, M. 2008. Challenging Cultural Stereotypes of "Scientific Ability." In M. Pollock, Ed., *Everyday Antiracism: Getting Real about Race in School.* New Press, New York, NY, 114-119.

[14] Traweek, S. 1988. *Beamtimes and Lifetimes: The World of High Energy Physicists.* Harvard University Press, Cambridge, MA.

[15] Hamilton, K. 2004. Faculty Science Positions Continue to Elude Women of Color. *Black Issues in Higher Education*, 21, 3, 36-39.

[16] Lugones, M. 1994. Purity, Impurity, and Separation. *Signs*, 19, 2, 458-79.

[17] Wei, V. W. 1996. Asian Women and Employment Discrimination: Using Intersectionality Theory to Address Title VII Claims Based on Combined Factors of Race, Gender and National Origin. *Boston College Law Review,* 37, 4, 771-812.

[18] Crenshaw, K., "Demarginalizing the Intersection of Race and Sex: A Black Feminist Critique of Antidiscrimination Doctrine, Feminist Theory and Antiracist Politics." In Feminist Legal Theory: Foundations, edited by D. K. Weisberg, Temple University Press, Philadelphia, 1993, pp. 383-95.

[19] Ong, M., Wright, C., Espinosa, L. L., and Orfield, G. 2011. Inside the Double Bind: A synthesis of Empirical Research on Undergraduate and Graduate Women of Color in Science, Technology, Engineering, and Mathematics. *Harvard Educational Review*, 81, 2, 181-196.

[20] Kvasny, L. (2006). Let the sisters speak: understanding information technology from the standpoint of the 'other'. *ACM SIGMIS, 37*, 4, 13-25.

[21] Varma, R. 2002. Women in information technology: A case study of undergraduate students in a minority-serving institution, *Bulletin of Science, Technology, and Society*, 22,4, 274–282.

[22] Varma, R., Prasad, A., and Kapur, D. 2006. Confronting the "socialization" barrier: Crossethnic differences in undergraduate women's preference for IT education. J. M. Cohoon and W. Aspray, Eds., *Women and Information Technology: Research on Underrepresentation*, MIT Press, Cambridge, MA, 301–322.

[23] Taylor, V. E. 2002. Women of Color in Computing. *ACM SIGCSE Bulletin*, 34, 2, 22-23.

[24] Taylor, V. E. 2009. *Women of Color in Computing.* Paper presented at The *Mini-Symposium on Women of Color in Science, Technology, Engineering, and Mathematics* (Arlington, VA, October 27 - 28, 2009).

[25] Glenn, E. and Tolbert, C. 1987. Technology and Emerging Patterns of Stratification for Women of Color: Race and Gender Segregation in Computer Occupations. In B. D. Wright, Ed., *Women, Work and Technology: Transformations*, University of Michigan Press, Ann Arbor, MI, 318-331.

[26] Ong, M. 2011. The Status of Women of Color in Computer Science. *Communications of the ACM,* 54, 7, (Jul. 2011), 1-3.

[27] Eisenhart, M., Morris, T., Kotys-Schwartz, D., Kantor, J., Prosser, R., and Starbird, K. 2009. *Empty choice: Can girls "want" engineering if they don't know what it is?* Paper presented at the *Annual Meeting of the American Educational Research Association* (San Diego, CA, April, 2009).

[28] Klassen, M., Stockard, R., and Akbari, A. 2004. Stimulating information technology education among underrepresented minorities. In *Proceedings of The 5th Conference On Information Technology Education (formerly CITC) (*Salt Lake City, UT, October 28-30, 2004). ACM, New York, NY, 278. DOI=10.1145/1029533.1029611

[29] Sader, J. L. 2007. *Beyond the First "Click": Women Graduate Students in Computer Science.* Doctoral Thesis. Publication No. 304898121, Retrieved from ProQuest Dissertations and Theses database.

[30] No author. A Pause for Reflection: The 2006 Black Engineers of the Year. 2006. *USBE & Information Technology,* Feb./Mar., 2006, 34.

[31] Gaidos, S. 2009. Flying High. *Science Careers.* Retrieved from http://sciencecareers.sciencemag.org/career_magazine/previous_issues/articles/2009_10_02/caredit.a0900117

[32] Riddle, J. 2007. Linda Gooden is now Exec. VP of Lockheed Martin IT Services. *USBE & Information Technology,* Feb./Mar., 2007, 11.

[33] Ko, L., Kachchaf, R., Ong, M., and Hodari, A. 2013. Narratives of the double bind: Intersectionality in life stories of women of color in physics, astrophysics, and astronomy. In *Proceedings of the Physics Education Research Conference (PERC)* (Philadelphia, PA, August 2012). American Institute of Physics, Melville, NY, 222-225. DOI= 10.1063/1.4789692

[34] Ko, L., T., Kachchaf, R. R., Hodari, A.K., and Ong, M. 2014. Agency of women of color in physics and astronomy: Strategies for persistence and success. *Journal of Women and Minorities in Science and Engineering* 20, 2, 171-195.

[35] No author. 2011. *Shaundra Daily: Education Engineer. PBS NOVA, The Secret Life of Scientists and Engineers.* PBS. Retrieved from http://www.pbs.org/wgbh/nova/secretlife/scientists/shaundra-daily/; retrieved 12 February 2013.

[36] Charmaz, K. 2006. *Constructing Grounded Theory: A Practical Guide Through Qualitative Analysis.* Sage Publications Limited, Thousand Oaks, CA.

[37] Riessman, C. 2007. *Narrative Methods for the Human Sciences.* Sage Publications, Newbury Park, CA.

[38] Creswell, J. W. 2009. *Research design: Qualitative, quantitative, and mixed methods approaches (3rd ed.).* Sage Publications, Inc., Thousand Oaks, CA.

[39] Ong, M. and Hodari, A. 2008-2014. *Beyond the Double Bind: Women of Color in Science, Technology, Engineering and Mathematics.* NSF/REESE funded project (DRL-0909762), TERC, Cambridge, MA.

# Graduating Students' Designs – Through a Phenomenographic Lens

Lynda Thomas
Department of Computer
Science
Aberystwyth University
Aberystwyth, Wales
ltt@aber.ac.uk

Anna Eckerdal
Department of Information
Technology
Uppsala University
Uppsala, Sweden
annae@it.uu.se

Robert McCartney
Department of Computer
Science and Engineering
University of Connecticut
Storrs, CT USA
robert@engr.uconn.edu

Jan Erik Moström
Department of Computing
Science
Umeå University
901 87 Umeå, Sweden
jem@cs.umu.se

Kate Sanders
Mathematics and Computer
Science Department
Rhode Island College
Providence, RI USA
ksanders@ric.edu

Carol Zander
Computing & Software
Systems
University of Washington Bothell
Bothell, WA USA
zander@u.washington.edu

## ABSTRACT

We expand upon previous research that looked at the question: "Can graduating students design software systems?" Specifically we want to examine students' understanding of the phenomenon "produce a design." What does this instruction mean to them? In order to investigate student understandings, we examined their designs using a phenomenographic approach.

Our outcome space includes six understandings: (0) the design a layman might produce; (1) a design with some formal notation; (2) a design that uses formal notations to express the static relationships among the parts; (3) a design that uses formal notation to express sequential (dynamic) information, but does not relate that to the static system parts; (4) a design that includes and relates multiple artifacts, both static and dynamic; and (5) a design that relaxes the notations and includes only essential artifacts. The last understanding was found only in our expert's design, and we do not expect it from undergraduates.

## Categories and Subject Descriptors

K.3.2 [**Computers and Education**]: Computers and Information Science Education—*Computer Science Education*

## Keywords

design; software engineering; assessment; replication

*ICER'14*, August 11-13, 2014, Glasgow, Scotland, UK.
Copyright 2014 ACM 978-1-4503-2755-8/14/08 ...$15.00.
http://dx.doi.org/10.1145/2632320.2632353.

## 1. INTRODUCTION

This paper expands on previous research into graduating students' designs. We administer the same task used in previous studies [4, 5, 6] – designing a "super alarm clock" – to a group of advanced students with fairly homogeneous backgrounds. The full text of the task is given in Figure 1.

Rather than investigating whether the students could produce a software design, as in earlier studies, our goal was to determine the students' understanding of the instruction "produce a design". We use a phenomenographic approach to get insights into the critical features of the phenomenon "produce a design."

### 1.1 A "good" design

Implicit in this research is our desire that students be able to produce good designs. As a point of comparison, we used a design produced by a professional with extensive industry experience given the same design task. This design is shown in Figure 2.

Why is this design good? It uses a sequence diagram to indicate the behavior of the system. The rectangles at the top of each "tram-line" implicitly indicate the classes that need to be designed. The rough draft of this design included some code and something that looked like the beginning of a class diagram; these were then abandoned in the final version. The design indicates static structure (the classes) and also the dynamic behavior – how the objects of those classes behave in relation to each other. It uses the language of computing, but not slavishly. Another professional could pick up this design and implement it.

### 1.2 Research questions

We focus our analysis on the details of what students produced when they were given a free-form "produce a design" brief. Specifically the research questions we consider are:

1. What can we learn about the students' understandings of what 'produce a design' means from their artifacts? In addition, through this analysis:

### Getting People to Sleep

Your brief is to design a "super alarm clock" for University students to help them to manage their own sleep patterns, and also to provide data to support a research project into the extent of the problem in this community. You may assume that, for the prototype, each student will have a Pocket PC (or similar device) which is permanently connected to a network.

Your system will need to:

- Allow a student to set an alarm to wake themselves up.

- Allow a student to set an alarm to remind themselves to go to sleep.

- Record when a student tells the system that they are about to go to sleep.

- Record when a student tells the system that they have woken up, and whether it is due to an alarm or not.

- Make recommendations as to when a student needs to go to sleep. This should include "yellow alerts" when the student will need sleep soon, and "red alerts" when they need to sleep now.

- Store the collected data in a server or database for later analysis.

- Report students who are becoming dangerously sleep-deprived to someone who cares about them (their mother?). This is indicated by a student being given three "red alerts" in a row.

The server/database system (which will also trigger the yellow/red alerts) will be designed and implemented by another team. You should, however, indicate in your design the behaviour you expect from the back-end system.

You only have 50 minutes, so produce the best design that you can in this amount of time – you are producing an initial solution that someone (not necessarily you) could work from. Include as many artefacts as needed so someone could fill in the details for your design.

**Figure 1: The design brief given to students in this study**

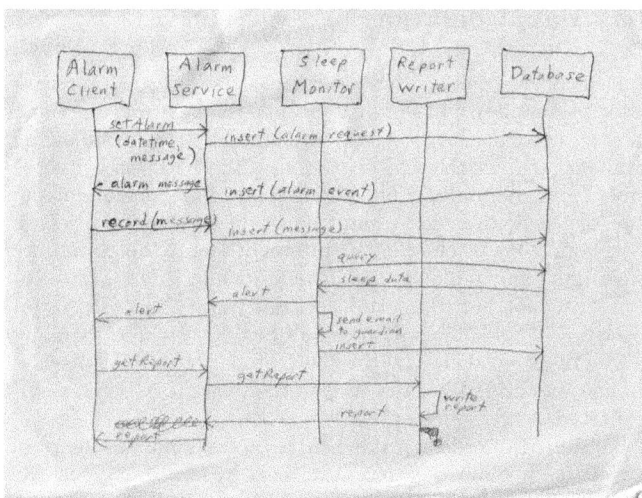

**Figure 2: Design produced by a software professional.**

2. What are the implications for teaching software design?

Section 2 examines the results of the previous studies and other relevant literature. Our methodology is described in Section 3, followed by results in Section 4. We further discuss these results and their implications for teaching in Section 5. Finally, in Section 7, we provide conclusions drawn from this work and suggest further work that might follow.

## 2. BACKGROUND

This work builds upon two studies of student software designs. The first [4] of these specifically asked the question "Can graduating students design software systems?" The authors of the paper looked at 149 designs produced by students nearing graduation in multiple countries and institutions, and concluded that "the majority of graduating students cannot design a software system." In order to reach this conclusion they placed each design into one of six categories that are reproduced (slightly abbreviated) in Figure 3, which also shows the results. Over 20% produced nothing, and over 60% communicated no significant progress toward a design (lowest three categories).

The conclusions of the Graduating Design paper were sobering and surprising for educators. This study was later revisited [6] in the context of a final year compulsory course that consolidates students' design knowledge while introducing Agile Methodologies. The researchers looked at whether graduating students could design software systems in groups; and also whether students were able to recognize good and bad designs produced by others. To assess the quality of designs, the authors produced a weighting system based on an attempt to answer the question: "if a system architect was presented with a design for a system that the architect was about to maintain or build, then what information would s/he hope to find in the perfect design document?" They then went on to produce relative weightings reflecting the importance attached to each design area: Analysis, Overall Architecture (structural and behavioral), Detailed design (structural, behavioral, database, GUI, security), and finally linkage between the design artifacts. The authors noted that different problems might require different weightings. For this problem, they identified: analysis, structure and behavior as the important categories; with use-case diagrams, class diagrams and sequence diagrams as examples of the artifacts. A further requirement of the linking of artifacts was identified.

In brief, that paper confirmed the findings of the original work. In addition it noted that the main things lacking from the students' designs were descriptions of the system behavior and linkages between the use-case diagrams and the designs that implemented them. That study did, however, conclude that students were on the whole able to recognize good design when they saw it. The authors noted that it was possible that the social dynamics of the groups may have impacted on the designs submitted.

There have been other phenomenographic studies of software design. In [2], Box examines the variation in approaches that information system analysts/designers use to do analysis and design. Box conducted a phenomenographic study in which she interviewed 20 professional software analyst/designers. She was looking at "approaches that the analysts/designers were aware of, not just approaches they were using. Look-

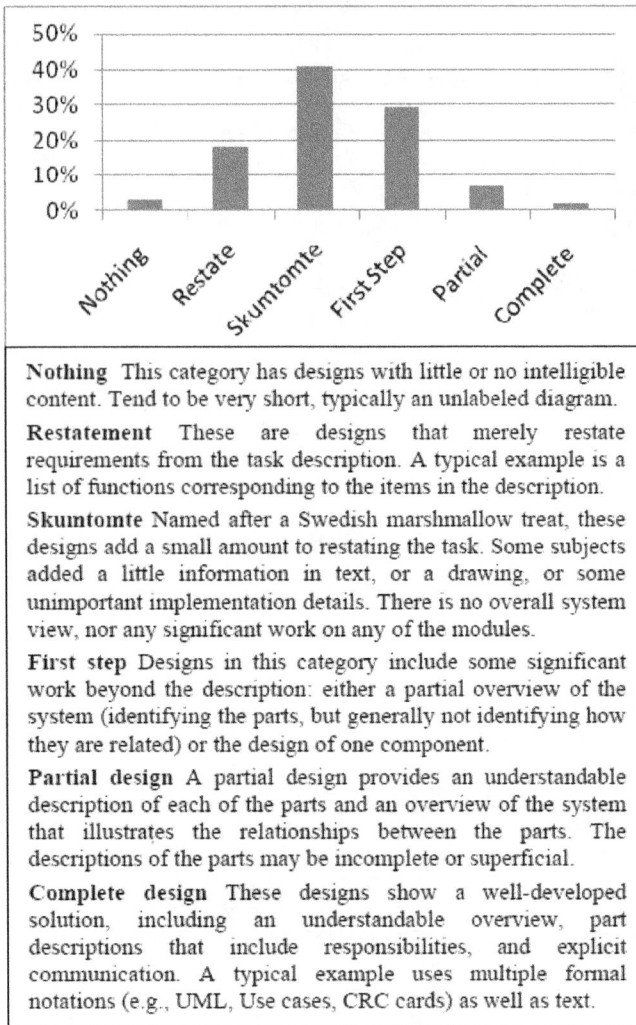

**Nothing** This category has designs with little or no intelligible content. Tend to be very short, typically an unlabeled diagram.

**Restatement** These are designs that merely restate requirements from the task description. A typical example is a list of functions corresponding to the items in the description.

**Skumtomte** Named after a Swedish marshmallow treat, these designs add a small amount to restating the task. Some subjects added a little information in text, or a drawing, or some unimportant implementation details. There is no overall system view, nor any significant work on any of the modules.

**First step** Designs in this category include some significant work beyond the description: either a partial overview of the system (identifying the parts, but generally not identifying how they are related) or the design of one component.

**Partial design** A partial design provides an understandable description of each of the parts and an overview of the system that illustrates the relationships between the parts. The descriptions of the parts may be incomplete or superficial.

**Complete design** These designs show a well-developed solution, including an understandable overview, part descriptions that include responsibilities, and explicit communication. A typical example uses multiple formal notations (e.g., UML, Use cases, CRC cards) as well as text.

**Figure 3: The categories of design and the results (from [4])**

ing at what approaches analysts/designers are aware of tells ... about the range of likely analysis/design practices." The outcome space of Box's research consists of four categories of approach to analysis and design:

**Category 1** an ad hoc strategy with the intention of solving the problem as quickly as possible;

**Category 2** a strategy of producing atomistic analysis and design artifacts with the intention of proving analysis/design has taken place;

**Category 3** a strategy of adhering to a method with the intention of producing a better solution; and

**Category 4** a strategy of adapting and scaling a method with the intent to accurately define the problem while sharing a vision of the project.

Our expert fits best into Box's Category 4 – he used the notation of a UML sequence diagram, but adapted it to fit the problem.

In [1], Boustedt reports on a phenomenographic study of students' understanding of UML class diagrams: what they are, what purposes they have, and what the two aggregation/composition relations mean. He interviewed 20 final-year Computer Science students from four different universities in Sweden. The students focused primarily on three different aspects: describing how an existing program can be documented, how class diagrams support the design process, and how a team can use class diagrams to aid in communication. Class diagrams were seen as specification of classes, and on to a more advanced view, showing relationships between classes. Composition is seen as two classes related and in the more advanced view, aggregation and composition are distinguished. Boustedt did not look at whole software designs.

## 3. METHODOLOGY

### 3.1 Perspective

Our main focus in this paper is a phenomenographic analysis of the phenomenon "produce a design." "Phenomenography is a research method adapted for mapping the qualitatively different ways in which people experience, conceptualize, perceive, and understand various aspects of, and phenomena in, the world around them." [7, p. 31, quoted in [2]]

The artifacts of a phenomenographic analysis are often interviews that seek to draw out understandings of a phenomenon. The reseachers, individually or in groups, search for patterns of distinctly different understandings in the data. The qualitatively different understandings emerge when the data is read and reread, and decontextualized parts of the data, often student quotes, are compared and grouped. This process does not aim at categorizing individuals, nor to identify the most common understandings, but rather to extract all different ways to understand the phenomenon found in the data irrelevant of the frequency.

The output of a phenomenographic analysis – the outcome space – typically describes the different ways in which researchers interpret how a phenomenon is experienced in a cohort, expressed in a qualitative hierarchy [8].

### 3.2 Data Collection

We collected data from 35 students who were taking a compulsory year-long final year projects course. Our task description (shown in Figure 1, above) is essentially the same as that used in the two earlier studies, with the following differences. The original brief (found in [4]) included some contextualizing paragraphs about the importance of getting enough sleep; these were omitted in [6] and in the brief we used here. Our brief added a statement about the 50-minute time limit, and replaced the instructions to divide the solution "into not less than two and not more than ten parts" (used in [4] and [6]) with instructions to "Include as many artefacts as needed ..." in the last paragraph. This last change was added because the word "parts" could be misinterpreted.

We added one design done by a professional to our pool of data as a point of reference. This expert was given the version of the task brief used in [4].

All of the students had taken an intense computing curriculum including courses on Java programming, software design, database, and data structures. Some students had also had a year long internship experience. In their first year, the students had been introduced to UML diagrams: use case, class, instance, and sequence. In addition, they had looked at software development methodologies with an emphasis on the waterfall method. In their second year they studied object-oriented design patterns and were being introduced to refactoring and anti-patterns in the Agile Methodologies course. These students are expected to document their software projects with formal notation that indicates behavior; the formalisms that are encouraged include sequence diagrams, state diagrams, and pseudocode.

In week 4 of the projects course, the students were asked to produce a design (see Figure 1) and told that while they could do the design anonymously if they wished, they would be given feedback that would help them in their project. Students were given about 50 minutes to produce their design. In the original study the time was not fixed and complete designs took on average 60 minutes, but this was not achievable within the constraints of the course. We note that in our study almost all students finished before the time was up.

## 3.3 Data Analysis

The analysis was done in several phases. In an initial deductive analysis we considered all the designs with respect to previous work [4, 6]. This initial analysis inspired us to treat the designs as data for a phenomenographic analysis.

### 3.3.1 Initial Deductive Analysis

To gain familiarity with the data, we read the designs individually and in groups. Using software engineering concepts and influenced by Loftus, Thomas, and Zander [6], we created a spreadsheet that corresponded to the categories: analysis, static design, dynamic design, and linkage. We refined each category by its artifacts (for example, use case diagram, GUI, class diagram, etc.). Each design was tagged with recognizable artifacts of the category.

After becoming accustomed to the data, we reviewed the expert's design which did not include as many details and artifacts, yet we believe to be a good design. That led to a re-analysis of the data on a less detailed level. We categorized all the designs with respect to understandings they exhibited of the design process so that we were able to concentrate on the abstract understanding rather than the idiosyncrasies and errors inherent in individual designs.

Additionally, as a measure of overall quality, we assigned each design into one of the six categories (see Figure 3) presented in [4].

The results of these analyses are presented in Section 4.

### 3.3.2 Phenomenographic Analysis

We seek to gain an understanding of how students experience the phenomenon "produce a design" by using the designs they produce as our raw data. The result of our analysis is thus a phenomenographic outcome space based on what students *do* when confronted with the phenomenon of design rather than what they *say* about it. In the outcome space, the latter categories describe more advanced ways to understand the phenomenon than the former.

The phenomenographic analysis builds on our initial analysis. Influenced by our experience as educators and by the categorization from [6], we investigated qualitatively different ways that students experience producing a design. In

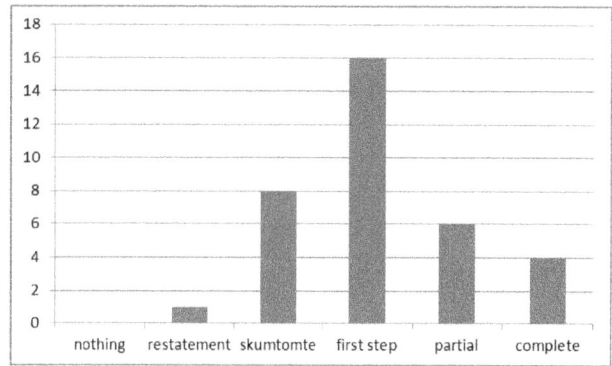

**Figure 4: New designs placed in categories of [4].**

a joint effort, the group of researchers analyzed the pool of data. The analysis was a time-consuming iterative process where we read and compared the designs. Individual, decontextualized features were grouped and re-grouped until the researchers reached consensus. In this way we sought to elicit critical features that differentiated the various ways students understood the phenomenon. This led to the outcome space discussed in Section 4.

## 3.4 Threats to validity

There were small changes in the design brief between this study and the previous studies [4, 6]; these changes could have affected the outcomes, making these results less directly comparable with the previous studies.

We collected designs from another group of students who did the design exercise the following week. As these data could have been contaminated by the students advance knowledge of the task, we did not include these students' designs in our analysis. We used those designs to verify the categories, and found that they fit well.

## 4. RESULTS

In our initial deductive analysis, we examined our dataset using the categories developed by Eckerdal et al. [4], and found a somewhat shifted distribution. As shown in Figure 4, there were a greater proportion of the top three categories (first step, partial, and complete designs) and a smaller proportion of the lowest three (nothing, restatement, and skumtomte designs) in our data than in the earlier paper. The data in the top three categories – those that illustrate at least a partial step towards creating a design – are the most useful to us in the current study, as we investigate the ways in which students understand the phenomenon of design.

Our phenomenographic analysis resulted in the outcome space presented in Figure 5. We discuss the categories in this outcome space one by one in the remainder of this section.

## 4.1 Category 0: informal design

The understanding of "produce a design" that is expressed in this category is that of a layman. We number this category 0 as it reflects no references to formal software design. An example of this category is shown in Figure 6. This student appears to be thinking in terms of a traditional alarm clock. He or she has created a detailed sketch of the device's interface, but it makes no reference to software.

| 0 | Informal design; does not include any formal artifacts. Generally text, but may include detailed pictures without reference to software. |
|---|---|
| 1 | Uses some formal notation for analysis, such as use case diagrams, but does not describe system structure nor behavior. |
| 2 | Focus on design techniques of software engineering, expressing the components and their structural (i.e., static) relationships using notations like class or architecture diagrams. |
| 3 | Focus on design techniques of software engineering, expressing the components and some sequential (dynamic) behavior using notations like sequence diagrams or flowcharts. |
| 4 | Uses multiple artifacts, and relates components across different artifacts - the static and the dynamic are linked |
| 5 | *The notations are relaxed and only the essential artifacts are included (see the expert)* |

**Figure 5: Outcome space: students' understandings of "produce a design". Category 5 is included for completeness, but was not exhibited by the students.**

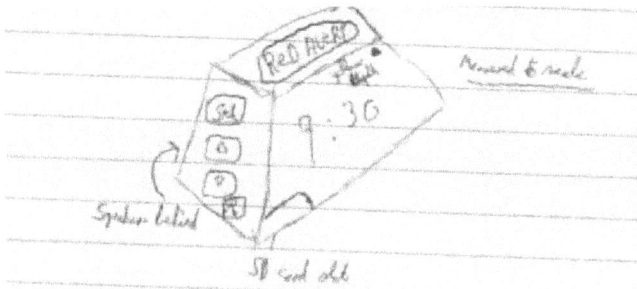

**Figure 6: Category 0**

## 4.2 Category 1: analysis

The understanding that is expressed in this category corresponds to producing software analysis artifacts, and is illustrated by user interaction diagrams, functional specifications (drawn from the problem specification or augmented), or use-case diagrams. There might be some consideration of data security requirements, or data integrity.

In theory, a use case diagram might serve as a transition from analysis to design, if it identified several different classes of people, hardware, or software involved in the system. For example, a detailed use-case diagram for this system might include icons for Student, System Administrator, Researcher, PersonWhoCares, the Database in which sleep histories are stored, and possibly ComputerNetwork, and associate system functionality with the appropriate icons.

Most often, however, the use-case diagrams were of the type shown in Figure 7. Since the only user class identified is Student, the diagram does not provide much assistance in understanding or mapping out the complete system, and in fact is simply a restatement of the problem, admittedly using UML notation.

## 4.3 Category 2: static structure

The understanding that is expressed in this category corresponds to producing artifacts that show the structural re-

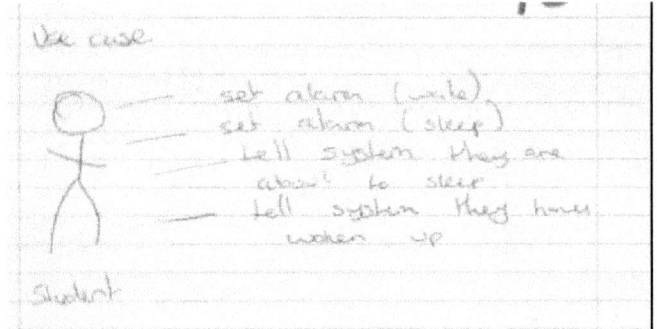

**Figure 7: Category 1**

lationships among the parts of the system. For example, physical parts, e.g., server, database, were shown in diagrams. More commonly, there might be a class diagram or text that describes classes. Figure 8 exemplifies this understanding.

Often the diagrams were non-standard. There might be a UML-like class diagram but with no data or methods; it might include only a description. Some classes were confusing in that they might be named "Main" or "Loop." Sometimes the database was shown as a class. Architecture components could be imbedded in other diagrams. Or there may be only text that describes the backend or the database.

Category 2 is related to Category 1 (Figure 5). Using formal notation for analysis is a necessary step before describing structural relationships since analysis is a preliminary and essential step to producing a design.

## 4.4 Category 3: dynamic behavior

The understanding that is expressed in this category corresponds to producing artifacts that show sequential relationships among the parts of the system. These relationships can be expressed, for example, in sequence diagrams, state diagrams, interaction diagrams. However, these were infrequently shown.

Most often seen were dataflow, flowchart-like diagrams, or non-standard diagrams. Many included text about behavior without showing any formal notation. For example, Figure 9 is considered Category 2 as it includes a class diagram, but it is also in Category 3 because it shows a relationship to the database (non-standard arrow) and the verbiage next to the class diagram describes the behavior of how objects would interact. Figure 10 is a flowchart diagram. It shows the behavior of the person sleeping and the clock. Only one component is described, although it alludes to the database.

Category 3 is related to Category 2 (Figure 5) in that all the designs that express dynamic behavior include some information about the static structure of the system, but there was no linkage between the two.

## 4.5 Category 4: multiple related artifacts

The understanding that is expressed in this category suggests that these students perceive design to include breaking up the solution into static elements, and also providing some evidence of a dynamic flow of control within between those elements.

The three Figures 11, 12, and 13 from the same design illustrate this category. The first diagram shows STUDENT as an input to the system. When the student sets an alarm

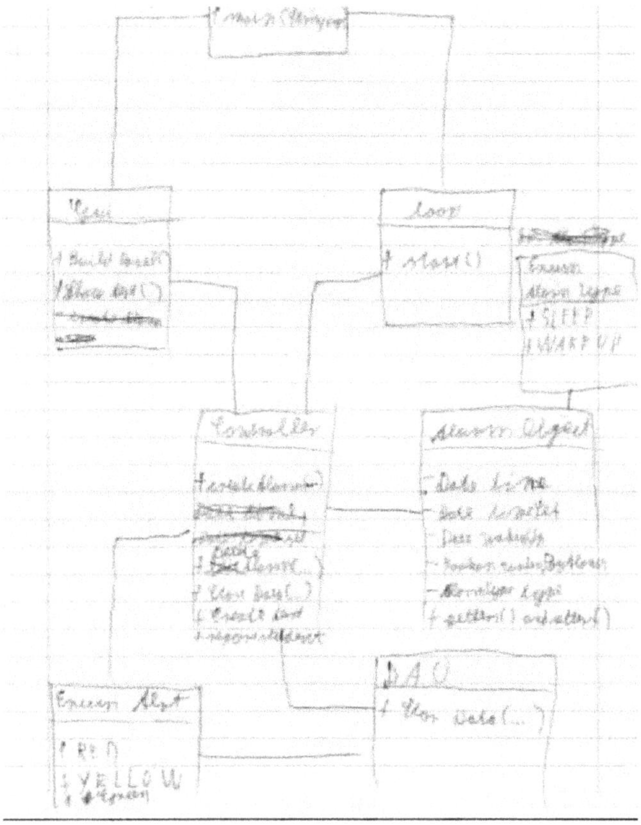

Figure 8: Category 2

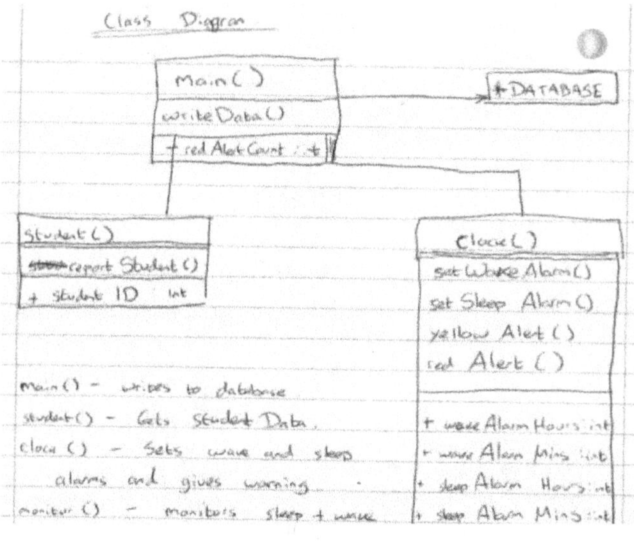

Figure 9: Category 3(1)

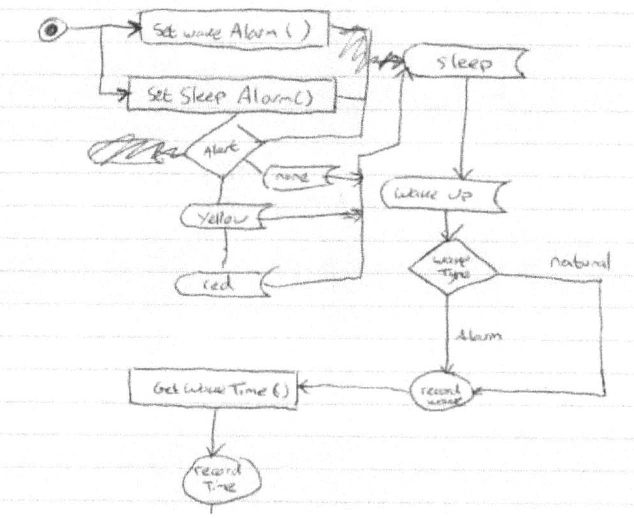

Figure 10: Category 3(2)

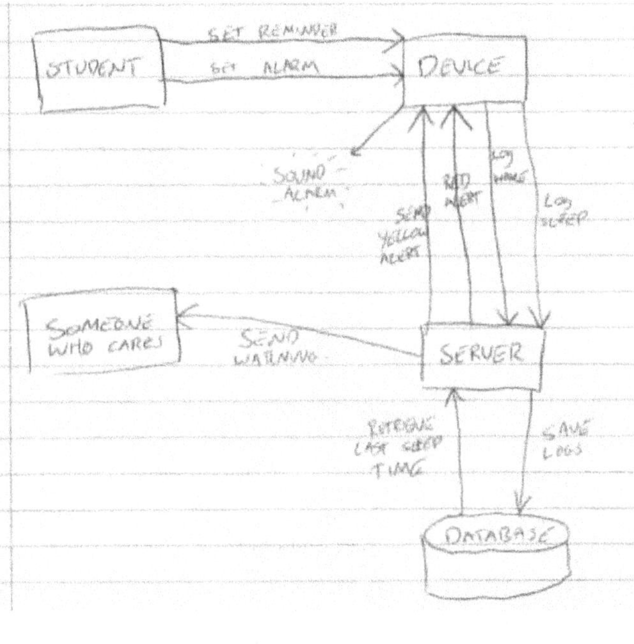

Figure 11: Category 4(1)

main actions. The second diagram is largely dynamic and then the design returns to the static classes. This iteration represents the desired approach of most software development processes.

Category 4 is an extension of Category 3 because there is an explicit realization that there needs to be a linking of the static and dynamic aspects of a software design.

## 4.6 Category 5: The expert category

The expert's design, Figure 2, includes multiple-related artifacts. The notation is relaxed, yet the components are clearly and elegantly presented.

on the DEVICE things happen with other components such as SERVER. In Figure 12 there is an elaboration of this behavior. Then in Figure 13 we can see the beginnings of a class diagram for the SERVER component. Although the naming is not totally consistent, there is a clear progression through the three diagrams linking static and dynamic aspects of the design. One interesting aspect is that the first diagram mainly represents the static components, linked by

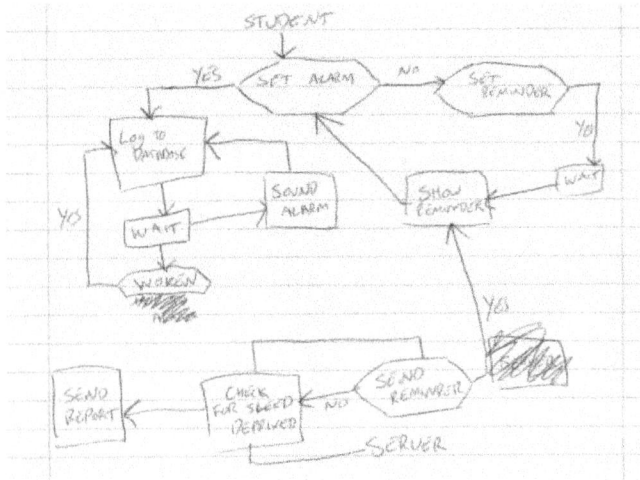

Figure 12: Category 4(2)

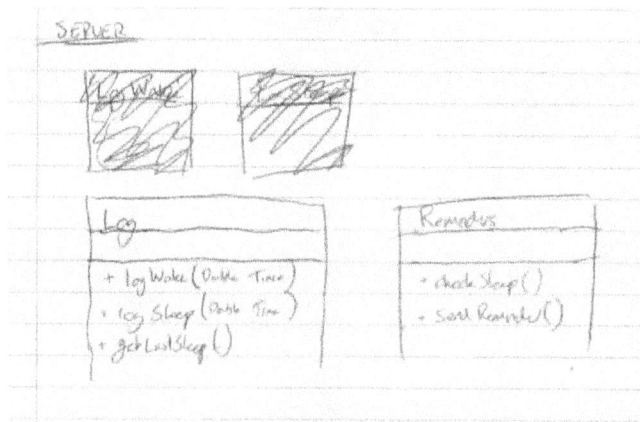

Figure 13: Category 4(3)

## 5. DISCUSSION

When the designs were examined in relation to the expert design from Figure 2, some points became clear:

- Some students interpreted design in the sense that they might have in a design and technology course in high school. Design meant drawing a picture and some students drew quite complex attractive GUIs.

- Some students restated the problem via the "correct" notation of the use-case diagram, but did little else. Their view of design is that some kind of special notation is required. In that sense they understand that there is a computer science language that is expected of them, but are not able to use it to produce a design.

- Some students understand that design is software design and that it requires artifacts like class diagrams, interaction diagrams etc. But these artifacts were presented independently from each other and not linked back to the original problem or to each other – this has resonance with Box's category 2. The students are proving that design and analysis has taken place.

- Our expert design included just one artifact, which both indicated static design and also how behavior

| 1 | Language of Computing |
| 2 | Structure of components |
| 3 | Behavior of components |
| 4 | Link structure and behavior |
| 5 | Appropriate artifacts as needed (expert) |

Figure 14: Critical Features of "produce a design"

linked the static components. It did not have any kind of analysis artifact. Given how clearly the problem was stated, we assume that the expert decided not to bother presenting this artifact.

In terms of Box's categories discussed in Section 2, all but the first of the categories we have identified are her category 2 (producing atomistic analysis and design artifacts with the intention of proving analysis/design has taken place). There were different levels here and the designs in our Category 4 went beyond simply proof of process and into the production of useful artifacts with links between them (Box's category 3). Some of these designs may be said to be approaching the expert design which could be considered to be her category 4, since it adapted typical design artifacts in order to demonstrate the essential behavior of the system and its relationship to static structure. These good designs though still did the fairly useless use-case diagram to "prove" they were following the method.

The findings of this work places a good deal of emphasis on formal notation, especially UML diagrams, consistent with university teaching. Boustedt [1] discusses students' understanding of UML class diagrams and aggregation/composition relations. Students in our study did use class diagrams but rarely used the symbol for composition. They included their own non-standard notation connecting classes or more often, showed no connections at all.

Although the expert used essentially formal notation, using formal notation may not, however, be consistent with industrial practice: [10] reports on an empirical study of 50 professional software engineers, where 35 reported that they use no UML in practice.

### 5.1 Implications for Teaching

One of the purposes of a phenomenographic analysis is to identify the critical features that distinguish understandings in different categories. As Bussey et al. stated,

> If we, as educators, can get our students to attend to certain critical features of the object of learning, we can help our students construct a more directed understanding of a given object of learning. Variation theory suggests that students' awareness can be focused on these critical features when they are allowed to experience variation in those features. [3, p.14]

The critical features for an understanding of "produce a design" identified in this study are summarized in Figure 14 where we lay out the differences between the understandings expressed in each category. These critical features are obvious things to emphasize in teaching and presenting examples of software design.

As educators we can create learning conditions that enable students to discern the educational critical features identified above. Patterns of variation [9, p. 16] can be used to create such conditions, as illustrated below.

Our data shows that there are students who have not discerned that there is a special, formal language of computing. Students need the language of "CS Speak" and of a problem domain language. The *contrast pattern* can be used to contrast differences between a layman's sense of design and a software design. Before learning formal notation, the student designs an alarm clock. This design example can then reoccur, and new designs of the same problem are created using more and more artifacts of the language of computing. By contrasting their first design attempt to later designs, students might discern and see the purpose of the artifacts.

To help students discern the importance of decomposition, the *generalization pattern* can be used. Common to problem solving is breaking a problem into its parts. Examples that students are already familiar with can be discussed and compared, and general ideas like divide and conquer introduced through appropriate artifacts.

Category 3 introduces the additional feature of the behavior of the system. This seems to be a crucial and difficult step for many students. Students generally understand that software performs tasks, but have difficulties expressing the behavior in formal notation. The purpose of the *separation pattern* is to vary one feature while keeping other features invariant. Students could be introduced to static designs for simple problems, and then shown variants of those designs that also incorporate dynamic behavior.

In Category 4, the relationships between artifacts come into focus. The *fusion pattern* involves simultaneously experiencing of several critical features. Marton et al. [9, p. 16] write however that first separating critical features so they are discerned individually before they are presented together is more powerful "than a global, undifferentiated way of seeing" the same thing. Linking structure and behavior should thus be introduced only once the students have discerned and mastered the critical features in the previous categories.

Understanding software design and learning how to do good design is, as we all know, a difficult endeavor. It requires both long experience and theoretical knowledge to be able to produce high-quality designs. Thus we should not expect our students, not even graduating students, to perform on the level of a professional software designer. However, it is important that we give them a solid starting point for their personal development.

Many of our courses are designed to give the students design problem-solving skills, but individual results show that we are not always succeeding. We can only speculate what causes this but the students in our study spent a large part of their design effort in reformulating the problem and, while it is important to understand the problem, many students seem to not be able to continue into problem solving and software design.

One positive sign is that students are, on the whole, aware of the same approaches as professional analysts/designers; in fact they attempt to prove to us that they are aware of the techniques. This suggests that these students have learned about analysis/design approaches and UML. But it is also clear that they need more practice before they are able to produce high quality solutions.

We believe that the best way to improve the design results is to have a carefully designed and implemented curriculum where students are constantly forced to improve their design abilities. A major improvement in these student designs might have followed from more emphasis in the curriculum on the purpose of use-case diagrams. Had designs been able to clearly indicate how to implement the use-cases then that diagram would have been useful. The creation of the diagrams is a round-trip process and all the artifacts of a design should serve to produce a better solution. This involves a less mechanistic approach on the faculty end – not just checkmarking the production of various artifacts but being sure that they work together to solve the problem.

## 6. ACKNOWLEDGEMENTS

Thanks to Neil Taylor for collecting the student designs.

## 7. CONCLUSIONS AND FUTURE WORK

This study tells us that things are not as bad in the area of graduating students' design abilities as first thought. These students (who had a fairly uniform preparation) performed better than those in [4] and [6]. However, while students are aware of the same methods/approaches as professionals they lack the experience to be able to produce elegant designs.

We have outlined some suggestions for teaching that arise out of our analysis of student designs. Further work needs to be done in order to test these suggestions empirically. It would also be interesting to repeat the experiment, then ask students about their understanding of design, and do a more conventional phenomenographic analysis.

## 8. REFERENCES

[1] J. Boustedt. Students' different understandings of class diagrams. *Computer Science Education*, 22(1):29–62, 2012.

[2] I. Box. Toward an understanding of the variation in approaches to analysis and design. *Computer Science Education*, 19(2):93–109, 2009.

[3] T. J. Bussey, M. Orgill, and K. J. Crippen. Variation theory: a theory of learning and a useful theoretical framework for chemical education research. *Chem. Educ. Res. Pract.*, 14:9–22, 2013.

[4] A. Eckerdal, R. McCartney, J. E. Moström, M. Ratcliffe, and C. Zander. Categorizing student software designs: Methods, results, and implications. *Computer Science Education*, 16(3):197–209, 2006.

[5] J. Tenenberg et al. Students designing software: a multi-national, multi-institutional study. *Informatics in Education*, 4(1):143–162, 2005.

[6] C. Loftus, L. Thomas, and C. Zander. Can graduating students design: Revisited. In *Proc. SIGCSE '11*, pages 105–110, New York, NY, USA, 2011. ACM.

[7] F. Marton. Phenomenography – a research approach to investigating different understandings of reality. *Journal of Thought*, 21(3):28–49, 1986.

[8] F. Marton and S. Booth. *Learning and Awareness*. Lawrence Erlbaum Ass., Mahwah, NJ, 1997.

[9] F. Marton and A. Tsui. *Classroom Discourse and the Space of Learning*. Lawrence Erlbaum Ass., Mahwah, NJ, 2004.

[10] M. Petre. UML in practice. In *35th International Conference on Software Engineering (ICSE 2013)*, pages 722–731, San Francisco, CA, USA, 2013.

# Computer Programs, Dialogicality, and Intentionality

Josh Tenenberg
University of Washington Tacoma
Institute of Technology
Tacoma, WA 98402
+1-253-692-5860
jtenenbg@uw.edu

Yifat Ben-David Kolikant
Hebrew University of Jerusalem
School of Education
Jerusalem, 91905
+972-2-588-2056
yifat.kolikant@mail.huji.ac.il

## ABSTRACT

Computer programs are addressed to two different audiences: to the computer, which interprets the program according to the formal semantics of the programming language in which it is written, and to human readers, who try to discern how the program will operate in a real-world context. In this paper, we use Bakhtin's notion of *dialogicality,* along with recent research in psycholinguistics and evolutionary psychology, as a theoretical basis for reflecting on the way in which computer programs embed cooperative communicative norms between programmers and program readers, and how these can be and sometimes are exploited in the program text. In doing so, this provides an important set of theoretical lenses for undertaking and interpreting empirical research in computer science education.

## Categories and Subject Descriptors

K.3.2 [**Computers and Education**]: Computer and Information Science Education—*Computer science education*

## General Terms

Human Factors, Languages.

## Keywords

Dialogicality; shared intentionality; collective intentionality; common ground; cooperative discourse maxims; Bakhtin.

## 1. INTRODUCTION

This paper began as a dialog between its authors about the relationship between dialogicality as originally conceptualized by Bakhtin [1, 2] and computer science education. Our argument in a nutshell is this. According to Bakhtin, human speech is explicitly shaped by the speaker with the addressee in mind. Each unit of speech uttered by a speaker during their speech turn references and responds to prior discourse and anticipates the response of the recipient that is yet to come. Such speech is constrained not only by the formal system of grammar that defines the language [7] but also by conventionalized speech forms or *genres* [1]. Recent empirical research in psycholinguistics, establishes that interlocutors, in whatever written or spoken genre that they use for communication, shape their speech cooperatively for mutual intelligibility. People follow normative cooperative speech maxims [17], and in so doing, rely upon the shared common ground between them, that is, the mutual knowledge that each has not only about the shared topic of interest but about one another's

ICER '14, August 11 - 13 2014, Glasgow, United Kingdom
Copyright is held by the owner/author(s). Publication rights licensed to ACM.
ACM 978-1-4503-2755-8/14/08?$15.00.
http://dx.doi.org/10.1145/2632320.2632351

knowledge [10]. They thus, for instance, take as normative that utterances are relevant, perspicacious, and honest. The cooperative motive in developing common ground *through* speech relies upon a tacit assumption that speakers have concerning themselves and one another not only as goal-directed intentional agents, but as agents capable of *shared* intentionality [28]. As a result, they rely upon their mutual capability to engage in socially recursive inference about one another's accruing mental state about the topic at hand as well as self-monitor their success at achieving mutual intelligibility [32].

These characteristics of human communication provide an important set of theoretical lenses for empirical research in computer science education, especially, the genres that emerge as students interact within their educational arena and the interlocutors they take into account. Looking at human communication as cooperative and dialogical helps to articulate processes of knowledge *creation* (of individual and groups), and emphasizes individual agency as an individual finds "voice" (without neglecting the power that the societal world puts on the individual).

To illustrate this perspective in relation to concrete research questions, we consider the question of whether novices consider computer programs to be a form of speech, and if so, who are the recipients for this speech, with what characteristics? If they consider the computer to be a recipient, then do they construe the computer as intentional, whether weakly, as they might consider a food-seeking animal, or strongly, in the human, socially recursive way? Taking this intentional stance concerning the computer may cause the learner considerable difficulty when the computer does not act as an intelligent interlocutor that responds to the learner's program as either a goal-seeking or socially recursive agent would. As importantly, there are additional research questions concerning the extent to which learners recognize that other people may be recipients of their program text, and hence these readers will seek to render the program intelligible with respect to the imputed intentions of the authoring programmer. If no such audience is recognized, then novice learners may see little reason to use conventionalized program genres to express their computational ideas nor for providing linguistic cues to aid the human who will read the program in pursuit of their goal of understanding the programmer's intentions. Although we have anecdotal information that some students treat the computer as having strong intentionality and that many students ignore other human readers as an audience, we have virtually no systematic studies of either of these beliefs and their prevalence (though [29], discussed below is an exception). And in particular, we have no theoretical account for when and why students might have these beliefs, without which it becomes difficult to structure educational interventions to help students develop more expert-like communicative beliefs and practices.

This paper, then, explicitly relies upon both old and new theoretical perspectives on social cognition and human communication, speculating that these may be crucial to understanding how people learn to program computers. In doing so, we situate this work amidst recent CS education research that borrows from an important strand of recent research in Science Education, in that learners of the discipline have internal cognitive resources developed from their work in other domains that they can and do bring to bear within the programming activity and learning, e.g. [12, 19]. In particular, by casting computer programs as speech acts, we consider that novices learning to program might, can, and sometimes do rely upon their prior (and extensive) experience as skilled natural language users.

## 2. BAKHTINIAN DIALOGICALITY

In his writings, Bakhtin asserts that human speech is *dialogical* [1, 2, 40]. That speech is dialogical means that it always occurs within some existing speech context, in which (other) people have already spoken beforehand and will speak afterward. "[A]ny speaker is himself a respondent to a greater or lesser degree. He is not, after all, the first speaker, the one who disturbs the eternal silence of the universe. And he presupposes not only the existence of the language system he is using, but also the existence of preceding utterances—his own and others'—with which his given utterance enters into one kind of relation or another (builds on them, polemicizes with them, or simply presumes that they are already known to the listener). Any utterance is a link in a very complexly organized chain of other utterances" [1]. Each new utterance adds meaning to the discourse as it unfolds through time.

An *utterance* is the primitive speech unit, and the corresponding atomic communicative event is the *speech turn*, the change of speakers from one to another (for a similar approach from a sociological perspective, see [27]). An utterance, then, is the speech that emerges from a single speaker from the beginning to the end of their speech turn. Speakers alternate their speech, giving a direction and linearity to it. In being dialogical, uttered speech always presupposes a hearer, an *addressee*, and so speech responds to prior utterances, and anticipates the responses of recipients to the utterance. Speech is therefore explicitly shaped with the addressee in mind.

Bakhtin also underscores the polyphonic, heteroglossic nature of speech: extant in any individual's utterance is reference to and echoes of prior utterances of self and others. This reference to past speech is what Garfinkel [16] and Cicourel [8] have called *indexicality*. The sedimentation of such past references to others from a discourse community are conventionalized in speech genres. To Bakhtin, such speech genres stand between the formal, generative grammar of any particular human language (e.g. as formalized by Chomsky [7]) and concrete utterances. That is, speech users are constrained not only by the grammatical structure of their particular natural language (even as they might extend, play with, and satirize this formal structure), they are also constrained to speak within particular genres (e.g. the joke, the greeting, the novel, the tweet) that are appropriate for the audience, the context, and their communicative goals. "We are given these speech genres in almost the same way that we are given our native language, which we master fluently long before we begin to study grammar. We know our native language—its lexical composition and grammatical structure—not from dictionaries and grammars but from concrete utterances that we hear and that we ourselves reproduce in live speech communication with people around us. We assimilate forms of language only in forms of utterances and in conjunction with these forms. The forms of language and the typical forms of utterances, that is, speech genres, enter our experience and our consciousness together, and in close connection with one another. To learn to speak means to learn to construct utterances (because we speak in utterances and not in individual sentences, and, of course, not in individual words)" [1].

Viewing human communication as dialogical thus can be viewed as operating at two distinct levels. On the first level, communication is mutualistic, a relation between the speaker and the recipient of the speech who in turn responds, reversing the speaking and recipient roles, and on and on. This mutualism diachronically unfolds in the back-and-forth of real voices in sequential utterance. On the second level, it is collectivized and conventionalized, abstracted above the specific utterances and experiences of pairs of individuals into generic forms that are shared by entire cultural communities. Natural language is the outermost and broadest form for human communication and speech genres are forms specialized to particular, repeated kinds of human interaction.

## 3. THE PSYCHOLINGUISTICS OF HUMAN COMMUNICATION

### 3.1 Cooperative discourse maxims

Psycholinguistic research within the last several decades has provided empirical support for this Bakhtinian perspective of dialogicality in human communication, at both the mutualistic and the collective levels. In his seminal work on speech use, Grice [17] argues that speakers shape their locutions and hearers make inferences from such locutions based on shared principles of cooperativeness that each implicitly and normatively follows; and that, in fact, mutual intelligibility is virtually impossible without such underlying assumptions. In short, speakers and hearers assume that the other uses *cooperative norms* (what Grice called *maxims*) in order to carry out discourse, which is always a joint production. These maxims relate to *quantity* ("make your contribution as informative as is required (for the current purposes of the exchange)" (p45)), *quality* ("do not say what you believe to be false" (p46)), and *manner* ("avoid obscurity of expression … be brief" (p46)). So for instance, if I say to you "I went shopping yesterday," you can, in general, infer that I in fact did go shopping, that this fact is relevant to a prior or upcoming conversation, and that I would not so inform of you of this fact if I believed you knew that I had gone shopping yesterday. Grice thus presupposes and explicates both levels of communication outlined in our discussion of dialogicality: cooperative mutuality between speaker and hearer, and conventionalized cultural norms about speech use.

### 3.2 Common ground

Clark [10, 11] extended Grice's cooperative principle by arguing that one of the key cooperative activities that interlocutors engage in is *grounding*, the establishment of common ground between them. Common ground is the knowledge that each holds in common, and that each knows the other knows is held in common, recursively ad infinitum. For instance, suppose that you and I are watching a classroom lecture, and the teacher has just written "$f = ma$" on the whiteboard. If I see that you are looking at the whiteboard, and I see that you see that I am looking at the whiteboard, then I can take it that not only do I know what is on the whiteboard, but that I know that you know what is on the whiteboard, and you know that I know what is on the whiteboard, and I know that you know that I know what is on the whiteboard, etc. In having common ground, you and I can and do make use of this mutually held knowledge in shaping and interpreting our utterances. So for example, I can say to you "I wonder if we'll get tested on this," under the assumption that you and I both understand what *this* refers to, since we both hold it in common, and we both assume that I am following the Gricean cooperative maxims (e.g. of relevance, informativeness, quantity, quality, etc.). But if you had not attended the lecture, and we are having coffee afterward, I will instead say "I wonder if we will get tested on the formula relating force to mass and acceleration" or similar. The concept of common ground is thus important because cooperative principles of speech such as what Grice propose exploit the common ground between interlocutors.

From any speaker's perspective, however, common ground is never guaranteed; I may shape my speech under assumptions about your knowledge that turn out to be false. According to Clark, in their turn-taking behavior, speakers *present* an utterance, which they do not take as being mutually understood (i.e. common ground) until there is *acceptance* by the hearer. 'Note that the acceptance process is recursive. B's evidence in response to A's presentation is itself a presentation that needs to be accepted. But where does the recursion stop? . . . What keeps the process from spinning out indefinitely?' [9]. What prevents infinite recursion is (a) that the interlocutors 'mutually believe that the partners have understood what the contributor meant to a criterion sufficient for current purposes' [11], i.e. they settle for weaker evidence depending on context, and (b) they settle for decreasing strength of evidence as the conversation continues [9].

Common ground occurs from several sources. First, we can have common ground due to shared background knowledge, e.g. that we are both lawyers and we each mutually know that we are lawyers, hence we can in mutual knowledge make reference to things that in common ground all lawyers know. Second, we can develop common ground from sharing experience in mutual knowledge, e.g. that we are both observing the same lecture and can see that we are doing so. Third, common ground emerges from the shared and ongoing conversation that we together create, i.e. we mutually assume that the other knows the conversation that has already transpired between us.

## 3.3 Least collaborative effort
Based on the notion of common ground, and recognizing that interlocutors never act simply as speakers but in both roles as speaker and hearer in an ongoing conversation, Clark and colleagues proposed a principle of communicative efficiency between conversational participants relative to the *joint* work that they undertake. This is in contrast to Grice's maxims, which are from the point of view of the speaker. Clark calls this *the principle of least collaborative effort*: "In conversation, the participants try to minimize their collaborative effort—the work that both do from the initiation of each contribution to its mutual acceptance" [11]. Thus, not only am I honest, perspicuous, unambiguous, relevant, etc., but you and I *together* as speakers and recipients who trade roles with each speech turn in an ongoing manner minimize our joint work in carrying out our joint communicative goals.

Rather than communication being a matter of simply transmitting "content" from speaker to hearer, then, communicators shape their communication and interpretation of the speech of others according to the principle of least collaborative effort, relying upon the common ground that the interlocutors share, and tacit assumptions about the kinds of inference that the other interlocutor carries out. The mutual inference and activity goes

something like this: "I intend that you know something, and so I refer your attention or imagination to some situation (my referential act) in the hope that you will figure out what I intend you to know (my communicative intention). Then you, relying on our common ground (both personal and cultural), hypothesize abductively what my communicative intention might be, given that I want you to attend to this referential situation" [32].

## 4. Intentionality
### 4.1 Theory of mind
From Grice and Clark, we have an account of human communication that accords with both the mutualism and the generic conventionalism inherent in dialogicality. Underlying these accounts are assumptions about human cognition that interlocutors make toward one another. The fundamental assumption that human interlocutors make about one another that we will be explicating is often referred to by the term *theory of mind* [22, 36], i.e. that people treat others as having mental activity (such as goals, desires, and plans) similar to themselves. As an assumption about another interlocutor, it is easy not only for interlocutors but for researchers in the social sciences to take these human capabilities for granted. But because computer programmers engage in discursive activity with both the computer and with other programmers—who differ in their cognitive capabilities—it is important to make explicit what it means to have a theory of mind *about other people*, and how this kind of cognition differs from other, weaker forms of cognition.

Tomasello and his colleagues have undertaken considerable research related to the development of human cognition and the associated forms of communication, theorizing from a series of empirical studies with great apes (chimpanzees, bonobos, orangutans, gorillas) and with human infants and children. They have done so both from a phylogenetic perspective concerning the evolution of the human species as distinct yet emergent from that of our nearest primate relatives, as well as from an ontogenetic perspective of the emergence of different communicative and cognitive competencies in individual human development [32, 34, 35]. Since the evidence indicates that the ontogenetic mirrors the phylogenetic, we will tell the phylogenetic story, mentioning only that, ontogenetically, shared intentionality emerges in early infancy and collective intentionality (both defined below) emerges during the fourth year of life (for an extended discussion of the ontogenetic story, see [36–38]). Our primary source for the account we provide here is Tomasello's most recent explication in *A Natural History of Human Thinking* [32], which encapsulates and unifies much of his and colleagues' research over the last three decades. We additionally reference some of Tomasello's prior research and that of others working in related fields.

### 4.2 Individual intentionality
There is considerable evidence that great apes (and hence the common ancestor to apes and humans from over 6 million years ago) are intentional creatures who mentally represent the world, make inferences from these representations, and self-monitor their thinking and behavior. By intentionality, we mean "the capacity of the mind to represent objects and states of affairs in the world other than itself" [28], i.e. "the way the individual mind is directed at objects by virtue of some mental content that represents them" [15]. The evidence suggests that great apes have intentionality: they mentally represent the world imagistically, schematically, and situationally with respect to their goals ("e.g. that food is present or that a predator is absent" (p28)). Their inferences allow them to make "off-line simulations in which the subject infers or

imagines nonfactual situations" (p28) and they have "proto-versions of everything from modus tollens to disjunctive syllogisms" (p28). In sum, the great apes have what Tomasello calls *individual intentionality* since they use their cognitive abilities to counterfactually simulate activity prior to in-the-world activity, thereby letting their thoughts "die in their stead". And although they can reason about social situations, they do so primarily in *competition* rather than cooperation with other individuals of the same species.

## 4.3 Shared intentionality

Tomasello asserts that the next form of intentionality began somewhere between 2 million and 400,000 years ago, shortly after the emergence of the genus *homo*. This change was due largely to increased pressure for small-scale cooperation in order to procure game animals that are too large for an individual human to reliably kill themselves [35]. With this increased pressure came considerable changes to human physiology, such as increased support for two-legged standing, walking, and (especially) running, and changes to the shape of the face, neck and throat to support articulate speech [20]. Most important, however, were the cognitive changes that led to what Tomasello calls *shared intentionality,* borrowing form notions of shared intentionality hypothesized by philosophers of language [28]. In shared intentionality, two individuals not only have goals and intentions, but they develop the mutual intention to do something *together*. This joint activity has a dual character, in that it involves not only something joint (the goal, the joint action), which must be mentally represented, but it also involves both actors taking separate but complementary roles in carrying out the joint action, and having the capability to take the perspective of the other in order to aid them in completing their role-specific responsibilities. Their mental representations thus had to explicitly include *both* individuals in the joint activity, their inferences had to be socially recursive, in the sense described above (where each in mutual knowledge knows that the other knows, ad infinitum), and they had to self-monitor, not only with respect to their success in their communicative activity, but to ensure that they are achieving their role-specific behavior that they have committed to jointly undertake. Along with these new cognitive capacities came new normative dimensions to human behavior, since undertaking joint activity commits its participants to ongoingly engage in this shared endeavor—and to publicly display this ongoing activity and commitment—in spite of individual incentives to pursue competing individual goals. Part of this normativity concerns uses of language that take account of socially recursive thought, in that "linguistic constructions are created with adaptations for the recipients' knowledge, expectations, and perspective in mind" [32].

## 4.4 Collective intentionality

Finally, starting approximately 200,000 years ago, humans began a new form of intentionally, largely because of demographic pressure from increased population, and the often lethal *inter*-group competition that arose in competition over finite resources [5, 6]. There were thus a number of cognitive changes that arose for small bands (approximately 200 people) of individuals to identify as a shared collective with a shared culture and group identity. What had earlier been mutualistic normative commitments and forms of communication between pairs of individuals among pre-modern humans gave way to "objective" knowledge, generalized, impersonal group norms and generic, conventionalized forms of communication among modern humans. Not only did individuals have to be able to take the perspective of a cooperative partner, they additionally had to develop abstracted, objective forms of knowledge (e.g. how the entities in the world are classified and named, their properties, their relations). As well they had to adopt institutionalized social practices, i.e. idealized ways of doing things that were not only functional to achieve valued goals, but had corresponding agent-neutral social roles with normative obligations for fulfilling responsibilities associated with each role. Being a member of the group meant "knowing what we all know" and "doing it the way we all do it," which was not only enforced mutually by committed cooperators, but, unlike any other species, enforced by uninvolved third parties [23]. Along with this came social forms of teaching children so that cultural forms of being and doing became common ground, not only among two individuals engaged in a spontaneous form of cooperation in the moment, but to all members of the cultural group [33]. This meant that any subgroup from within the larger tribal band could generate stable expectations for behavior in order to flexibly and spontaneously engage in cooperative activity as demanded by whatever contingency the group faced. This conventionalized form of intentionality is what Tomasello calls *collective intentionality*. "Everything is genericized to fit anyone in the group in an agent-neutral manner, and this results in a kind of collective perspective on things, experienced as a sense of the 'objectivity' of things, even those we have created" [32]. And along with it came the kind of conventionalized, generic forms of communication that Bakhtin speaks of. Conforming to shared cultural forms of speech at the same time signals membership and affinity toward the group, enhances mutual intelligibility, particularly with other members of the cultural community with whom we share no direct common ground, and reproduces the cultural form across time.

## 4.5 Three forms of intentionality

To summarize, we can talk about three distinct forms of intentionality. The first, individual intentionality, characteristic of the great apes, involves possessing mental representations, making inferences from these to replace, supplant, and/or anticipate action in the world, and to self-monitor with respect to achieving ones goals. Shared intentionality, characterizing the genus *homo*, involves developing joint goals and plans that explicitly include both participants acting in complementary roles, making socially-recursive inferences, along with the second-personal normative commitments associated with undertaking joint goals and plans. With this form of intentionality, interlocutors explicitly create and interpret speech with respect to their communicative goals and what they take to be shared common ground. And finally, collective intentionality, possessed only by modern humans, involves generalized cultural forms of knowing and doing within a group (including generic forms of speech), and generic (rather than mutual) forms of normativity that are common ground among all members of the cultural group, enforced by third parties.

## 5. DIALOGICALITY, INTENTIONALITY, AND COMPUTER PROGRAMS

Having undertaken this review of intentionality and dialogicality, we can now connect the theoretical framework discussed above to our illustrative research concern within computer science education, that of treating computer programs as communicative objects. In doing so, it is important to recognize that computer programs as utterances have two distinct recipients—1) computers and 2) other programmers—hence two different "interpreters" of these texts and two distinct senses of "meaning" [30].

## 5.1 The computer interpreter

From an expert perspective, the computer interprets a program in precise ways according to the formal semantics associated with each syntactic construct, as documented in such things as programming language reports and embodied in software interpreters. We also recognize that this interpretation is mediated through various "layers" or "levels," e.g. from a user interface to an Integrated Development Environment, to an interpreter that may use one or more intermediate languages before these are interpreted for the particular hardware that we happen to running, etc. Nonetheless, each level translates through well-defined semantics to the next level below. This view of the meaning of a computer program treats computers as hermetically sealed, so that semantics in this formal sense is only with respect to the ways in which particular operations (e.g. an assignment statement or a conditional) change the computer's internal state. Under this view, such things as conventionalized linguistic genre and style are simply irrelevant as far as the interpreted computer action is concerned: the identifier `Rose` by any other name is just as sweet from the interpreter's point of view. This treats the computer from a point of view that Dennett calls the *design stance* [13], where one can make predictions of its behavior based on an understanding of its functional design properties. To reiterate, this is an expert perspective on the computer. We thus take as an assumption that expert computer scientists and software developers, when programming a computer, take the design stance with respect to the computer, a stance that both authors of this paper share. In doing so, we set aside the larger question of whether computers actually *have* intentionality, one of the most contentious philosophical questions of the latter part of the 20th century [13, 14]

Novice programmers and "just plain folks" (a phrase coined by Jean Lave [18]), on the other hand, may treat the computer as having intentionality, i.e. such cognitive things as beliefs, goals, plans, etc., especially if novices do not have a sufficiently well-developed model of the computer's operation to take the design stance. Such intentional attributions can be seen in statements that any introductory computer science teacher has heard such as "the computer doesn't like me," "it is acting up," "it has a mind of its own," "it just does what it wants" and similar. This is what Dennett calls taking the *intentional stance* or *intentional strategy*. "To a first approximation, the intentional strategy consists of treating the object whose behavior you want to predict as a rational agent with beliefs and desires and other mental stages exhibiting what Brentano and others call *intentionality*" [13].

## 5.2 The human interpreter

Let us now consider the other recipient of computer programs: all of the programmers who might happen to read the program, human beings who may be charged with having to debug the program, port it to another language, write a unit test suite for it, or any of a countless number of programming-related activities. These program readers consider that the original programmer *is* intentional, and that the computer program is written so as to carry out some humanly-devised goal with respect not only to internal changes of computer state, but how such computer state changes affect the larger state of affairs out in the world. So, for example, what a program statement "means" for a human program reader (and the original programmer, who is self-reflectively also a reader) is not simply that some memory location called "`Order`" receives the value "`Rose`" but that this state change is one part of a larger sociotechnical process that will result in someone having a rose delivered to him or her, such as when someone orders

flowers for his or her mother from a florist's website. And so anyone reading the program not only has to internalize the interpreter, so that she can simulate what the program will do in execution, but at the same time has to infer a model of the intentions of the person who programmed the computer. In addition, and particularly for programming teachers when they read student code, the teacher has to infer the student's model of the interpreter that this student has internalized, particularly if there are systematic kinds of errors in the program. Readers are thus socially recursive, in that they have to think about the intentions of the original programmer. Hence, expert programmers are socially recursive in their software development activities, recognizing that their programs will be read by others who will have to infer the program author's intentions. These program authors thus add particular linguistic elements to aid the reader in this task, such as comments, identifier names that suggest larger goals and intentions, unit tests, documentation, and the like. Finally, programmers and readers are collectively intentional, since, as members of programming organizations and communities, they develop and use conventionalized stylistic elements, as well as programming genres in order to "minimize the joint collaborative effort" of programmer and (human program reader), even if neither has ever established direct common ground in the past. That is, experts follow conventionalized ways of expressing programs because of general normative requirements associated with being members of particular cultural programming communities (e.g. put curly braces in these places, put constants before variables before methods, and so on). As a result, program readers can develop stable expectations about how computer programs will be written.

There are a number of empirical research studies on expert/novice differences in reading and comprehending computer programs, such as that of Petre [25], who reports that experts "see" computer programs differently than novices based on different expectations about how programs are written. There is also research on teaching and learning general cultural norms within computing communities [3, 4] But these do not take the perspective that program readers and writers are bound by cooperative *discursive* norms such as those that Grice describes for natural language, nor are such programming norms explored and enumerated. In the only empirical study that we know of related to the cooperative linguistic norms of programmers and program readers, Soloway and Ehrlich [29] identify several such norms, such as "variable names should reflect function" and "don't include code that won't be used." They conclude: "[I]t is not merely a matter of aesthetics that programs should be written in a particular style. Rather there is a psychological basis for writing programs in a conventional manner: programmers have strong *expectations* that other programmers will follow these discourse rules. If the rules are violated, then the utility afforded by the expectations that programmers have built up over time is effectively nullified." To clarify, we are not claiming that programmers and program readers are not bound by discursive norms; on the contrary, we believe that they are. Rather, discursive norms (and the collective intentionality that they imply) have rarely been used as the theoretical framing for empirical studies of programmers, whether expert or novice.

To summarize, to experts, computer programs have two audiences, two distinct readers, one of whom is non-intentional, the other of whom is fully, collectively, socially-recursively intentional. And we can "see" this intentionally inscribed directly in the program: the identifier `Rose` by any other name might make a large difference with respect to the way in which I as the original programmer intend for this program to function in the world and you as the (human) program reader are to understand my intentions. As a result, computer programs embed the dialogicality of human programmers in all of the Bakhtinian senses mentioned above: addressable (to its human readers), heteroglossic (in carrying the "voice" of past programmers in the program code, perhaps in conventionalized programming schemas [21]), and expressed within conventionalized programming genres (which vary within different programming communities, even if they share the same programming language or paradigm).

# 6. AN EMPIRICAL RESEARCH PROGRAM

Taking programs as utterances with two distinct audiences, one of which is a computer and non-intentional, the other of which is human and collectively intentional, opens a space of empirical investigation with respect to novices learning how to program. We see two ways in which novices might construe programs in ways that differ from the dual-recipient view outlined above. And these misconstruals may serve as considerable hindrances to learning.

## 6.1 Treating the computer as intentional

In an earlier, study, Pea [24] identified that many students treat computers as intentional, which he termed a "superbug" that has a number of different manifestations. He warns, however, "[i]t is not that students *literally* believe that the computer has a mind, or can think, or can interpret what was not explicitly stated. In our experience, novice programming students are likely to vehemently deny that the computer can think or that it is intelligent. … But students' behaviors when working with programs often contradict their denials; they act *as if* the programming language is more than mechanistic. Their default strategy *for making sense* when encountering difficulties of program interpretation or when writing programs is to resort to the powerful analogy of natural language conversation, to assume a disambiguating mind which can understand" (p33).

Given these results, where might the theoretical borrowings that we explicate in prior sections provide additional insight? One is in studying why some students take the intentional stance and others do not. And, given our distinction of kinds of intentionality, individual, shared, and collective, which kinds are attributed to computers? Are there students who believe that they and the computer they are programming are accumulating common ground based on the *history of interaction* that they are jointly accruing, as a human partner would? Do they believe that the interpreter's linguistic output (such as prompts, auto-completions, dialogs, and error messages) should follow the cooperative maxims and principle of least collaborative effort as human interlocutors are obliged to follow?

Perhaps most importantly, might different kinds of instructional interventions, perhaps some that explicitly link forms of intentionality to communicative competence, help students to take the design stance rather than the intentional stance when programming computers?

## 6.2 Not fulfilling communicative obligations to anticipated human readers

The second set of empirical investigations concerns the extent to which novices are aware of the intentional, human recipient for their programs. To what extent do they see themselves as participating in human-to-human discourse about computational things expressed in a programming language? What do students believe that human readers require in order to infer the programmer's intentions? That is, what norms do they have about *how* programs should be written so as to be read and understood *by others*? What conventionalized forms of programming discourse (if any) do students believe they should internalize (in addition to internalizing the interpreter)? We conjecture that it is likely that novices (as well as most programming teachers and CS Ed researchers) are unaware of the normative principles (i.e. Gricean cooperative axioms, exploitation of common ground, principle of least collaborative effort) that they use in inter-human communication, just as we ourselves were unaware of such practices prior to reading the research summarized above. And this is because such communicative practices are learned socially at an early age through imitation, implicit use, and correction by experienced others, in the same way that children implicitly learn the grammar of their native languages (a recursive, infinitely generate grammar), and hence become expert users of grammar without any awareness of it. And if this is the case, then novice programmers may see little reason to write their programs in conventionalized ways.

# 7. IMPLICATIONS OF ADOPTING THE INTENTIONAL AND DIALOGIC PERSPECTIVE

There are several implications of studies concerning the intentional stance of novices toward the computer and of their awareness of human program readers and their normative obligations toward them. *If* some novices believe that the computer is intentional (and we speculate that this is the case), then this suggests that these novices have appropriated cognitive resources that they use in communicative activity with human beings (or perhaps a weaker form such as they might use with pet dogs), and that it will be problematic for them if they persist in taking the intentional stance with the computer. Similarly, *if* a novice does not recognize that there is a strongly intentional human agent that may have to read their code (to figure out what it does, to change it, etc), then it may be problematic for this student to both read and understand programs, particularly with respect to adopting certain genre norms and other linguistic conventions that make computer programs intelligible to other people.

The perspective that we have outlined in this paper, which we shorthand as the *dialogic perspective* (and all that it implies about intentionality) also provides an alternative reading for some prior research on student misconceptions and epistemology. For example, in their oft-cited paper "Epistemological Pluralism," Turkle and Papert [39] lament what they claim to be dominant cultural ways of thinking about computer programs, particularly by computer scientists teaching novices at such places as Harvard. These culturally dominant ways of thinking, they state, privilege the use of black-boxed, computational abstractions rather than code written "from scratch" anew by each programmer, thereby alienating many students—many of whom are women—who prefer a more concrete, bottom-up form of thinking and programming. An anchoring belief that Turkle and Papert express is "*the computer is an expressive medium that different people can make their own in their own way* [emphasis in original]" (p165). In speaking of the computer as an *expressive* medium, but ignoring the *communicative* aspects of computer programs, Turkle and Papert treat individuals as social isolates. Computers are thus naturalized as found objects, rather than bequests from cultural predecessors.

Taking a dialogical perspective on cultural forms for writing and thinking about programs, yields a different insight into Turkle and

Papert's data, and leads to different conclusions. And that is that cultural communities develop programming genres, conventionalized ways of writing programs (e.g. black-box, top-down) that have deontic requirements for members of these communities: in order to be one of us, this is how we write programs. Simply having functionally correct programs is not sufficient; rather, programs have to be expressed in ways that meet the genre norms of the community. Expressive artifacts come with no such obligations, but communicative artifacts do.

Moreover, these conventions, these genres, are not mere caprice, but rather are community wisdom which evolved through much experience and interaction. These norms should not be considered as suppressing students' expression but rather as empowering them to express themselves *within and in relation to the community*. Furthermore, norms constantly evolve as new members of communities introduce new practices, and communities encounter and adapt norms from other communities [26]. For example,, "concrete ways of thinking", such as the *bricolage* that Turkle and Papert [39] advocated, is now more legitimate within the computing education community. In fact, part of being "in the game", we hope, involves challenging its rules. But in order to do so, students should be immersed in the community wisdom, its discourse, and aim at improving it, thereby expressing themselves within their community.

As Tomasello explains: "Communicative conventions thus come to be governed by constitutive norms in the sense that if I do not use them in the conventional way, I am just not in the game. As Wittgenstein (1995) argued so trenchantly, the criteria for conventional use are determined not by the individual but by the community of users. I can rebel, but to what effect? ... Anyone not comprehending this communicative convention is just not one of us—which makes it culturally normative" [32].

Though we sympathize that entering new cultural communities, with cultural practices that might be different than what one is familiar with—including discourse practices—may present considerable challenges, we nonetheless believe that lamenting the fact that such conventionalized discourse practices exist and wishing them away is to overlook the fact that cultural practices (including communicative ones) become normative [3, 31].

The debate on genre conventions versus. freedom of expression is timely today, too, given that we want to teach K-12 students computational thinking and that there are a variety of languages today available for their use (e.g., Scratch). What genres emerge as students interact with these languages in the classrooms and outside? What aspects of computational thinking—what discourse genres—are expressed? Further research is required to address these question, future dialogue to discuss the direction(s) this community takes.

# 8. CONCLUSION

This paper presents the argument that viewing computer programs as linguistic acts, as *utterances* that function with human communities, opens a space for empirical research and theorizing related to the learning of computer programming, surely one of the enduring concerns of computer science education. As utterances, computer programs not only *express* computational ideas that are interpreted mechanically by a digital computer in order to control its operation, but at the same time *communicate* human intentions about the way that the computer will effect change in the ontic world to other human beings. As a result of the human recipient, expert-written computer programs embed dialogicality, in that they are addressable to other programmers who will have to read the program, heteroglossic, in that they reference computer programs written previously by others, and written in conventionalized programming genres specific to programming communities. This dialogicality takes for granted but depends upon uniquely human forms of intentionality, not only involving goals and plans, but *joint intentions* and socially recursive inference within conventionalized and normative programming genres. As a result, we posit that there are two primary ways in which this dialogical perspective can serve as a basis for an empirical research program. On the one hand, because of past language use that novices have with natural language and the relative ease with which people impute intentionality to others, there are a number of research questions related to the intentional stances that novices might take toward the computer that they are attempting to program, and learning about what these stances are is worth understanding. On the other hand, novices may either be unaware of the communicative function of the computer programs that they write with respect to human recipients, or more likely, unaware of their normative obligations to shape their programming utterances so as to facilitate the understanding of their intentions by a program reader from within their programming community, much as they already do so in natural language. Undertaking research to better understand novice intentional stances can then serve as a basis for teaching that is explicitly designed to foster programmer dialogicality.

# 9. ACKNOWLEDGEMENTS

Initial discussion between the authors started at a workshop supported by the National Science Foundation under Grant No. 1332686. Any opinions, findings, and conclusions or recommendations expressed in this material are those of the author(s) and do not necessarily reflect the views of the National Science Foundation. We are grateful to Steve Cooper for inviting us to participate in this workshop.

# 10. REFERENCES

[1]    Bakhtin, M. 1986. *Speech genres and other late essays*. University of Texas Press.

[2]    Bakhtin, M. 1981. *The dialogic imagination: Four essays by M. M. Bakhtin*. University of Texas Press.

[3]    Ben-David Kolikant, Y. 2011. Computer science education as a cultural encounter: a socio-cultural framework for articulating teaching difficulties. *Instructional Science*. 39, (2011), 543–559.

[4]    Ben-David Kolikant, Y. and Pollack, S. 2004. Establishing Computer Science Professional Norms Among High-School Students. *Computer Science Education*. 14, 1 (2004), 21–35.

[5]    Boehm, C. 2012. *Moral Origins: The Evolution of Virtue, Altruism, and Shame*. Basic Books.

[6]    Bowles, S. and Gintis, H. 2011. *A cooperative species: human reciprocity and its evolution*. Princeton University Press.

[7]    Chomsky, N. 1965. *Aspects of the Theory of Syntax*. MIT Press.

[8]    Cicourel, A. V. 1974. *Cognitive sociology: Language and meaning in social interaction*. Free Press.

[9]    Clark, H.H. 1993. *Arenas of language use*. University of Chicago Press.

[10] Clark, H.H. 1996. *Using language*. Cambridge University Press.

[11] Clark, H.H. and Brennan, S.E. 1991. Grounding in communication. *Perspectives on socially shared cognition*. 13, 1991 (1991), 127–149.

[12] Danielak, B. 2014. *How electrical engineering students design computer programs*. University of Maryland, College Park.

[13] Dennett, D. 1987. *The Intentional Stance*. MIT Press.

[14] Dietrich, E. ed. 1994. *Thinking Computers and Virtual Persons: Essays on the Intentionality of Machines*. Academic Press.

[15] Dreyfus, H. 1991. *Being-in-the-World: A Commentary on Heidegger's Being and Time, Division I*. MIT Press.

[16] Garfinkel, H. 1967. *Studies in ethnomethodology*. Prentice Hall.

[17] Grice, P. 1975. Logic and conversation. *Syntax and Semantics, 3: Speech Acts*. P. Cole and J. Morgan, eds. Academic Press.

[18] Lave, J. 1988. *Cognition in Practice: Mind, Mathematics, and Culture in Everyday Life*. Cambridge University Press.

[19] Lewis, C.M. 2012. *Applications of out-of-domain knowledge in students' reasoning about computer program state*. University of California at Berkeley.

[20] Lieberman, D.E. 2013. *The Story of the Human Body: Evolution, Health, and Disease*. Pantheon Books.

[21] Linn, M.C. and Clancy, M.J. 1992. The case for case studies of programming problems. *Communications of the ACM*. 35, 3 (Mar. 1992), 121–132.

[22] Meltzoff, A.N. 2011. Social cognition and the origins of imitation, empathy, and theory of mind. *The Wiley-Blackwell handbook of childhood cognitive development*. U. Goswami, ed. Wiley-Blackwell. 49–75.

[23] Nowak, M.A. and Sigmund, K. 2005. Evolution of indirect reciprocity. *Nature*. 437, (2005), 1291–1298.

[24] Pea, R.D. 1986. Language-independent conceptual "bugs" in novice programming. *Journal of Educational Computing Research*. 2, 1 (1986), 25–36.

[25] Petre, M. 1995. Why looking isn't always seeing: readership skills and graphical programming. *Communications of the ACM*. 38, 6 (Jun. 1995), 33–44.

[26] Rogoff, B. 2003. *The Cultural Nature of Human Development*. Oxford University Press.

[27] Sacks, H. et al. 1974. A simplest systematics for the organization of turn-taking for conversation. *Language*. 50, 4 (1974), 696–735.

[28] Searle, J. 1995. *The Construction of Social Reality*. The Free Press.

[29] Soloway, E. and Ehrlich, K. 1984. Empirical studies of programming knowledge. *IEEE Transactions on Software Engineering*. SE-10, 595-609 (1984).

[30] Tenenberg, J. 2001. On the meaning of computer programs. *Cognitive Technology: Instruments of Mind, Proceedings of the 4th International Conference of Cognitive Technology* (Coventry, UK, 2001).

[31] Tenenberg, J. and Knobelsdorf, M. 2014. Out of our minds: a review of sociocultural cognition theory. *Computer Science Education*. (2014).

[32] Tomasello, M. 2014. *A Natural History of Human Thinking*. Harvard University Press.

[33] Tomasello, M. et al. 1993. Cultural Learning. *Behavioral and Brain Sciences*. 16, (1993), 495–552.

[34] Tomasello, M. 2011. Human culture in evolutionary perspective. *Advances in culture and psychology*. M.J. Gelfand et al., eds. Oxford University Press.

[35] Tomasello, M. et al. 2012. Two Key Steps in the Evolution of Human Cooperation: The Interdependence Hypothesis. *Current Anthropology*. 53, 6 (2012), 673–692.

[36] Tomasello, M. et al. 2005. Understanding and sharing intentions: The origins of cultural cognition. *Behavioral and Brain Sciences*. 28, (2005), 675–691.

[37] Tomasello, M. 2009. *Why we cooperate*. MIT Press.

[38] Tomasello, M. and Vaish, A. 2013. Origins of Human Cooperation and Morality. *Annual review of psychology*. 64, (2013), 231–55.

[39] Turkle, S. and Papert, S. 1991. Epistemological Pluralism and the Revaluation of the Concrete. *Constructionism*. Ablex Publishing Company.

[40] Wertsch, J. 1993. *Voices of the Mind: A Sociocultural Approach to Mediated Action*. Harvard University Press.

# Academic Integrity Perceptions Regarding Computing Assessments and Essays

**Simon**
University of Newcastle, Australia
simon@newcastle.edu.au

**Beth Cook**
University of Newcastle, Australia
beth.cook@newcastle.edu.au

**Judy Sheard**
Monash University, Australia
judy.sheard@monash.edu

**Angela Carbone**
Monash University, Australia
angela.carbone@monash.edu

**Chris Johnson**
Australian National University
chris.johnson@anu.edu.au

## ABSTRACT

Student perceptions of academic integrity have been extensively researched in relation to text-based assessments, but there is rather less research relating to non-text-based assessments such as computer programs, databases, and spreadsheets. This paper reports the findings from a survey of computing students and academics to investigate perceptions of particular academic practices with regard to both essays and computing assessments. For each practice the research sought to discover whether it was perceived to constitute plagiarism or collusion and whether it was considered to be acceptable in an academic environment. While there was general agreement between academics and students regarding some practices, both groups displayed high levels of uncertainty about other practices. There was considerable variation between their attitudes to similar practices in the text and non-text environments, and between what was seen as plagiarism/collusion and perceptions of unacceptability. That is, there were practices that were perceived to be plagiarism or collusion but were considered acceptable, and others that were considered not to be plagiarism or collusion but were nevertheless thought unacceptable. These findings suggest a need for academic integrity policies and procedures specific to computing, accompanied by discipline-specific student education.

## Categories and Subject Descriptors

K3.2 [**Computers and education**]: Computer and Information Science Education – *computer science education*
K.4.1 [**Public Policy Issues**]: ethics, intellectual property rights

## Keywords

Academic integrity, computing education, non-text-based assessment

## 1. INTRODUCTION

A number of factors have been linked to the widely held view that plagiarism and collusion are common practices in higher

*ICER '14*, August 11 - 13 2014, Glasgow, United Kingdom.
Copyright 2014 ACM 978-1-4503-2755-8/14/08...$15.00.
http://dx.doi.org/10.1145/2632320.2632342

education. Some commentators link the perceived prevalence to developments in higher education, such as increased class sizes [20] and the rapid expansion in student numbers and changes in the types of student [12]. Some point to the exponential growth in the availability of information on the internet as a major factor in plagiarism [9, 12, 18, 25]. The increased use of group work has been recognised as blurring the boundaries between acceptable collaboration and unacceptable collusion [19].

Concerns about the adverse impact of plagiarism and collusion have motivated extensive research into academic integrity and the development of detailed definitions, educational materials, policies and procedures in higher education institutions internationally. While there is an extensive body of literature on academic integrity issues relating to prose text, there is much less literature relating to computing assessments, and we are not aware of any comparative studies of perceptions relating to text and non-text assessments. This paper reports on a nationwide Australian investigation into the perceptions of computing academics and students, in relation to plagiarism and collusion in both text-based and computing assessments.

## 2. BACKGROUND

Plagiarism and collusion are two of the major concerns in academic integrity. While some writers use the single word 'plagiarism' to cover both, we believe that the distinction is important in some disciplines, including computing, so we maintain the distinction in our research, and define it briefly here. Both plagiarism and collusion entail using the work of others without properly attributing that work. With plagiarism, the 'others' are typically people that the writer does not know, and the writer has found their work in some public medium such as a book, a journal, or the web. With collusion, the 'others' are typically people that the writer knows, and who tend to collaborate with the writer to produce the finished work. A common example of plagiarism would be including in one's work something found on the web and not referencing it; a common example of collusion would be two or more students in a class working together on an assessment item that is required to be done individually.

It is a continuing theme in the literature relating to academic integrity that students understand extreme examples of plagiarism but lack the skills to discriminate with less clear-cut scenarios [4, 8, 9, 10, 15, 16]. Numerous studies have found that the majority of students surveyed did not consider the resubmission of work previously submitted elsewhere to be plagiarism [4, 8, 15, 17]. Some studies have found that a majority of students thought collusion was an acceptable practice [1, 17], while others found that only a minority viewed collusion as serious cheating [10, 16].

Although there is some agreement that academics have more consistent interpretations of what constitutes acceptable academic behavior, and generally view breaches of academic integrity more seriously than do students [7, 10, 16, 18], there is evidence that academics also struggle to recognise plagiarism in particular circumstances [7].

Most of the literature of academic integrity deals with prose text assessment items. This is often not made explicit, but examples will tend to be couched in such terms as text, paraphrasing, direct quotation, in-text references, and more, all of which are specific to the written word [4, 9, 13, 19]. The different nature of assessments completed by computing students brings into question whether academics and students in this discipline will have the same perceptions of practices such as reusing the work of others in computing assessments as they might have in text-based assessments [22]. Even within the bounds of prose text, a number of authors have acknowledged the need for discipline-specific standards [9, 13, 15, 25].

Perceptions aside, the detection of plagiarism and collusion in computing is complicated by the fact that computer programs, databases, and other computing deliverables tend to have somewhat uniform structures, making similarity detection more difficult than with text [2, 23].

Research into perceptions of academic integrity in computing assessments has mirrored work in the text field by investigating the reasons why student plagiarise or collude [5, 20, 24] and by asking students and/or academics whether specific scenarios constitute plagiarism, collusion or cheating [2, 3, 5, 11, 24].

Dennis [5] took four scenarios identified by staff as collusion and presented them to first-year computing students in the UK. Three of the scenarios were identified as collusion by over 90% of students, while around 75% correctly identified the sharing of methods (the Java term for subroutines) as collusion. Around 16% of students admitted to sharing methods and thought that this was an acceptable practice.

Research conducted in Australia used 18 scenarios to investigate computing students' perceptions of cheating, plagiarism and collusion [6]. This research found that students perceived it as unacceptable to submit work that was wholly or partly someone else's, but thought it acceptable to resubmit one's own assignment from a previous subject or to acquire what the researchers considered to be excessive assistance from a friend [6]. However, these practices were viewed as somewhat less acceptable when the survey was repeated a decade later [20].

An online survey of 313 computing students and 25 staff in Slovakia established that the majority of both groups thought that copying source code and documentation was plagiarism [2]. However, only 40% of academics and 11% of students agreed that copying the input data of the program constituted plagiarism.

In a survey of 59 computing academics conducted in the UK, a majority agreed that reproducing or copying source code and submitting it without acknowledgement constitutes plagiarism [3]. A subsequent survey involving 770' students revealed that the majority of students did not consider it as plagiarism to substantially re-use one's own code from a former assessment item, or to translate a program from another programming language, without referencing [11].

In this paper we report on the results of an online survey of computing academics and students in Australian universities that investigated perceptions of plagiarism and collusion. The results provide a greater understanding of where the boundaries of plagiarism and collusion lie, and help lay the groundwork for the codification of acceptable practices and the development of educational resources to inform staff and students. Specifically this paper reports on:

- Academics' and students' perceptions of plagiarism and collusion in regard to essays and to computing assessment items
- Differences between perceptions relating to essays and to computing assessments
- Differences between perceptions of acceptability and of plagiarism and collusion

## 3. RESEARCH APPROACH

The research used a mixed methods approach to gain insights into the perceptions of academic integrity of academics and students who use non-text-based assessments. The project covered two disciplines that use two quite different forms of non-text-based assessment: computing, which uses such items as computer programs, databases, and spreadsheets; and visual design, which uses visual images. The research comprised:

- a qualitative component that used focus groups of academics and students to canvass the major academic integrity issues; and
- a quantitative component consisting of an online survey of academics and students from Australian universities.

In this paper we report on the responses from academics and students who identified as being from a computing discipline.

## 3.1 Focus groups

Focus groups were conducted at three Australian universities: two focus groups facilitated by non-teaching staff involved 12 computing students; three groups involved 18 computing academics. The focus group discussions were led by a few questions along the lines of

- What is plagiarism in the context of a written assessment item such as an essay?
- What is plagiarism in the context of a non-written assessment item?
- Do you work with assessment items where you (or your students) think unreferenced copying is legitimate so long as you add enough of your own work to the copy?
- What is collusion in the context of a written assessment item such as an essay?
- What is collusion in the context of a non-written assessment item?
- Do you work with assessment items where you (or your students) think unreferenced copying cannot be detected because all correct answers will be identical?
- When coding a program for an assignment, you use a couple of methods that you find on the web. You don't reference the source of these methods, but argue that as all the rest of the code is your own, the program is truly your own work and is not plagiarised. Discuss.

## 3.2 Online survey

Following the focus groups, an online survey was developed based upon the focus group findings and on surveys reported in the literature. The first section of the survey focused on academic integrity issues in relation to text-based assessments such as essays. This was followed by a section that explored similar issues in relation to non-text-based assessments. The remainder of the survey collected demographic information and focused on issues around academic integrity policies and how breaches of academic integrity are detected and dealt with.

Much of the survey was in four distinct branches, for computing academics, computing students, design academics, and design students. The survey was quite substantial, consisting of some 30 questions, four or five of which require responses to multiple scenarios. It was expected that participants would take 20-30 minutes to complete the survey, so as an incentive they were invited to take part in a draw to win one of five tablets or comparably priced devices.

The survey was promulgated by way of direct contacts. The team's project manager conducted web searches to identify people at each Australian university who might be able to assist, telephoned those people, and if necessary telephoned further contacts until she found one who was able and willing to inform relevant staff and students of the survey. When the survey was released she sent the link to all of these contacts, and halfway through the survey period she sent a reminder.

## 4. FINDINGS

Participants in the focus groups suggested that there are substantial differences between academic integrity issues in text-based assessments and computing assessments. All focus groups emphasised that plagiarism and collusion are more difficult to define in computing and that the boundaries between acceptable and unacceptable practices are more blurred than with text. It was observed that even if one chose to reference one's computing work, there are no standard guidelines for doing so. Further, while an in-text reference is clearly evident when one is reading an essay, there is no comparable way of referencing, say, a segment of program code so that the reference will be obvious to the user running the program. The findings from the focus groups have been reported in more detail elsewhere [22].

People from all 39 Australian universities participated in the survey of academics and students who use non-text-based assessments. A total of 1315 responses were received, with a final sample of 990 after eliminating inappropriate or incomplete responses.

The sample consisted of a computing and a design cohort. Some findings from the design cohort have been presented at a venue better suited to that cohort [21]. They bear some similarity to those presented here for the computing cohort, but there are also notable differences. For example, design students generally consider it academic misconduct to discuss work in progress with other students, whereas computing students are split fairly evenly on this question.

The remainder of this paper presents an analysis of the perceptions of plagiarism and collusion, and of acceptability, of the 70 computing academics and 486 computing students who responded to the survey.

We have no idea how many staff and students at each university are involved with computing or design courses, and given the

means by which the survey was promulgated we have no idea how many of these were informed of the survey. Therefore we cannot even begin to estimate a response rate for the survey.

Sections 4.4 to 4.6 of this paper compare the respondents' perceptions in three different ways, using appropriate tests to look for differences that are statistically significant. Some readers will be aware of what statisticians call 'the p-value problem': that for very large samples almost everything is statistically significant and gives rise to low p-values. However, discussions of this phenomenon [14] refer to sample sizes in the tens of thousands or hundreds of thousands, not to the tens and hundreds reported in this paper. Furthermore, if our sample size were large enough to be subject to the p-value problem, we would expect almost every difference to be statistically significant, and that is patently not the case. For these reasons we do not believe that the p-value problem is an issue in the research reported here.

The students who completed the survey were predominantly under 25 (72%), undergraduate (84%), and Australian (81%). Around three-quarters of academics and students were male. About a third of the academics had been teaching in higher education for less than 10 years, a third between 10 and 19 years, and a third for 20 years or more.

This section outlines the perceptions of computing academics and students concerning plagiarism/collusion and acceptability in relation to both text-based assessments such as essays and non-text-based assessments such as computer programming. Prior to a detailed analysis of the survey results we consider briefly the data describing the environments within which those perceptions have developed.

Only 30% of academics and 42% of students agreed that the academic integrity policy at their institution adequately addressed non-text-based assessment items. The lack of clear definition of standards was further evidenced by the fact that two-thirds of academics and 38% of students agreed that different staff members have different interpretations of academic integrity that lead to differences in their treatment of students. Supporting the findings from the literature and the focus groups, around three in five participants agreed that it is more difficult to define plagiarism/collusion with non-text-based assessments, while around 70% agreed that there is a grey area between plagiarism/collusion relating to computer code and standard practices such as using message boards and online tutorials.

One question in the survey presented 14 specific scenarios relating to essays, and a separate question presented 14 parallel scenarios for computing assessments. For each scenario respondents were asked whether the described practice constituted plagiarism or collusion and also whether it was acceptable (see Table 1). Note that while we distinguish clearly between plagiarism and collusion, and while these terms were defined at relevant points in the survey, we did not ask respondents to distinguish between the two. The question 'Does this constitute plagiarism or collusion?' had three possible answers: yes, unsure, and no.

## 4.1 Practices considered by participants to be plagiarism or collusion

Eight of the 14 scenarios were considered to be plagiarism or collusion by a majority of students and academics for both essays and computing assessments (Figure 1).

| | Essay Scenarios | Computing Scenarios |
|---|---|---|
| 1 | Copying or paraphrasing the words of others and fully referencing them. | Basing an assessment on code that is freely available from some source, such as the web, and referencing the source. |
| 2 | Copying or paraphrasing the words of others and not fully referencing them. | Basing an assessment on code that is freely available from some source, such as the web, without referencing the source. |
| 3 | Purchasing an essay from the internet and submitting it as one's own work. | Purchasing code written by others to incorporate into one's own work. |
| 4 | Paying another person to write the essay and submitting it as one's own work. | Paying another person to write the code and submitting it as one's own work. |
| 5 | Basing one's essay largely on an essay that one wrote and submitted for a previous course, without acknowledging this. | Basing an assessment largely on work that one wrote and submitted for a previous course, without acknowledging this. |
| 6 | Posting one's essay to an online forum and asking for feedback on it. | Posting troublesome code on a message board and asking for help with it. |
| 7 | Incorporating the work of another student without their permission. | Incorporating the work of another student without their permission. |
| 8 | Borrowing another student's essay and rewriting it in one's own words. | Borrowing another student's code and changing it so that it looks quite different. |
| 9 | Borrowing an early draft of another student's essay and developing it into one's own work. | Borrowing an early draft of another student's work and developing it into one's own. |
| 10 | Discussing with another student how to approach an essay and what literature to read, then researching and writing the essay independently. | Discussing with another student how to approach a task and what resources to use, then developing the solution independently. |
| 11 | Discussing the detail of one's essay with another student while working on it. | Discussing the detail of one's code with another student while working on it. |
| 12 | Showing one's essay to another student and asking them for advice on how to improve it. | Showing troublesome code to another student and asking them for advice on how to fix it. |
| 13 | Giving one's completed essay to another student and asking them to improve it. | Asking another student to take troublesome code and get it working. |
| 14 | Completing an essay and then expanding it to include an issue that one found out about by reading another student's essay. | Completing an assessment and then adding features that one noticed when looking at another student's work. |

A clear majority of participants agreed that it was plagiarism/collusion to purchase the work of others and submit it as one's own (scenarios 3 and 4); to incorporate the work of another student without their permission (scenario 7); or to include the work of others without referencing the source (scenario 2). A number of other scenarios were also seen as plagiarism/collusion, but by diminishing majorities: borrowing and using another student's work (scenarios 8 and 9); giving completed work to another student and asking them to improve it (scenario 13); and using work that had been written and submitted for a previous assignment (scenario 5) – a very slim majority.

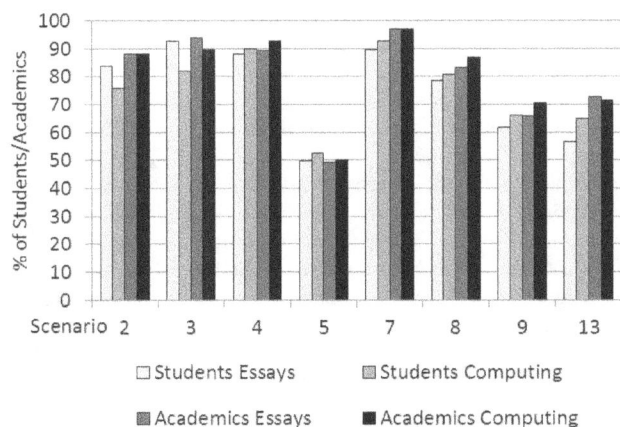

**Figure 1: Practices considered to be plagiarism or collusion**

There was very little variation in the results for academics between the essay and computing scenarios. On the other hand, there were two scenarios in which students distinguished between essays and computing. With scenario 3, 93% of students viewed it as plagiarism to purchase an essay, but this fell to 82% for computer code (although the computing scenario left open the possibility that only part of the assignment was being purchased). Similarly, with scenario 2, 84% of students thought it was plagiarism/collusion to copy or paraphrase other people's words in an essay without reference, but only 76% thought it was plagiarism/collusion to do the same with program code. For most of the other scenarios, marginally more students perceived plagiarism/collusion in the computing environment than in the essay equivalent.

## 4.2 Practices not considered by participants to be plagiarism or collusion

The remaining scenarios (Figure 2) were perceived as plagiarism/collusion by fewer than half of the respondents. As expected, the vast majority of respondents did not consider using another's work and fully referencing it (scenario 1) to be plagiarism. The other scenarios related mainly to interaction with other students: discussing how to approach a task and then working independently (scenario 10); discussing the detail of work in progress (scenario 11); and showing completed work to a friend and asking for advice on how to improve it (scenario 12). Assistance from others in the form of posting work to an online forum and asking for feedback (scenario 6) and changing completed work to incorporate an issue or feature from another

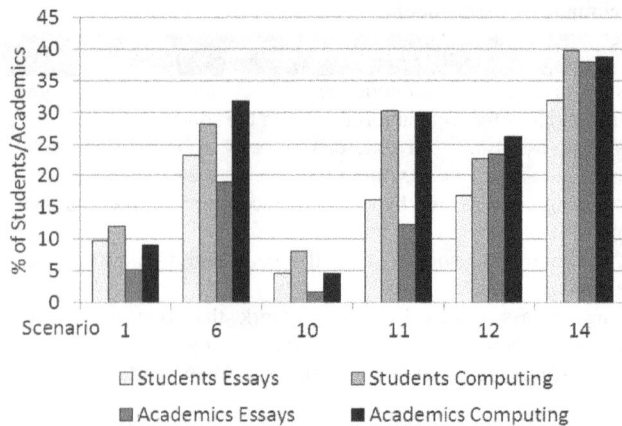

**Figure 2: Practices not considered to be plagiarism or collusion (bars show percentage of responses indicating that the practice constitutes plagiarism/collusion)**

student's work (scenario 14) were also only identified as plagiarism/collusion by a minority of participants.

With every one of these scenarios, a higher proportion of participants indicated that they were plagiarism/collusion for computing assessments than for essays.

## 4.3 How much uncertainty was there?

In response to concerns about the perceived level of plagiarism, Australian universities have progressively introduced initiatives to educate students about academic integrity, predominantly in relation to prose text. Given the abundance of education for text situations, compared with an apparent dearth of information and education in relation to non-text situations, we would expect that academics and students would be much more accomplished at recognising plagiarism in essays than in computing assessments.

This view is not fully supported by the findings of this research. A relatively large proportion of academics and students indicated that they were unsure whether some scenarios were plagiarism/collusion, both in the essay and computing contexts. Figure 3 shows the scenarios where 20% or more of the respondents indicated that they were not sure if a scenario constituted plagiarism/collusion.

In relation to essays, more than a third of both students and academics indicated that they were not sure whether scenarios 6 (posting an essay to an online forum) and 14 (expanding an essay to include an issue found by reading another student's essay) were plagiarism or collusion. More than one in five were unsure about scenarios 5, 9, 11, 12 and 13.

For the non-text scenarios, about half of the scenarios showed uncertainty levels of 20% or more, and students tended to be less sure than academics. Around a third of students were unsure about scenarios 6, 11 and 14, and more than a fifth for scenarios 5, 9, 12 and 13.

Overall levels of uncertainty were slightly higher for students than academics, but there was very little difference between uncertainty levels for essays and computing.

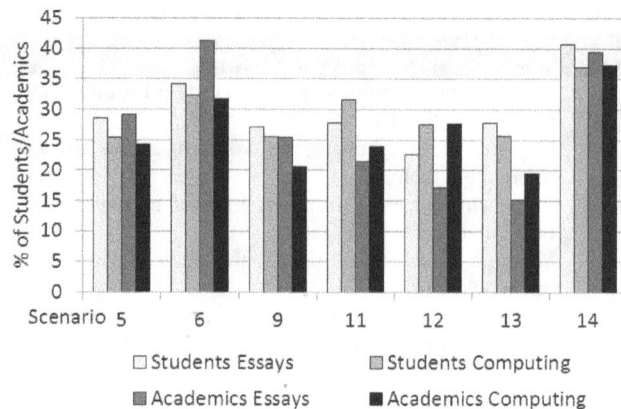

**Figure 3: Unsure if practice is plagiarism/collusion**

## 4.4 Differences between the perceptions of academics and students

For each essay scenario and each computing scenario we used chi-square tests to test for differences in the perceptions of academics and students, both for the question of whether the scenario constituted plagiarism/collusion and for the question of whether it was considered to be an acceptable academic practice. Table 2 shows the differences that were significant at the 0.05 level.

**Table 2: Differences between perceptions of academics and students**

|    | Essays/ Comp | Acceptable Plag/Coll | df | N | Chi-Square | *p* |
|----|------|------|----|-----|------|------|
| 13 | essays | plag/coll | 2 | 530 | 6.50 | 0.04 |
| 12 | essays | acceptable | 2 | 547 | 11.50 | 0.00 |
| 13 | essays | acceptable | 2 | 536 | 7.80 | 0.02 |
| 1 | comp | acceptable | 2 | 549 | 9.78 | 0.03 |
| 2 | comp | acceptable | 2 | 531 | 6.59 | 0.04 |
| 5 | comp | acceptable | 2 | 538 | 6.70 | 0.04 |

To the question of whether a practice constitutes plagiarism/ collusion there was only one statistically significant difference, for scenario 13 for essays: significantly more academics than students thought it was plagiarism/collusion to give a completed essay to another student and ask them to improve it.

To the question of whether a practice was acceptable academic conduct, there were statistically significant differences for both essays and computing, but with different scenarios. For essays, significantly more students than academics thought it acceptable to show one's essay to another student and ask them how to improve it (scenario 12) and to give one's completed essay to another student and ask them to improve it (scenario 13). For computing assessments, significantly more students than academics thought it acceptable to base an assessment on freely available code and reference the source (scenario 1), to base an assessment on freely available code and not reference the source (scenario 2), and to base an assessment largely on one written for a previous course without acknowledging this (scenario 5).

## 4.5 Differences between perceptions for essays and computing assessments

It was seen in figures 1 and 2 that the proportion of respondents categorising particular scenarios as plagiarism/collusion varied according to whether the scenarios related to essay or computing assessments. We used McNemar-Bowker tests to determine whether differences in answers to the essay and computing scenarios (no, unsure, yes) were statistically significant at the 0.05 level.

Table 3 reports for each scenario the statistically significant differences and the setting that drew the higher proportion of agreement. For example, significantly more students thought scenario 13 unacceptable in the essay setting than in the computing setting. On the other hand, significantly more students deemed the same scenario to be plagiarism/collusion in the computing setting than in the essay setting. For a number of the scenarios, denoted "a" in Table 3, the test could not be computed for academics because at least one cell of the data table was empty.

**Table 3: Differences in perceptions between essays and computing assessments**

|  | More unacceptable | | More plag/coll | |
|  | Academics | Students | Academics | Students |
|---|---|---|---|---|
| 1 | computing | computing | - | computing |
| 2 | a | essays | - | essays |
| 3 | a | essays | - | essays |
| 4 | a | - | - | - |
| 5 | - | essays | - | - |
| 6 | - | essays | - | - |
| 7 | a | - | a | - |
| 8 | - | - | a | - |
| 9 | - | - | - | - |
| 10 | a | computing | - | computing |
| 11 | - | computing | computing | computing |
| 12 | - | - | computing | computing |
| 13 | - | essays | - | computing |
| 14 | - | computing | - | computing |

*Note: a. The McNemar-Bowker test could not be calculated.*

In relation to computing assessments, a higher proportion of academics found copying and fully referencing (scenario 1) unacceptable than for essays. Similarly, a higher proportion of academics classified discussing the detail of work in progress (scenario 11) and asking another student for advice on how to fix troublesome code (scenario 12) as plagiarism/collusion than for the essay equivalent. These are possibly academics who require their students to create their own assignments alone and from scratch, but who would not apply the same strictures to essay-writing.

Computing students differentiated between essays and computing assessments for several scenarios. Practices such as copying and not fully referencing (scenario 2) and purchasing work from the internet (scenario 3) were regarded as more acceptable in computing than for essays, and fewer students classified these as plagiarism/collusion in computing than in essays. Conversely, discussing a task and then working alone (scenario 10), discussing the detail of work in progress (scenario

11), and adding features from another student's work (scenario 14) were less acceptable in computing than in essays, and more students classified these as plagiarism/collusion in computing.

Although a higher proportion of students classified asking another student to improve completed work (scenario 13) as plagiarism/collusion for computing, this practice was regarded as more acceptable in computing assessments than in essays.

As described earlier, all participants responded to the essay scenarios first and the computing scenarios later. This could perhaps have led to an ordering effect in the responses, but if there was such an effect it does not appear to have been substantial, as some of the differences favour essays while others favour computing assessments.

## 4.6 Differences between perceptions of plagiarism/collusion and unacceptability

While it might have seemed redundant to ask both whether a practice was plagiarism/collusion and whether it was acceptable, this was done deliberately in order to examine whether some participants thought that individual scenarios were:

- considered to be plagiarism or collusion but still considered acceptable; or
- not considered to be plagiarism/collusion but nevertheless considered unacceptable.

We used McNemar-Bowker tests to determine whether there were significant differences between perceptions of what constituted plagiarism/collusion and of what was considered unacceptable.

Table 4 shows the statistically significant differences between perceptions of plagiarism/collusion and unacceptability, most of which were for students. Note that these measures are just of the differences, not of the majority view. For example, in Table 4 there are 12 scenarios marked 'not plag/coll but unacceptable'. As it happens, every one of these 12 was identified as plagiarism/collusion by a majority of respondents. Table 4 tells us only that significantly fewer identified it as acceptable than identified it as plagiarism/collusion.

Of the practices considered by some respondents to be unacceptable but not to constitute plagiarism/collusion, some displayed large differences:

- Scenario 5, often called recycling or self-plagiarism: for essays, only 48% of academics and students indicated that this was plagiarism/collusion but 79% and 64% respectively said it was unacceptable; for computing assessments 49% of academics and 52% of students thought it was plagiarism/collusion but 71% of academics and 59% of students thought it was unacceptable.
- Scenario 13, asking another student to improve an essay: only 56% of students thought that this was plagiarism/ collusion, but 70% indicated that it was not acceptable.

## Table 4: Differences in perceptions of plagiarism/collusion and unacceptability

| | Essays | | Computing | |
| | Academics | Students | Academics | Students |
|---|---|---|---|---|
| 1 | - | Prop 1 | Prop 2 | - |
| 2 | a | - | - | - |
| 3 | a | not plag/coll but unacceptable | a | - |
| 4 | a | not plag/coll but unacceptable | a | not plag/coll but unacceptable |
| 5 | not plag/coll but unacceptable | not plag/coll but unacceptable | not plag/coll but unacceptable | not plag/coll but unacceptable |
| 6 | - | - | - | plag/coll but acceptable |
| 7 | a | not plag/coll but unacceptable | a | - |
| 8 | a | not plag/coll but unacceptable | - | - |
| 9 | not plag/coll but unacceptable | - | | not plag/coll but unacceptable |
| 10 | a | plag/coll but acceptable | - | plag/coll but acceptable |
| 11 | - | plag/coll but acceptable | - | plag/coll but acceptable |
| 12 | - | plag/coll but acceptable | plag/coll but acceptable | plag/coll but acceptable |
| 13 | - | not plag/coll but unacceptable | - | plag/coll but acceptable |
| 14 | - | plag/coll but acceptable | - | plag/coll but acceptable |

*Note: a. The McNemar-Bowker test could not be calculated*

Practices considered acceptable by some, despite being identified as plagiarism/collusion, related to scenarios that could be classified as collusion. These involved interaction with others, either discussing assessment tasks or seeking assistance to complete the work. Major differences were recorded for:

- Scenario 11 for computing, discussing the detail of code while working on the assessment: 30% of students identified this as plagiarism/collusion but only 20% thought it was unacceptable.

- Scenario 12 for computing, asking another student for assistance to fix troublesome code: 22% of students thought this was plagiarism/collusion but only 13% thought it was unacceptable.

## 5. CONCLUSION

This research has contributed to the literature on academic integrity issues relating to computing assessments. The Australian national survey of academics and students has revealed that there is a high level of agreement between students and academics in their assessment of whether particular scenarios constituted plagiarism/collusion and whether they were acceptable practices in an academic environment. However, there were also high levels of uncertainty for some scenarios.

The results also indicate that there are statistically significant differences between perceptions for essays and computing assessments, suggesting the need for further research to ascertain why these differences exist and whether there is a case for different academic integrity standards and procedures for computing assessments.

Having investigated perceptions both of whether scenarios constitute plagiarism/collusion and of whether they are acceptable practices, we find that some scenarios were viewed as unacceptable by some participants even though they did not think they constituted plagiarism/collusion. Conversely, some participants who identified practices as plagiarism/collusion nevertheless considered them to be acceptable, suggesting that there may be deep-seated differences with existing academic integrity policies.

This discrepancy suggests that educating students about academic integrity policies is a necessary but insufficient strategy for implementing effective policies. Education in the formal identification of practices that breach academic integrity standards should be accompanied by strategies to imbue students with an understanding of and genuine commitment to these standards. Further, so long as the university-level policies and education fail to address the issues and practices specific to the computing discipline, it must be the responsibility of departments and of individual academics to ensure that they work to agreed guidelines, and that they clearly educate their students about those guidelines and about the reasons for them.

## Acknowledgements

Support for this project has been provided by the Australian Government Office for Learning and Teaching. The views expressed in this publication do not necessarily reflect those of the Australian Government Office for Learning and Teaching.

The authors are grateful to Susan Snowdon for her guidance on the p-value problem. Any continuing misunderstanding is that of the authors alone.

## 6. REFERENCES

[1] Baker, R.K., Berry, P. and Thornton, B. (2008). Student attitudes on academic integrity violations. Journal of College Teaching & Learning 5(1): 5-13.

[2] Chuda, D, P Navrat, B Kovacova and P Humay (2012). The issue of (software) plagiarism: a student view. IEEE Transactions on Education 55(1): 22-28.

[3] Cosma, G. and M Joy (2008). Towards a Definition of Source-Code Plagiarism. IEEE Transactions on Education 51(2): 195-200.

[4] Curtis, GJ and R Popal (2011). An examination of factors related to plagiarism and a five-year follow-up of plagiarism at an Australian university. International Journal for Educational Integrity 7(1): 30-42

[5] Dennis, L (2004). Student attitudes to plagiarism and collusion within computer science. Paper presented at the First International Plagiarism Conference 2004.

[6] Dick, M, J Sheard, and S Markham (2001). Is it okay to cheat? The views of postgraduate students. ACM SIGCSE Bulletin 33(3): 61-64.

[7] Foltýnek, T., Rybička, J. and Demoliou, C (2013). Do students think what teachers think about plagiarism?

Proceedings of International Conference Plagiarism across Europe and Beyond, 12-13 June 2013, Brno, Czech Republic, 127-135.

[8] Forster, P (2010). Academic integrity initiatives: have they made a difference? Paper presented at the Fourth International Plagiarism Conference, 21-23 June 2010, Northumbria University, Newcastle upon Tyne, UK.

[9] Gullifer, J and GA Tyson (2010). Exploring university students' perception of plagiarism: a focus group study. Studies in Higher Education 35(4): 463-481.

[10] Gynnild, V. and P Gotschalk. (2008). Promoting academic integrity at a Midwestern University: Critical review and current challenges. International Journal for Educational Integrity 4(2): 41-59.

[11] Joy, MS,JE Sinclair, R Boyatt, JY-K Yau and G Cosma (2013). Student perspectives on source-code plagiarism. International Journal for Educational Integrity 9(1): 3-19.

[12] Joyce, D (2007). Academic integrity and plagiarism: Australasian perspectives. Computer Science Education 17(3): 187-200.

[13] Lampert, LD (2004). Integrating discipline-based anti-plagiarism instruction into the information literacy curriculum. Reference Services Review 32(4): 347-355.

[14] Lin, M, HC Lucas Jr, and G Shmueli (2013). Too big to fail: large samples and the p-value problem. Information Systems Research 24(4): 906-917.

[15] Marshall, S, and M Garry (2005). How well do students really understand plagiarism? In H. Goss (Ed.), Balance, fidelity, mobility: Proceedings of the 2005 ASCILITE Conference. Brisbane: Queensland University of Technology, 457-467.

[16] McCabe, DL (2005). Cheating among college and university students: a North American perspective. International Journal for Educational Integrity 1(1).

[17] Owunwanne, D, N Rustagi and R Dada (2010). Students' perceptions of cheating and plagiarism in higher institutions. Journal of College Teaching and Learning 7(11): 59-68.

[18] Park, C (2003). In other (people's) words: plagiarism by university students-literature and lessons. Assessment & Evaluation in Higher Education 28(5): 471-488.

[19] Pickard, J (2006). Staff and student attitudes to plagiarism at University College Northampton. Assessment & Evaluation in Higher Education 31(2): 215-232.

[20] Sheard, J and M Dick (2011). Computing student practices of cheating and plagiarism: a decade of change. ITiCSE'11, Darmstadt, Germany, 233-237.

[21] Simon, B Cook, M Minichiello, and C Lawrence (2014). Academic integrity: differences between design assessments and essays, Design Research Society Conference (DRS 2014), Umeå, Sweden.

[22] Simon, B Cook, J Sheard, A Carbone, and C Johnson (2013). Academic integrity: differences between computing assessments and essays, 13th International Conference on Computing Education (Koli Calling 2013), Koli, Finland.

[23] Vandeventer, J and B Barbour (2012). CodeWave: a real-time, collaborative IDE for enhanced learning in computer science. SIGCSE 2012, 75-80.

[24] Vogts, D (2009). Plagiarising of source code by novice programmers a "cry for help"? 2009 Annual Research Conference of the South African Institute of Computer Scientists and Information Technologists, 141-149.

[25] Yeo, S. (2007) First-year university science and engineering students' understanding of plagiarism. Higher Education Research & Development 26(2): 199-216.

# How CS Undergraduates Make Course Choices

Michael Hewner
Rose-Hulman Institute of Technology
5500 Wabash Avenue
Terre Haute, IN
hewner@rose-hulman.edu

## ABSTRACT

Students in most CS curricula have to make a wide variety of educational decisions including what courses to take. Frequently, they must make these decisions based on a very limited knowledge of the content of the topics they are choosing between. In this paper, I describe a theory of CS undergraduate course choices, based on 37 qualitative interviews with students and student advisors, analyzed with grounded theory. Most students did not have specific educational goals in CS and, as long as their classes were enjoyable, tended to assume that any course required by the curriculum had useful content (even if they could not articulate way). Particularly enjoyable or frustrating courses caused them to make long term course/specialization decisions and use a more strategic goal–oriented approach.

## Categories and Subject Descriptors

K.3.2 [**Computers and Education**]: Computer and Information Science Education — Curriculum

## General Terms

Design, Documentation, Experimentation, Management

## Keywords

Curriculum, Concentrations, Multi–disciplinary

## 1. INTRODUCTION

"Like I was signing up for fall classes. Okay, do I want to take processer design or operating systems class? And, to be honest, that stuff looks very similar to me from my shoes, right. I don't know anything about either one, so how am I supposed to distinguish them?

So is there anything I wish like I'd been told? Well, yeah. I wish people would say like - I mean

it's sort of impossible to tell you about it until you're actually in it and doing it ... they don't sit you down and say, okay, look at this screen of assembly code. That's what you're gonna do if you go into platforms."

—3rd Year, Georgia Tech

Undergraduate students in Computer Science find themselves in a difficult position. Their understanding of the field of Computer Science is still evolving, and yet in most curricula they must make decisions about what to learn. Often these choices are extremely subtle: operating systems or processor design. Both topics have their utility, but understanding the trade-offs requires a solid knowledge of the topics covered. Yet students make these decisions routinely.

A student's decision is likely influenced by many factors [7]. If a student has specific goals in Computer Science, they will need to reason about the courses they are selecting and their benefits. This is complicated by the fact that students generally do not have a detailed view of the subfields of CS and how they are useful [9].

If a student does not have specific goals in CS, how do they make important courses decisions? They could choose courses based on causal interest. They could attempt to choose the easiest courses possible. They could attempt to select courses that would 'keep their options open' and expose them to a wide range of the field (although this requires detailed reasoning about the field of CS itself).

Based on my interviews, there is are two modes of student decision making. One mode is an exploratory: students take courses of casual interest, working within the framework of the curriculum. The second mode is goal directed; students do have a particular plan and are willing to do detailed research to achieve them. What motivates the transition between these two modes seems to be a strong emotional experience in a course. When students greatly enjoy or greatly dislike a course, it motivates them to make long term educational decisions (e.g. selecting a particular major, selecting a particular specialization within a major, or just deciding on a few courses) and begin acting more strategically.

This work presents a theory of student course choices in CS, based on 37 interviews with students and student advisers and analyzed with a grounded theory approach. The goal of this research was to understand how undergraduate CS majors choose their courses or make other educational decisions and if misconceptions about CS cause problems. This paper first presents the design of the research study, then discusses the resultant theory, then compares the theory previous work in CS and other disciplines.

## 2. METHOD

My study was an open–ended qualitative interview study designed to understand how students think about computer science and their choices throughout their undergraduate program. I interviewed 33 students, the majority of whom were undergraduate CS majors (a few were recent graduates or students who had not yet chosen to major in CS). The interviews were between 45 and 60 minutes. I also interviewed four student advisors about their experience advising undergraduate CS majors.

### 2.1 Sampling and Recruitment

Recruitment was done through presentations in CS classes. Students were asked to volunteer and offered a gift certificate to compensate them for participating. To select students to interview, I used the grounded theory practice of theoretical sampling [2]. In theoretical sampling, a researcher begins with an initial population to interview and then selects future candidates based on what would further help elaborate the developing theory. This allows the researcher to discover factors that seem to have an effect on interview responses and pursue them. However, this method does not attempt to make the sample statistically representative.

I selected students to interview in order to get a range of academic success, gender, and ethnicity. Students were recruited from CS programs at three different US schools:

- *Georgia Tech* is a competitive engineering school with a curriculum that allows a great degree of student choice in CS courses.

- *Duke University* is a competitive liberal arts school with a more proscribed CS curriculum but greater focus on multi–degree programs.

- *Spelman College* is a traditionally African–American Woman's college. Students interviewed usually had not taken CS course prior to coming to Spelman.

Students were interviewed at all stages of their 4–year undergraduate careers, with particular focus on students in the 2nd and 3rd year. Note that students are identified by their approximate place in the curriculum (and therefore the courses they have had) not the absolute number of years they have been within the program (e.g. an accelerated 1st year student might be identified as a 2nd year student).

This study is focused on US students and 4–year CS curricula. The three schools were selected to give variation within those parameters. Although it is hoped that these results are suggestive to international CS educators, there are some clear limits to generalizability. First, curricula and the course choices available to students vary significantly between country and that will obviously affect student processes. Second, different cultural contexts (both cultural perceptions of CS and more general ideas like the purpose of college) are likely to have large effects.

### 2.2 Interview Method

The initial goal was to explore if student misconceptions of the field of CS caused educational problems when students attempted to select their classes or otherwise made educational decisions that required them to reason about CS as a field. The initially proposed study included detailed questions about computer architecture, compilers, to probe if students understood the relationship of these sub–disciplines as they made educational decisions.

As is common in a qualitative approach, the initial research questions proved to not match the participants' understanding of the situation. Initial interviews used fairly focused questions, asking students about specific courses or topics and reflect on their relationships with their goals. E.g, "Do you think you might use [topic X] in the future . . . How?" Initially, it was quite clear that students had no familiarity with the topics of future CS courses. Some students were adept at reasoning about what might be covered in the future, some were very far off base (e.g. operating systems being about configuring Unix servers) but for both groups it was clear that they did not use similar reasoning when selecting courses. Even when selecting courses that students presumably had some familiarity with (e.g. courses they had already chosen to take next semester), students repeatedly reiterated that it was their expectation to have the course syllabus on the first day be their first introduction to the topics of a course.

In later interviews, questions began with asking students about their own experiences in the major. I asked students to describe their courses and courses they were interested in the future. Usually this would naturally segue into a discussion of decisions they had made and why they made them. Students would reflect more freely on their own processes and even occasionally probe their own decision making reasons.

### 2.3 Checks to Ensure Validity

When attempting to understand student conceptions, there is a risk of misinterpretation and bias. This is a common problem in qualitative research; even when participants and researchers act in good faith, it is difficult to understand when backgrounds and assumptions are different. There are a variety of techniques to mitigate this risk [10]. I used two: triangulation from multiple data sources and member checking.

For triangulation, I used a written survey instrument with concrete questions about CS, handed to students after the in person interview. However, there was difficulty taking the very open ended approach used in the interview process and turning them into questions of sufficient specificity in a written form. Given the completed theory, I think it would be possible to design an appropriate questionnaire but the surveys I used focused on issues of student conceptions and therefore do not provide an effective triangulation,

With three students, I also used member checking: providing the student with my analysis of their educational decision approach and asking for feedback. In one case, I contacted the research participant after the initial interview and reinterviewed them with the my interpretation of their viewpoint. In two others, I presented my analysis after the regular interview process concluded. The students agreed quite strongly with my analysis (even after careful probing to attempt to mitigate power differential that makes agreement suspect [2]). Still, a greater amount of member checking would be preferable.

### 2.4 Grounded Theory Analysis

A grounded theory is based off careful line–by–line analysis of interview transcripts. My process was based off the approach outlined by Charmaz [2]:

1. First I read through the transcripts line–by–line and developed initial codes that describe what is being expressed in each line of the data (similar to Strauss and Corbin's open coding [4]).

2. Second, I went back through the body of research accumulated and selected 'focused' codes that explain larger segments of the data. This is similar to the axial coding described in Strauss and Corbin 2nd edition, but not exactly the same thing ([2], pg. 57–60).

3. Third, the focused codes are abstracted into categories in a tentative theory that is then checked against other parts of the data to test its explanatory power. There are several techniques I used to help to attempt to develop the categories in this larger theory including theoretical coding [2] and situational maps [3].

For example, consider the quote below:

> "Software engineering, it looked like it was more offered by lower tier colleges...I figured, even though I don't really like theory, there's probably some stuff in it that's useful and probably would make me a better programmer overall. So I figured I'll stick with Computer Science but try to take more practical side of classes."
>
> —2nd Year, Georgia Tech

One of the things I coded about this quote was the student's decision to rely on the reputation of the CS curriculum, despite negative experiences with CS theory in high school. The initial coding was abstracted into the focused code "trust in the curriculum," which included several other students who specifically mentioned they chose particular specializations because the specializations were considered "traditional" CS. When comparing student responses, I saw similar but different responses: students who argued that specializations were unimportant because they knew the curriculum would cover any really essential CS topics. I created a superordinate code about how students assume the CS curriculum will teach them everything they need to know, even when they often don't know what they really want from CS. Eventually, this code became called "abdicating responsibility to the curriculum."

## 2.5 Revising the Theory

Throughout the grounded theory process, there are tentative theories. These theories are being put to the test in later interviews, and during analysis processes like situational analysis. Usually, initial generalizations turn out to not to be universally true. Contradictions triggered me to revisit the source data and to become more nuanced which moves the grounded theory forward.

For example, at one point in the analysis, the idea that enjoying classes was the main determinant for student course choices was a major part of the tentative theory. There were a variety of codes having to do with student enjoyment like "frustration causing reconsideration", "enjoying classes involved in educational decisions", and "just choosing what sounds 'interesting' ". But, by looking at the counts of each code, other codes like "parental involvement" were almost as common. That seemed wrong insofar as enjoyment seemed to figure greatly into student decisions, but parental involvement definitely seemed more peripheral. It was clear that something about student enjoyment was being missed, so I went back through the codes and attempted to understand the role of enjoyment more clearly.

> "I got [to my architecture course] and I was like, 'I don't understand any of this. I don't really like it.' So I switched to [the people specialization] which I like a lot more. I have a lot of interest in psychology. I'm actually getting a certificate in social and personality psychology . So I switched.
>
> And I was kind of hesitant at first when I talked to my — the advisor in the CS department, because I was like, 'This - that really isn't as good for a career in video game animation and special effects or whatever I decided to go into.' She was like, 'It's not.' "
>
> —4th Year, Georgia Tech

Quotes like the one above made me realize that there were different kinds of enjoyment experiences. Weaker positive experiences encourage students to explore. But when a student has a very negative experience in a course, it often triggered them to make an educational decision. Then when they're making that decision, they solicit advice from parents or advisers (as in the quote above). But the experience triggering the sudden reorinetation is the emotional experience of enjoyment, which is why enjoyment seemed abstractly to be more important than, for example, parental advice. This idea eventually was revised even further into the overall idea of student course choices that is discussed below.

## 3. A THEORY OF STUDENT COURSE CHOICES

In this section, I propose a theory of CS student educational decision making based on my interviews. I begin with some of the puzzling student behaviors that suggests that students make decisions differently than one might expect. The overall theory is this:

1. Students initially start focused on *exploration*. They have *no concrete goal in CS*, and they don't attempt to gain a detailed view of the field quickly. Instead, they take courses as prescribed by the curriculum. They make the assumption that the curriculum is designed so that (regardless of what they might eventually pursue) it will put them in a good position. I described these students as *abdicating responsibility to the curriculum*. If the curriculum forces them to make choices, they will select them mostly based on casual interest, confident they all options are equally viable.

2. The exploratory approach continues until students experience a contrasting enjoyment experience: a course that is either much more or much less enjoyable than the others (most commonly less). Then *contrasting enjoyment experience triggers the student to make choices*. Often, they will narrow their educational focus and more clearly define their goals. The student may choose majors, specializations within majors, etc. Usually the student also solicits advice from parents, advisors, and websites at this point.

3. Once their educational focus is sufficiently narrow, students develop a concrete goal. At that point, students' approach changes to *making choices based on long term goals*. At this stage, they do attempt to reason about future courses and make strategic educational decisions. For most students, this occurs late in the undergraduate career if at all. Note that a student can make an educational decision at one level of detail (e.g. picking a particular CS specialization) and then act in an exploratory way within that decision (e.g. trying various subspecialties).

The following sections explain the various parts of this process in more detail.

## 3.1 No Concrete Educational Goals

"It's hard to remember [why I took a CS class at first] ... I thought I was kind of interested in, cognitive psychology and stuff and there's basically one — cognitive science actually. There's basically [one] cognitive science course and it has as its prerequisites one of the following and the intro to Computer Science was one of them. So I kind of had it in my head like 'Oh, I'll take that and that's offered in the fall.' So I couldn't take that in the freshman fall 'cause I hadn't taken any of the prerequisites. And then I ended up taking, like, all of [the prerequisites] and never taking that other class."

—3rd Year, Duke University

The first thing to know about students' decision making is that most do not have a concrete educational goal in Computer Science. As with the student in the quote above, a student's decision to take classes in CS might have nothing to do with a particular interest in the major. Even for students who select the CS major before they come to college, they may have enjoyed programming on their own but they almost never have researched the field of CS or what job they would like after graduation. Not having a goal makes the process of course selection much different than you would expect.

For example, when talking with a student advisor, the advisor estimated that a third of incoming CS students have a very off–base view of what CS is about. Given that, one might expect to see a fair number of students initially major in CS and then quickly shift to another major that is more in–line with their goals. According to the advisors, students don't change majors just because CS was radically different from their expectations. Instead students start leaving when their GPAs begin to go down. The advisor estimated that only two percent of major changes are students who are doing well academically but find CS doesn't match their expectations. Even acknowledging that off–the–cuff statistics probably have a fair degree of inaccuracy, this suggests that many students enter CS with an inaccurate conception of what CS is, yet — once they change their view of CS is — most students (at least initially) persist in CS. Poor grades are what motivate students to leave CS, not innaccurate views of the field.

A second example of student decision making without concrete goals is how students choose which courses to specialize

in. When I explicitly asked students about their post graduation goals, they rarely had a specific job or category of job in mind. Except for students recently involved in a job search, students' goals usually were not committed enough to suggest specific educational paths. One student was deciding between continuing in CS to get a Masters or Ph.D., joining the Navy, or web programming. The student did not have a plan for how to purse any of these goals by taking courses in CS. Some students suggested they might want to become a professional programmer for a company like Google, although they could not give any specifics about what they would like to do in such a job or what Google might be looking for. Many students admitted they had no idea where they would like to work or what they would like to do.

The fact that students don't have concrete goals early in their CS education is not necessarily an educational problem. But it does raise a question: how do students make educational decisions without a goal? What made students select CS initially if not an idea of what they might do after graduation?

## 3.2 Abdicating Responsibility to the Curriculum

"[I found my classes valuable not because] I had some predefined idea of 'this is what's important in this topic' and 'he should be teaching this'. It was because all of [my school]'s professors are very well-known ... so when you go into a [class] and you sit down in front of a professor, it doesn't matter what he wants to say. You kind of listen because you know it's gonna be important. It's just the people they are, that you trust them to know what they're teaching is important, and that's why we come to [this school]."

—3rd Year, Georgia Tech

At all the schools we talked to, CS students had a great trust that the content they learned in their CS courses would be valuable to them. Even when they were not able to articulate why a particular topic was valuable, they were confident they learned it for some reason (or at least that it was useful to some particular kind of CS major even if it was not useful to them). Students were also confident that whatever they would be taught would be useful in accomplishing their career goals, even though in general they were not sure what those goals were. As a result, students generally selected courses by looking at the degree requirements and selecting the next courses off the list.

Although the students are described as 'abdicating responsibility' this process was not necessarily a bad thing. For example, students' trust in the curriculum meant that students were often exposed to different kinds of CS content and believed it was valuable. However, it did often seem to be in conflict with curricula that gave the students a lot of choices. For example, a student who disliked architecture felt free to not take a second course in architecture, even though it significantly limited future course options. Because that was allowed within the framework of the curriculum, the student felt it was safe (i.e. would not limit their future career options). This is not to say that the decision to leave the course was a bad one: simply that the decision about whether a particular course is valuable would ideally be about the CS content covered and a particular student's goals. Given students' lack of detailed knowledge about CS [9] this approach is understandable. However, curriculum designers need to take this reliance into account and ensure that the curriculum really is as safe as students believe it to be.

## 3.3 Exploration

"So basically what I figured I wanna be kind of like well rounded ...[Networking] was the other one and I figured that that would come in handy like pretty much anywhere, you know? Because I have a feeling there's lots of jobs for that ...I mean, media seemed like a lot more interesting like the classes you take and such rather than modeling. I mean, those are pretty interesting too but I just, I felt like this was more interesting."

—3rd Year, Georgia Tech

When students were enjoying most of their CS courses, they selected courses in what I called an "exploratory" way. They selected courses they were curious about, given descriptions on the school website. They occasionally considered what might be good for a job after graduation, but this was usually based on instinct rather than any concrete data or specific companies they were aiming at. They did not get advice from instructors or advisors. Only rarely did they consider course difficulty. Overwhelmingly, what was most important was that the course or specialization seem interesting.

This exploratory behavior can continue even until 3rd and 4th year. Obviously by the 4th year students need to start making decisions about careers post graduation, but students with an exploratory approach still did not have a specific goal. They had some areas they were considering going forward (either in graduate school or in industry) but it was still an interest rather than a specific commitment. Students with a strong specific commitment generally could describe an experience of contrasting enjoyment that triggered their focus.

## 3.4 Contrasting Enjoyment Triggers Choices

"Well, I just wanna explore more aspects of where I could go and what I could do in the future, and so maybe having a more people-oriented major, more literature basically, which might involve the major computational media, so maybe I could explore that, but I just - I know that I'm interested in languages, and I've become more interested in history, so instead of just technology ...I found [my computer architecture class] boring, and I didn't grasp it so quickly, so that generally discouraged me and what was good about that AP computer science class was that it was really slow and everyone was at your same level or below you."

—2nd Year, Georgia Tech

Students used course enjoyment as a mechanism to test their own suitability for the field of CS. If they found a CS course

enjoyable, that was generally construed as confirmation that CS was a good choice. Enjoyment was not the only aspect that students consider, but, when students reflected on their own significant curriculum choices, it was almost always an unenjoyable class experience that initially triggered the crisis and forced the student to make the decision. Occasionally, a particularly good course amount otherwise average courses could trigger a similar experience. Either way, it is the strong contrast in enjoyment that makes the student reconsider and begin thinking about making a new educational decision. This was true even when students were aware that other non–content factors (e.g. unhelpful TAs) affected their enjoyment. Grades did effect student enjoyment (e.g. students found courses they did particularly bad in unenjoyable) but simply getting good grades was not enough to ensure a student would enjoy the course.

Unenjoyable experiences caused a student to reevaluate their options. This was when they would reach out and begin to do research into the various options within CS. This often gave them a more detailed view of the subfields of CS than other students. Students would also make decisions about themselves in relationship with Computer Science. Students would decide they didn't like the hardware–level parts of CS, or that they didn't want to program professionally:

"I think that — I know I don't want to program, so I'm going to try to stay away from that ...Yeah, after my C++ course, I liked it and I still had to do it, of course. But, I just knew that I don't think I want to sit here up all night doing this. I think that I would much rather — actually, I took a course, too. It was a software engineering course. And, so that was the life cycle — a life cycle process, and project management. And, I really, really liked that. I was kind of able to see a task through, and I didn't have to be the sole one programming, or the sole one doing one thing. I was able to talk to people, gather information, gather requirements — I really liked that."

—4th Year, Spelman College

Students who had a contrasting experience would often explain themselves in terms of being a particular kind of person (e.g. a *social* person who doesn't like just programming all the time). Students before this would usually talk about being curious about different areas of CS but not saying they were unsuited for a particular area of CS.

This overall process of educational decision making seemed to occur at two levels during a student's undergraduate career: the selection of a particular major, and the selection of a particular specialization with in the major. A student would have a experience that would commit them to CS, for example, and then begin engaging in exploratory behavior to find a specialization within the major. Not every student talked about both stages — and for many students the selection of CS as a major came from an experience in high school.

## 3.5 Making Choices Based on Long–Term Goals

"Well, I got interested in robotics. I was enjoying the class. Things were going well ...but I wasn't sure exactly what I should go to towards learning robotics on my own and in the classroom. So I went to my robotics professor and asked him for some direction, and one of the things I asked was simply what threads would you choose ... And I suppose the difference between when I changed my threads from when I originally picked my threads was originally I was thinking from what I like and what I do what would be good threads. But then when I chose the threads I'm working with now, it was more where do I want to go and how do I get there that made me choose them."

—3rd Year, Georgia Tech

Up to this point, we've discussed students who are choosing based on enjoyment and adopted an exploratory strategy. A minority of students had a different approach to choosing courses: they chose based on a relatively specific long–term goal for themselves. Most of these students had a contrasting experience that focused them in a particular area and encouraged them towards a particular long term goal. For example, the student quoted above had a very good experience in a robotics course. He changed his specialization and started strategically selecting courses to further a career in robotics — a change from his previous exploratory strategy. Not every contrasting experience would completely change a students strategy: for example, a student might have an experience that settled them on majoring in CS versus something else, but within CS classes the student would still adopt an exploratory approach.

Students approaching CS based on long term goals had much more use for reasoning about the field of Computer Science. They often had done research beyond their classes into what was necessary for their long–term goal. They would even take non–required classes that they anticipated disliking, because they believed they would be useful for their goal. This was very different from students adopting the exploratory approach, who would exclusively select classes based on what they imagined they would enjoy (within the framework of the curriculum).

## 3.6 Peers, Parents, Advisors, and Professors

A little should be said about the involvement of other people in student's process of making educational decisions. The first is that students were fairly independent: although many students did mention some others at some point in their process, generally they described most decisions as being self–made (perhaps with a little advice). The departmental website was by far the most commonly referenced resource. But when students did solicit external advice, they tended to use each group in different ways:

- *Peers.* What was most surprising was how little peers tended to come up in student discussion of course choices. Although students definitely talk with each other, they generally do not talk about (or at least retain) information about the concepts discussed in later CS classes. They do talk about the difficulty of courses, although plenty of students I talked to did not even have information about that. Students did not evangelize particular specializations, and it was even rarer for students to talk about being attracted to the major by others. What peers did seem to provide was gossip about par-

ticular specializations (e.g. 'everyone knows' the theory specialization is really hard), which students did occasionally use in their decision making process.

- *Parents.* Parents were heavily involved in some students' decision making, especially when initially selecting a major. Parents generally seemed to encourage students to make educational decisions with an eye towards careers. Some students seemed to talk about consulting with their parents frequently, some mentioned it hardly at all.

- *Advisors.* Only the engineering school had explicit departmental advisors that students had to meet with every year. At other schools, students were required to meet with CS professors yearly. Students did mention going to advisors when they experienced a contrasting experience. The advisors themselves mentioned that students mostly sought them out to ask about graduation requirements. No student mentioned an advisor that they regularly met with for advice.

- *Professors.* Some students had a professor they had developed a personal relationship with after enjoying a particular course. Students in a such a relationship frequently talked about getting advice about educational decisions. Most other students did not mention getting advice from professors, even when considering changing specializations or having a bad experience in a particular course.

## 4. RELATIONSHIP WITH EXISTING THE-ORIES

The majority of CS education literature regarding student goals in CS focuses on pre–college or early college students. Margolis and Fisher's work [11] studied students across their CS undergraduate career and finds enjoyment a significant aspect of student decision making, although the students interviewed seem to have stronger goals earlier than observed in my interviews. Biggers et. al [1] finds differences between student perceptions of the field, but the survey nature of the work makes it difficult to isolate causes. Other work has also been done on how students think about the field of CS (see [9] for a summary) but not how that understanding relates to educational decisions.

General education literature has done considerable research into student decision making processes [8]. In general, these models tend to be complex with a variety of factors influencing student decisions. The difficulty in applying these models to a educational situation tends to be identifying which of the factors are most salient for most students.

### 4.1 Eccles's Model of Achievement–Related Choices

One model that is particularly well suited to student course choices is Eccles's model of achievement–related choices, which has been applied to a variety of educational choices including selection of major and courses [6]. The Eccles model is an expectancy–value model: students made decisions based on both their estimated expectation of success and what they expect to gain (called the subjective task value). These general aspects are further subdivided in several parts including values of society, individual utility, enjoyment, expectations of success, personal goals (both short and long term), and others [7].

Studies have shown that the factors outlined in Eccles model do affect student educational choices [7]. In my interviews, most of these issues did also make an appearance to some degree. But there are some clear differences between the Eccles model and my results.

Firstly, there is much less of a delineation between the various aspects of the model in my interviews. Students, for example, would routinely alternate in their discussion between their enjoyment of a subject (subjective-task value) and their feeling of skill in the subject (expectation of success). While it may be true that students subconsciously associate their expectation of success with enjoyment, it definitely seemed to be enjoyment that they used when explaining their own processes.

Second, many of the aspects of the model break down when students seem to have no explicit goals. What does 'utility' correspond to in such a student? How can students be thought to be doing expectancy–value analysis when they are unaware of their options? I think although the behavior we saw in students could fit within the general framework the Eccles model, the aspects it highlights are not the ones that seemed most relevant in exploritory decision making processes.

## 4.2 Deci and Ryan's Model of Intrinsic Motivation

After discovering the importance of enjoyment in the interviewed students' decision making, we also examined enjoyment focused models of decision making processes. Deci and Ryan's model [5] seemed the closest. The model emphasize what factors are necessary for an activity to be subjectively enjoyable, which develops into intrinsic motivation.

Deci and Ryan identify three main needs that drive intrinsic motivation: competence (feeling skillful at a particular activity), relatedness (feeling connected to others), and autonomy (feeling in–control and consistent with one's sense of self) [5]. In this model, there is a more explicit relationship between the subjective experience of enjoyment and factors such as expectations of success.

Deci and Ryan use their model to explain how motivation develops over time. In that sense, it explains how despite the fact that students are aware their enjoyment/frustration in a class may be caused by other factors than natural affinity for the discipline, an enjoyable class causes a feeling of affinity. Over time (and after some long term educational decisions have been made) the activities of the discipline become internalized and intrinsic motivation emerges.

## 5. DISCUSSION

## 5.1 Detailed Conceptions of CS Don't Help Make Course Choices

The way students approach choices is related to their conceptions of the field of CS. Students use enjoyment to measure their suitability for a particular major or specialization. A detailed understanding of CS would not let a student know what he or she is really interested in: 'What part of CS is enjoyable to me personally?'

Once a student has a particular goal, a detailed conception of CS becomes useful. With a particular goal in mind, a student can reason about courses that would or would not

be valuable — independent of the question of whether a particular course would be enjoyable. If the students I interviewed are representative then students do not generally decide on a particular goal in CS until late in their undergraduate curriculum after many major educational decisions have already been made.

Given that students use enjoyment as a measure of suitability, the strategy students adopt makes sense. Students take courses required by the curriculum. Students rely on the curriculum to ensure they are exposed to a variety of areas all of which are potentially valuable long–term. Where choices exist within the curriculum, students select what sounds interesting but it is not a problem if they are surprised.

## 5.2 Student Enjoyment

Enjoyment turned out to be a large component of student educational decision making. Students attributed enjoyment in a class to be a sign that they were well suited for a particular discipline. This was true even though students could often identify reasons for their enjoyment (or lack of enjoyment) that had more do to with pedagogical factors (e.g. frustration with TAs). Strong contrasts in enjoyment motivated students to make choices and narrow their long–term options.

While it is not surprising that enjoying classes motivated students, what is surprising is the extent to which students conflated enjoying courses and being well suited for a particular discipline. From an educational perspective, this can be problematic because there are many factors that influence student enjoyment: difficulty in getting TAs, courses with too much required content due to curricular issues, etc. A bad experience in a particular course has a potential to be much farther reaching than instructors might expect. A bad experience in a course may convince a student they are poorly suited for a subdiscipline of Computer Science.

This suggests that unenjoyable classes, especially unenjoyable classes that are prerequisite for many others, can make students consider themselves unsuited for (and avoid) large areas of Computer Science. Courses of this sort often have many stakeholders which can encourage too much material in the curriculum. Obviously no teacher intends to make a course unenjoyable, but most curricula have a few courses that are considered especially frustrating. These frustrating courses may cause students to prematurely decide that they are not suited for certain areas of CS that they might otherwise enjoy.

## 5.3 Lack of Student Goals

In our interviews, students definitely liked curricula which gave them control over their classes. However, very few students used the freedom to select specific classes for specific goals. Instead, students tended to make choices fairly arbitrarily, in line with their exploration of the major.

Based on my interviews, encouraging students to specialize early in their academic careers seems to be counterproductive. Before I undertook this project, I imagined that greater control of their curriculum might encourage students to develop a more detailed conception of CS in order to make good choices. This does not seem to have happened: students rarely talk about researching specializations or talking with their peers about CS content. When students are forced to make educational decisions prematurely, they choose without much consideration. If they have to specialize early, it reduces their ability to explore.

Students rely on the curriculum and assume that any really essential content will be taught to them regardless of their educational decisions. Students ignore the fact that a decision to specialize early inevitably comes at the cost of some other material. Early in the design of the survey instrument, I asked students to select elective courses for a student who wanted to 'keep their options open' in CS. Students found this question quite difficult, and it is difficult question for CS educators as well. My research suggests that many students actually really do want to keep their options open in CS, and I think the curriculum needs to provide guidance in that regard.

# 6. CONCLUSION

Students do not approach course choices in the way we might initially expect. Even when students found their classes to cover content very different from their expectations, that did not motivate them to switch classes or majors. In our interviews, even students with detailed understandings of the field of CS treated choices like which area to specialize in very casually. Students did not seem to get much advice from advisors or professors. In short, students do not seem to be reasoning about the field of CS when making educational decisions.

The theory of how students make educational decisions comes from two basic ideas. One: students do not have a concrete idea of what career or skillset they would like to pursue in CS; they are trying to figure out their goals within the CS program. Two: the primary way students evaluate what their goals ought to be is by examining their enjoyment of classes. Enjoyment of particular classes is used as a test for how suitable that area of CS is for them.

This situation creates three main behaviors:

1. *Exploration.* Students do not have a concrete goal when they begin studying in a particular field, but rather than attempting to gain a detailed view of the field for themselves, students rely on the curriculum to teach them. They choose their courses based on casual interest, but within the framework of the overall curriculum.

   This process rests on the assumption that is safe to abdicate responsibility to the curriculum, i.e. that the curriculum is built in such a way that anything which is possible within the requirements is viable in terms of a long–term career. Abdicating responsibility is not always a bad thing from an educational perspective. Students arrive in class with very few preconceptions about what they expect to learn and (at least initially) assuming the professor is an expert with their best interests in mind. It does put students at risk for ignoring valuable content or by relying too much on the curriculum to ensure bad choices are impossible.

2. *Contrasting Enjoyment Triggering Choices.* They view their enjoyment of their classes as a useful measure of whether they would enjoy pursing a particular area more. If all their classes are equally enjoyable, students select courses in an exploratory way. They choose courses of casual interest, while keeping in mind course requirements. If they notice a strong difference in how

enjoyable some courses are (especially if they have a bad experience in a particular course), it motivates them to make larger decisions. Often, they will narrow their educational focus and more clearly define their goals. This is when they often seek advice from parents, advisors, and websites. It also motivates refining a conception of the field.

3. *Making educational decisions based on long term goals.* Once their educational focus is sufficiently narrow, students develop a concrete goal. At this stage, they do use their conception of the field to make educational decisions towards their goal, and often describe research activities to refine their conception. They also engage in behaviors that are very unlike students making educational decisions based on enjoyment, like taking non–required courses they expect to dislike because they will be useful.

Overall, student decision making follows a process that makes sense. Students do not generally make faulty decisions based on incorrect reasoning about the field. However, students do tend to over–value how enjoyable courses are in their decisions. Although students enjoy curricula where they can make a lot of educational decisions, early decisions may not be being made in the way the curricula designers intended.

# 7. ACKNOWLEDGMENTS

This research supported in part by a grant from the National Science Foundation BPC Program #0634629.

# 8. REFERENCES

[1] M. Biggers, A. Brauer, and T. Yilmaz. Student perceptions of computer science. In *Proceedings of SIGCSE 2008*, pages 402–406, Portland, 2008. ACM.

[2] K. Charmaz. *Constructing Grounded Theory*. Sage Publications Ltd, 1 edition, Jan. 2006.

[3] A. Clarke. *Situational Analysis: Grounded Theory After the Postmodern Turn*. Sage Publications, 2005.

[4] J. Corbin and A. C. Strauss. *Basics of Qualitative Research*. Sage Publications, Inc, 3rd edition, 2008.

[5] E. L. Deci and R. M. Ryan. The "what" and "why" of goal pursuits. *Psychological Inquiry*, 11(4):227–268, 2000.

[6] J. S. Eccles. Understanding women's educational and occupational choices. *Psychology of Women Quarterly*, 18:585–609, 1994.

[7] J. S. Eccles. Who am i and what am i going to do with my life? personal and collective identities as motivators of action. *Educational Psychologist*, 44(2):78, 2009.

[8] J. S. Eccles and A. Wigfield. Motivational beliefs, values, and goals. *Annual Review of Psychology*, 53:109–132, 2002.

[9] M. Hewner. Undergraduate conceptions of the field of computer science. ICER '13, pages 107–114, New York, 2013. ACM.

[10] Y. S. Lincoln and E. G. Guba. *Naturalistic inquiry*. Sage, 1985.

[11] J. Margolis and A. Fisher. *Unlocking the Clubhouse: Women in Computing*. The MIT Press, Apr. 2003.

# Measuring Enrichment: The Assembly and Validation of an Instrument to Assess Student Self-Beliefs in CS1

Michael James Scott
Information Systems, Computing & Mathematics
Brunel University
Uxbridge, Middlesex, UB8 3PH
United Kingdom
michael.scott@brunel.ac.uk

Gheorghita Ghinea
Information Systems, Computing & Mathematics
Brunel University
Uxbridge, Middlesex, UB8 3PH
United Kingdom
george.ghinea@brunel.ac.uk

## ABSTRACT

Educational research has shown that self-beliefs can have profound influences on learning behaviour and achievement. It follows, then, that beliefs about the nature of programming aptitude (e.g., students' mindset) and the way in which individuals perceive themselves as programmers (e.g., students' self-concept) could also have a salient impact on programming practice behaviour and the development of programming expertise. However, in order to test this hypothesis, a valid and reliable measurement instrument is needed. This paper draws upon the Control-Value Theory of Achievement Emotion to assemble such a measurement instrument. An evaluation of the proposed measurement instrument with three cohorts of undergraduate computing students ($N = 239$) then demonstrates that reliability and construct validity are adequate, while the concurrent validity of the conceptual framework is satisfactory. This suggests that the measurement instrument is suitable for further research into students' self-beliefs within the introductory programming context. However, it is important to note that this work represents only a first step and further validation is required to establish whether the measurement instrument is valid across different contexts and populations.

## Categories and Subject Descriptors

J.4 [**Social and Behavioral Sciences**]: Psychology; K.3.2 [**Computers and Education**]: Computer and Information Science Education—*Computer Science Education*.

## General Terms

Human Factors, Measurement.

## Keywords

Measurement; Self-Beliefs; Self-Concept; Self-Efficacy; Mindset; Anxiety; Interest; Practice; Programming; CS1.

## 1. INTRODUCTION

Reliable and valid measurement is critically important in educational research. Variables of interest should be clearly defined and measured with minimal error in order to make meaningful conclusions from an analysis [8, 44]. However, there is not a strong history of instrument development and validation in computer science education research. Two systematic reviews of the literature found that the quantitative research in the field would benefit from improvements in methodology and reporting [37, 46]. Of particular interest, only 1.5% of articles published between 2000 and 2005 reported adequate psychometric information to support the validity, the reliability, and the generalisability of their claims [37].

A number of measurement instruments have since been developed and evaluated. For example, the Foundations of CS1 Test (FCS1) assesses students' performance in the cognitive-domain of introductory computing [45]. However, few instruments address the affective-domain of learning computing (e.g., attitude development [9]). In particular, there is a need to explore the emotive aspects of learning computer programming as, for some students, programming invokes strong negative feelings [19, 24, 38] and shapes their self-beliefs in counter-intuitive ways [22]. This is important to consider because self-beliefs play an important role in academic development [5, 26]. As an example, beliefs about the nature of programming aptitude, extending Dweck's mindset theory (see [7, 10, 11, 32, 42]), can lead to significant differences in the time that students report practising programming [41]. Nevertheless, to pursue this line of research, a valid measurement instrument is needed.

As such, this article will propose one such measurement instrument and will then address the research question: is the proposed measurement instrument reliable and valid? The following section will highlight a number of challenges encountered in introductory programming and will then situate these challenges within the Control-Value Theory of Achievement Emotions to illustrate the potential role which students' self-beliefs may play. Drawing from the theory, a parsimonious set of key variables is then identified to include in the measurement instrument. The next section then describes how the proposed measurement instrument was assembled. This leads into an evaluation with three cohorts of undergraduate computer students. The paper then closes with a brief discussion of the potential uses of the measurement instrument, its limitations, and a conclusion on its adequacy for future research.

## 2. BACKGROUND

### 2.1 Challenges in Programming Education

Programming is a craft which many would seem to find challenging to learn [21]. Notwithstanding practices that have been shown to improve retention and success [36], failure rates can be high [4] and there is a history of poor outcomes in the higher education context [17, 45]. The reasons for these poor outcomes are complex and multifaceted (see [3]). However, for this reason, introductory is considered a challenge for computer science education research [17, 30].

A key issue can sometimes be the amount *and the quality* of practice that novice programmers engage in [40]. This is because the discipline can require a substantial level of deliberate practice to master [13, 51]. That is, practice which is ongoing, focused, reflective, and situated at the right level of challenge for any individual student [13]. This type of practice, however, is inherently uncomfortable and demands that learners remain motivated.

Despite the best efforts of instructors (e.g., through encouraging and motivating students [20]), learners regularly report negative experiences when they engage with programming tasks [22, 38]. Some authors describe this phenomenon as *programming trauma* [19] and, to reinforce such striking language, there is some evidence which indicates that the type of task anxiety these experiences invoke are related to the activation of brain regions associated with visceral threat detection and pain [27]. Another concern is evidence suggesting that such affective factors worsen over a course of instruction [31, 41].

With this being the case, the emotions that learners feel may prompt them to reflect on themselves and their ability in several different ways [22]. Potentially, learners may start to believe that they no longer have the time or the motivation to overcome these challenges as they cannot envision success in the future [23]. In other words, learners may change their self-beliefs based on their experiences, through a process of self-appraisal, potentially diminishing the way that they identify with programming as a discipline and disengaging with deliberate forms of practice [35, 40].

### 2.2 The Control-Value Theory of Achievement Emotions

A framework that considers the role of self-beliefs and emotions in learning is the Control-Value Theory of Achievement Emotion [33, 34]. In this framework, students' self-appraisal of ongoing achievement activities, and of their past and future outcomes, are of key importance. This is because the emotions that they experience during a particular task will depend upon whether they feel in control of the outcome and that the outcome is subjectively important to them.

These emotions then influence academic engagement and performance through the model shown in Figure 1. The model proposes that instruction and support have an influence on the way in which individuals form the control and value appraisals. These appraisals then shape the specific achievement emotions that students may experience based on whether they feel they can control activities and outcomes that are subjectively important to them. These emotions then have a direct impact on self-regulated learning and performance. Specifically, emotions seem to influence

cognitive resources, use of strategies, and dependence on external regulation of learning [33]. The overall model is also reciprocal in nature, such that outcomes can shape emotions while both emotion and performance shape the way students form their self-appraisals. In some cases, instruction and support may also respond to student needs. In particular, offering a range of interventions which could influence any part of the model. As this process continues over time, it could have substantial impact on learning behaviour and subsequently performance; as evidenced through the known co-variance between self-efficacy beliefs and success [47, 50].

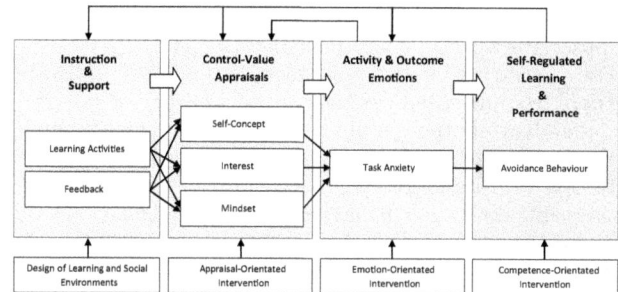

**Figure 1: Overview of the Control-Value Theory of Achievement Emotion with an Embedded Conceptual Framework (Adapted From [33, 34])**

As each component of the framework represent a broad range of different constructs, a parsimonious conceptual framework has been embedded within the model. This example has been derived from factors hypothesised to influence student programming practice [40] and illustrates how learning activities and feedback influence students' self-beliefs. Namely: self-concept, which is is understood to be a composite of "self-perceptions that are formed through experience with and interpretations of one's environment" [29]; interest, which is the extent to which an individual enjoys engaging with a set of tasks; and mindset, based on Dweck's [10] notion of mindsets. That is, students have a growth mindset, where they believe their capacities can be developed through practice, or students have a fixed mindset, where they believe their capacities are natural, inherent qualities. These, in turn, influence task anxiety which, consequently, may encourage avoidance behaviour.

### 2.3 Proposed Conceptual Framework and Instrument Assembly

To validate the framework and test such a hypothesis, it is necessary to develop an appropriate measurement instrument. Therefore, in line with the proposed conceptual framework shown in Figure 2, items for the key variables were assembled.

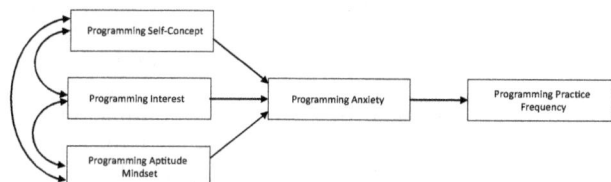

**Figure 2: A Conceptual Framework for Enhancing Students' Programming Practice**

The measurement model for the proposed measurement instrument consisted of four constructs: Programmer Self-Concept (PSC); Interest in Software Development (INT); Programming Anxiety (ANX); and Mindset Towards Programming Aptitude (APT). Additionally, in order to ensure appropriate discriminatory power between constructs, such as differences between self-concept and self-efficacy [6], items relating to software debugging task self-efficacy are also included (DSE). As existing instruments target similar constructs of interest, items were drawn from the literature and adapted to the introductory programming context. A self-report of programming practice behaviour, for the purpose of establishing the concurrent validity of the proposed framework, is also included (see [41]).

The construct debugging task self-efficacy captures learners' cognitive self-assessments of whether or not they are confident in their ability to write and debug simple programs. This is based on the theoretical construct proposed by Bandura [1], as it relates to how self-assessments influence behaviour change. The items for this construct were created using guidelines regarding the domain-specificity of self-efficacy and its association with particular criterial tasks.

The construct of programmer self-concept has some conceptual overlap with debugging self-efficacy, however there are a range of theoretical and empirical differences [6, 14]. It represents a composite of self-perceptions that one can be a good programmer, which is "formed through experience with and interpretations of one's environment". This construct drives the affective elements of being a programmer as opposed to a cognitive assessment of success at programming because "self-concept better predicts affective reactions such as anxiety, satisfaction, and self-esteem, whereas self-efficacy better predicts cognitive processes and actual performance" [6]. The items for this construct were adapted from scales used by Ferla et al. [14] and Eccles & Wigfield [12]. These focus on the ability-belief component of self-concept.

The construct for interest in software development measures the extent to which an individual enjoys engaging with programming-related activities. This construct is believed to have a reciprocal relationship with self-concept, resulting in the pursuit of more achievement experiences in a domain [16]. The items for this construct were adapted from the scale used by Wigfield et al. [48], focusing on the enjoyment aspect of interest.

The programming anxiety instrument construct measures the self-reflected state of experiencing negative emotions, such as nervousness or helplessness, while writing and debugging programs. The items were drawn and adapted from the worry-component of the instrument used by Wigfield and Meece [49].

The mindset towards programming aptitude instrument construct represents the strength of a learners' belief in the notion of a fixed programming aptitude (e.g., aptitude is inherent and cannot change). The items were drawn from Dweck [10].

These items were then put together as a 5-point Likert instrument, with each item rated from strongly disagree to strongly agree. Each item was reviewed by 2 colleagues and a small convenience sample of undergraduate students, and revised to improve content validity and readability. This resulted in the instrument shown in Table 1.

## 3. METHOD

In order to evaluate the proposed measurement instrument, the psychometric properties are examined. Namely, based on the recommendations of Straub *et al.* [43] and other authors (e.g. [8, 44]), reliability and validity need to be established in order to deem a measurement instrument adequate. This involved a trial of the instrument with three cohorts of students at the conclusion of their first programming course and an analysis of their responses using a confirmatory factor analysis technique (see [18]).

### 3.1 Data Collection

The sampling frame for each cohort was set to all students who had submitted at least one assignment or code review to ensure participants had indeed attended the course. Minimum sample size requirements were calculated using Cochran's formula for continuous data with finite population correction and adjusted for anticipated non-response [2].

A random sampling procedure was used to select participants. Data was collected in three rounds: a paper-based survey was distributed to all students in the lab environment (unselected cases are not considered in analysis); a digital version was then advertised on the virtual learning environment and email alerts were distributed to those whom had not responded to the paper-version; after ten days, an additional series of follow-up emails were distributed to the non-respondents. All participants were offered an opt-out for further communication at each stage.

From 126, 115 and 98 invitations for each respective cohort, 91, 84, and 64 responded. This represents an overall response rate of 70%, noting that 34 cases in 2011-12, 30 cases in 2012-13, and 21 cases in 2013-14 were classified as late respondents. This is because their response was elicited after considerable follow-up during a third round of data collection.

### 3.2 Participants

Participants were all first undergraduate students following the sequential pathway for either 'Computer Science' or 'Business Computing'. The descriptive statistics show that less than 20% of the respondents were female, while the average age was 20 years, with approximately 15% respondents being mature students (over the age of 23 at entry).

Admission to the pathway required at least 300 UCAS Points (University & College Admission System Points), with a strong preference for STEM subjects (science, technology, engineering, and mathematics). Prior programming experience was not required. However, students without a relevant STEM qualification, or the required points, could opt to pursue a relevant foundation course.

During the introductory programming course, students would learn object-orientated design and the fundamental constructs of the Java language. This was conducted through a sequence of laboratory-based assignments and a collaborative project. The assignment for the 2011-12 cohort was a website and a lab-based programming examination. The assignments for the 2012-13 and 2013-14 cohort were robot scripting tasks, where students would program robots to complete activities such as maze navigation or communication in Morse Code. These assignments were examined by code review and oral viva.

# 4. DATA ANALYSIS

According to Straub *et al.* [43], there are three main forms of validity and reliability which are important in instrument development: content validity, construct validity and internal reliability. Content validity is the level at which items used to measure a construct reflect the meaning of the construct (and breadth of possible items which could represent the construct) to which the items will be generalised. Construct validity is the form of validity that deals with the degree to which items are an effective measure of a theoretical construct. This is often sub-divided into convergent validity and discriminant validity as evidence for both *imply* construct validity [18]. Convergent validity refers to the level at which multiple items which theoretically should be related are actually related. Conversely, discriminant validity assess the extent to which items which should be unrelated are actually unrelated. Reliability refers to the extend with which parallel items are consistent in what they are intended to measure (e.g. responses to a set of related items are internally consistent). Concurrent validity is also a consideration in cases where constructs should be related. That is, a construct is related to, or able to predict, another in the same instrument.

The data was analysed in PASW v20 and AMOS 21. All data was analysed. Items under consideration were modified to reflect feedback received from the 2011-12 cohort (see [39]), as such items were analysed on a pair-wise basis. This section follows the factor analysis procedure outlined by Hair *et al.* [18].

## 4.1 Descriptive Statistics

Descriptive statistics for the three samples are shown in Table 1 on the following page. This shows that learners tended to report high DSE, PSC, and INT. Many reported low ANX and, as indicated by low APT, many endorsed a growth view of programming aptitude.

Some analyses require the distribution of the data to follow a normal distribution. This was verified through an examination of skew and kurtosis, with skew indices greater than 3.0 and kurtosis indices greater than 10.0 often indicative of severe non-normality [25]. Table 1 shows these indices are within these guidelines.

## 4.2 Measurement Model

To verify the structure of the items for the proposed measurement model (i.e., checking that it was appropriate to group variables together into meaningful constructs), the proposed five-construct solution was evaluated using maximum-likelihood confirmatory factor analysis. As advised in [18], several fit indices were used to determine fit. One APT item was eliminated at this stage due to a low regression weight. Modifications were also made based on the modification indices to improve overall fit. These fit indices for the final set of items, shown in Table 2, indicate that the hypothesised model was 'not a bad fit' to the data (i.e., accepting the null hypothesis of having no significant difference between the prediction and the data).

This suggests that the expected model was adequately reflected by the structure of the data. However, it should be noted that alternative models with superior fit could still exist. An exhaustive review of alternative candidate models is beyond the scope of this article.

**Table 2: Fit Indices and Criteria for the Measurement Model**

| Fit Index | Measurement Model | Adequate Fit Criteria [18] |
|---|---|---|
| $\chi^2 (df = 153)$ | 267.312 | *N/A* |
| $\chi^2/df$ | 1.747 | < 3.00 |
| $p$ | 0.000 | > 0.05 |
| NNFI | 0.950 | > 0.90 |
| CFI | 0.960 | > 0.90 |
| SRMR | 0.044 | < 0.08 |
| RMSEA | 0.056 | < 0.08 |

*Note: df: degrees of freedom, NNFI: non-normed fit index, CFI: comparative fit index, SRMR: standardised root mean square residual, RMSEA: root mean square error of approximation.*

**Table 4: Regression Results for Relations in the Proposed Structural Model**

| Relationship | Estimate | Standard Error | Critical Ratio | $p$ |
|---|---|---|---|---|
| APT → ANX | 0.310 | 0.084 | 3.685 | < 0.001 |
| INT → ANX | -0.020 | 0.149 | −0.135 | 0.893 |
| PSC → ANX | -0.534 | 0.085 | −6.301 | < 0.001 |
| ANX → PRACT | -2.335 | 0.389 | −6.004 | < 0.001 |

*Note: APT: programming aptitude mindset, PSC: programming self-concept, ANX: programming anxiety, PRACT: frequency of programming practice.*

### 4.2.1 Reliability

Reliability is assessed through examining the Composite Reliability (CR) of each construct. Values close to 1.0 indicate reliablilty, with 0.7 considered minimal [18]. Table 3 shows that the values are consistently above 0.7. Thus, the measurement instrument was reliable with this sample.

### 4.2.2 Construct Validity

In order to establish construct validity, each construct should demonstrate convergent and discriminant validity. Adequate convergent validity is demonstrated by an Average Variance Extracted (AVE) greater than 0.5 [18]. Table 3 shows all values were above this threshold. Adequate discriminant validity is demonstrated by the $\sqrt{AVE}$ being greater than any correlation with another construct [15]. Table 3 shows that the $\sqrt{AVE}$ of each construct was greater than its most significant correlation with another construct. Subsequently, these results imply construct validity.

### 4.2.3 Concurrent Validity

Adequate concurrent validity is established through a cursory examination of the correlation matrix and an examination of hypothesised relationships in a structural model. Table 3 does not show any anomalies within the correlation matrix. As such, the proposed structural model was assessed along with a self-report measure of programming practice. The results, shown in Table 4, reveal that most of the expected regression relationships were statistically significant. However, the regression between INT and ANX was not statistically significant. This suggests that either there is no relationship or the size of effect is small. Nevertheless, with the exception of INT, the conceptual model appears to be valid.

## Table 1: Mean, Standard Deviation, Skewness and Kurtosis of the Instrument Items

| Item | Item Description | M | SD | Sk | K |
|------|------------------|----|----|----|----|
| *Debugging Self-Efficacy* | | | | | |
| DSE1 | I am confident that I can understand Java exceptions (e.g., NullPointerException) | 3.65 | 0.96 | -0.27 | -0.61 |
| DSE2 | I am confident I can solve simple problems with my programs | 3.48 | 1.02 | -0.18 | -0.55 |
| DSE3 | I am confident I can implement a method from a description of a problem or algorithm | 3.87 | 0.98 | -0.68 | -0.26 |
| DSE4 | I am confident I can debug a program that calculates prime numbers | 3.68 | 0.92 | -0.35 | -0.37 |
| *Programming Self-Concept* | | | | | |
| PSC1 | I am just not good at programming | 2.44 | 1.18 | 0.44 | -0.67 |
| PSC2 | I learn programming quickly | 3.42 | 1.11 | -0.28 | -0.58 |
| PSC3 | I have always believed that programming is one of my best subjects | 3.41 | 1.17 | -0.28 | -0.82 |
| PSC4 | In my programming labs, I can solve even the most challenging problems | 3.34 | 1.10 | 0.07 | -1.01 |
| *Programming Interest* | | | | | |
| INT1 | I enjoy reading about programming | 3.66 | 1.10 | -0.44 | -0.50 |
| INT2 | I do programming because I enjoy it | 3.93 | 0.95 | -0.75 | 0.13 |
| INT3 | I am interested in the things I learn in programming classes | 3.72 | 0.98 | -0.52 | -0.39 |
| INT4 | I think programming is interesting | 3.87 | 1.03 | -0.72 | 0.67 |
| *Programming Anxiety* | | | | | |
| ANX1 | I often worry that it will be difficult for me to complete debugging exercises | 2.77 | 1.06 | -0.27 | -0.85 |
| ANX2 | I often get tense when I have to debug a program | 2.83 | 1.18 | -0.08 | -0.95 |
| ANX3 | I get nervous when trying to solve programming bugs | 2.82 | 1.16 | 0.06 | -0.96 |
| ANX4 | I feel helpless when trying to solve programming bugs | 2.76 | 1.21 | 0.11 | -0.83 |
| *Programming Aptitude Mindset* | | | | | |
| APT1 | I have a fixed level of programming aptitude, and not much can be done to change it | 2.08 | 0.97 | 0.82 | 0.35 |
| APT2 | I can learn new things about software development, but I cannot change my basic aptitude for programming | 2.22 | 0.95 | 0.34 | -0.59 |
| APT3 | To be honest, I do not think I can really change my aptitude for programming | 1.90 | 0.92 | 0.87 | 0.23 |

Note: Pooled Sample (N = 175); M: mean, SD: standard deviation, Sk: skew, K: kurtosis.

## Table 3: Construct Validity of the Latent Constructs in the Measurement Model

| | Loadings | Reliability | Variance Explained | | | Correlations | | | | |
|---|---|---|---|---|---|---|---|---|---|---|
| Items | FL | CR | AVE | MSV | ASV | DSE | PSC | INT | ANX | APT |
| *Debugging Self-Efficacy* | | 0.868 | 0.624 | 0.530 | 0.418 | (0.790) | | | | |
| DSE1 | 0.776 | | | | | | | | | |
| DSE2 | 0.808 | | | | | | | | | |
| DSE3 | 0.696 | | | | | | | | | |
| DSE4 | 0.870 | | | | | | | | | |
| *Programming Self-Concept* | | 0.703 | 0.655 | 0.494 | 0.413 | 0.703 | (0.809) | | | |
| PSC1 | -0.710 | | | | | | | | | |
| PSC2 | 0.800 | | | | | | | | | |
| PSC3 | 0.882 | | | | | | | | | |
| PSC4 | 0.835 | | | | | | | | | |
| *Programming Interest* | | 0.842 | 0.579 | 0.530 | 0.363 | 0.728 | 0.686 | (0.761) | | |
| INT1 | 0.781 | | | | | | | | | |
| INT2 | 0.847 | | | | | | | | | |
| INT3 | 0.846 | | | | | | | | | |
| INT4 | 0.522 | | | | | | | | | |
| *Programming Anxiety* | | 0.888 | 0.664 | 0.475 | 0.364 | -0.681 | -0.689 | -0.507 | (0.815) | |
| ANX1 | 0.817 | | | | | | | | | |
| ANX2 | 0.762 | | | | | | | | | |
| ANX3 | 0.834 | | | | | | | | | |
| ANX4 | 0.844 | | | | | | | | | |
| *Programming Aptitude Mindset* | | 0.865 | 0.682 | 0.262 | 0.214 | -0.431 | -0.462 | -0.439 | -0.512 | (0.826) |
| APT1 | 0.782 | | | | | | | | | |
| APT2 | 0.858 | | | | | | | | | |
| APT3 | 0.836 | | | | | | | | | |

Note: Values on the diagonal represent $\sqrt{AVE}$; FL: factor loading, CR: composite reliability, AVE: average variance explained, MSV: maximum shared variance, ASV: average shared variance, DSE: debugging self-efficacy, PSC: programming self-concept, INT: programming interest, ANX: programming anxiety, APT: programming aptitude mindset.

## 5. DISCUSSION

Adequate measurement in computing education research is important. This is because researchers need to know whether the measures being selected and used by other researchers are valid. Straub *et al.* [43] highlight several key concerns that researchers may have: Does the instrument truly represent the essence or content of the target construct? Is the instrument unidimensional and therefore only representing the target construct? Has the target construct been confused with another similar construct? Are the estimates of the true values of latent constructs appropriate? Rigorous approaches to measurement address such questions.

Unfortunately, there has not been a strong history of reporting psychometric information in the field [37] and few measurement instruments are readily available to researchers in the computing education community. Particularly, measurement instruments that capture constructs concerned with the affective-domain of learning computer programming. This may be because developing adequate measurement instruments can be fraught with difficulties [43]. However, there is a strong case for pursuing such work [43, 44] and there is a range of literature which can be drawn from for support (e.g. [8, 18, 43]).

This paper has assembled one such measurement instrument and demonstrated that it has adequate psychometric properties in terms of reliability, construct validity, and concurrent validity. This instrument focuses on student self-beliefs in the introductory programming context and measures five different constructs: programming aptitude mindset, programming self-concept, debugging self-efficacy, programming anxiety, and programming interest.

It is interesting to note that interest in software development did not predict programming anxiety. In hindsight, other value appraisals such as 'importance of programming for future prospects' may have been more appropriate for anxiety. Nevertheless, programming self-concept and mindset towards programming aptitude were shown to be related to programming anxiety and, subsequently, programming practice behaviour. These relationships have not been firmly established as causal relationships nor are the directions of the relationship clear. This suggests that the measurement instrument will be useful for future work investigating hypotheses raised by the theory in, for example, longitudinal survey studies.

The measurement instrument may also be useful in other similar areas of work. There is a vast range of techniques which educators could attempt to apply in order to enrich their students' beliefs, practice, and performance (see [28]). Using a validated instrument, such as the one proposed here, will improve the rigor of such explorations. To illustrate, the authors previously embedded a fantasy role-play within an e-learning tool to evaluate its impact on students' programming self-concept through a pre-post experiment [39]. The ongoing development of this measurement instrument will support future such experiments, increasing confidence that such design experiments present useful and meaningful conclusions. Other uses of the measurement instrument may include educators using the measurement instrument to identify potential problems in their introductory programming classes or researchers evaluating student outcomes across different course designs and cohorts.

## 6. LIMITATIONS

It should be noted that this work only represents a first step and future development is needed to overcome a number of limitations. Most importantly, the instrument has only been administered to students at a single institution. Therefore, it may not generalise to populations from other higher education institutions; particularly, those with a different culture. Therefore, there is a need to further validate the tool beyond the institution. Of particular note, the cross-cultural validity of the measurement instrument also needs to be considered in addition to the appropriateness of adapting the framework for different educational contexts. In its present form, it is not clear whether the instrument would be suited for a range of programming topics or age groups.

A small number of items have been included in this scale to facilitate the collection of data from a large group with a short questionnaire. As such, it should not be used to make fine-grain judgements about any individual student. However, estimation of the true values of the latent constructs for individual students would likely improve with additional items.

## 7. CONCLUSION

Valid measurement is important, however only a small number of validated measurement instruments are available to computing education researchers. This limits research being conducted into educational theory, teaching practice and the the use of instructional technologies which aim to enrich beliefs and learning behaviour. The study presented in this paper contributes to this gap in the literature through the assembly and validation of a measurement instrument that could be used for such research. Specifically, for the investigation of student self-beliefs within the introductory programming context.

Three administrations of the instrument at the authors' institution demonstrated that the proposed measurement model had a good fit to the data. Furthermore, there was adequate support for reliability, construct validity, and concurrent validity. However, there are a number of limitations. Critically, the results may not generalise to different age-groups, cultures or educational contexts.

Future work will involve further validation of the conceptual framework in addition to an examination of appropriate descriptive statistics across a range of students and contexts. This will support further research into teaching practice and instructional technology used in introductory programming.

## 8. REFERENCES

[1] A. Bandura. Self-efficacy: Toward a unifying theory of behavioral change. *Psychological Review*, 84(2):191 – 215, 1977.

[2] J. E. Bartlett, J. W. Kotrlik, and C. C. Higgins. Organizational Research: Determining Appropriate Sample Size in Survey Research. Information Technology, Learning, and Performance Journal. 19(1):43 – 50, 2001.

[3] T. Beaubouef and J. Mason. Why the High Attrition Rate for Computer Science Students: Some Thoughts and Observations. *SIGCSE Bulletin*, 37(2):103 – 106, 2005.

[4] J. Bennedsen and M. E. Caspersen. Failure rates in introductory programming. *SIGCSE Bulletin*, 39(2):32 – 36, 2007.

[5] L. Blackwell, K. Trzesniewski, and C. S. Dweck. Implicit Theories of Intelligence Predict Achievement Across an Adolescent Transition: A Longitudinal Study and an Intervention. *Child Development*, 78:246 – 263, 2007.

[6] M. Bong and E. Skaalvik. Academic Self-Concept and Self-Efficacy: How Different Are They Really? *Educational Psychology Review*, 15(1):1 – 40, 2003.

[7] Q. Cutts, E. Cutts, S. Draper, P. O'Donnell, and P. Saffrey. Manipulating mindset to positively influence introductory programming performance. In *Proceedings of the 41st ACM technical symposium on Computer science education*, pages 431 – 435, 2010.

[8] R. F. DeVellis. *Scale Development: Theory and Applications*. Sage: London, 3rd edition, 2012.

[9] B. Dorn and A. E. Tew. Becoming experts: Measuring attitude development in introductory computer science. In *Proceeding of the 44th ACM technical symposium on Computer science education (SIGCSE '13)*, pages 183 – 188, 2013.

[10] C. S. Dweck. *Self-Theories: Their Role in Motivation, Personality, and Development*. Psychology Press, Philadelphia, PA, 1999.

[11] C. S. Dweck and A. Master. Self-Theories Motivate Self-Regulated Learning. pages 31 – 51. Lawrence Erlabaum, New York, NY, 2008.

[12] J. S. Eccles, Wigïñ\eld, and A. In the mind of the actor: The structure of adolescents' achievement task values and expectancy-related beliefs. *Personality and Social Psychology Bulletin*, 3:215 – 225, 1995.

[13] K. Ericsson, R. Krampe, and C. Tesch-Romer. The Role of Deliberate Practice in the Acquisition of Expert Performance. *Psychological Review*, 100(3):363 – 406, 1993.

[14] J. Ferla, M. Valcke, and Y. Cai. Academic Self-Efficacy and Academic Self-Concept: Reconsidering Structural Relationships. *Learning and Individual Differences*, 19(4):499 – 505, 2009.

[15] C. Fornell, Larker, and D. F. Evaluating Structural Equation Models with Unobservable Variables and Measurement Error. *Journal of Marketing Research*, 18:39 – 50, 1981.

[16] F. Guay, H. W. Marsh, and M. Boivin. Academic self-concept and academic achievement: Developmental perspective on their causal ordering. *Journal of Educational Psychology*, 95:124 – 136, 2003.

[17] M. Guzdial. From Science to Engineering. *Communications of the ACM*, 54(2):37 – 39, 2011.

[18] J. Hair, B. Black, B. Babin, and R. Anderson. *Multivariate Data Analysis*. Psychology Press, NJ, USA, 7th edition, 2009.

[19] M. Huggard. Programming Trauma: Can it be Avoided? In *Paper presented at the BCS Conference on Grand Challenges in Computing: Education*, page 50, 2004.

[20] T. Jenkins. Teaching Programming: A Journey from Teacher to Motivator. In *2nd HEA Conference for the ICS-LTSN*, pages 53 – 58, 2001.

[21] T. Jenkins. On the Difficulty of Learning to Program. *3rd HEA Conference for the ICS-LTSN*, pages 1 – 8, 2002.

[22] P. Kinnunen and S. Beth. My Program is OK – Am I? Computing Freshman's Experience of Doing Programming Assignments. *Computer Science Education*, 22(1):1 – 28, 2012.

[23] P. Kinnunen and L. Malmi. Why Students Drop Out CS1 Courses? In *Proceedings of the 2006 International Computing Education Research Workshop*, pages 97 – 108, 2006.

[24] P. Kinnunen and B. Simon. Experiencing Programming Assignments in CS1: The Emotional Toll. In *Proceedings of the 6th International Workshop on Computing Education Research*, pages 77 – 86, 2010.

[25] R. B. Kline. *Principles and Practice of Structural Equation Modeling*. New York, NY: The Guilford Press, 2nd edition, 2005.

[26] D. R. Krathwohl, B. S. Bloom, and B. B. Masia. New York, NY: David McKay Co, 1973.

[27] I. M. Lyons and S. L. Beilock. When Math Hurts: Math Anxiety Predicts Pain Network Activation in Anticipation of Doing Math. *PLOS One*, 7:e48076, 2012.

[28] E. MacLellan. How might teachers enable self-confidence? A Review Study. *Educational Review*, 66(1):59 – 74, 2014.

[29] H. Marsh and A. Martin. Academic Self-Concept and Academic Achievement: Relations and Causal Ordering. *British Journal of Educational Psychology*, 81(1):59 – 77, 2011.

[30] A. McGettrick, R. Boyle, R. Ibbett, J. Lloyd, G. Lovegrove, and K. Mander. Grand Challenges in Computing: Education - A Summary. *The Computer Journal*, 48(1):42 – 48, 2005.

[31] D. McKinney and L. F. Denton. Houston, We have a Problem: There's a Leak in the CS1 Affective Oxygen Tank. *SIGCSE Bulletin*, 36(1):236 – 239, 2004.

[32] L. Murphy and L. Thomas. Dangers of a Fixed Mindset: Implications of Self-Theories Research for Computer Science Education. *SIGCSE Bulletin*, 40(3):271 – 275, 2008.

[33] R. Pekrun. The control-value theory of achievement emotions: Assumptions, corollaries, and implications for educational research and practice. *Educational Psychology Review*, 18(4):315 – 341, 2006.

[34] R. Pekrun and E. J. Stephens. Achievement Emotions: A Control-Value Approach. *Social and Personality Psychology Compass*, 4:238 – 255, 2010.

[35] A.-K. Peters and A. Pears. Engagement in Computer Science and IT – What! A Matter of Identity? In *Learning and Teaching in Computing and Engineering Conference*, pages 114 – 121, 2013.

[36] L. Porter and B. Simon. Retaining nearly one-third more majors with a trio of instructional best practices in CS1. In *Proceedings of the 44th ACM Technical Symposium on Computer Science Education*, pages 165 – 170, 2013.

[37] J. Randolph, G. Julnes, E. Sutinen, and S. Lehman. A Methodological Review of Computer Science Education Research. *Information Technology Education*, 7(1):135 – 162, 2008.

[38] C. Rogerson and E. Scott. The Fear Factor: How it Affects Students Learning to Program in a Tertiary Environment. *Information Technology Education*, 9(1):147 – 171, 2010.

[39] M. J. Scott and G. Ghinea. Integrating Fantasy Role-Play into the Programming Lab: Exploring the 'Projective Identity' Hypothesis. In *Proceedings of the 44th ACM Technical Symposium on Computer Science Education*, pages 119 – 122.

[40] M. J. Scott and G. Ghinea. Educating Programmers: A Reflection on Barriers to Deliberate Practice. In *Proceedings of the 2nd HEA Conference on Learning & Teaching in STEM Disciplines*, pages 85 – 90, 2013.

[41] M. J. Scott and G. Ghinea. On the Domain-Specificity of Mindsets: The Relationship Between Aptitude Beliefs and Programming Practice. *IEEE Transactions on Education*, in print.

[42] B. Simon, B. Hanks, L. Murphy, S. Fitzgerald, R. McCauley, L. Thomas, and C. Zander. Saying Isn't Necessarily Believing: Influencing Self-Theories in Computing. In *Proceedings of the 4th Int. Workshop on Computing Education Research*, pages 173 – 184, 2008.

[43] D. Straub, M.-C. Boudreau, and D. Gefen. Validation Guidelines for IS Positivist Research. *Communications of the Association for Information Systems*, 13:380 – 427, 2004.

[44] A. E. Tew and B. Dorn. The Case for Validated Tools in Computing Education Research. *Computer*, 46(9):60 – 66, 2013.

[45] A. E. Tew and M. Guzdial. The FCS1: A Language Independent Assessment of CS1 Knowledge. In *Proceedings of the 42nd ACM Technical Symposium on Computer Science Education*, pages 111 – 116, 2011.

[46] D. W. Valentine. CS Educational Research: A Meta-Analysis of SIGCSE Technical Symposium Proceedings. In *Proceedings of the 35th ACM Technical Symposium on Computer Science Education*, pages 255 – 259, 2004.

[47] S. Wiedenbeck. Factors affecting the success of non-majors in learning to program. In *Proceedings of the 1st Int. Workshop Computing Education Research*, pages 13 – 24, 2005.

[48] A. Wigfield, J. S. Eccles, K. S. Yoon, R. D. Harold, A. J. A. Arbreton, and C. Freedman-Doan. Change in children's competence beliefs and subjective task values across the elementary school years: A 3-year study. *Journal of Educational Psychology*, 89:451 – 469, 1997.

[49] A. Wigfield, Meece, and J. L. Math anxiety in elementary and secondary school students. *Journal of Educational Psychology*, 80(2):210 – 216, 1988.

[50] B. C. Wilson and S. Shrock. Contributing to success in an introductory computer science course: A study of twelve factors. *SIGCSE Bulletin*, 33(1):184 – 188, 2001.

[51] L. E. Winslow. Programming Pedagogy - A Psychological Overview. *SIGCSE Bulletin*, 28(1):17 – 22, 1996.

# Measuring Cognitive Load in Introductory CS: Adaptation of an Instrument

### Briana B. Morrison
Georgia Institute of Technology
85 5th Street NW
Atlanta, GA, 30332-0760
bmorrison@gatech.edu

### Brian Dorn
University of Nebraska at Omaha
6001 Dodge St
Omaha, NE 68182
bdorn@unomaha.edu

### Mark Guzdial
Georgia Institute of Technology
85 5th Street NW
Atlanta, GA, 30332-0760
guzdial@cc.gatech.edu

## ABSTRACT

A student's capacity to learn a concept is directly related to how much cognitive load is used to comprehend the material. The central problem identified by Cognitive Load Theory is that learning is impaired when the total amount of processing requirements exceeds the limited capacity of working memory. Instruction can impose three different types of cognitive load on a student's working memory: intrinsic load, extraneous load, and germane load. Since working memory is a fixed size, instructional material should be designed to minimize the extraneous and intrinsic loads in order to increase the amount of memory available for the germane load. This will improve learning. To effectively design instruction to minimize cognitive load we must be able to measure the specific load components for any pedagogical intervention. This paper reports on a study that adapts a previously developed instrument to measure cognitive load. We report on the adaptation of the instrument to a new discipline, introductory computer science, and the results of measuring the cognitive load factors of specific lectures. We discuss the implications for the ability to measure specific cognitive load components and use of the tool in future studies.

## Categories and Subject Descriptors

K.3.2 [**Computers and Education**]: Computer and Information Science Education—*computer science education*

## Keywords

cognitive load theory, measuring cognitive load, confirmatory factor analysis, survey

## 1. INTRODUCTION

Cognitive Load can be defined as "the load imposed on an individual's working memory by a particular (learning) task" [42, p.599]. The resultant performance for a student to learn a specific concept is directly related to how much cognitive load is used to comprehend the material. If instruction

overloads the student's working memory, then knowledge retention and any possible transfer will suffer. As designers of instructional material, it is our responsibility to ensure that we do not overload the learner's working memory where possible when presenting new material. That is, we should help ensure that students' attentional abilities are directed to key aspects of the content and learning activities that have maximum value, rather on than extraneous aspects of the material. But how can we know if we are successful?

The central problem identified by Cognitive Load Theory (CLT) is that learning is impaired when the total amount of processing requirements exceeds the limited capacity of working memory [30]. According to Cognitive Load Theory [34, 36, 44], instruction can impose three different types of cognitive load on a student's working memory: intrinsic load, extraneous load, and germane load. Intrinsic load (IL) is defined as a combination of the innate difficulty of the material being learned as well as the learner's characteristics [20]. A topic is considered to have a high IL if the material being learned is interconnected; that is, learning requires processing several elements simultaneously to understand their relations and interactions [35]. Intrinsic load can also vary with the domain expertise and previous knowledge of the learner [37] in that learners with a higher level of previous knowledge may chunk the material differently than novices [6], allowing them to hold more information in working memory. Extraneous load (EL) is the load placed on working memory that does not contribute directly toward the learning of the material—for example, the attentional resources consumed while understanding poorly written text or diagrams without sufficient clarity [20]. The IL and EL are the factors that can be controlled through instructional design. The final category is that of germane load (GL) which are the instructional features that are *necessary* for learning the material [20].

One of the assumptions of CLT is that these three components are additive [30]; thus if the extraneous load is using the capacity of working memory, little can be devoted to the germane load. Because working memory is considered to be a fixed size [22, 5], it behooves the instructional designer to minimize the EL, design appropriately for the IL, and emphasize the GL. To accomplish this, we must be able to measure the specific load components for any pedagogical intervention. Until recently, there were no effective instruments to measure the different components of cognitive load.

This paper reviews previous attempts to measure cognitive load as both an overall entity and with respect to its defined factors. It then describes the specifics of the study conducted. The statistical results are reported and the paper concludes with a discussion on the implications of being able to measure cognitive load components within introductory computer science. We also describe future use for the instrument in measuring pedagogical interventions as well as limitations of the survey.

## 2. MEASURING COGNITIVE LOAD

Since the discovery and identification of CLT, researchers have searched for a means to measure cognitive load. To date, this has been accomplished through indirect, subjective, and direct measures.

### 2.1 Indirect Measures of CLT

Researchers began exploring cognitive load when they saw how problem-solving activities actually interfered with learning. Computational models provided independent evidence that working memory was strained to accomplish both problem-solving and learning, so decreasing cognitive load became an important instructional design goal. Problem solving that required more searching of knowledge led to inferior learning outcomes [37]. This led Sweller and his colleagues [33, 3] to develop production system models to simulate the problem solving using both high-intensive and low-intensive search strategies. Results demonstrated that high-intensive search methods required a more complex model to simulate the problem solving process.

Another indirect measure of CLT is based on learner performance indicators during the acquisition of the material. Without a direct measure, Chandler and Sweller [9, 10] used instructional time as a proxy for cognitive load. Error rates were higher during acquisition of knowledge under conditions in which the expected time to solve was higher. This corresponded to their measurement of a higher cognitive load. Error rates have also been used to identify differences in cognitive load within problems [3, 4].

### 2.2 Subjective Measures of CLT

In 1992, Paas theorized that learners are able to assess the amount of mental effort required during learning and testing and that this 'intensity of effort' may be considered to be an 'index' of cognitive load [26, p.429]. A 9-point Likert scale ranging from very, very low mental effort (1) to very, very high mental effort (9) was used to ask learners to rate their mental effort at various points during the learning and testing cycle. Paas found that there was a correlation between self-rated mental effort and test performance. A follow-up study [28] replicated the findings and also found that the subjective ratings were more sensitive and less intrusive than an objective physiological measure also captured during this study. The 9-point scale was also found to be highly reliable [29]. The success of these initial instruments to measure cognitive load led others to adopt the subjective scale. However, during the adoption process, the wording of survey questions were changed and the term *mental effort* was changed to *difficulty* or *easy*, thus measuring something different. While subjective measures of difficulty and mental effort may be related, they are not interchangeable; difficulty does not always match effort [41].

However the subjective rating scale, regardless of the wording used, has been shown to be the most sensitive measure available to differentiate the cognitive load imposed by different instructional methods [37]. The subjective measures have also been consistent in matching performance data predicted by CLT [23]. The subjective scale has been used extensively to measure the relative cognitive load of different instructional methods with over 25 studies having used it between 1992 and 2002 [25].

Building on the initial self-rating scale, Paas and van Merriënboer developed an efficiency measure for cognitive load [27]. This efficiency measure combined both mental effort with task performance indicators. This measurement allowed instructors to determine whether specific pedagogical interventions yielded high or low instructional efficiency results. Over 30 cognitive load theory related studies have used this efficiency measure [41]. However the adoption of this measurement tool also resulted in changes from the original use: measuring the mental effort changed the efficiency of learning. Obviously measurement in and of itself adds to cognitive load for participants. Also, *when* the mental effort was measured changed what the efficiency was measuring. For those studies where mental effort was measured immediately following the acquisition phase and prior to the testing phase, training efficiency was measured. For those studies where mental effort was measured after test performance, learning efficiency was measured.

### 2.3 Direct Measures of CLT

Two basic means of measuring cognitive load through direct measures have been used: using a dual task and physiological measurements. A secondary or dual task study requires learners to engage in an additional cognitive activity that is secondary to the primary task of learning. If a higher cognitive load is required for the primary task, performance on the secondary task will suffer. Usually the secondary task is quite dissimilar and requires less working memory than the primary task, such as recognizing when a letter changes color or when a specific tone is heard. Examples of cognitive load studies using the dual task methodology can be found in [8, 11, 40]. In general, CLT research has made far less use of the dual task method than the subjective method for measuring cognitive load. However the advantage of using a dual task method is that it can provide an almost continuous measure of cognitive load during a task.

Physiological measures can also provide a continuous measure of cognitive load during a task. Researchers have used measurements of heart rates [28], pupillary response [39], EEGs [1], and eye tracking [43, 38]. Others have even advocated using fMRI [45]. In general the results support measuring CLT using physiological measures, but the studies have only been run in laboratory settings due to the requirement of specialized equipment. This raises questions about the ecological validity of such studies and highlights the impracticality of using these approaches in most applied educational research.

### 2.4 Critique of CLT Measurements

The basic question of a cognitive load measurement method is whether it is valid, reliable, and practical. Subjective rating scales are simple and practical to use and have proven reliable through repeated use. However, they only deliver a one point post hoc assessment of the cognitive load imposed by the learning task. It remains unclear which of the specific aspects of the learning situation caused the level of cognitive load reported by the student. Although it is assumed that learners are able to be introspective about their own cognitive processes and quantify their perceived mental load during learning, the measures are unable to provide information regarding which processes caused the perceived amount of mental load. It is also not possible to determine which of the three types of load (IL, EL, or GL) originated the report of mental effort.

Objective methods yield data for more than a single point in time by providing information about instantaneous, peak, average, accumulated, and overall load [1]. However these measurement techniques are far from practical for the majority of any large scale study based on the specialized equipment needed. Objective measurement methods also suffer from the ability to determine which type of load was responsible for the resultant physiological changes.

Several researchers have attempted to distinguish between and measure the different types of cognitive load. Ayres attempted to keep the extraneous cognitive load (EL) constant between treatments thus attributing the differences to a change in intrinsic load (IL) [2]. DeLeeuw and Mayer used a mixed approach (both subjective measures and a secondary task method) to investigate if different instruments could measure the three loads separately [14]. The results indicated that different measures do tap into different processes and show varying sensitivities.

A widely used multidimensional scale is the *NASA Task Load Index (NASA-TLX)* [17], which consists of six subscales that measure different factors associated with completing a task. An overall measure of task load is achieved by combining the subscales of the NASA-TLX. One of those subscales is mental demand/load. However the NASA-TLX was designed for use with interface designs and specifically for the aeronautical industry. In an attempt to measure the different cognitive load categories, Gerjets, Scheiter, and Catrambone selected three items from the NASA-TLX associated with task demands [15, 16]. The researchers argued that the three items selected (mental and physical activity required, effort to understand the contents, and navigational demands of the learning environment) could be mapped to the intrinsic, germane, and extraneous loads, respectively. The test manipulated the complexity of worked examples. There was broad agreement with the test performance data in that groups with the highest learning outcomes reported the lowest cognitive load. However there was no corroborating evidence that the three measures corresponded to the different types of cognitive load as proposed.

However in 2013, Leppink et al. [20] developed an instrument specifically for measuring different types of cognitive load which consists of a ten question subjective survey. (We will refer to this survey as the *Cognitive Load Component Survey.*) The researchers developed the questions and tested them using a set of four studies. The overall purpose of the studies was to compare their instrument as a measurement tool for the three types of cognitive load to other existing subjective measurement tools. The first study used exploratory analysis to determine if the questions developed did indeed load onto the three types of cognitive load (IL, EL, and GL). The second study used confirmatory factor analysis (CFA) to test the existing measurement tools [2, 12, 32, 26] for measurement of specific cognitive load factors. This study revealed that none of the existing survey tools adequately separated the three types of cognitive load in that each had significant cross-loading between factors. The newly developed Cognitive Load Component Survey was also tested using confirmatory factor analysis in the third study. The final study then used the Cognitive Load Component Survey to examine the effects of experimental treatment and prior knowledge on the cognitive load components and learning outcomes of students within a statistics

course. The results of the final study were consistent with outcomes based on CLT.

Leppink et al. [21] recently extended their 2013 work by adapting the survey instrument to another domain, that of learning languages, and replicated their analyses. These new findings reinforce the strong support for the survey measuring both intrinsic and extraneous load, but found less support for the direct measure of germane load.

Here, we report on a study to adapt the Cognitive Load Component Survey for use in an introductory computer science context. We detail how the instrument was adapted to a different discipline and the results of measuring the cognitive load factors of specific lectures during the course.

## 3. METHOD OF STUDY

Development and initial validation work on the original Cognitive Load Component Survey identified a set of three underlying dimensions (factors): 3 items related to intrinsic load, 3 items measuring extraneous load, and 4 items measuring germane load [20, 21]. Participants respond to each item using an 11-point semantic differential scale from 0 to 10 anchored at "0-not at all the case" and "10-completely the case". Multiple CFA studies using data from different undergraduate statistics lectures confirmed that this three factor model consistently performs well [20, 21].

Given the consistent findings related to using the cognitive load questionnaire in statistics lectures, we sought to adapt and verify its applicability for computer science. Since the underlying cognitive load theory dimension tied to each factor should be independent of any particular discipline, our method for validating this adaptation hinges on verifying that the original factor model holds true for the newly reworded items in the new disciplinary context of computing. That is, the structure of items on the questionnaire should be robust to slight alterations in question wording better suited to terminology used in computer science coursework.

Similar to the changes done by [21], the wording was changed in a total of three questions. In questions 2 and 9 the word "formulas" was changed to "program code". In question 8, the word "statistics" was changed to "computing / programming". These word changes were piloted with a small group of students to determine if they were understood by participants and were appropriate for the concepts addressed during lectures. The final modified instrument instructions and items are provided in Figure 1.

As posited by Leppink et. al. [20], items 1, 2, and 3 measure the intrinsic load (IL); items 4, 5, and 6 are the extraneous load (EL) factors; and items 7 through 10 measure the germane load (GL). Note that the wordings for items 1 through 6 are negatively worded, in the sense that a response of "10-completely the case" indicates a very high detriment to learning. This is in comparison to items 7 through 10 which are positively worded. Because items 1 through 6 are measuring factors (IL and EL) that we want to minimize, the higher the response indicates that more working memory is being allocated toward undesirable components; while higher scores on items 7 through 10 indicate a desirable use of working memory.

The CS Cognitive Load Component Survey (CS CLCS) was administered twice during the term of an introductory course in computing using Python designed for non-CS majors that utilizes a media computation context. The students were declared majors in Liberal Arts (mostly literature, public policy, and international affairs), Business, and Architecture. Data was collected from two different sec-

*Instructions:* All of the following questions refer to the lecture that just finished. Please respond to each of the questions on the following scale by circling the appropriate number (0 meaning not at all the case and 10 meaning completely the case):

1. The topics covered in the activity were very complex.
2. The activity covered program code that I perceived as very complex.
3. The activity covered concepts and definitions that I perceived as very complex.
4. The instructions and/or explanations during the activity were very unclear.
5. The instructions and/or explanations were, in terms of learning, very ineffective.
6. The instructions and/or explanations were full of unclear language.
7. The activity really enhanced my understanding of the topic(s) covered.
8. The activity really enhanced my knowledge and understanding of computing / programming.
9. The activity really enhanced my understanding of the program code covered.
10. The activity really enhanced my understanding of the concepts and definitions.

**Figure 1: CS Cognitive Load Component Survey**

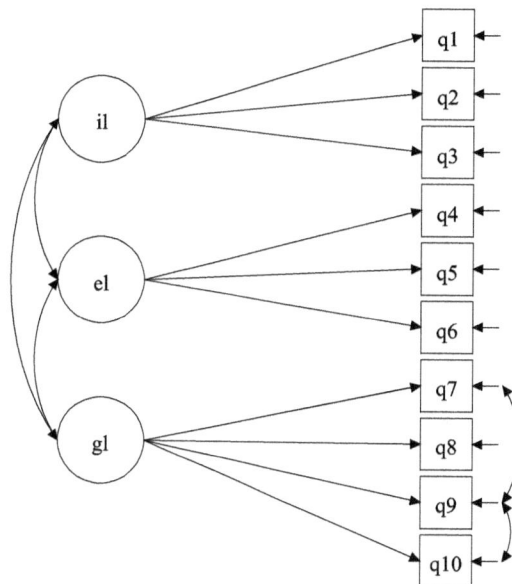

**Figure 2: Factor Model**

tions of the course. Both sections were taught by the same instructor and covered the same material on the days of collection. The first dataset (Lecture 1) was collected mid-way through the course. Students had already completed several assignments involving text and list manipulations and image processing. The first dataset was collected after a lecture on generating HTML for web pages using Python functions. The second dataset (Lecture 2) was collected in the last 20% of the course and followed the initial lecture on sound processing. Students saw visualizations of different sounds, heard an explanation for how sound is digitized, and saw demonstrations of code for manipulating volume.

Surveys were paper-based and distributed at the end of each lecture. Approximately 10 minutes at the end of class was allocated to explaining the purpose of the survey, distribution and collection of the instrument. The survey items were presented in three different orders (see Table 1). The three versions were put into randomized order so that people sitting next to each other were not necessarily answering the questions in the same order. This mitigates ordering effects within the questions that might skew the results.

After each collection of data, surveys with obvious patterns (e.g., all 5's, zig-zag responses) were filtered out to ensure participants had appropriately considered each question prompt. For Lecture 1, only one invalid survey was removed from processing, and for Lecture 2, two invalid surveys were eliminated. The survey yielded a total of 156 valid responses from both sections following lecture 1 and a total of 117 valid responses following lecture 2.

**Table 1: Question Ordering**

| order | Item Order | Count in Lecture $L_1$ | $L_2$ |
|---|---|---|---|
| A | 1, 7, 4, 2, 8, 5, 3, 9, 6, 10 | 53 | 40 |
| B | 6, 10, 9, 3, 5, 8, 2, 7, 1, 4 | 52 | 43 |
| C | 9, 3, 6, 8, 2, 4, 10, 5, 7, 1 | 51 | 34 |

Each data set was then analyzed using confirmatory factor analysis (CFA). CFA allows the researcher to propose and test underlying relationships between items on a survey [7]. It is commonly used within instrument validation to determine whether groups of survey questions that theoretically relate to one another also relate statistically. CFA uses the co-variance matrix of item responses to investigate the degree to which a specified model explains the observed variation in the data set. It produces a set of model fit statistics and parameter estimates that are interpreted to evaluate how well a proposed model captures these relationships.

This data was analyzed using MPlus for confirmatory factor analysis. We replicated the factor model found by the earlier work (see Figure 2) [20]. In this model each item serves as an indicator of a single factor (i.e., it loads on only one factor), and the error terms of two pairs of items to covary (q7 & q9, q9 & q10) due to similarities in the wording of question stems. While Leppink et. al. [20] failed to indicate the statistical estimation algorithm used in their CFA on the original questionnaire, it is probable that maximum likelihood (ML) was used as it is the default in most CFA software packages and is the one most commonly used [7, 19]. Thus, we employed the ML estimator in our analysis. The results of the CFA analysis for the adapted questionnaire are outlined in the following section.

## 4. RESULTS

### 4.1 Lecture 1

Fit statistics provided by confirmatory factor analysis on data collected following lecture 1 (N=156) indicated that the model specified in Figure 2 fit the data well ($\chi^2(30) = 36.92, p = 0.18; RMSEA = 0.04, pclose = 0.67; CFI = 0.99; TLI = 0.99$). The $\chi^2$ test yielded a non-significant p-value, indicating that the observed co-variance matrix was not significantly different from the expected matrix specified by the model. Further, this model exhibited other fit statistics meeting or exceeding cutoff criteria for well-fitting models specified by Hu and Bentler [18]. The root mean

**Table 2: Factor Loadings and Reliability (Lecture 1)**

| Factor/Item | Factor Loading | Std Err | p-Value |
|---|---|---|---|
| IL - Intrinsic Load ($\alpha = 0.85$) | | | |
| Q1 | 0.75 | 0.043 | < 0.001 |
| Q2 | 0.93 | 0.031 | < 0.001 |
| Q3 | 0.76 | 0.040 | < 0.001 |
| EL - Extraneous Load ($\alpha = 0.80$) | | | |
| Q4 | 0.92 | 0.030 | < 0.001 |
| Q5 | 0.71 | 0.046 | < 0.001 |
| Q6 | 0.69 | 0.048 | < 0.001 |
| GL - Germane Load ($\alpha = 0.92$) | | | |
| Q7 | 0.91 | 0.023 | < 0.001 |
| Q8 | 0.86 | 0.027 | < 0.001 |
| Q9 | 0.87 | 0.030 | < 0.001 |
| Q10 | 0.80 | 0.034 | < 0.001 |
| Residual Covariance | | | |
| Q7 with Q9 | -0.19* | 0.157 | 0.230 |
| Q9 with Q10 | 0.40* | 0.091 | < 0.001 |

*denotes a correlation rather than a loading

**Table 3: Factor Correlations (Lecture 1), all significant at $p \leq 0.001$**

| | IL | EL | GL |
|---|---|---|---|
| IL | 1.0 | 0.435 | -0.282 |
| EL | | 1.0 | -0.749 |
| GL | | | 1.0 |

**Table 4: Factor Loadings and Reliability (Lecture 2)**

| Factor/Item | Factor Loading | Std Err | p-Value |
|---|---|---|---|
| IL - Intrinsic Load ($\alpha = 0.86$) | | | |
| Q1 | 0.77 | 0.050 | < 0.001 |
| Q2 | 0.95 | 0.037 | < 0.001 |
| Q3 | 0.75 | 0.047 | < 0.001 |
| EL - Extraneous Load ($\alpha = 0.85$) | | | |
| Q4 | 0.90 | 0.033 | < 0.001 |
| Q5 | 0.81 | 0.043 | < 0.001 |
| Q6 | 0.72 | 0.051 | < 0.001 |
| GL - Germane Load ($\alpha = 0.93$) | | | |
| Q7 | 0.85 | 0.033 | < 0.001 |
| Q8 | 0.91 | 0.026 | < 0.001 |
| Q9 | 0.89 | 0.032 | < 0.001 |
| Q10 | 0.83 | 0.035 | < 0.001 |
| Residual Covariance | | | |
| Q7 with Q9 | -0.08* | 0.156 | 0.620 |
| Q9 with Q10 | 0.13* | 0.143 | 0.361 |

*denotes a correlation rather than a loading

**Table 5: Factor Correlations (Lecture 2), all significant at $p \leq 0.01$**

| | IL | EL | GL |
|---|---|---|---|
| IL | 1.0 | 0.403 | -0.272 |
| EL | | 1.0 | -0.739 |
| GL | | | 1.0 |

square error of approximation (RMSEA) was less than 0.06, and both the comparative fit index (CFI) and Tucker-Lewis Index (TLI) are greater or equal to 0.95.

Table 2 presents standardized item loadings for each of the factors in the well-fitting model. Loading values range from 0.0–1.0 and indicate the degree to which an item serves as a measure of a factor. Values closer to one signify that the item is a pure measure of that factor. Here we note that all items load significantly and highly ($\approx 0.7$ or more) on their corresponding factor. Further, Cronbach's alpha values for each factor met or exceeded 0.8, indicating good internal consistency within each factor, and the overall survey internal reliability was $\alpha = 0.89$. The two residual co-variance paths in the model did not exhibit high correlations, as had been the case in some of the original development studies by [20]. Inspection of the modification indices revealed no suggestions that would markedly improve model fit.

Theoretically, factors that measure EL and GL should be negatively correlated. The more EL that exists, there is less working memory available for GL. Components that measure IL and GL should have a correlation around 0 indicating that the relationship between IL and GL is non-linear. Extremely low or extremely high levels of IL may lead to a lower GL score. If a learning task is too easy for a student, the explanations and instructions in the task may not contribute to actual student learning. On the other hand, if the learning task is too complex for a particular student, working memory available for GL activity may be limited.

The observed inter-factor correlations (see Table 3) support this theoretical interpretation. Overall, observed correlations were all less than 0.8, indicating a reasonable degree of discriminant validity (i.e., each factor measures a unique facet of cognitive load) [7, 24]. We observed a weak, positive correlation between intrinsic and extraneous load and a moderate, negative correlation between extraneous and germane load. Negative correlations in the table involving germane load are due to the negated language used in items 7–9

as compared to those on the rest of the survey (as previously discussed). With respect to the relationship between IL/GL, there was only low correlation ($r = -0.272$) accounting for just 7.4% of the co-variance between the two factors.

## 4.2 Lecture 2

Analysis of the data collected during a subsequent class lecture (N=117) also demonstrated excellent model fit ($\chi^2(30) = 39.7, p = 0.11; RMSEA = 0.053, pclose = 0.43; CFI = 0.99; TLI = 0.98$). As shown in Table 4, the standardized item loadings for this set of data followed a very similar pattern to that found with Lecture 1 responses. All items strongly loaded on their respective factors. Cronbach's alpha values demonstrated good internal consistency within the factors, and the overall reliability for the scale here was $\alpha = 0.87$. Again, none of the modification indices suggested further substantive additions to the model. Lastly, the two residual/error paths in the model (between items q7/9 and q9/10) were not significantly correlated here. Taken in combination with the low correlations between these items observed with the Lecture 1 data, they could likely be removed from the factor model entirely without negatively impacting overall model fit or its interpretation significantly. (Removing the two residual/error paths was originally suggested by [20] after analysis of Study 3; we have kept the co-variance pairs in an effort to be faithful to the original study.) Simplifying the model in this way and verifying it with additional data is one avenue of our future work.

The factors correlated (Table 5) in a nearly identical pattern to what was observed with the Lecture 1 data. Again IL and EL had a weak, positive correlation and EL and GL showed a moderate, negative correlation.

Overall, we conclude that the CS Cognitive Load Component Survey as adapted for introductory computer science validly replicates the original findings in statistics and can reliably reproduce them across multiple lectures in a CS1 class. In the next section we discuss the implications of measuring cognitive load components within a CS1 class.

## 5. DISCUSSION

The contribution of this paper is the creation of the instrument, adapted from an existing instrument for measuring cognitive load. We use the instrument to explore hypotheses about these two lectures, to demonstrate how the instrument might be used in experiments. A thorough exploration of the differences between the two lectures would require a deeper and broader analysis than just considering cognitive load.

To analyze the perceived cognitive load levels during each of the two lectures we needed to determine metrics for each of the factors. These metrics are computed as the average rating given all of the items within a factor and thus falls in the range 0–10. Table 6 presents the mean and standard deviation ($\sigma$) for each survey item and survey factor. Metrics from Lecture 1 are shown on the left-hand side of the table, while corresponding metrics from Lecture 2 are on the right.

We hypothesized that the lecture on sound processing (Lecture 2) should have posed a lower intrinsic load than the lecture on processing lists to produce HTML (Lecture 1). Recall that the IL component measures the innate connectedness or inherent difficulty of a topic (for a novice). The introduction of sound processing requires only the knowledge of sampling sounds to generate digital representations, while processing lists to create HTML code requires knowledge of strings, lists in Python, and valid HTML code. Analytically speaking, Lecture 1's content requires holding multiple concepts in working memory at one time; more so than Lecture 2's content. The data collected in this study supports this hypothesis, and IL during Lecture 1 was statistically significantly greater than during Lecture 2 ($t(271) = 4.43, p < 0.001$).

With respect to extraneous load, we also believed that Lecture 2 would pose lower demands on mental resources, and this was confirmed with statistical significance ($t(271) = 3.08, p = 0.002$). EL consists of instructional material that serves to distract the student from learning. Split attention between two elements, using only text explanations, and unnecessary redundant material all contribute to a higher EL score. In our case, we hypothesized that Lecture 2 would have a lower EL score because it makes use of dual input channels—both audio as well as visual inputs [13]. A known multimedia learning principle to reduce extraneous cognitive load is to use both pictures and sound rather than text only to explain a concept [13]. Even though students were most likely more familiar with HTML and web pages than with sound manipulation, the sound processing lecture produced the lower EL average. The sheer number of items being manipulated to produce the web page with Python code (Python editor window, HTML code editor window, browser window) forces split attention for the student. Even though with sound processing the editor window and sound visualization are both on screen, the student does not attempt to interpret or "read" the visualization; it is merely a placeholder and representation for the sound which is heard.

The final cognitive load factor is that of germane load, in which Lecture 1 had a statistically significantly lower score ($t(271) = -3.91, p < 0.001$). Any reduction in GL would indicate that students are utilizing too much working memory for IL and EL, thus reducing the amount of learning. According to cognitive load theory, students may have learned less from Lecture 1 than they did from Lecture 2. This could

### Table 6: Average Factor Scores by Lecture

| | Lecture 1 (N=156) | | | Lecture 2 (N=117) | | |
|---|---|---|---|---|---|---|
| Q | Avg | $\sigma$ | Factor Avg | Avg | $\sigma$ | Factor Avg |
| 1 | 6.32 | 2.28 | IL=6.33 $\sigma = 2.07$ | 5.18 | 2.38 | IL=5.19 $\sigma = 2.16$ |
| 2 | 6.35 | 2.36 | | 5.21 | 2.49 | |
| 3 | 6.32 | 2.45 | | 5.18 | 2.45 | |
| 4 | 3.67 | 2.45 | EL=3.59 $\sigma = 2.11$ | 2.74 | 2.18 | EL=2.81 $\sigma = 1.98$ |
| 5 | 3.47 | 2.45 | | 2.62 | 2.18 | |
| 6 | 3.62 | 2.60 | | 3.07 | 2.41 | |
| 7 | 5.63 | 2.40 | GL=5.54 $\sigma = 2.20$ | 6.63 | 2.07 | GL=6.53 $\sigma = 1.87$ |
| 8 | 5.58 | 2.40 | | 6.38 | 2.05 | |
| 9 | 5.51 | 2.51 | | 6.58 | 2.00 | |
| 10 | 5.47 | 2.43 | | 6.52 | 2.14 | |

be determined through student performance on questions addressing the concepts covered during the two lectures. Because surveys were collected anonymously, correlation with test question performance was impossible here—and beyond our focus on the instrument itself. We discuss how correlation with performance could be done in the next section.

### 5.1 Future Work

Now that an instrument to measure cognitive load dimensions has been constructed, it can be used within other experimental situations.

The purpose of the CS Cognitive Load Component Survey (CS CLCS) is to compare pedagogical interventions. We can use it to evaluate multiple sets of instructional materials developed along with a hypothesis that one set of materials would be higher (or lower) in either EL (the most common) or IL. Participants could then be randomly assigned to a specific treatment. Upon completion of the learning activity, the participant could be asked to complete the CS CLCS. Metrics for each cognitive load factor can be calculated by averaging all the responses to the questions contributing to that factor. For example, calculate the average to all the responses for questions 1, 2, and 3 to calculate the IL.

The CS CLCS can also be combined with learner performance indicators such as retention or transfer questions. Here it would be important to have participants complete the CS CLCS immediately following knowledge acquisition or learning so as to measure the components of the training material specifically. Once the performance data and survey data have been collected, it should be analyzed to determine if the survey results correlate with the post-test results. Questions to be asked include:

- Does a higher GL score indicate better learning?
- Does a higher pre-test score affect the IL score?
- Does a higher EL score indicate lower performance?

Having the ability to correlate the cognitive load components and learning results gives the researcher the ability to test for and quantify specific elements of the instructional material for iterative design improvement.

The authors plan to use the CS CLCS to determine the cognitive load components for understanding code segment explanations via text or auditory explanations. It is currently unknown what the most effective modality for code segment explanations is for those just learning to program. We will use the CS CLCS along with performance indicators to explore how modality affects learning. Our process can be seen in Figure 3. CLT and multi-media principles suggest that auditory only explanations should yield a lower overall

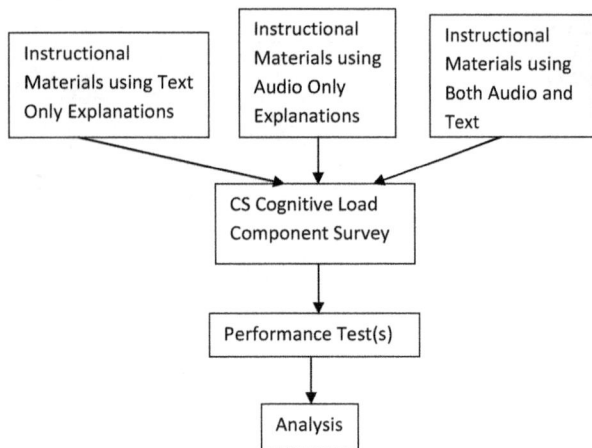

**Figure 3: Using CS Cognitive Load Component Survey to Determine Modality Learning Effects**

EL due to the use of dual channels [13], however this result remains to be proven empirically.

## 5.2 Limitations

While we have adapted and initially verified the use of the CS CLCS here, there are some limitations and opportunities for further survey refinement. We acknowledge that this study used data collected in two sections of a single introductory CS class with lectures given by the same instructor. These lectures were chosen in part because of opportunity (we wanted to ensure the same lecturer and identical lecture content) and because of the topics. Both lectures were the introduction of new topics. Wider data collection with other courses and instructors was done by [21], but the study has not yet been replicated in computer science.

Elements of our survey construction warrant further investigation. In particular, more experimentation should be conducted to explore different wordings of the questions in the survey. While our method here randomized question presentation to control for ordering-effects, item phrasing could be confounding the factor groupings we observed. It is possible that at least some of the inter-item co-variance was due to common stems across multiple items. For example, "The activity really enhanced my understanding of ...," used in questions 7–9 which all contribute to the germane load factor. Further, in each set of factor questions, all the questions are positively (or negatively) worded. Such concerns about inadvertent bias due to wording are common in survey design; however, in this initial study we opted to use language that matched the original phrasing from Leppink et al [20] as closely as possible. In future follow-on studies, we plan to examine the impact of randomizing positively and negatively worded items within each subscale along with minimizing shared prompt substrings to the extent possible. Further, a qualitative study using a think-aloud protocol during survey completion would uncover how learners *interpret* these items which could aid in further item refinement.

## 6. CONCLUSION

The contribution of this paper is the adaptation and collection of initial validity evidence for an instrument to measure cognitive load components within introductory CS class lectures. The high Cronbach's alpha values, the high fit indices (i.e., the CFI and TLI), and the low RMSEA in the data for both lectures support the three-factor cognitive load structure of CLT and provide validity evidence for the CS Cognitive Load Component Survey in measuring cognitive load components in a CS1 class. We describe how the instrument could be used, along with student performance indicators, to investigate specific pedagogical interventions.

We know that computer science is difficult to learn. For example, the Learning Edge Momentum theory [31] suggests that the deep interconnections in CS topics leads to bimodality in grades. Deep interconnections are measured by IL. An instrument to measure cognitive load helps us to ask research questions about the amount of cognitive load and how we can manage the cognitive load through careful instructional design. We hope that CS CLCS (with further development) and its successors give computing education researchers a new tool for developing theory and better interventions to address the unique learning challenges of computer science.

## ACKNOWLEDGMENTS

We would like to thank the students who participated in multiple versions of the survey. We also thank the anonymous reviewers who supplied a wealth of comments (and an important reference) which further enhanced the paper.

This work is funded in part by the National Science Foundation under grant 1138378. Any opinions, findings, and conclusions or recommendations expressed in this material are those of the authors and do not necessarily reflect the views of the NSF.

## References

[1] P. D. Antonenko and D. S. Niederhauser. The influence of leads on cognitive load and learning in a hypertext environment. *Computers in Human Behavior*, 26(2):140–150, 2010.

[2] P. Ayres. Using subjective measures to detect variations of intrinsic cognitive load within problems. *Learning and Instruction*, 16(5):389 – 400, 2006. ISSN 0959-4752.

[3] P. Ayres and J. Sweller. Locus of difficulty in multistage mathematics problems. *The American Journal of Psychology*, 1990.

[4] P. L. Ayres. Systematic mathematical errors and cognitive load. *Contemporary Educational Psychology*, 26(2):227–248, 2001.

[5] A. Baddeley. Working memory. *Science*, 255(5044): 556–559, 1992.

[6] J. D. Bransford, A. L. Brown, and R. R. Cocking. *How People Learn: Brain, Mind, Experience, and School*. National Academy Press, Washington, D.C., expanded edition, 2000.

[7] T. Brown. *Confirmatory Factor Analysis for Applied Research*. Guilford Press, New York, NY, 2006.

[8] R. Brunken, J. L. Plass, and D. Leutner. Direct measurement of cognitive load in multimedia learning. *Educational Psychologist*, 38(1):53–61, 2003.

[9] P. Chandler and J. Sweller. Cognitive load theory and the format of instruction. *Cognition and instruction*, 8 (4):293–332, 1991.

[10] P. Chandler and J. Sweller. The split-attention effect as a factor in the design of instruction. *British Journal of Educational Psychology*, 62(2):233–246, 1992.

[11] P. Chandler and J. Sweller. Cognitive load while learning to use a computer program. *Applied cognitive psychology*, 10(2):151–170, 1996.

[12] G. Cierniak, K. Scheiter, and P. Gerjets. Explaining the split-attention effect: Is the reduction of extraneous cognitive load accompanied by an increase in germane cognitive load? *Computers in Human Behavior*, 25(2):315–324, 2009.

[13] R. C. Clark and R. E. Mayer. *E-learning and the science of instruction: Proven guidelines for consumers and designers of multimedia learning*. John Wiley & Sons, 2011.

[14] K. E. DeLeeuw and R. E. Mayer. A comparison of three measures of cognitive load: Evidence for separable measures of intrinsic, extraneous, and germane load. *J. of Educational Psychology*, 100(1): 223, 2008.

[15] P. Gerjets, K. Scheiter, and R. Catrambone. Designing instructional examples to reduce intrinsic cognitive load: Molar versus modular presentation of solution procedures. *Instructional Science*, 32(1-2):33–58, 2004.

[16] P. Gerjets, K. Scheiter, and R. Catrambone. Can learning from molar and modular worked examples be enhanced by providing instructional explanations and prompting self-explanations? *Learning and Instruction*, 16(2):104–121, 2006.

[17] S. G. Hart and L. E. Staveland. Development of nasa-tlx (task load index): Results of empirical and theoretical research. *Advances in psychology*, 52: 139–183, 1988.

[18] L.-t. Hu and P. M. Bentler. Cutoff criteria for fit indexes in covariance structure analysis: Conventional criteria versus new alternatives. *Structural Equation Modeling: A Multidisciplinary Journal*, 6(1):1–55, 1999.

[19] D. L. Jackson, J. A. Gillaspy, and R. Purc-Stephenson. Reporting practices in confirmatory factor analysis: An overview and some recommendations. *Psychological Methods*, 14(1):6–23, 2009.

[20] J. Leppink, F. Paas, C. P. Van der Vleuten, T. Van Gog, and J. J. Van Merriënboer. Development of an instrument for measuring different types of cognitive load. *Behavior research methods*, 45(4): 1058–1072, 2013.

[21] J. Leppink, F. Paas, T. van Gog, C. P. van der Vleuten, and J. J. van Merriënboer. Effects of pairs of problems and examples on task performance and different types of cognitive load. *Learning and Instruction*, 30:32–42, 2014.

[22] G. A. Miller. The magical number seven, plus or minus two: some limits on our capacity for processing information. *Psychological review*, 63(2):81, 1956.

[23] R. Moreno. Decreasing cognitive load for novice students: Effects of explanatory versus corrective feedback in discovery-based multimedia. *Instructional science*, 32(1-2):99–113, 2004.

[24] J. Nunnally. *Psychometric theory*. McGraw-Hill, New York, NY, 2nd edition, 1978.

[25] F. Paas, J. E. Tuovinen, H. Tabbers, and P. W. Van Gerven. Cognitive load measurement as a means to advance cognitive load theory. *Educational psychologist*, 38(1):63–71, 2003.

[26] F. G. Paas. Training strategies for attaining transfer of problem-solving skill in statistics: A cognitive-load approach. *J. of educational psychology*, 84(4):429, 1992.

[27] F. G. Paas and J. J. Van Merriënboer. The efficiency of instructional conditions: An approach to combine mental effort and performance measures. *Human Factors: The Journal of the Human Factors and Ergonomics Society*, 35(4):737–743, 1993.

[28] F. G. Paas and J. J. Van Merriënboer. Variability of worked examples and transfer of geometrical problem-solving skills: A cognitive-load approach. *Journal of educational psychology*, 86(1):122, 1994.

[29] F. G. Paas, J. J. Van Merriënboer, and J. J. Adam. Measurement of cognitive load in instructional research. *Perceptual and motor skills*, 79(1):419–430, 1994.

[30] J. L. Plass, R. Moreno, and R. Brünken. *Cognitive load theory*. Cambridge University Press, 2010.

[31] A. Robins. Learning edge momentum. In *Encyclopedia of the Sciences of Learning*, pages 1845–1848. Springer, 2012.

[32] G. Salomon. Television is" easy" and print is" tough": The differential investment of mental effort in learning as a function of perceptions and attributions. *J. of educational psychology*, 76(4):647, 1984.

[33] J. Sweller. Cognitive load during problem solving: Effects on learning. *Cognitive science*, 12(2):257–285, 1988.

[34] J. Sweller. Element interactivity and intrinsic, extraneous, and germane cognitive load. *Educational Psychology Review*, 22(2):123–138, 2010.

[35] J. Sweller and P. Chandler. Why some material is difficult to learn. *Cognition and instruction*, 12(3): 185–233, 1994.

[36] J. Sweller, J. J. Van Merriënboer, and F. G. Paas. Cognitive architecture and instructional design. *Educational psychology review*, 10(3):251–296, 1998.

[37] J. Sweller, P. Ayres, and S. Kalyuga. *Cognitive load theory*, volume 1. Springer, 2011.

[38] G. Underwood, L. Jebbett, and K. Roberts. Inspecting pictures for information to verify a sentence: Eye movements in general encoding and in focused search. *Quarterly Journal of Experimental Psychology Section A*, 57(1):165–182, 2004.

[39] P. W. Van Gerven, F. Paas, J. J. Van Merriënboer, and H. G. Schmidt. Memory load and the cognitive pupillary response in aging. *Psychophysiology*, 41(2): 167–174, 2004.

[40] P. W. van Gerven, F. Paas, J. J. van Merriënboer, and H. G. Schmidt. Modality and variability as factors in training the elderly. *Applied cognitive psychology*, 20 (3):311–320, 2006.

[41] T. Van Gog and F. Paas. Instructional efficiency: Revisiting the original construct in educational research. *Educational Psychologist*, 43(1):16–26, 2008.

[42] T. van Gog and F. Paas. Cognitive load measurement. In *Encyclopedia of the Sciences of Learning*, pages 599–601. Springer, 2012.

[43] T. van Gog and K. Scheiter. Eye tracking as a tool to study and enhance multimedia learning. *Learning and Instruction*, 20(2):95–99, 2010.

[44] J. J. Van Merriënboer and J. Sweller. Cognitive load theory and complex learning: Recent developments and future directions. *Educational psychology review*, 17(2):147–177, 2005.

[45] R. R. Whelan. Neuroimaging of cognitive load in instructional multimedia. *Educational Research Review*, 2(1):1–12, 2007.

# Self-explaining from Video Recordings as a Methodology for Learning Programming

Viviane C. O. Aureliano
IFPE - Campus Belo Jardim
UFPE - Center of Informatics
Av. Jornalista Aníbal Fernandes, s/n
Recife, PE, 50740-560, Brazil
vcoa@cin.ufpe.br

## ABSTRACT

The literature has shown that novice learners have several difficulties in acquiring programming skills. As a way to overcome these difficulties, novice learners should be guided in the process of studying the programming process. One evidence-based practice for improving student learning by guiding them while they are studying from instructional material is through the use of self-explanations. Videos have been proposed as an ideal instructional material for presenting the dynamics of programming to novices. In this context, my research proposes that novices should be guided in the process of studying videos by means of self-explanation. In order to evaluate the benefits of using this methodology, two studies will be realised as part of the research.

## Categories and Subject Descriptors

K.3.2 [**Computers and Education**]: Computer and Information Science Education – *computer science education.*

## Keywords

Learning programming; novices; video recordings; self-explanations.

## 1. RESEARCH SITUATION

I am enrolled in an academic PhD programme in Computer Science at the Center of Informatics of the Federal University of Pernambuco, Brazil. I am also a teacher at the Federal Institute of Pernambuco, Brazil, where I mainly teach programming language subjects to technical high school students. My main supervisor is Dr. Patrícia Tedesco.

The PhD programme in which I participate must be completed in four years and I am at the beginning of the fourth year. I defended my research proposal in November 2013. Since December 2013, I am working as a visiting PhD student with Prof. Michael Caspersen at Centre for Science Education at Aarhus University, Denmark.

## 2. CONTEXT & MOTIVATION

Years of research have shown that novice learners experience several difficulties in acquiring programming skills. Novices

struggle when they have to apply the knowledge learned in new situations of use [1]. However, the major difficulty experienced by novices is how to combine and properly use basic structures to build a program [1, 5].

As a way to overcome these difficulties, novice learners should be guided while they are learning the programming process. One evidence-based practice for improving student learning by guiding them while they are studying from some instructional material is through the use of self-explanations [2, 3]. In particular, this practice is especially important for novice learners in programming and contributes to their learning while they are studying alone [3].

Video recordings have been proposed as an ideal instructional material for presenting the dynamic process of programming for novice learners [4]. In the presented context, my PhD research proposes a methodology to promote and guide novices' self-explanations while they are learning programming languages from video recordings. Through the use of this methodology I would like to teach technical high school students how to study properly in a programming course and encourage them to become deep learners.

## 3. BACKGROUND & RELATED WORK

Currently, numerous video recordings for teaching programming are available over the internet. Instead of textbooks that are static, video recordings are an important instructional material to expose the programming process since they are essentially a dynamic medium [4].

Stepwise Improvement framework describes programming as an incremental process [5]. It provides guidance regarding the structure of instructional material and, consequently, the manner novices learn programming by extending, refining and restructuring small pieces of code systematically and incrementally during the course.

In this sense, Stepwise Improvement was employed in the structure of the videos of the Joy of code channel on Youtube [6] and also in a set of worked examples in videos [5]. However, the framework does not provide any guidance regarding the way that students may study and comprehend this instructional material. One way of providing this kind of guidance is through self-explanations.

Self-explanation is a type of dialog that learners have with themselves while they are learning from different instructional materials [2, 3]. The process of self-explaining benefits the building of new knowledge through the refinement of the given information [8].

## 4. STATEMENT OF THESIS

I agree with Bennedsen and Caspersen (2008) that video recordings are an important medium for exposing the programming process. In particular, I believe that videos are an important resource when students are studying programming alone and outside the classroom. Also, I believe that the process of studying programming can be guided by prompting self-explanations from the students while they are studying these video recordings.

In this context, the main objective of this PhD dissertation is to propose a methodology to promote and guide novices' self-explanations while they are learning programming languages from video recordings which are structured according the ideas of Stepwise Improvement framework. In order to do that, the main research question that guides this PhD is *how could novice learners in programming benefit from using self-explanations while studying videos that expose the programming process?* In this sense, novice learners would benefit if they achieve better results, obtain higher grades, code faster or make fewer errors.

## 5. RESEARCH GOALS & METHODS

Aiming to answer the question which conducts this research, I am realizing two different studies. Both studies are based on the previous works by Bielaczyc and colleagues (1995) and Chi and colleagues (1994), but instead of studying plain texts, learners are using video recordings as instructional material.

The first study has the following objectives: (i) check whether the proposed self-explanations prompts are appropriate for the video recordings; (ii) analyse when to use the self-explanations prompts and the videos together; (iii) verify if there is any benefit of using self-explanations while studying video recordings (if so, which are these benefits); and (iv) refine the self-explanations prompts and the manner that they should be used. The participants in the study will be divided in three groups: (i) the instructional group in which the self-explanations are prompted while watching the video; (ii) the instructional group in which the self-explanations are prompted only when the video finishes; and (iii) the control group.

This first study consists of three phases. The first phase aims to provide the participants with a common prior knowledge of the programming language chosen and familiarize them with the think aloud process. The second phase aims to train the two instructional groups in how to use the self-explanation prompts. The third phase aims to collect data from all participants after the second phase. The students will be assessed by means of the explanations provided by them while studying the video recordings. Together with these explanations, students are asked to solve similar problems in order to assess their process of transfer of knowledge.

Aiming to answer the question which conducts this research, I believe that is an effective approach to vary the kind of video recordings adopted in the studies. For this reason, the second study will be similar in structure to the first one regarding the objectives, group participants, sequence of phases, programming language and development tool. However, it will vary regarding the following characteristics: (i) a refined set of self-explanations prompts and practice problems; and (ii) worked examples in videos as instructional materials, enriched with the self-explanations prompts.

## 6. DISSERTATION STATUS

As I mentioned before, I am a PhD student in Brazil, but I am working as visiting PhD student in Denmark. I expect that the first study occurs next August in Denmark. Currently, I am preparing the instructional materials that will be used in the first study. Also, I am planning each phase of the study in detail.

After the preparation for the first study, I will start to organize the instructional materials for the second study which I expect to occur next October in Brazil. Then, from the ICER Doctoral Consortium, I expect to discuss and obtain feedback mainly about the two studies that I am planning.

## 7. EXPECTED CONTRIBUTIONS

The expected contributions of this PhD research are: (i) a methodology for studying programming from video recordings in a deeper manner by self-explaining them; (ii) a study to analyse how novice learners in programming would benefit from using self-explanations while studying video recordings; and (iii) a suite of worked examples structured according the Stepwise Improvement framework, enriched with self-explanations prompts.

## 8. ACKNOWLEDGMENTS

I would like to thank CAPES Foundation for the scholarship provided under report n° 1127-91-3.

## 9. REFERENCES

[1] Robins, A.; Rountree, J.; Rountree, N. (2003) Learning and Teaching Programming: A Review and Discussion, Computer Science Education, v. 13, n. 2, p. 137-172.

[2] Chi, M. T. H.; Bassok, M.; Lewis, M.; Reimann, M., & Glaser, R. (1989). Self-explanations: How students study and use examples in learning to solve problems. Cognitive Science, 13, 145-182.

[3] Bielaczyc, K.; Pirolli, P.; Brown, A. L. (1995). Training in self-explanation and self-regulation strategies: Investigating the effects of knowledge acquisition activities on problem solving. Cognition and Instruction, 13, 221-253.

[4] Bennedsen, J.; Carpersen, M. E. (2008). Exposing the Programming Process. In Reflection on the Theory of Programming: Methods and Implementation, J. Bennedsen, M. E. Carpersen, M. Kölling (Eds.) Springer-Verlag, 6-16.

[5] Caspersen, M. E. (2007) Educating novices in the skills of programming. PhD dissertation PD-07-4, Department of Computer Science, University of Aarhus.

[6] Kölling, M. (2012). *The Joy of code* [Video recordings]. Retrieved from http://bit.ly/1jbTbHq

[7] Chi, M. T. H; deLeeuw, N.; Chiu, M.; LaVancher, C. (1994). Eliciting self-explanations improves understanding. Cognitive Science, 18, 439-477.

[8] Chiu, J. L.; Chi, M. T. H. (2014). Supporting Self-Explanation in the Classroom. In V.A. Benassi, C.E. Overson, C.M. Hakala (Eds.). Applying science of learning in education: Infusing psychological science into the curriculum. Retrieved from: http://bit.ly/KbYLtG

# Identification and Measurement of Computer Science Competencies in the Area of Software Development, Software Engineering and Programming

Kathrin Bröker
University of Paderborn
Fürstenallee 11
33102 Paderborn, Germany
kathyb@upb.de

## ABSTRACT

Many challenges exist at today's universities. Next to all these challenges students should get the best education. To improve the educational process and to overcome students' deficits, we need to know the competencies of our students.

This paper presents a methodology to find out these competencies and how to build a competence model accordingly. Such a competence model is necessary for our next step: Building an assessment to measure competencies. Measuring competencies is useful, for example, to value the benefit of interventions during educational processes.

## Categories and Subject Descriptors

K.3.2 [**Computers and Education**]: Computer and Information Science Education – *computer science education.*

## General Terms

Computer science education, Model curricula, Software engineering education

## Keywords

competence measurement, competence model, eAssessment

## 1. RESEARCH SITUATION

I'm a research associate and Ph.D.-Student at the University of Paderborn, Germany since 2012. There I'm responsible for the Computer Science Learning Center and associate to the CSE research group of Prof. Dr. Johannes Magenheim. Next to my full-time job as research associate I have the opportunity to do my Ph.D.

## 2. CONTEXT AND MOTIVATION

Many challenges exist at today's Universities in Germany and other countries, for example: increasing numbers of students, tightening up the study process after Bologna and an internationalization of the majors. Next to all these challenges our students should get the best education and furthermore we want to have only small drop out rates. Major reasons for dropping out are subject related problems.

To improve the educational process and to overcome student deficits, we need an instrument to identify the deficits. Moreover, we need such an instrument to measure the benefit of educational interventions. The basis for such an instrument is a competence model that describes which competencies our students should have.

## 3. BACKGROUND & RELATED WORK

Many of the existing national and international projects, especially in computer science, focus on the competences in schools, for future teachers, key competencies or on ICT key competencies in different subjects [10], [2]. That implies that their main focus is not on subject specific competence. In contrast, there are only a few projects where subject specific competence models are developed. The German projects MoKoM [5] and KUI [1] are two of these. The MoKoM project has its focus on developing a competence model for informatics modeling and system comprehension for students at schools. In contrast to that, the project KUI focuses on competences for future teachers. The KUI competence model is divided into three parts: competencies on subject matter knowledge (CK), competencies on pedagogical content knowledge (PCK) and non-cognitive competencies (NCC) [3], [7]. In addition, there are some projects with research in students' competencies at universities. Nevertheless until now, no national or international project has developed a concrete competence model for subject specific competences in computer science for academics. The only existing models are, for example, the IEEE Software Engineering Body of Knowledge (SWEBOK)[9], the ACM/IEEE Curriculum [10] or the IEEE Software Engineering Competency Model (SWECOM)[4]. Nevertheless the first two documents rather describe knowledge, which should be part of a curriculum than real competencies. The SWECOM describes competencies but for software engineers who participate in development of and modifications to software-intensive systems not for academics directly after their study. Unfortunately, these documents are additionally not empirically verified. Consequently we don't know if universities teach the topics mentioned in these curricula/competence models. Only accreditation rules give us a first hint. Moreover, they are not as specific as the ACM/IEEE Curriculum. However, these documents are a good basis for the developing of a concrete competence model. In addition to the missing competence models, there is no assessment for the competences by now.

*ICER '14*, Aug 11-13 2014, Glasgow, United Kingdom
ACM 978-1-4503-2755-8/14/08.
http://dx.doi.org/10.1145/2632320.2632322

# 4. STATEMENT OF THESIS/PROBLEM

The previous motivation for developing a competence model and an additional assessment results in the following research questions for my thesis:

1. Which facets include computer science competencies in the Area of Software Development, Software Engineering and Programming? (developing a competence model)

2. Can we measure an increase of computer science competencies in the Area of Software Development, Software Engineering and Programming? (developing and evaluation of the test instrument)

# 5. RESEARCH GOALS & METHODS

Computer Science is a widespread subject with many different areas. This is the reason I focus on the areas of Software Development, Software Engineering and Programming. For these areas, I describe the process of developing the competence model and the assessment for measuring the competencies.

To develop the Competence Model I first analyze different Computer Science Bachelor Curricular from all over the world with the deductive content analysis. The content analysis has the aim to find common competences in the different study programs.

The basis for my analysis and my category system is the ACM/IEEE Curriculum [9]. In this curriculum experts defined a catalog with 18 knowledge areas belonging to computer science. Each knowledge area consists of different knowledge units. I use these knowledge areas and units as category system during the content analysis [6]. As text corpus, I use different international computer science bachelor curricula.

The results of this curricula analysis give an overview about what the different universities teach and if there is anything like a core knowledge. Referring to this analysis, I will develop a first competence model. Following by a validation of experts, a comparison with other existing research and standards should be done. After this step, I will build the competence model that structures the competencies in competence dimensions and graduate levels for each of these dimensions.

The results of the content analysis are the starting point to develop an assessment for competence measurement. For this, I have to create different exercises and items. Finally, I need at least one item for each competence mentioned in the competence model. In addition, I have to add the difficulty for each item. This gives the opportunity to measure levels of competences. Consequently levels of competences help to create more specific offers for our students. Furthermore, it gives the opportunity measure the development of competences in a more specific way.

With a competence model, items and a psychometric model we can start to measure competencies. However, my aim is to build an eAssessment for the competence measurement. Reasons are different advantages of eAssessment like the instant feedback and the greater flexibility with respect to location and time.

# 6. DISSERTATION STATUS

After coding the curricula, I have analyzed the results. Because the richness in details of the different curricula descriptions varies considerably we do not consider the number of occurrences of a single coding, but only the existence of a coding for a category/subcategory in a curriculum. Half of these subcategories occur in 50% or more of the curricula. For building the competence model I decide to concentrate on the coding of these subcategories.

After developing the competence model, I have to evaluate my competence model with experts, to check if I have considered all important aspects. This competence model is then the basis for the assessment I will develop and test in the last step.

# 7. EXPECTED CONTRIBUTIONS

In my thesis, I want to develop a Computer Science Competence Model for the needs of curriculum development and evaluation in Higher Education. The methodology I will use to develop the competence model for the areas of Software Development, Software Engineering and Programming can also be used to develop competence models for other areas of Computer Science.

With the competence model and the additional assessment I will create, we have the ability to find out the deficits of our students. These concrete results will give computer science departments the opportunity to develop specific interventions to help students in overcoming their deficits and in addition to measure the effect of these interventions accordingly.

# 8. REFERENCES

[1] M. Berges, P. Hubwieser, J. Magenheim, E. Bender, K. Bröker, M. Margaritis-Kopecki, J. Neugebauer, N. Schaper, S. Schubert, and L. Ohrndorf. 2013. Developing a competency model for teaching computer science in schools. In Proceedings of the 18th ACM conference on Innovation and technology in computer science education (ITiCSE '13). ACM, New York, NY, USA, page 327, 2013.

[2] P. J. Denning, Great principles of computing, Communications of the ACM, ACM, Volume 46, Issue 11, pp. 15-20, November 2003.

[3] P. Hubwieser, J. Magenheim, A. Mühling, and A. Ruf, "Towards a conceptualization of pedagogical content knowledge for computer science," in Proceedings of the ninth annual international ACM conference on International computing education research, 2013, pp. 1–8.

[4] IEEE Computer Societey, "Software Engineering Competency Model (SWECOM)", 2014 IEEE, online reference https://computer.centraldesktop.com/home/viewfile?guid=53 076640805C22BA4AC16312FABAAB1D33917BDEA&id= 30862727, last access:12.05.2014

[5] B. Linck, L. Ohrndorf, S. Schubert, P. Stechert, J. Magenheim, W. Nelles, J. Neugebauer, N. Schaper, "Competence model for informatics modelling and system comprehension," Global Engineering Education Conference (EDUCON), 2013 IEEE , vol., no., pp.85,93, 13-15 March 2013.

[6] P. Mayring, Qualitative Inhaltsanalyse: Grundlagen und Techniken. Beltz Pädagogik, Beltz, Weinheim 2010.

[7] N. Schaper, J. Magenheim, S. Schubert, P. Hubwieser, E. Bender, M. Margaritis, L. Ohrndorf, and M. Berges, "Competences for Teaching Computer Science. In KoKoHs Working Papers, [no. 4].," KoKoHs Work. Pap. 3, no. 3, pp. 32–34, 2013.

[8] Society, I. C. & Bourque, P. & Dupuis, R. (eds.), Software Engineering Body of Knowledge (SWEBOK). EUA: Angela Burgess, 2004.

[9] The Joint Task Force on Computing Curricula Association for Computing Machinery IEEE-Computer Society 2012. Computer Science Curricula 2013 - Ironman Draft, 2013.

[10] UNESCO: UNESCO ICT Competency Framework for Teachers, UNESCO, 2012, online reference: http://unesdoc.unesco.org/images/0021/002134/213475E.pdf, last access: 14.10.2014.

# CS Outreach to High School Enrollment: Bridging the Gap

Veronica Cateté
NC State University
Raleigh, NC, 27695, USA
vmcatete@ncsu.edu

## ABSTRACT

Researchers in CS have heard of disparities between under-represented groups and the lack of people to fill future jobs. Initiatives focus on strengthening the computing pipeline and getting more students interested. This research goes further by analyzing factors that affect behavioral change and get students to enroll in computing courses. We focus on a middle grades outreach program called SPARCS that has a 84% transfer rate into high school courses. We approach with a lens on identity, social cognitive career theory, and other attitudes and demographics perspectives.

## Categories and Subject Descriptors

K.3.2 [**Computers and Education**]: Computers and Information Science Education—*Computer Science Education*.

## Keywords

Outreach; Retrospective

## 1. RESEARCH SITUATION

I am a second year Ph.D. student at North Carolina State University in the Center for Educational Informatics. I plan on completing the second stage of my program, the research proposal, this fall and graduating by December of 2015. In my research on computer science outreach, I have conducted a case study for one program, SPARCS, analyzing previous data collected over the last five years, in addition to running follow up surveys with the alumni from the program to identify long term impacts. When continuing my research, I plan to conduct interviews with these students to get more in depth reports. Our end goal is to develop a model to determine the likelihood of a student continuing into the next stage of the computing pipeline, with a primary focus on the middle to high school transition and then using this model to create a checklist for curriculum and pedagogy.

## 2. CONTEXT AND MOTIVATION

*ICER'14*, August 11-13, 2014, Glasgow, Scotland, UK.
ACM 978-1-4503-2755-8/14/08
http://dx.doi.org/10.1145/2632320.2632323.

Students plan future career ideas as early as middle school[10]. Van Leuvan's 2004 study, found that female interest in math and science declines rapidly by the time students reach high school [12]. Although personal interest has been found to be one of the most important factors when choosing a major, many students do not realize they are interested in something until they start exploring careers [6, 1]. This leaves computer science in quite a predicament, as students are not properly exposed to computer science until later in their academic career if at all.

Trying to recruit students to take computing courses in high school is an issue when at the middle school level, the only computing courses they've been exposed to are primarily word processing and spreadsheets. Outreach programs and informal learning opportunities are key to getting middle school students interested in computing, and understanding the full spectrum of computing fields. There are many grassroots outreach programs, however, very little research has been done to investigate whether or not the participants continue into CS courses in high school or if they have any lasting impact. Following Breckler's ABC model of affect, behavior, and then cognitive change, we want to know if we can move past the affective level, and identify program features that enact behavioral change (taking a course).

## 3. BACKGROUND & RELATED WORK

Middle school students are both developmentally broad-minded enough and capable of understanding computational theories [4]. Although research in *computer science* outreach is still fairly new, there have been studies into informal STEM programs such as Meredith Kier's doctoral research on using a 6 week STEM-video intervention to increase interest in STEM in a rural school [7]. Kier found science identity to play a key part in STEM attitude change. We use Lent's framework of Social Cognitive Career Theory (SCCT) and Markus' possible selves to examine the outcomes of the computing outreach program SPARCS [8, 9], utilizing a similar analytic lens to Kier.

SCCT combines a student's environmental and internal factors towards accomplishing a goal, including self-efficacy, goals, and contextual influences. Additional research by Mei Tang et al. shows that self-efficacy in a subject is the number one factor influencing high school students' career aspirations [11]. The SCCT framework also incorporates personal factors such as ethnicity, gender and contextual factors (supportive structures and barriers) to help explain influences on students' perceptions of careers. Role models such as family, friends, and mentors have been shown to be predictors of student interest and motivates students without explicit external rewards [8]. This is even more relevant for interventions with women and underrepresented groups, as strong role models and positive learning experiences have been shown to outweigh the negative stereotypes, leading to a persistence in STEM [5].

The possible selves framework focuses on the concept of a science identity and being able to see yourself in that career. Possible selves, is based off of Markus' model of science identity which incorporates performance, competence, and recognition, recognition being the most prominent [9]. Carlone and Johnson's study found that not only recognition by one's self as a scientist, but also by one's professors, and peers is critical to being successful in science [2].

We believe that by immersing students into deeper, agile, computational activities where role models are present we can influence them to try out computing courses in high school. We will integrate the aforementioned frameworks and investigate whether they and our intervention that is informed by that research (SPARCS) is effective in long-term behavior change and possibly cognitive change or career choices.

## 4. PROBLEM, GOALS, & METHODS

In order to test the above hypothesis we must figure out which factors related to gender, performance, identity, etc. have the biggest impact on students who persisted in computing. Using these factors to create a model, we then hope to predict how likely new students are to persist in computing. Persistence as measured by enrollment in computing courses or major.

I begin this research investigating one particular CS outreach intervention, SPARCS, with the goal of being able to identify the key aspects of the program that led to such high retention rates. In this case study I have three goals in mind: (i) figure out how students perceive the program itself (do they think they are learning, are they having fun, content) (ii) figure out if students retain knowledge learned in the program (do students remember skills taught in previous sessions) (iii) figure out which students decided to take computing in high school, and what makes them different than those who hadn't (gender, efficacy, identity, etc). I plan on adapting analysis metrics and frameworks used by Kier and other scientists as a lens for analyzing student differences.

Our outcome will be a curriculum design that incorporates factors associated with persistence in computing and pedagogical strategies to complement.

## 5. DISSERTATION STATUS

We have looked at past SPARCS data and determined that attrition rates are highly correlated with enjoyment. If students are having fun they will return to the next session [3]. We found that how much students think they learned to be less of an impact factor. I have also sent surveys to the alumni students (10th grade or higher) covering computing identity, affective, behavioral change, and demographics. Data shows that 84% of the respondents have taken CS courses in high school. We are matching alumni data with past data to get a full spectrum view. SPARCS is unique in that each session teaches something different, ranging from security to video games. Students spend 5 hours learning a topic, and then the next month get something new to explore. We are trying to identify which aspects of the program seem the most beneficial. We will be publishing papers one both the alumni data and on our initial model framework.

As I am currently completing my proposal, the dissertation is not yet drafted. Future plans are to tie up this case study on SPARCS and begin to see if this program can be replicated. All major analysis should be completed by early fall, and factor testing should be completed by winter. In the spring we will begin replication attempts.

From this consortium I would like help in which direction I should take the model, either in a practical applications standpoint, theoretical, or a more computational based approach.

## 6. EXPECTED CONTRIBUTIONS

By developing this model and consequent curriculum design, our goal is to develop a checklist that groups can use to enhance their BPC efforts and cause not only affective change but behavioral change in participants of CS outreach.

## 7. REFERENCES

[1] J. M. Beggs, J. H. Bantham, and S. Taylor. Distinguishing the factors influencing college students'choice of major. *College Student J.*, 42(2), 2008.

[2] H. B. Carlone and A. Johnson. Understanding the science experiences of successful women of color: Science identity as an analytic lens. *J. Research in Science Teaching*, 44(8):1187–1218, 2007.

[3] V. Cateté, K. Wassell, and T. Barnes. Use and development of entertainment technologies in after school stem program. In *Proc. of the 45th ACM Tech. Symp. Comp. Sci. Ed.*, pages 163–168. ACM, 2014.

[4] J. S. Eccles. *Where Are All the Women? Gender Differences in Participation in Physical Science and Engineering.* Amer. Psychol. Assoc., 2007.

[5] A. L. Griffith. Persistence of women and minorities in stem field majors: Is it the school that matters? *Econom. Ed. Rev.*, 29(6):911–922, 2010.

[6] C. Hall, J. Dickerson, D. Batts, P. Kauffmann, and M. Bosse. Are we missing opportunities to encourage interest in stem fields? *J. Tech. Ed.*, 23(1), 2011.

[7] M. W. Kier. *Examining the effects of a STEM career video intervention on the interests and STEM professional identities of rural, minority middle school students.* PhD thesis, NC State University, 2013.

[8] R. W. Lent, S. D. Brown, and G. Hackett. Toward a unifying social cognitive theory of career and academic interest, choice, and performance. *J. Vocat. Behav.*, 45(1):79–122, 1994.

[9] H. Markus and P. Nurius. Possible selves. *Amer. Psychol.*, 41(9):954, 1986.

[10] R. H. Tai. Career choice: Enhanced: Planning early for. *Life Sci.*, 1:0–2, 2006.

[11] M. Tang, W. Pan, and M. D. Newmeyer. Factors influencing high school students' career aspirations. *Prof. Sch. Counsel.*, 11(5):285–295, 2008.

[12] P. VanLeuvan. Young women's science/mathematics career goals from seventh grade to high school graduation. *J. Ed. Res.*, 97(5):248–268, 2004.

# Adaptive Parsons Problems with Discourse Rules

Barbara J. Ericson
Georgia Institute of Technology
801 Atlantic Drive
Atlanta, GA, 30332, USA
+1-404.385.2107
ericson@cc.gatech.edu

## ABSTRACT

Parsons problems are code segments that the user must put in the correct order with the correct indention. Research on Parsons problems suggests that they might be a more effective and efficient learning approach than writing equivalent code, especially for time-strapped secondary teachers. I intend to explore this hypothesis with empirical experiments, observations, and log file analysis.

## Categories and Subject Descriptors

K.3.2 [**Computers and Education**]: Computer and Information Science Education – *computer science education.*

## General Terms

Design, Experimentation, Measurement

## Keywords

Parsons problems; Learning programming

## 1. RESEARCH SITUATION

I have just completed the 2nd year of my Human-Centered Computing (HCC) PhD program. In April of 2014 I passed my written and oral qualifying exams, which are intended to show competency in:

- Technical skills
- Written and oral research communication
- Core HCC knowledge
- Core knowledge in my specialization area of learning sciences and technology
- The design and evaluation of HCC systems

There are two more courses that I have to take, so I should finish coursework by the end of spring 2015. I hope to complete my research proposal by fall 2015 and my PhD defense by fall 2017.

My research group is creating and testing features for e-books to help people learn programming. One of the features that I have focused on is Parsons problems [8]. Parsons problems are code segments that are mixed up and have to be placed into the correct

*ICER'14*, August 11–13, 2014, Glasgow, Scotland, UK.
ACM 978-1-4503-2755-8/14/08.
http://dx.doi.org/10.1145/2632320.2632324

order and may have to be indented correctly as well. I created 11 Parsons problems for a chapter of a Python e-book. I also created a short introduction to programming in Python for the Hour of Code, which also included the same 11 Parsons problems. In the spring of 2014 I created 9 more Parsons problems for a Java e-book to help students review for the Advanced Placement Computer Science A exam. Advanced Placement courses are high school (secondary) courses intended to be equivalent to introductory university courses.

In the fall of 2013 and spring of 2014 I conducted an observations of four teachers working though the Python e-book chapter that contained the first set of 11 Parsons problems. I plan on doing additional teacher observations this summer on both sets of Parsons problems. Our research group is currently analyzing the data from the detailed log files from the three e-books.

## 2. CONTEXT AND MOTIVATION

The National Science Foundation (NSF) wants to prepare 10,000 United States of America high school teachers to teach a new course, Advanced Placement (AP) Computer Science Principles (CS-P), by the beginning of the 2016-2017 school year. This effort is called the CS 10K effort. Many researchers in the computer science education community are focusing on this effort, including the members of the CS Learning 4U project at Georgia Tech.

The new AP CS-P course covers several big ideas in computing, including programming. It would be very expensive and difficult to provide face-to-face professional development for thousands of teachers before 2016. Much of the professional development will have to be done using distance learning.

One of the difficulties in preparing teachers to teach programming is that programming can be difficult to learn. Reported failure rates in introductory computer science courses at the university level are as high as 90% [2]. A large multi-institutional study found that many undergraduate students can't program as well as expected after either their first or second computer science course [7]. Studies of expert programmers show that experts recognize and apply many "programming plans" as well as "rules of programming discourse" [9]. Teachers who are new to programming will need to learn these "programming plans" and "rules of programming discourse". Soloway and Guzdial recommend using scaffolding to support learners as they learn a new task [10]. Examples include providing hints, correcting mistakes, and coaching. As the learner progresses, scaffolding can fade.

The pace of on-line learning can be problematic for teachers. A study of adult learners in two online introductory computer science university courses found that success in the course was dependent on having sufficient time to dedicate to the course work and that working adults often did not have sufficient time [1]. Students had difficulty in learning to program and the time it took to create working programs was unpredictable. Even simple syntax errors like having a comma out of place could take hours to fix [1].

## 3. BACKGROUND & RELATED WORK

One way to make the learning of computer science more efficient and effective is to reduce the amount of time that teachers struggle with syntax errors. One approach is to use Parsons problems [8]. There are several variants of Parsons problems, such as including extra code as distractors.

Work in this area [4] has found that Parsons problems scores highly correlate with code writing scores. This means that Parsons problems might be a more effective and efficient way to learn than the traditional approach, which requires teachers to spend an unpredictable number of hours writing code. Denny, Luxton-Reilly et al. felt that students would be able to solve the Parsons problems more quickly than writing the equivalent code. But, they did not test this hypothesis. The researchers also tested several variants of Parsons problems and found that students had the most trouble with Parsons problems with one distractor per code block and had the easiest time solving Parsons problems when they were given the structure of the solution (the number of lines in each code block and the indention).

In the e-books we are using an open-source tool called js-parons. Researchers using this tool have found that even though Parsons problems remove syntax errors, users can get stuck and repeat the same incorrect solution [5]. Some users also exhibit a "trial and error" approach. They drag a single code block into the solution area and ask for feedback to see if it is in the correct place.

One group, [6] who also used js-parsons, tried to limit "trial and error" behavior by restricting the use of feedback if this behavior was detected. They wanted students to think about the solution rather than just try different combinations. They informed the user if the user repeated the same incorrect solution. The feedback they gave was "Your current code is identical to one you had previously. You might to stop going in circles and think carefully about the feedback shown here".

Research on learning highlights the importance of explanatory feedback [3]. Rather than simply recommending that the user "think carefully" I propose exploring adaptive Parsons problems in an on-line e-book where the difficulty of the problem is adjusted dynamically depending on the teachers' performance. I will also add hints to help a teacher learn the "discourse rules" that guide placement of the code block, such as "declarations are usually done near the top of a method".

## 4. STATEMENT OF THESIS/PROBLEM

Do adaptable Parsons problems with discourse rule feedback help students, and particularly teachers, learn programming effectively and efficiently? I will extend the js-parsons tool to allow for adaptive Parsons problems with discourse rule feedback. I will test if solving these Parsons problems is more efficient than writing the equivalent code and leads to similar learning outcomes.

## 5. DISSERTATION STATUS

I created two sets of Parsons problems and have done observations of teachers solving one set. The only difficulty the teachers had was with realizing that they needed to indent the code. However, these teachers all had prior programming experience. I plan to observe additional teachers this summer.

My research group has started analyzing the log file data to look for evidence of difficulties solving the Parsons problems. We have found that not every person who attempted a Parsons problem solved it. We will do more in-depth analysis of the log file data this summer to determine what percentage of users had difficulty and the types of difficulties they had.

## 6. EXPECTED CONTRIBUTIONS

Research on Parsons problems suggests that they might be a more effective and efficient learning approach than writing equivalent computer programs. However, more research is needed to solidify this claim and to test methods to help students who use "trial and error" approaches or get stuck. If this research helps teachers learn programming on-line in an efficient and effective manner, it could provide a scalable solution to allow the US to prepare 10,000 computing teachers by 2016-2017.

## 7. ACKNOWLEDGEMENT

This work is supported by the National Science Foundation grant CNS-1138378.

## 8. REFERENCES

[1] Benda, K. and A. Bruckman (2012). "When life and learning do not fit: Challenges of workload and communication in introductory computer science online." ACM Transactions on Computing Education.

[2] Bennedsen, J. and M. E. Caspersen (2007). "Failure rates in introductory programming." SIGCSE Bull. **39**(2): 32-36.

[3] Clark, R. C. and R. E. Mayer (2011). E-Learning and the Science of Instruction: Proven Guidelines for Consumers and Designers of Multimedia Learning. , Pfeiffer.

[4] Denny, P., et al. (2008). Evaluating a New Exam Question: Parsons Problems. International Computing Education Research Conference. Sydney, Australia, ACM.

[5] Helminen, J., et al. (2012). How Do Students Solve Parsons Programming Problems? - An Analysis of Ineraction Traces. International Computing Education Research Conference. Aukland, New Zealand, ACM: 119-126.

[6] Karavirta, V., et al. (2012). A mobile learning application for parsons problems with automatic feedback. Proceedings of the 12th Koli Calling International Conference on Computing Education Research. Koli, Finland, ACM: 11-18.

[7] McCracken, M., et al. (2001). "A multi-national, multi-institutional study of assessment of programming skills of first-year CS students." SIGCSE Bull. **33**(4): 125-180.

[8] Parsons, D. and P. Haden (2006). Parson's programming puzzles: a fun and effective learning tool for first programming courses. Proceedings of the 8th Australasian Conference on Computing Education - Volume 52. Hobart, Australia, Australian Computer Society, Inc.: 157-163.

[9] Soloway, E. and K. Ehrlich (1984). "Empirical Studies of Programming Knowledge." IEEE Transactions on Software Engineering **SE-10**(5): 595–609.

[10] Soloway, E., et al. (1994). "Learner-Centered Design: The Challenge For HCI In The 21st Century." Interactions **1**(2) 36-48

# Big Data and Data Management:
# A Topic for Secondary Computing Education

Andreas Grillenberger
Computing Education Research Group
Friedrich-Alexander-Universität Erlangen-Nürnberg (FAU)
Martensstraße 3, 91058 Erlangen, Germany
andreas.grillenberger@fau.de

## ABSTRACT

The topics data management and data analysis are currently discussed in various contexts, e.g. in Computer Science but also in daily life and society. The recent developments in this field, which are often summarized under the term *Big Data*, did not only lead to the emergence of new database models, but also comprise new threats, e.g. for data privacy. These topics include many aspects that are important for everyone, but they only gain in relevance slowly in higher education and hardly in secondary education. Hence, I will evaluate data management as a topic for secondary education, with a view on the long-lasting concepts and aspects in this field.

## Categories and Subject Descriptors

K.3.2 [**Computers and Education**]: Computers and Information Science Education—*Computer Science Education*

## Keywords

Data Management; Big Data; Secondary Schools; Daily Life; Databases; Data Privacy; Data Analysis; NoSQL

## 1. RESEARCH SITUATION

I am a first-year doctoral candidate in computing education research at the University of Erlangen-Nürnberg, Germany, under supervision of Prof. Dr. Ralf Romeike. As usual in Germany, my doctoral study is not part of a PhD program, instead it is an individual part-time study alongside a (full-time) employment as research assistant.

Since my work is right at its beginning, I expect to defend my thesis in about 4.5 years. Until now, I focused especially on narrowing the field, as data management covers various different aspects. Yet, some first ideas on this topic have been developed and published as conference papers [5, 6].

## 2. CONTEXT AND MOTIVATION

Despite their influences on CS as well as on daily life and society, the topics data management and Big Data only play

*ICER'14*, August 11-13, 2014, Glasgow, Scotland, UK.
ACM 978-1-4503-2755-8/14/08.
http://dx.doi.org/10.1145/2632320.2632325.

a minor role in current CS education. Additionally, the relevance of various concepts and topics currently taught in computing education is challenged by the recent developments. Today, education in this field focuses on "databases", while in the future the impact of other aspects will increase: data privacy, data safety/security, data analysis, Open Data, distributed data, cloud storage, data backup, and so on. Therefore, CS education research needs to analyze the influences of these developments on current teaching. Overall, the current emphasis on relational database management systems (RDBMS) results in the main topics data modeling, normalization, redundancy-free and consistent data storage, SQL, and so on. While these aspects are clearly fundamental to RDBMS, their relevance is changing when considering other modern databases, like the NoSQL[1] ones. For example, such newly emerging databases often use redundancy for speeding up the access to distributed stored data. As topics considered as fundamental so far may lose importance in the future, the current focus of database education is being questioned.

Therefore, current education on this topic is not able to fulfill the task of preparing students for handling the large amounts of data in their daily and probably in their later vocational life. Nor can it sufficiently support understanding of current issues like the threats of large data collections.

## 3. BACKGROUND & RELATED WORK

This focus of teaching was last discussed in the 1990s: e.g. Witten [8] emphasizes the relevance of (R)DBMS for CS education. Later, mainly learning environments (especially for teaching SQL, e.g. [4]) were presented, while only few work on approaches for teaching databases and SQL was published: e.g. Antonitsch [1] questions current approaches for database education by discussing databases in context of information retrieval. At the moment, a discussion on these topics seems to emerge: at the SIGCSE'14 multiple papers in this field were presented, mainly suggesting data management as a topic for higher education. However, Buffum et. al. [2] set their focus on middle schools, especially on integrating Big Data aspects into other subjects in order to teach CS principles by using these as a tool.

Another field that is also strongly related to data management and (CS) education is learning analytics / educational data mining. This topic is already being discussed in detail in various other publications and research projects. Hence, I will not cover such aspects in my research.

---

[1] Nowadays, NoSQL is commonly interpreted as "not only SQL" [3] in contrast to its original meaning "no SQL".

## 4. STATEMENT OF THESIS/PROBLEM

The shortage of publications shows that data management is only considered as a marginal topic so far. Today, data become visible for everyone, as their value is clearly increasing and even popular media are talking about data analysis. In this context, everyone needs knowledge, skills and competencies for handling data. Therefore, the key question guiding my research is: *"Which are the influences of current developments in data management on secondary computing education and how can CS education handle the newly arising requirements in this field?"*. This especially includes a broader view on the topic "data" in future CS education, instead of focusing mainly on databases.

## 5. RESEARCH GOALS & METHODS

In order to answer the key question stated before, I will focus on the following research questions:

**What knowledge and skills does everyone need to have concerning data management?** A first step to answering this question was having a view on current topics in society and daily life that are often strongly related to data and data management. On this basis, some ideas on key competencies for handling data in a proper way were derived inductively [6]. In the future, it is planned to expand and systematize this catalog, e.g. by applying a competence model. Additionally, I plan to design some checklists that can be used as learning material (for example on topics like *"What can I do to make my data secure?"*) in order to raise learners' and teachers' awareness on this topic.

**Which are the fundamental and long-lasting aspects of data management that are important for computing education?** Data management is a topic that is continuously changing and developing. In contrast, the aspects brought to school must be stable during these changes in order to prevent teaching of outdated knowledge and skills. A starting point for analyzing such aspects is focusing on databases: today, various concepts supposed to be fundamental so far are changing; in this context, stable concepts can be found by comparing the concepts of newly arising database models with the proven ones.

**Which attitudes do learners currently have on the chances and threats of data management?** Today, learners are mostly confronted with data management long before secondary and even before primary education. Hence, an important basis for teaching are their prejudices and preknowledge on this topic, which may range from "excitement" to "helplessness". Dealing with these attitudes is fundamental for finding the main aspects of data management for secondary education. Therefore, analyzing these attitudes and knowledge by a questionnaire study is an important task.

**Which are the new requirements computing education has to deal with in the future?** For finding these requirements, a first step was taken: first ideas on challenges for CS education were collected based on the literature review and will be presented at ISSEP'14 [5]. In the future, these challenges need to be detailed and more well-founded, e.g. by comparing the current CS education with the findings in the other questions described before.

## 6. DISSERTATION STATUS

As my research is at a preliminary stage, writing the thesis was not started yet. However, some first ideas were gained while narrowing the field of research and were / will be presented in form of conference papers. These include a catalog of key competencies everyone needs for handling data that was presented at KEYCIT'14 [6], as well as first ideas for the challenges that lie ahead for CS education [5]. These will be published at ISSEP'14 together with a poster that discusses the influences of data management on secondary education in general and outlines the gaps of current education on these topics [7].

At the doctoral consortium I am looking forward to others' estimations on my research topic and would be interested in additional ideas or aspects I have not considered so far. Especially, as no empirical research has been done yet, the doctoral consortium may help refining the research questions stated above. By having a look on others' ongoing work, I also expect having new ideas for how to deal with my own research. At last, meeting people who possibly work at related topics and establishing contacts is an important reason for attending the conference for me.

## 7. EXPECTED CONTRIBUTIONS

The ongoing work provides a clear contribution to computing education: a main topic of CS, "data", will be analyzed for teaching purposes in the context of current developments but with a strong emphasis on the long-lasting ideas and concepts of data management. This will not only prepare including these ideas into curricula, but can also enable students to understand current developments and handle data in a more responsible way in their daily life.

## 8. REFERENCES

[1] P. Antonitsch. Databases as a tool of general education. In R. Mittermeir, editor, *Informatics Education - The Bridge between Using and Understanding Computers*, volume 4226 of *Lecture Notes in Computer Science*, pages 59–70. Springer Berlin Heidelberg, 2006.

[2] P. Buffum et al. CS Principles Goes to Middle School: Learning How to Teach "Big Data". In *Proceedings of the 45th ACM Technical Symposium on Computer Science Education*, SIGCSE '14, pages 151–156, New York, NY, USA, 2014. ACM.

[3] S. Edlich et al. *NoSQL [in German]*. Hanser, Carl Gmbh + Co., 2011.

[4] A. Grillenberger and T. Brinda. eledSQL: A New Web-based Learning Environment for Teaching Databases and SQL at Secondary School Level. In *Proceedings of the 7th Workshop in Primary and Secondary Computing Education*, WiPSCE '12, pages 101–104, New York, NY, USA, 2012. ACM.

[5] A. Grillenberger and R. Romeike. Big Data - Challenges for Computer Science Education [in print]. In *Proceedings of ISSEP 2014*.

[6] A. Grillenberger and R. Romeike. Teaching Data Management: Key Competencies and Opportunities [in print]. In *Proceedings of KEYCIT 2014*.

[7] A. Grillenberger and R. Romeike. Data Management: More Than a Matter of CS. In *Local Proceedings of ISSEP 2014*, 2014.

[8] H. Witten. Datenbanken - (k)ein Thema im Informatikunterricht? [Databases - (No) Topic in Computer Science Education?]. *LOG IN*, 2, 1994.

# Allegories for Learning Abstract Programming Concepts

Jeisson Hidalgo-Céspedes
Universidad de Costa Rica
San José 2060, Costa Rica
jeisson.hidalgo@ucr.ac.cr

## ABSTRACT

Constructivism theory states that learning is unavoidably done through association of new concepts with existing ones. Although programming concepts are abstract metaphors of some colloquial concepts, they seem to be not enough to overcome learning difficulties. We hypothesize that interrelated systems of metaphors (allegories) of abstract programming concepts can ease the association process and improve student learning. Our research introduces *allegoric development environments* and proposes to experimentally evaluate their effects on learning of programming concepts reported as difficult by students.

## Categories and Subject Descriptors

K.3.2 [**Computers and Education**]: Computer and Information Science Education – *computer science education.*

## General Terms

Design; Human Factors; Languages; Theory

## Keywords

Learning; programming language; metaphor; allegory

## 1. RESEARCH SITUATION

I am half way through of the three-year long doctorate program in Computer Science at the University of Costa Rica. Specifically, I am preparing my research proposal which should be defended by the end of the year. Background, related work, and problem definition have been completed. We are working on methodology aspects.

## 2. CONTEXT AND MOTIVATION

Students must demonstrate proficiency in several programming paradigms, and deep knowledge in at least one programming language in order to obtain a Computer Science degree. Nevertheless many students find this difficult and an unpleasant activity [4]. Several universities worldwide have reported a 33% failure rate in the first two programming courses [5]. There is also evidence of students who approve their courses without basic knowledge of programming [5]. This is an important problem for computer education researchers.

*ICER '14,* Aug 11-13 2014, Glasgow, United Kingdom
ACM 978-1-4503-2755-8/14/08.
http://dx.doi.org/10.1145/2632320.2632326

## 3. BACKGROUND & RELATED WORK

Constructivism theory states learning is done by *association* of new *concepts* with existing ones [1]. When learning computer programming, students must mentally construct abstract concepts like pointers and threads, by associating them with other concepts acquired in their life experience. Because abstract concepts cannot be experienced by the senses, students must resort to imagination in order to make these associations. When left to the imagination alone, these associations can be weak or incorrect.

Computer Science concepts are named as metaphors. Shopping carts, mice, servers, ports, files, folders, trees, stacks, memory leaks, garbage collectors, and throwing-catching exceptions are some examples [2]. A *metaphor* in Computer Education is a representation of an abstract concept (target) with another more familiar concept (source). In that way, students can naturally associate them, easing the learning process. Good metaphors allow students to intuitively infer fundamental properties of abstract concepts from familiar concepts. For example, throwing and catching a physical ball helps explain how the processing control is passed from one place in the code to another when an exception is raised [2].

Professors usually teach programming concepts using verbal metaphors, while writing source code examples and doing abstract drawings for representing the program state (i.e., graphical metaphors). Students receive a mixture of metaphors that seems to be insufficient to overcome the learning difficulties reported by several researchers.

*Allegories* are interrelated systems of metaphors. They are quite appropiate to represent abstract programming mechanisms. Little work on allegories has been done. For example, Waguespack used consistent drawings for representing data types [6], and Forišek & Steinová used heterogeneous metaphors to explain algorithms [3]. No empirical evaluation of allegory's effects in programming learning are provided by them.

Teachers can naturally use metaphors in lessons when introducing abstract programming language concepts. But this is a behaviorist approach. Constructivist suggests that students must work directly with metaphors, so they can infer the fundamental properties of abstract programming concepts by themselves. We propose to construct and allow to students use *allegoric development environments* where objects represent simultaneously both worlds: a familiar real life group of concepts and an interrelated group of abstract programming concepts. Allegoric development environments can have ludic rules. So, when students follow natural gameplay rules for the objects, they automatically infer and learn abstract programming rules. Some video game related systems such as Robocode (2001), Greenfoot (2003), CodeCombat (2013) and CodeSpells (2013), have been developed for learning computer programming. However their game concepts (e.g., tanks and crates) are not direct metaphors of abstract programming concepts.

## 4. PROBLEM, GOALS & METHODS

The aim of our research is to answer the question of whether playing with allegoric development environments has a meaningful effect in learning abstract programming language concepts or not. If it does, Computer Scientists would have an innovative tool for improving the programming learning process. The following steps aim to answer this question.

1. Determine abstract programming language concepts that students consider difficult to be learnt. Method: survey. Main contribution: knowledge about difficult experiences of programming learners.

2. Design an allegoric development environment that represents difficult concepts found in the previous step, and implement a prototype. Method: software development process. Main contribution: a tool for programming learning and for testing the hypothesis.

3. Evaluate whether students playing with the prototype of the allegoric development environment have better performance in learning tasks than students who learn with traditional material. Method: quasi-experiment. Main contribution: scientific knowledge about allegoric development environments and their effect on abstract programming learning.

## 5. DISSERTATION STATUS

For the first step, in November 2013 we surveyed 144 students of six programming-related courses of our Computer Science bachelor program. Results revealed C++ is the most used programming language (51%), followed by Java (33%). Students considered "parallel/concurrent programming" as the most difficult topic when learning C++, followed by "memory handling."

For step 2 we designed an allegoric development environment that represents concurrency and memory handling with familiar concepts from puppetry (Figure 1) called *Puppeteer++*. Puppets are characters (objects) that act in the scenery (heap segment) controlled by puppeteers (execution threads). Puppeteers are not supposed to act. Therefore, they never appear in scenery. They work over a platform (stack segment) at the top of the theatre, hidden from the audience. A puppeteer controls its puppet in the scenery through strings (pointers). Puppeteers animate their marionettes following a script (code segment) step by step. A puppeteer could control several puppets, but not at the same time. Switching from one puppet to another introduces a visible delay. If several puppets must act simultaneously in the same scene, several puppeteers must work together (concurrence). A large puppet, for example a Chinese dragon, requires several coordinated puppeteers (shared memory).

In order to conceptually validate the proposed allegoric development environment, a focus group was conducted with all our seven programming professors of our Computer Science department (except the author). Three of the seven professors expressed that the game idea would positively impact the learning and motivation of students; one professor said there would be both positive and negative effects; and three professors were unsure. Professors expressed that they would require empirical results. Five participants emphatically suggested using a

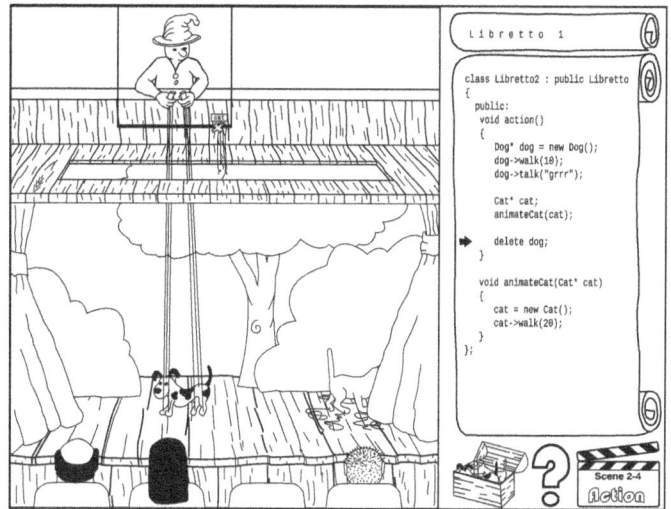

**Figure 1. Paper prototype of a puppet theatre game**

simplified visual model of the machine, for the empirical evaluation.

We are currently implementing the Puppeteer++ prototype and designing the quasi-experiment. A dissertation proposal will be defended by the end of 2014. The quasi-experiment would be conducted in first half of 2015 with Programming II students. Data analysis and final defense is expected by the end of 2015. We hope to get assistance in the Doctoral Consortium from international experts in order to criticize and strength the proposal before defending it.

## 6. EXPECTED CONTRIBUTIONS

My dissertation main contribution is the evaluation of allegory effects on learning abstract programming concepts. We hypothesize positive results, and we will propose a methodology for building allegorized development environments. Hopefully, these tools would help students learn difficult concepts of programming languages.

## 7. ACKNOWLEDGMENTS

Thanks to Marta Calderón, and Ministry of Science, Technology and Telecommunications (MICITT) of Costa Rica.

## 8. REFERENCES

[1] Bogoyavlensky, D.N. and Menchinskaya, N.A. 2011. La psicología del aprendizaje desde 1900 a 1960. *Psicología y pedagogía*. Ediciones Akal. 119–188.

[2] Colburn, T.R. and Shute, G.M. 2008. Metaphor in computer science. *Journal of Applied Logic*. 6, 4 (Dec. 2008), 526–533.

[3] Forišek, M. and Steinová, M. 2012. Metaphors and analogies for teaching algorithms. *SIGCSE '12* (Feb. 2012), 15.

[4] Li, F.W.B. and Watson, C. 2011. Game-based concept visualization for learning programming. *MTDL '11* (Dec. 2011), 37.

[5] Mccracken, M. et al. 2001. A multi-national, multi-institutional study of assessment of programming skills of first-year CS students A framework for first-year learning objectives. *ACM SIGCSE Bulletin, Volume 33 Issue 4*.

[6] Waguespack, L.J. 1989. Visual metaphors for teaching programming concepts. *ACM SIGCSE Bulletin* (Feb. 1989), 141–145.

# Computational Thinking Curriculum Development for Upper Elementary School Classes

Charlotte Hill
UC Santa Barbara
Santa Barbara, CA, 93106, USA
charlottehill@cs.ucsb.edu

## ABSTRACT

As computer science plays an increasingly large role in our lives, it is important to also move it into our classrooms. Computer science careers are among the fastest growing jobs, yet large groups of the population are severely underrepresented in computer science. Elementary school is a key time to introduce computer science or computational thinking because students are capable of programming and they will soon be deciding whether they see a future in the sciences. Including computational thinking as a part of the elementary school general education would give all children an introduction to the subject. In addition, elementary schools are looking for computational thinking material. We need appropriate, research-based tools and curricula for them to use.

Unlike the natural sciences, computer science's domain is pliable. Through language and programming environments, developers can create new ways to represent computational thinking concepts. My research seeks 1) to understand how 4th through 6th grade students learn computational thinking, 2) to develop computational thinking learning progressions and curricula, and 3) to create a language and programming environment suitable for elementary school classes and teachers who do not have a computer science background.

## Categories and Subject Descriptors

K.3.2 [**Computers and Education**]: Computer and Information Science Education; K.4.m [Computers and Society]: Miscellaneous—Diversity and Outreach

## General Terms

Design; Human Factors

## Keywords

diversity; K-12 education; outreach

## 1. RESEARCH SITUATION

I am a second year PhD student at UC Santa Barbara in the computer science department. I am currently working on my course requirements and research. I plan to finish my course requirements and Major Area Exam next year, submit my proposal by 2017, and graduate the following year.

## 2. CONTEXT AND MOTIVATION

Eleven states have adopted the Next Generation Science Standards, which list computational thinking as one of the eight key practices of science and engineering [2,3]. However, more research must be done in order to successfully introduce computational thinking in schools. Teaching computational thinking as a part of the school day brings challenges not present when teaching it in enrichment programs. Classes are less likely to have multiple volunteers for support, and activities must tie to standards. Additionally, elementary school teachers are expected to teach all subjects, but are unlikely to have had any training in teaching computational thinking because it is a new addition to the science standards. Elementary school students are capable of programming [4,5], but new research and tools are needed to make computational thinking and computer science successful in the classroom.

Students often decide if they want to pursue a career in the sciences by eighth grade [1]. Unfortunately, students rarely have the opportunity to learn about computer science before high school. Computer science has not been a part of traditional K-8 curricula so early exposure to computer science is limited to outreach opportunities, summer camps, and projects with family members with computer science knowledge. These options are less likely to be feasible for students from underrepresented populations. Adding computational thinking to the curriculum for earlier grade levels would potentially get more students from these populations interested in computer science.

## 3. BACKGROUND & RELATED WORK

CSTA and CS Unplugged provide computer science activities and resources for teachers and outreach providers [6,7]. Much of our learning progressions are based on the standards developed from CSTA, and many of our curriculum's off-computer activities are based on CS Unplugged activities.

Mike Clancy surveyed prior work on sources of misconceptions and the misconceptions that lead to student errors [8]. In particular, commonly used words (e.g., as if, else, and while) have slightly different meanings when used in programming and lead to confusion. We use snapshots of student work, focus groups, and observations from the classrooms to identify students' misconceptions when learning computational thinking.

Piech et al researched the paths students take when completing a programming project [9]. They used machine learning on sets of snapshots and found that the path a student takes to complete the

*ICER'14*, August 11–13, 2014, Glasgow, Scotland, UK.
ACM 978-1-4503-2755-8/14/08.
http://dx.doi.org/10.1145/2632320.2632327

project had a much stronger correlation to future success than the final state of the project. However, they did not look at the content of the snapshots to see what those different paths represented. Our programming environment saves snapshots of student work, which we use to find partial understandings and the routes students take to complete assignments.

## 4. STATEMENT OF THESIS/PROBLEM

My thesis will address the question: How do 4th through 6th graders learn computational thinking? Current computer science curriculums (e.g. Scratch, Alice, etc.) may include an assessment piece, but they do not detail how students learn to program. We will find the lower anchor points, or baseline knowledge students have before they begin formal computational thinking instruction. We will develop learning progressions for 4th through 6th grade computational thinking classes. These progressions will be used to create a curriculum for computational thinking and to design a programming environment geared to the specific requirements of the elementary school setting.

## 5. RESEARCH GOALS & METHODS

My thesis research is made up of four components:

- What are the lower anchor points, or knowledge that students have of computational thinking before formal instruction?

- What are the learning progressions $4^{th}$ through $6^{th}$ graders follow when learning computational thinking?

- How can these learning progressions be successfully implemented in an elementary school classroom?

- What types of tools are needed in an elementary school computational thinking class?

We created a theoretical set of learning progressions based on existing curricula by CSTA and used focus groups to test the lower anchor points [6,10]. Using a drawing activity based on the Marching Orders activity by CS Unplugged, we found that fourth graders recognized the need for but struggled to produce specific instructions [10]. We also tested prior knowledge for our algorithms learning progression strand. We found that, with little to no instruction, students were able to create an algorithm for sorting six canisters and identified the limitations of their algorithms when scaled to a larger number of items [11]. The students also struggled with the distinction between speeding up the algorithm and speeding up its implementation, so we adjusted our curriculum to go over this distinction [11].

We used our learning progressions to create a scaffolded $4^{th}$ grade curriculum. We then spent the first year piloting a curriculum and observing how students progressed through it, categorizing student challenges by programming environment, programming language, curriculum, and concepts. We introduced LaPlaya, a Scratch variant for scaffolding instruction. We are currently modifying the language, programming environment, and curriculum based on what we learned.

Next year, we will study closely how students learn the basic concepts, as well as pilot the second module. We will continue to blend qualitative analysis to identify students' conceptual challenges and the reasons for them (classroom observations in about 6 classrooms) with quantitative analysis to find out how prevalent those challenges are across different student populations

and learning environments (project snapshots in about 30 classrooms).

## 6. DISSERTATION STATUS

As described above, we have identified and revised some of our learning progressions based on focus groups. In addition, we identified several challenges that students faced in the traditional Scratch language and interface, which was designed for middle school students, not $4^{th}$-$6^{th}$ graders. We are currently in the midst of making changes to the language, environment, and curriculum. I will spend the next two years exploring the above questions related to how students learn computational thinking concepts in upper elementary school.

## 7. EXPECTED CONTRIBUTIONS

Understanding how students learn computational thinking will allow computational thinking curricula to be more successful overall. Developing new tools specifically for elementary school classrooms will give teachers without a computer science background the resources and confidence to bring computer science or computational thinking into their classrooms. Elementary school computational thinking lessons will create a public that is more knowledgeable about computers, and a computer science field made stronger by increased diversity.

## 8. REFERENCES

[1] R. Tai, C. Liu, A. Maltese, and X. Fan, "Planning early for careers in science," *Science*, vol. 312, no. 5777, pp. 1143–1144.

[2] L. Heitin, "It's Official: Illinois Adopts Common Science Standards", *Education Week*, 2013. http://blogs.edweek.org/edweek/curriculum/2014/03/illinois_science_standards_ado.html

[3] I. Achieve, The Next Generation Science Standards. The National Academies Press, 2013. Anderson, R.E. Social impacts of computing: Codes of professional ethics. Social Science Computing Review 10, 2 (1992), 453-469.

[4] C. Lewis, "Is pair programming more effective than other forms of collaboration for young students?", *Computer Science Education. 21(2)*. 105-134.

[5] J. Vahrenhold and A. Pasternak, "Design and evaluation of a braided teaching course in sixth grade computer science education", *SIGCSE*, 2012.

[6] C. S. T. Force, *CSTA K-12 Computer Science Standards*. 2011.

[7] T. Bell, I. H. Witten, and M. Fellows, *Computer Science Unplugged*. 2006. www.unplugged.canterbury.ac.nz/en/.

[8] M. Clancy, *Misconceptions and attitudes that interfere with learning to program*. Taylor and Francis, 2004.

[9] Piech et al. Modeling how students learn to program. In *SIGCSE*, pages 153–160, 2012.

[10] H. Dwyer, B. Boe, C. Hill, D. Franklin, and D. Harlow. "Computational Thinking for Physics: Programming Models of Physics Phenomenon in Elementary School", *PERC*, 2013.

[11] H. Dwyer, C. Hill, S. Carpenter, D. Harlow, and D. Franklin. "Identifying Elementary Students' Pre-Instructional Ability to Develop Algorithms and Step-by-Step Instructions", *SIGCSE*, 2014.

# The Effect of Robotics Activities on Students' Learning and Attitudes

Fatima Kaloti-Hallak
Weizmann Institute of Science
P. O. Box 26
Rehovot 76100, ISRAEL
fatima.hallak@weizmann.ac.il

## ABSTRACT

My research investigates students' learning of and attitudes toward STEM (Science, Technology, Engineering, and Mathematics) in general and Computer Science (CS) in particular during their participation in robotics activities. The research population consists of middle-school students who participated in robotics competitions. The methodology used is both qualitative and quantitative, using questionnaires, observations and interviews. A representational model is used to facilitate the interviews by externalizing the students' understanding of STEM concepts. The revised Bloom Taxonomy was used in the analysis. The research achieved preliminary results for CS and engineering which show that the students can achieve a satisfying level of learning CS and Engineering when they participate in the robotics activities.

## Categories and Subject Descriptors

K.3.1 [**Computers and Education**]: Computer Uses in Education – *collaborative learning, computer-assisted Instruction*

K.3.2 [**Computers and Education**]: Computer and Information Science Education – *Computer science education*

## General Terms

Human Factors

## Keywords

Robotics; STEM; Meaningful Learning; Attitudes

## 1. RESEARCH SITUATION

I am a PhD student in the science teaching department at the Weizmann Institute of Science. My research proposal has been approved two years ago (2012). The department requires an interim report to be submitted and examined at the mid phase of the PhD program. My interim report was approved last year (2013). The data collection and interviews were conducted throughout the year of 2012/2013. Currently, I am analyzing the data. I started with the learning of the disciplines of CS and engineering and achieved preliminary results. I anticipate during the upcoming year and a half to a) expand the analysis of learning to cover also concepts from the disciplines of science and mathematics; and b) analyze the data collected about attitudes.

## 2. CONTEXT AND MOTIVATION

Robotics can attract and inspire students who are often unmotivated by conventional classroom curricula [4]. Therefore, it has been suggested as a way to help students who experience substantial difficulties in learning scientific concepts and often exhibit significant misconceptions [6]. In order to improve learning of STEM disciplines, educators have suggested that robotics should be integrated into schools at levels from middle school through college [1]. Despite the high expectations from educational robotics activities in these contexts, and its hypothesized potential to improve motivation and learning, relatively few research projects have been carried out to study these issues.

The literature showed that students can be motivated and enthusiastic about participation in robotics activities and that they are capable of building sophisticated robots [5]. However, there are very few empirical studies that demonstrate improvement in students' learning and attitudes.

The research investigates middle-school students learning of and attitudes toward STEM in general and CS in particular (in the context of this study, CS represents the "T" of "STEM"), during their participation in robotics activities. The results of this research can aid in arriving to a rationalized decision as to integrating robotics activities into schools, and can also contribute to the development of a robotics curriculum that may be integrated into school curriculum in general and a CS curriculum in particular.

## 3. BACKGROUND & RELATED WORK

Many schools participate in Robotics activities through competitions such as FIRST LEGO League (FLL). Others participate with robotics as after school activities, while some have integrated robotics in their curriculum.

Robotics enables students to be active as they construct knowledge by manipulating technology. Lauwers, et al. [5] collaborated with CS educators to layout the features of robots that are well-suited to the learning goals of CS. Sullivan [7] found that the affordances of the robotics environment, with pedagogical approach emphasizing inquiry, prompts the utilization of science literacy-based thinking and science process skills to solve a robotics challenge, and leads to increased systems understanding as a result of participating in the robotics activities.

*ICER'14*, Aug 11–13, 2014, Glasgow, Scotland, UK.
ACM 978-1-4503-2755-8/14/08.
http://dx.doi.org/10.1145/2632320.2632328

Similarly and in term of attitudes, a survey evaluated students' skills and changes in attitudes toward robotics activities [9] found that the majority of students mentioned a positive impact of the robotics project on their motivation to learn and interest in specializing in science and engineering.

## 4. STATEMENT OF THESIS/PROBLEM

The general goal of my research is to investigate the effect of integrating robotics activities into middle-school education on students' learning of and attitudes toward STEM in general and CS in particular. When students are intentionally active, constructive, and engaged in authentic robotics activities in a cooperative setting, they are participating in a process that employs student-centered and guided discovery-based learning to achieve meaningful learning [2, 3] in line with constructionism [8]. The research questions (RQ) are:

1. What scientific content knowledge do students learn through their robotics activities?
   a. To what extent are the various STEM disciplines represented in the content knowledge that is learned?
   b. To what extent is the students' learning meaningful?
2. Attitudes:
   a. What are the students' attitudes towards learning STEM and how do the attitudes change after participating in robotics activities?
   b. What are students' attitudes towards learning about robots and how do the attitudes change after the robotics activities?

My conjecture is that robotics activities will positively affect students' learning of STEM, and specifically of CS, to achieve meaningful learning and boost their attitudes toward STEM, and CS in particular.

## 5. RESEARCH GOALS & METHODS

In order to assess students' learning I defined for each of the four disciplines a set of concepts, the learning of which can be affected by robotics activities, and I measure learning of these concepts.

The research population consists of 62 middle-school students from 8 schools who participated in robotics competitions. Most of the students participated in the competition for the first time; only ten students had already participated in previous competitions.

The research instruments were: Pre and post-questionnaire that were used to check the students attitudes before and after the activities (RQ 2); Observations used to record students verbal and physical acts during the robotics activities and follow closely their learning evolvement (both RQs 1 and 2); and semi-structured interviews with two or three students from each group, total of 17 interviewed students, to deeply assess the students' learning of STEM disciplines (RQ 1). The interviews used what I called *Representational Model (RM)* as a tool to externalize student understanding through the use of drawing, pictures or symbols.

The revised Bloom Taxonomy and the framework of meaningful learning [2, 3] are used as tools to analyze the students' learning of STEM disciplines during the activities. The learning of the set of concepts is analyzed according to operational categories, which are based on the revised Bloom Taxonomy. A triangulation among observation and interviews will be used to ensure accuracy of the reported results.

The data collected through the questionnaires will be grouped and analyzed according to categories defined regarding students' attitudes toward learning STEM and robots. These include categories that measure intrinsic motivation, self-determinacy, self-efficacy, and extrinsic motivation. Cornbach's alpha was calculated to measure the reliability of the questionnaires, $\alpha = 0.7$.

## 6. DISSERTATION STATUS

Preliminary results for section (a) of the first research question showed that the students can achieve a satisfying level of learning CS and Engineering when they participate in the robotics activities. Many students achieved the *understanding* or *applying* level of the Bloom Taxonomy for the CS concepts, while few achieved *analyzing* or *evaluating*. For the engineering concepts, most of the students achieved the *analyzing / evaluating* level in research / decision making and construction phases of the engineering design process, while few achieved that level in the testing and diagnosis phase.

The research continues with the analysis of the CS and engineering disciplines according to section (b) of the first RQ regarding meaningful learning. The phases of the research that remain to be done are: a) expanding the analysis of learning to cover concepts from science and mathematics (RQ 1); and b) analyzing the data about attitudes (RQ 2).

## 7. EXPECTED CONTRIBUTIONS

The research outcomes may be used to improve the integration of robotics activities as a tool for affecting students' learning of and attitudes toward STEM in general and CS in particular.

## 8. REFERENCES

[1] Anderson, M., McKenzie, A., Wellman, B., Brown, M., Vrbsky, S. (2011) Affecting Attitudes in First-year Computer Science using Syntax-free Robotics Programming, *ACM Inroads, 2*(3), 51-57.

[2] Ausubel, D. (1963) *The Psychology of Meaningful Verbal Learning.* New York, NY: Grune & Stratton.

[3] Howland, J., Jonassen, D., & Marra, R. (2011) *Meaningful Learning with Technology.* (4th Ed.) Pearson Education, Inc.

[4] Hamner, E., Lauwers, T., Bernstein, D., Stubbs, K., Crowley, K., & Nourbakhsh, I. (2008) Robot Diaries Interim Project Report: Development of a Technology Program for Middle School Girls. *Carnegie Mellon Uni.* CMU-RI-TR-08-25.

[5] Lauwers, T., Nourbakhsh, I., & Hamner, I. (2009) CSbots: Design and Deployment of a Robot Designed for the CS1 Classroom. *ACM SIGCSE Bulletin, 41*(1), 428-432.

[6] Reif, F. (1987) Interpretation of Scientific or Mathematical Concepts: Cognitive Issues and Instructional Implications. *Cognitive Science 11*, 395-416

[7] Sullivan, F. R. (2008) Robotics and Science Literacy: Thinking Skills, Science Process Skills and Systems Understanding. *The Journal of Research in Science Teaching. 45*(3), 373-394.

[8] Turkle, S. & Papert, S. (1991) Epistemological pluralism, in Harel, I. & Papert, S. (Eds), *Constructionism.* Norwood, NJ: Ablex, 116-126.

[9] Verner, I. M. & Ahlgren, D. J. (2004) Robot Contest as a Laboratory for Experiential Engineering Education. *ACM Journal on Educational resources in computing 4*(2), 1-15

# Cartographies of Practice

Daniel Knox
University of Kent
S.15 School of Computing
Canterbury, Kent, Ct27NF, England
dk242@kent.ac.uk

## ABSTRACT

In contrast with other vocational disciplines, such as law, architecture and medicine, computer science is a young, emerging discipline. The development of new technologies and methods, which are used to teach the skills and knowledge that computing students require, are informed by our research on how current students engage with the curriculum.

For this research, we decided to look at the curriculum through a different lens and in doing so, developed a set of complimentary methods and instruments to help us investigate student practices in disparate parts of the computer science curriculum.

## Categories and Subject Descriptors

K.3.2 [**Computers and Education**]: Computers and Information Science Education—*Computer Science Education*.

## General Terms

Human Factors

## Keywords

place, practice, mapping

## 1. RESEARCH SITUATION

I will soon enter my continuation year of a UK PhD, during which I shall be expected to produce and submit my thesis.

## 2. CONTEXT AND MOTIVATION

Computer Science is a discipline that has changed substantially in a short period of time. The availability of digital resources and tools, in combination with our students ready acceptance to use them in their lives, has radically changed the way that they can engage in academic study.

*ICER'14*, August 11-13, 2014, Glasgow, Scotland, UK.
ACM 978-1-4503-2755-8/14/08.
http://dx.doi.org/10.1145/2632320.2632329 .

These tools not only provide new kinds of spaces for our students to use, but also allows them to participate with people and access information at an unprecedented global scale.

For us, as computing education researchers, this change has an important impact on our teaching and research. When students are studying computer science they are developing a set of practices that are comprised of interconnected and inseparable elements, situated in space and time. However, much of our current education research studies learning at the micro-level, focusing on a single element and the 'learning effect' that it has on an individual student, for example the importance and the role of the compiler's warning messages. Whilst this is useful, if we wish to better understand the *practices* of computer science, we must recognise that it is a social process that can only be researched by taking a step back and looking at academic study as a whole, with reference to the spaces that students use, their navigation between them and their commitment to participate in them [9].

By looking at 'how, when and where' students study computer science, we are provided with a macro-perspective on student learning across the computer science curriculum and are able to look at factors beyond the cognitive, such as socio-cultural learning.

## 3. BACKGROUND & RELATED WORK

One of the first tasks for this research was to identify the spaces that students use for academic study. However, this is not an easy problem. Students do not necessarily interact in a single space at any one moment, the use of mobile devices allows the boundary between physical and virtual spaces to become blurred.

For example, a student can be sitting in a lecture theatre, but also simultaneously interacting with peers (who may also be in the same room) in a virtual space, such as Facebook.

A key question arises from this: Is the student maintaining a presence in two different kinds of space at the same time? Or, is the student acting in a single space, but is utilising different kinds of media to afford his/her's actions?

My resolution to this question is informed by literature on space and place. Hubbard [6] and Dourish [5] make a distinction between 'spaces' and 'places'. For them, a space is a volume that provides affordances for interactions to occur, whereas the term 'place' is used to describe spaces that are invested with meaning and action (a person's 'lived experience'). Therefore, in the case of the student in the lecture theatre, they were interacting within a single place, whilst using the affordances of two spaces.

The next task is to start identifying and mapping student navigation of place in relation to their practice. To do this, a number of research methods were found in related literature [10, 4, 1]. The researchers use a variety of techniques including, mapping exercises of virtual space use to elicit a discussion at interview and the keeping of journals, comprised of captured photographs and videos, in order to "probe the more subtle, affective and abstract aspects of experience which may be difficult to express verbally" [4]. Another researcher [1], who conducted a localised ethnomethodology by utilising webcam and audio capture in a classroom environment, provides an important contribution because it shows that students utilise an 'anarchistic bricolage' of practices in order to get work done. It also identified that these 'banned practices' would emerge whenever a carriage of laptops was bought into the room, which highlights an important issue with the current methods used in this area; practices can be afforded by completely unrelated events, which despite being in plain sight, are otherwise invisible to us.

## 4. STATEMENT OF THESIS PROBLEM

The related work informs and motivates the thesis question:

**How do students develop competence and meaning when they are studying computer science?**

Several tasks arise from this:

- To develop research methods to identify the places that computer science students use to support their academic study.

- To develop an artefact that visualises the navigation of these places and the academic activity within them.

- To produce a picture of student engagement in the computer science curriculum and their motivation to participate in the study of computing.

## 5. METHOD

Informed by a method first presented in "Research design: necessary bricolage" [3], I have developed a set of complimentary instruments called 'My Programming Week' (MPW):

1. A diary exercise - Where students keep a diary for one-week of their programming related activity by using a supplied web-application. With this tool, students are able to take pictures of the spaces that they use and record details about the interactions that occurred within them.

2. A one-to-one interview - The diary materials are used at interview to elicit a rich-narrative to provide context for the data collected.

3. A focus group interview - To discuss cohort perceptions of practice and identity.

## 6. THESIS STATUS

Using the MPW instruments, several publications have been produced from the data that has been collected:

The first paper, 'Why does place matter?' [8] attempts to raise awareness of the importance in studying place from a pedagogical standpoint.

The second paper, 'The porous classroom' [2], of which Sally Fincher is the principle author, provides examples of practical experience being incorporated into the classroom environment.

The third paper, 'Where students go for knowledge' [7], presents a sophisticated array of help-seeking behaviours used by students. These were discovered using the MPW interviews and an accompanying set of observations.

I have begun work on two chapters of the thesis, the literature review (existing mapping techniques) and the methodology (My Programming Week). A recently submitted paper was produced from this work.

## 7. EXPECTED CONTRIBUTION

I believe that my research contributes to the field by providing a macro-perspective of 'how, when and where' students engage in the practices of computer science and provides new methods to investigate this.

## 8. REFERENCES

[1] I. Bhatt. Digital literacy practices and their layered multiplicity. *Educational Media International*, 49(4):289–301, 2012.

[2] S. Fincher and D. Knox. The porous classroom: Professional practices in the computing curriculum. *Computer*, 46(9):44–51, Sept. 2013.

[3] S. Fincher, J. Tenenberg, and A. Robins. Research design: necessary bricolage. In *Proceedings of the seventh international workshop on Computing education research*, ICER '11, pages 27–32, New York, NY, USA, 2011. ACM.

[4] L. Gourlay. Multimodality, visual methodologies and higher education. *New Approaches to Qualitative Research*, page 80, 2010.

[5] S. Harrison and P. Dourish. Re-place-ing space: the roles of place and space in collaborative systems. In *Proceedings of the 1996 ACM conference on Computer supported cooperative work*, CSCW '96, pages 67–76, New York, NY, USA, 1996.

[6] P. Hubbard and R. Kitchin. *Key Thinkers on Space and Place*.

[7] D. Knox and S. Fincher. Where students go for knowledge and what they find there. In *Proceedings of the Ninth Annual International ACM Conference on International Computing Education Research*, ICER '13, pages 35–40, New York, NY, USA, 2013. ACM.

[8] D. Knox and S. Fincher. Why does place matter? In *Proceedings of the 18th ACM Conference on Innovation and Technology in Computer Science Education*, ITiCSE '13, pages 171–176, New York, NY, USA, 2013. ACM.

[9] K. Kuutti and L. J. Bannon. The turn to practice in hci: Towards a research agenda. In *Proceedings of the SIGCHI Conference on Human Factors in Computing Systems*, CHI '14, pages 3543–3552, New York, NY, USA, 2014. ACM.

[10] D. White and A. L. Cornu. Visitors and residents: A new typology for online engagement. *First Monday*, 16(9), 2011.

# Using Case-Based Reasoning to Improve the Quality of Feedback Generated by Automated Grading Systems

Angelo Kyrilov
University of California, Merced
5200 N Lake Rd
Merced, CA, 95340, USA
akyrilov@ucmerced.edu

## ABSTRACT

My research is focused on developing e-learning systems that provide high-quality feedback on student submitted programming exercises. To create such systems we use a new approach of applying case-based reasoning (CBR) techniques which proved to be successful in other areas such as technical support departments and financial institutions. The increased quality of feedback delivered by our system will help to keep students engaged, which in turn will reduce attrition rates. A prototype system has been tested in several undergraduate Computer Science courses with promising preliminary results. The effectiveness of the completed system will be thoroughly evaluated in CS classrooms.

## Categories and Subject Descriptors

K.3.2 [**Computers and Education**]: Computers and Information Science Education—*Computer Science Education*.

## General Terms

Algorithms, Design, Measurement, Experimentation

## Keywords

Case-based reasoning, e-learning, e-assessment

## 1. RESEARCH SITUATION

I am a third-year PhD student in the Electrical Engineering and Computer Science graduate program at the University of California, Merced. The program includes a two-year long curriculum of graduate CS courses, which I have completed. My research is focused on computer science education, specifically on developing e-learning systems with automated grading modules that provide high quality feedback for programming exercises. The program requires candidates to submit a research proposal to the thesis committee and present this research at a qualifying exam. I have completed the proposal and submitted it to my thesis committee. My qualifying exam presentation is scheduled for

*ICER'14*, August 11-13, 2014, Glasgow, United Kingdom.
ACM 978-1-4503-2755-8/14/08.
http://dx.doi.org/10.1145/2632320.2632330.

August 2014. Upon successful completion of the qualifying exam, I will advance to candidacy, and will be expected to graduate in Summer 2016.

My research focus is to use machine learning techniques in order to enable automated graders to offer meaningful feedback to students who submit incorrect solutions to programming exercises. We have identified case-based reasoning (CBR) as a promising strategy for this task due to its ability to learn from concrete past examples. We have created a prototype system and validated it using data collected in two upper division undergraduate CS courses. The main ideas and preliminary results of the project have been summarized in a manuscript that has been accepted for publication. Over the next two years I plan to further develop the algorithms at the base of the system, implement the complete e-learning framework, and thoroughly test it in undergraduate courses.

## 2. CONTEXT AND MOTIVATION

The United States, as well as other countries, are currently experiencing underproduction of CS graduates [4], which can be partly attributed to high attrition rates. [3] points out that high attrition is caused by the insufficient amount of practical training in undergraduate CS courses. [7] describes typical lab sessions as "teacher-assisted debugging sessions". Students experiencing problems will often wait passively for a TA to provide guidance, which is frustrating and inefficient because they may need to wait a long time to get help, while TAs may end up explaining the same concept numerous times. This leads to *disengagement* from the course.

Automated grading systems can be used to remedy the situation by allowing students to complete exercises at their own pace, with immediate feedback, which would keep them motivated. One shortcoming of automated graders for programming exercises is the binary feedback they provide [6]. The authors suggest that binary feedback may, in fact, have a detrimental effect on students because it discourages them. This is consistent with observations of high disengagement rates in our own labs, where binary feedback is given.

My research is focused on addressing the problem of binary feedback by exploring machine learning techniques that can be trained to recognize bugs in students' code and provide meaningful guidance to students on how to remedy their programming errors. Case-based reasoning was found to be particularly suitable for this task as it had been previously used to solve problems of a similar nature in other application areas. It is known that CBR systems perform well when similar problems are encountered numerous times and when similar problems have similar solutions. This fits in well with Computer Science laboratory sessions, where many students make the same mistake, and similar bugs can be addressed in similar ways. If the new e-learning platform we develop is successful, it will significantly improve the quality of students' experience, ensure their engagement in the course and reduce attrition rates in Computer Science courses.

## 3. BACKGROUND & RELATED WORK

CBR is a machine learning technique that uses knowledge from past experiences (or *cases*) to find solutions to current problems [5]. CBR has been successfully applied in many areas of business, including customer support centers and financial departments [1]. In [2] the authors found that CBR systems are used in health sciences for a wide variety of tasks, such as diagnosis, treatment planning, and training of medical personnel. There are few examples of CBR being applied in education. RubricAce, presented in [8], is a CBR system designed to assist instructors who use rubrics for grading students' work. RubricAce suggests feedback comments to instructors once they have assigned grades according to a rubric. Instructors then decide how to use the suggested feedback to provide summative evaluations to students. The aim of our research is to provide automated high quality immediate formative feedback to computer science students. To our knowledge there have been no previous attempts to use CBR for this task and our research is the first attempt to design a CBR e-learning systems.

## 4. PROPOSED RESEARCH

The main goal of my research is to develop an effective e-learning system that will enable students to receive prompt and meaningful feedback on their programming assignments that will help to keep students engaged and to improve their learning of programming and performance in computer science courses. The proposed project consists of three major phases: (I) development of algorithms underlining automated analysis of student assignment submissions, clustering of incorrect solutions and identification of the appropriate feedback to students, (II) implementation of the complete e-learning system, (III) deployment and testing of the system in the undergraduate CS courses and evaluation of its effectiveness.

To accomplish phase (I) we employ CBR techniques to create a system able to process student assignment submission in a desired way. An important part of this task is the development of an algorithm and a suitable similarity metric that ranks two programs as similar if and only if they suffer from the same error. We have tested with promising results a simple similarity metric based on the performance of a program on a set of test cases, however we plan to improve the accuracy of this algorithm by including static analysis of the source code. The resulting system will be implemented as part of an e-learning platform we developed and deployed in several CS courses. The current version of the e-learning system constitutes progress towards completing phase (II) of the project and enables administration of the courses and collection and analysis of student performance data. To complete this phase we will integrate the automated grading and feedback option into the system. In phase (III) a completed e-learning platform will then be deployed in several CS courses such as the Intro-duction of Object-Oriented Programming and the Introduction to Java Programming. In collaboration with education researchers and cognitive scientists we will design controlled experiments to test the effectiveness of the system and measure the benefits it provides to students.

## 5. DISSERTATION STATUS

I have developed a prototype system that is based on the new idea of using CBR for automated grading of programming exercises. I have also created a portal that enables administration of the class (i.e. student account creation, logins, and assignments submission and grading) as well as a system that analyzes student assignment submissions and clusters them by the types of errors using the similarity metric I described in the previous section. I have tested both of these components in two undergraduate CS courses and obtained promising results. This research was accepted as a conference publication at the International E-Learning Conference (Lisbon, July 2014). Based on these results I have also written and submitted a doctoral candidacy proposal which will constitute about a third of my Ph.D. thesis. My plan for the remaining portion of my doctoral research includes further refining the algorithms underlining the generation of the automated feedback, implementation of these techniques and their integration into the e-learning portal. In addition, an important aspect of the research will be thorough testing of the e-learning platform performance in several upper division undergraduate CS courses.

The main reason I am applying for the Doctoral Consortium is to get feedback on my work from established Computer Science Education researchers and an opportunity to network in the field. There is no one working on Computer Science Education at my university so I feel isolated at times. My advisor, who is an expert in Computational Cognitive Neuroscience and Machine Learning, provides great advice and support in many aspects. In addition, I am continuously reviewing the current literature in my field and actively seeking chances to present my work at conferences. However, an opportunity for in-depth, extensive interaction with people working directly in my field through the Consortium would be invaluable to accelerating progress in my research.

## 6. REFERENCES

[1] B. Allen Case-Based Reasoning: Business Applications. *Communications of the ACM*, 37(3):40–42, 1992.

[2] S. Begum *et al.* Case-based reasoning systems in the health sciences. *Systems, Man, and Cybernetics*, 41(4):421–434, 2011.

[3] T. Beaubouef *et al.* Why the high attrition rate for computer science students. *SIGCSE Bull.*, 37(2):103–106, 2005.

[4] T. Lacey *et al.* Occupational employment projections to 2018. *Monthly Labor Review*, 132(11), 2009.

[5] B. López. Case-Based Reasoning: A Concise Introduction. *Morgan & Claypool Publishers*, 2013.

[6] J. Ridgway *et al.* Literature review of e-assessment. *Technical report*, University of Durham, 2007.

[7] G. N. Walker. Experimentation in the computer science lab. *SIGCSE Bull.*, 36(4):69–72, 2004.

[8] N. Wiratunga *et al.* RubricAce: A Case-based Feedback Recommender for Coursework Assessment. *Proceedings of 16th UK Workshop on Case-Based Reasoning*, 2011.

# Promoting Constructive Mindsets for Overcoming Failure in Computer Science Education

Emily Lovell
University of California, Santa Cruz
1156 High Street, #SOEGRAD
Santa Cruz, CA 95064 USA
emme@soe.ucsc.edu

## ABSTRACT

Encountering failure while cultivating computational literacy is inevitable, as debugging is a normal and necessary part of any programmer's workflow. Unfortunately, internalization of this failure is one discouraging factor in many students' choice not to pursue computer science. In this proposal, I outline my dissertation research on constructive mindsets for overcoming failure in introductory programming contexts. This work is motivated by an overarching interest in broadening participation in computing – and, in particular, attracting and retaining more female computer science students. My doctoral research examines the differences in how technical students and non-technical students approach learning to code, with the goal of generating best practices for other educators.

## Categories and Subject Descriptors

K.3.2 [**Computers and Education**]: Computer and Information Science Education – *computer science education.*

**Keywords:** Tinkering, growth mindset, self-theories, failure, computer science education, CS0, CS1.

## 1. RESEARCH SITUATION

I am currently a first year doctoral student in Computer Science at UC Santa Cruz, although I have three prior years of graduate research experience at the MIT Media Lab, where I completed a master's degree and began my doctoral research. (I left this program for UCSC only because my previous advisor exited academia, thereby dissolving my research group.)

I have spent my first year at UCSC completing the majority of the coursework required by my new department and familiarizing myself with the literature of the space in which I plan to pursue dissertation work. I have especially gone out of my way to pursue methodologically focused coursework in UCSC's education department, which has provided grounding in the philosophy of educational research as well as qualitative and quantitative methods.

I had already advanced to candidacy at MIT and am planning to do so again in my new department at UCSC in the fall of 2014. I expect to complete data collection and any associated classroom/teaching interventions by the following fall. I anticipate spending the 2015-2016 school year analyzing my data and writing my dissertation, with an expected graduation date of spring 2016. This timeline takes into consideration both my prior research experience at MIT as well as the research freedom afforded by my NSF Graduate Research Fellowship.

*ICER '14*, Aug 11-13, 2014, Glasgow, United Kingdom.
ACM 978-1-4503-2755-8/14/08.
http://dx.doi.org/10.1145/2632320.2632331

By the time of the Doctoral Consortium this summer, I will be immersed in designing the study that I will run during the 2014-2015 school year. It will be the perfect timing and opportunity for me to receive feedback on my plans before undertaking this work.

## 2. CONTEXT AND MOTIVATION

There are numerous complex reasons that underrepreted minority groups, such as women, either do not enter the field of computer science to begin with – or exit the field prematurely. Margolis and Fisher illuminated many of these issues in their seminal study, Unlocking the Clubhouse [3], which helped to inspire years of subsequent research in this space. However, much work remains to be done as we strive for greater gender parity within the field.

Issues around attracting and retaining a broader range of students to computer science are both theoretical and practical in nature; theoretical in terms of considering why interested, capable students do not persist in the field – and practical in terms of classroom implementation and potential for long-term impact. Some of the many considerations include curriculum, choice of teaching programming language, and facilitation of the learning environment. In tackling such a wide-reaching problem, I would like to focus my research on examining novice programmer mindsets. I believe that this is an area of research which has been less explored than curricular reform and teaching languages, yet harnesses a great deal of potential in terms of impact on students. In particular, I am interested in investigating the infusion of tinkering and growth mindsets into computer science education – thereby equipping and empowering students to face inevitable feelings of failure as they learn to write and debug programs.

## 3. BACKGROUND & RELATED WORK

Background work exists across a web of related contexts, including: tinkering as a way of learning, tools/languages for learning to program, and self-theories.

The Tinkering Studio is a progressive working group and physical space within San Francisco's Exploratorium science museum. The studio's directors have prominently advocated for a discourse around tinkering as a way of learning – one which they practice within their own space at the museum [5]. Tinkering Studio staff thoughtfully facilitate spaces in which learners are encouraged to embrace failure as a key component of intellectual growth; failure is celebrated, shared, and reflected upon, rather than avoided. This approach has begun to take root in after-school science learning contexts [8], and I now seek to evaluate its potential for positively impacting the culture of computer science education.

Within the field of computer science, a significant amount of research has gone into developing environments and programming languages which strive to improve the accessibility of programming for novices. Of particular note is the Scratch programming language, which not only promotes learning about computational concepts (variables, loops, etc.), but does so in a way which also supports tinkering [6]. Because Scratch is a blocks language, students can snap together code snippets to write programs without the risk of generating syntactical errors. The worst that may happen is for a program to output different behavior than what the programmer was expecting.

Finally, of great complement from the field of social psychology is the research of Carol Dweck on self-theories [2]. Over many years, Dweck has studied what she refers to as a growth mindset, or the belief that one's own intelligence is malleable. Equipped with such a mindset, students can appreciate that hard work leads to intellectual growth – and reject the notion of being born with a fixed level of intelligence. Early studies have shown promise in promoting growth mindsets within computer science education [1, 4, 7], and I hope to build upon the foundation laid by this work.

## 4. PROBLEM, GOALS & METHODS

Inspired in part by my own teaching experience, I hypothesize that there is something distinctly different about how non-computer scientists approach learning to program. I am consequently interested in learning about the various constructive mindsets that non-computer scientists bring to novice programming pursuits and, in particular, how we can learn from this diversity of approaches. More specifically, I would like to study how to promote tinkering and growth mindsets in novice computer scientists – as these suggest how one might overcome failure as an obstacle to learning.

Although I plan to survey curricular and programming language choices in the course of my research, my focus will be on studying novice programmers who persist in the face of failure. I believe that helping early computer science students to adopt constructive mindsets may be one effective approach to changing the perception of failure within the computer science classroom. As it stands, computer science culture does not always encourage asking for help or admitting failure. If we can facilitate more effective strategies for students to overcome repeated feelings of failure, this may ultimately contribute to the retention of women and other minorities. My ultimate goal is to intervene in such a way that creates long-term shifts in student mindset. It will be difficult to measure long-term effects in the course of my degree, but I plan to interview students to obtain data on the effectiveness of my approach and to track retention across computer sciences courses on a short-term scale.

## 5. DISSERTATION STATUS

While part of the High-Low Tech research group at MIT, I pursued research on electronic textiles (e-textiles) as an alternative avenue for learning about computer science and electronics. I was especially interested in how such a creative, hands-on approach might invite a more diverse set of end-users and students to the field. During this time, I designed hands-on activities/curricula and taught workshops to a wide variety of participants including hobbyists, designers, technologists, educators, and students. Throughout these experiences facilitating technical workshops, I have observed that those with non-technical backgrounds are especially apt to tinker, failing often and without dire consequence.

Since returning to UCSC (where I also completed my bachelor's degree in Computer Science), I have thus far focused on coursework and reading to prepare for my dissertation research. I feel that this summer would be the ideal time for me to receive constructive feedback on my research, prior to starting work on my dissertation document. I feel uniquely poised to tackle the questions I've put forth, due to my prior experience teaching introductory programming and electronics across a wide range of disciplines.

I will be teaching UCSC's undergraduate Introduction to Computer Science course this summer, which will offer a preliminary opportunity to explore influence upon students' programming mindsets. I am currently auditing the present offering of the course in order to observe student-instructor interactions and what mindsets students bring to class. Before teaching the course, I also plan to interview department faculty on their experiences iteratively revising the curriculum. This pilot teaching experience will directly inform the longer study which I am planning for the academic year.

In the 2014-2015 academic year, I will partner with introductory computer science teaching faculty to undertake a mixed-methods approach to both learning about and influencing student mindset. I will begin with a qualitative data collection phase, in which I will interview students in various disciplines who are learning to program (e.g. design, psychology, and of course, computer science). I will compare my findings across fields and, in response, design an intervention which attempts to cultivate constructive mindsets in computer science classrooms. I intend to collect both qualitative and quantitative data to measure impact, for example: student retention throughout the course of a single class, student enrollment rates in follow-up classes, and pass/fail rates for the class in question. I also plan to interview some of the same computer science students at various points in their coursework/academic trajectory.

I hope that participation in the Doctoral Consortium will allow me to receive feedback on both the narrative that I am developing around my work as well as the specific study design and implementation going forward.

## 6. EXPECTED CONTRIBUTIONS

The outcome of my work will consist of insights into how non-computer scientist novices exhibit mastery of constructive programming mindsets. More formally, I expect to be able to present my findings in the form of best practices for teaching early computer science courses. I hope that these recommendations will help to support other educators interested in infusing growth and/or tinkering mindsets into their own practices.

## 7. ACKNOWLEDGMENTS

This material is based upon work supported by the National Science Foundation Graduate Research Fellowship Program under Grant No. DGE-1339067.

## 8. REFERENCES

[1] Cutts, Q., Cutts, E., Draper, S., O'Donnell, P., and Saffrey, P. 2010. Manipulating Mindset to Positively Influence Introductory Programming Performance. *Proceedings of SIGCSE*, 431-435.

[2] Dweck, C. 2000. *Self-Theories: Their Role in Motivation, Personality, and Development.* Psychology Press.

[3] Margolis, J. and Fisher, A. 2001. *Unlocking the Clubhouse.* MIT Press.

[4] Murphy, L. and Thomas, L. 2008. Dangers of a Fixed Mindset: Implications of Self-theories Research for Computer Science Education. *Proceedings of ITiCSE*, 271-275.

[5] Petrich, M., Wilkinson, K., and Bevan, B. 2013. It looks like fun, but are they learning? In *Design, Make, Play: Growing the Next Generation of STEM Innovators.* M. Honey and D. Kanter, Eds. Routledge, 50-70.

[6] Resnick, M, et al. 2009. Scratch: Programming for All. *Communications of the ACM 52* (11), 60-67.

[7] Simon, B., Hanks, B., Murphy, L., Fitzgerald, S., McCauley, R., Thomas, and L., Zander, C. 2008. Saying Isn't Necessarily Believing: Influencing Self-Theories in Computing. *Proceedings of ICER*, 173-184.

[8] Vossoughi, S., Escudé, M., Kong, F., and Hooper, P. 2013. Tinkering, Learning & Equity in the After-School Setting. In *Proceedings of FabLearn*.

# What Pedagogical Content Knowledge Competencies do Computer Science Pre-Service Teachers have?

Melanie Margaritis
University of Paderborn
Fürstenallee 11
Paderborn, NRW, 33102, Germany
melanie.margaritis@upb.de

## ABSTRACT

This document aims at identifying important competencies for pedagogical content knowledge of Computer Science pre-service teachers at the end of the theoretical part of their education by means of empirical research. The goal of this study is to detect whether pedagogical content knowledge courses for Computer Science pre-service teachers are sufficient or whether the curriculum should be adapted. For my research, I am using video recordings and interviews to measure these competencies. Moreover, I based my study on the pedagogical content knowledge competence model developed by the "Competencies for Teaching Computer Science" research group.

## Categories and Subject Descriptors

K.3.2 [**Computers and Education**]: Computer and Information Science Education – *computer science education, curriculum, self-assessment*

## General Terms

Measurement, Verification

## Keywords

Computer Science Education; Competence Measurement; Video Analysis; Pedagogical Content Knowledge.

## 1. RESEARCH SITUATION

I started my research position at the University of Paderborn in Germany in January 2013 at the department of Computer Science Education. My work at the University is divided into three parts. The first part is participation in an external funding project, which lasts until June 2015. The project is called "Competencies for teaching Computer Science" (KUI) and is about the development of a competency model for Computer Science (CS) teachers to clarify what competencies CS teachers should have for teaching that subject [1]. The second part comprises a teaching assignment for CS students at the University of Paderborn. And the third part is my research about pre-service teachers' competencies. It is planned to complete my thesis by the beginning of 2016.

My research involves the identification of competencies for pedagogical content knowledge (PCK) that CS pre-service teachers have at the end of their theoretical education. To measure these competencies, I am using video recordings of school lessons and interviews regarding fields of pedagogical operations and aspects of teaching and learning.

The KUI project forms the basis for my dissertation, so it is possible for me to take advantage of some of the materials and results.

## 2. CONTEXT AND MOTIVATION

Becoming a good teacher is a long process of learning and teaching relevant subject matter and relevant PCK. Teacher education in Germany is divided into two parts: a theoretical part at the university and a practical part in school. The theoretical part is scheduled for 160 hours per semester where pre-service teachers get subject matter knowledge and PCK for their subjects. In addition, the theoretical part is also scheduled with 14 hours of practice for a first practical insight into school teaching to apply their knowledge. [6]

The practical education is scheduled for 18 months, where for several hours a week CS pre-service teachers get the opportunity to teach classes independently. During these 18 months, pre-service teachers are accompanied by an advisor, who sometimes observes their teaching. Moreover, pre-service teachers also have to attend professional seminars for teaching their subjects. After this short period of time and a successful examination at the end, the pre-service teachers should be ready to take responsibility for teaching their own classes.

In this context, my study proposes to find out what PCK competencies CS pre-service teachers have at the end of their theoretical education. By means of the results, I would like to find out if the competencies are adequate to teach classes independently or whether the curricula should be adapted.

## 3. BACKGROUND & RELATED WORK

The focus on educational research, especially in the exploration of teachers' competencies, has grown in the last few years. There are several prominent surveys like "Technological Pedagogical Content Knowledge (TPCK)" [3], "Professional Competence of Teachers, Cognitively Activating Instruction, and Development of Student's Mathematical Literacy (COACTIV)" [2] or KUI [1] that have all researched the field of PCK based on Shulman's definition [5]. The definition of competencies can be understood in many different ways. This study follows Weinert's notion of competency [7].

The KUI project group researches for competencies for German CS teachers and develops a corresponding competence model. This competence model is divided into three parts: (1) Competencies for subject matter knowledge (SC), (2) Competencies for PCK and (3) Competencies for non-cognitive aspects.

In my study, I am using the PCK-Model of that project as a scale to measure pre-service teachers' competencies. This PCK-Model shows what PCK competencies German CS teacher should have. [1]

## 4. STATEMENT OF THESIS/PROBLEM

The research questions, which lead my dissertation, are: (1) What PCK competencies do CS pre-service teachers have at the end of the theoretical education? (2) How do CS pre-service teachers self-estimate their competencies? (3) How do these competencies differ from competencies of professional CS teachers?

The reason these questions are worth answering is that CS pre-service teachers have PCK courses at the University with varying opportunities to practice their knowledge in school. 18 months for the practical part of teacher education is a very short period to learn how to apply PCK for teaching students in a class. Often pre-service teachers try to teach under the trial-and-error-principle at the expense of their students. To see if the PCK that is taught at university is sufficient to let pre-service teachers teach classes independently, it is vitally important to measure what kind of PCK these pre-service teachers have and what competencies have to be improved by, for example, adapting the curriculum.

## 5. RESEARCH GOALS & METHODS

The goal of my research is figuring out what PCK competencies CS pre-service teachers have and how these competencies differ from competencies of professional teachers. To achieve my goal I will use video recordings and interviews to measure these competencies. For the measurement, I conduct interviews with a group of CS pre-service teachers and a group of professional CS teachers. The scenarios for the interviews were developed together with the KUI project group by means of a qualitative content analysis of school curricula. The scenarios contain situations regarding fields of pedagogical operations (planning, reacting and evaluating) and aspects of teaching and learning. [4] Moreover, I take a sample of each group and record them during a CS school lesson to see if they can transfer their knowledge during teaching.

As a next step, I am going to measure the CS pre-service teachers' self-estimation regarding their PCK. To achieve this goal, I measure the pre-service teachers' self-estimation at three different times during the seminar. The first time is directly after their school lesson. The pre-service teachers will get the opportunity to talk freely about their lesson guided by some questions from their advisor. The next time will be some days after the school lesson. At this stage I am going to conduct interviews with the pre-service teachers and ask them specific questions regarding their planning of, reaction to and evaluating of their lesson. The third time will be at the end of their seminar. At this stage, the CS pre-service teachers get the chance to review their video recordings and self-estimate themselves afterwards. All parts will be audio recorded and transcribed.

In addition, I am going to perform a qualitative content analysis by means of the video recordings and the transcribed interviews using the PCK-Model as a scale to see what competencies are covered and what are not. By means of the analysis, it is possible to see what kind of PCK these two groups have and how these competencies may differ from each other. Furthermore, the results will show to what degree the pre-service teachers' competencies cover the competencies of the PCK-Model and what competencies should be improved.

## 6. DISSERTATION STATUS

The current status of my dissertation is that I have already conducted all the video recordings and interviews mentioned in point 5 in this article. Moreover, all the interviews have already been transcribed.

The next step in my research is to take the collected material and conduct a qualitative content analysis. There will be three parts, which have to be analyzed for each group: (1) The video recordings, (2) The self-estimation and (3) The interviews regarding typical and critical school situations. I am planning to start with the first part of the analysis at the beginning of June. To ensure reliability for the analysis, 25 % of each part will be coded by a second person. All parts should be analyzed by September of this year, so that I can make an initial estimation of to what degree competencies of PCK are covered in the theoretical part of the education.

## 7. EXPECTED CONTRIBUTIONS

My research findings will support the improvement of CS teacher education in Germany by learning what PCK competencies pre-service teachers have by attending the PCK courses at university. The results of my research and my dissertation will help to adapt the CS curricula regarding PCK and will provide the CS education research community with new insights.

## 8. REFERENCES

[1]    Berges, M. et al. 2013. *Developing a Competency Model for Teaching Computer Science in Schools.*

[2]    Krauss, S. and Kunter, M. 2004. COACTIV: Professionswissen von Lehrkräften, kognitiv aktivierender Mathematikunterricht und die Entwicklung von mathematischer Kompetenz. ... *als Strategien der ....* (2004).

[3]    Mishra, P. and Koehler, M.J. 2006. Technological Pedagogical Content Knowledge: A Framework for Teacher Knowledge. *Teachers College Record.* 108, 6 (Jun. 2006), 1017–1054.

[4]    Hubwieser, P., Berges, M., Magenheim, J., Schaper, N., Bröker, K., Margaritis, M., Schubert, S. and L.O. 2013. Pedagogical content knowledge for computer science in German teacher education curricula. ... *Computing Education.* (2013), 95–103.

[5]    Shulman, L. 1986. Those who understand: Knowledge growth in teaching. *Educational researcher.* 15, 2 (1986), 4–14.

[6]    Studienordnung - Inhaltsübersicht: 2003. *http://ddi.uni-paderborn.de/fileadmin/Informatik/AG-DDI/Studium/StO_2004/studienordnung_gymgs_informa tik_2004.pdf.*

[7]    Weinert, F. 2001. *Concept of Competence: A conceptual clarification. In Defining and Selecting Key Competencies.*

# Developing Students' Problem-Posing Skills

Shitanshu Mishra
Indian Institute of Technology Bombay
Mumbai, Maharashtra, 400076, India
shitanshu@iitb.ac.in

## ABSTRACT

Problem posing involves the asking of new questions around a given situation. It is highly desirable that students pose quality problems to address their knowledge deficit and unfold new knowledge. The Ph.D. work discussed in this document aims at devising interventions to develop students' Problem Posing Skills. We anticipate that by the completion of this doctoral thesis we would be able to contribute with a validated assessment instrument to evaluate PP skills, an efficient instructional intervention to develop PP skills, and models of PP strategies that students employ while doing knowledge discovery through Problem Posing in CS applications domain. The research is being carried out in CS applications domain and the target population is engineering undergraduates.

## Categories and Subject Descriptors

K.3.2 [**Computers and Education**]: Computer and Information Science Education – *computer science education.*

## Keywords

Problem Posing; Problem Posing Skills; Instructional Strategies; Exploration Based Learning;

## 1. RESEARCH SITUATION

I am currently a fulltime Ph.D. candidate in the Interdisciplinary Program in Educational Technology at Indian Institute of Technology, Bombay. I have successfully completed the academic credit requirements and enrolled as a fulltime research scholar in teaching assistant category in July 2013, and anticipate that I will graduate in the next 2.5 – 3 years.

As far as my state of research is concerned, I have explored how students pose problems in a semi-structured problem posing (PP) situation [1]. I found seven PP strategies with which students use their prior knowledge, and the given "seed" knowledge to pose questions, (where "seed" knowledge is the content presented to students before they are asked to pose problems around them). Future goals of the research are to devise an assessment instrument to assess students PP skills, and design, implement, and evaluate an intervention which can improve students' PP skills.

## 2. CONTEXT AND MOTIVATION

Human PP is extremely limited in both quantity and quality [2]. PP is an important skill of intelligent inquiry, and is highly useful

*ICER'14,* August 11-13, 2014, Glasgow, Scotland, UK.
ACM 978-1-4503-2755-8/14/08.
http://dx.doi.org/10.1145/2632320.2632333

to enhance learning, and address knowledge deficit. Most people lack this skill and pose very few and shallow problems [3]. According to Graesser, a typical student in a class asks less than 0.2 questions per hour in a classroom [3]. It is not just the quantity of posed-problems by learners, but the quality of posed-problems that also effects learning [3]. It is highly desirable that students pose more and good quality problems [2].

In this way the need for an effective instructional intervention to improve PP Skills in students, becomes very much relevant. To the best of our knowledge, PP (by students) has been explored mostly in domains of Mathematics and Prose Comprehension [4], and no other research has been found that explores PP in CS education research. Moreover, no significant research work has been traced, which uses PP (skills) as an object of instruction.

## 3. BACKGROUND & RELATED WORK

As discussed before the PP research community resides mostly in the Mathematics Education domain [4]. There is literature which talks about PP domain in general, as an instructional strategy, and as an assessment tool. As far as "PP Skills" are concerned, some researchers [5] establish the need for effective strategy for developing PP-Skills. But only a few talk about ways of developing PP skills. For example, in [6], students were given guidelines of what type of problems to pose before performing PP; they found that the quality of problems improves gradually with more and more PP practice. Another research [7] used demonstration of the "What if" strategy of PP, and found improvement in posing problems of "What if" type by the students. The notion of "PP Skills" in these papers is different from our notion of "PP Skills". In existing research of PP Skill development the PP situation [1] considered is either completely structured (problems are generated around a specific problem solving task), or completely open (there are no restriction on PP context). Our notion of PP, on the other hand, involves the generation of new problems (questions/ issues) around a given semi-structured [1] PP situation. We want students to pose such problems, which can help students to explore or unfold new knowledge, around conceptually preceding and/or related seed knowledge, in a given domain.

Therefore the gap in the existing research is three fold: firstly PP has not been found to be explored in CS education research; secondly there is a scarcity of research that aims at improving PP skills; and thirdly there is no research about improving PP skill for semi-structured PP situation, where the PP aims at unfolding new knowledge.

## 4. STATEMENT OF THESIS/PROBLEM

With a broad goal of devising an efficient instructional strategy that could improve students' PP Skills, the broad research question (RQ) is *"How to develop students' PP Skills, where PP refers to the generation of problems leading to exploration or unfolding of new knowledge, in CS applications domain?"* More specific research problems that the research would be answering are:

1. What strategies do students organically use to generate problems to unfold new knowledge around any given seed knowledge?
2. How to assess the goodness of a posed problem?
   a. How to evaluate PP skills of a given student?
3. How to devise an instructional strategy for training students on PP skills?
   a. How could the PP based activities be used as an instructional strategy to develop PP skills?
4. What is the effect of students' PP skills on their learning and motivation in CS applications courses?

## 5. RESEARCH GOALS & METHODS

Following research goals (and research methods) have been identified till now:

(1) *Identifying a range of PP strategies that students employ to generate problems to unfold new knowledge around any given seed knowledge.*

To achieve this goal, I performed a field study, where students were asked to generate problems in a semi-structured PP situation to either propose a new idea, or to unfold new knowledge, or to clarify any muddy points. All generated problems were collected and analyzed using grounded theory based inductive qualitative data analysis method to answer a very vague question: "What do students do during such a PP task?"

(2) *Identifying a goodness metrics to evaluate the PP skill level of any given student.*

To achieve this goal, it is required that we operationalize the PP skills into measurable behaviors. A further literature review and field studies are needed to identify the traits of good problems, and good problem posers.

(3) *Devising an instructional strategy to develop students PP skills.*

Once the goodness measure for problems and PP skills are determined, we will go ahead with iteratively designing and refining the instructional strategy.

(4) *Measuring the effect of the instructional strategy devised in the goal 3.*

After the instructional strategy is devised, we would deploy the strategy in a classroom setting to test for its effects on learning, engagement, motivation, and other affective and learning behaviours.

## 6. DISSERTATION STATUS

To address the first research goal, as mentioned in the previous section, a field study was conducted and problems generated by students were collected and qualitatively analyzed. The aim of the study was to understand how students use their prior knowledge and the seed knowledge (the semi-structured PP situation) to generate new questions. The key finding of this study was that students generated two categories of questions, (i) Clarification, and (ii) Exploratory. To generate exploratory questions, students employed one or more of the seven PP strategies with which they used their prior knowledge, and the seed knowledge and generated new problem in CS application domains (Data

Structures, and AI). These 7 strategies are: Application, Organization, Probe, Comparison, Connection, Variation, and Procedure. The problems generated using these strategies always result in unfolding of some new knowledge. The details of this study have been communicated for publication. The next goal of the research would be to identify which of these strategies are more desirable for generating 'good' problems.

Apart from this study, there are two key publications which were produced while exploring the possibilities in PP domain. One paper talks about a PP based instructional model to teach CS1 [4]. It discusses how the model affects students' learning and motivation. Another study has exploited PP, as an assessment tool to assess the learning in CS1 [8]. I have documented my research work, done till date, in the form of these three publications. In my future work, I will be addressing the goals 2, 3 and, 4 mentioned in the previous section. From the ICER community I hope to gain appropriate research methodology that should be employed to decide 'goodness' measures of PP skills (goal 2). Also, I would like discuss how to approach the design of a new instructional strategy, and what are the related standard research practices.

## 7. EXPECTED CONTRIBUTIONS

One of the key contributions of my research (till date) is the identification of PP strategies to generate exploratory problems in CS applications domain. By the completion of my dissertation, I anticipate that we would have a validated PP skill assessment instrument/ guidelines, and an efficient instructional strategy to improve students' PP skills in CS applications domain.

## 8. REFERENCES

[1] Stoyanova, E., & Ellerton, N. F. (1996). A framework for research into students' problem posing in school mathematics. Tech. in mathematics education. Melbourne: Mathematics Education Research Group of Australia.

[2] Graesser, A., Otero, J., Corbett, A., Flickinger, D., Joshi, A., & Vanderwende, L. (2008). Guidelines for question generation shared task evaluation campaigns. In The QGSTEC Workshop Report, University of Memphis. http://www. questiongeneration.org/

[3] Graesser, A. C., & Person, N. K. (1994). Question asking during tutoring. American educational research journal, 31(1), 104-137.

[4] Mishra, S. & Iyer, S. (2013), Problem Posing Exercises (PPE): An Instructional Strategy for Learning of Complex Material in Introductory Programming Courses. Technology for Education (T4E).151-158.

[5] McComas, W. F., & Abraham, L. (2004). ASKING MORE EFFECIVE QUESTIONS. Rossier School of Education.

[6] Gubareva, A. E. (1992). Teaching by posing questions. Biochemical Education, 20(4), 226-227.

[7] Pintér, K. (2012) On Teaching Mathematical Problem-Solving and Problem Posing.

[8] Mishra, S., Balan S., Iyer, S., & Murthy S. (2014). Innovation and Technology in Computer Science Education (ITiCSE), in press.

# User Groups: Community Collaborative Learning

Daniel deOliveira
University of Kent
School of Computing
Canterbury, Kent, CT2 7NF, UK
dioa2@kent.ac.uk

Ian Utting
University of Kent
School of Computing
Canterbury, Kent, CT2 7NF, UK
I.A.Utting@kent.ac.uk

## ABSTRACT

This work explores the behaviour of User Groups -- the ad hoc, geographically-based, socio-technical networks formed by users of particular software technologies as networking, self-help and mutual learning spaces. We compare these networks to the discussion lists, (general) social networks and communities of practice which these users also inhabit. We situate the work in ideas from Computer Supported Collaborative Learning and Communities of Practice, as well as the ongoing research into discussion list and social network use.

We have postulated a taxonomy of the modes of participation in these User Groups, looking at both the structure of the Groups and the way that participants' engagement varies over time. We are now moving on to validate that taxonomy with a more formalised investigation of participants' interactions and particularly the role that Peripheral Members and Visitors (external speakers and technology evangelists) might play as Weak Ties transferring teaching, learning and innovation between the Groups.

## Categories and Subject Descriptors

K.3.1 [**Computers and Education**]: Computer uses in Education – *collaborative learning*

## General Terms

Informal learning.

## Keywords

Social Networks; Communities of Practice; Discussion Lists; Computer-Supported Collaborative Learning; Weak Ties; User Groups.

## 1. RESEARCH SITUATION

Full time Doctoral student, currently starting the second year, and planning to defend the thesis in December 2015. Models of the structure and dynamics of (Java) User Groups have been created. I am now starting the development of instruments to validate these models, like questionnaires and a personal diary of community learning.

## 2. CONTEXT AND MOTIVATION

A professional suddenly finds himself hard pressed to find a solution to a problem. He looks at various sources of information such as books, magazines, Internet search engines, and friends but no answer meets his needs. Finally he discovers that there is a User's Group - UG where he can meet hundreds of people like him who will be very happy to help him to solve his problem. He tries ... and it works. Cases like this are happening every day, all the time, across the planet. People who do not know each other are collaborating to solve their mutual problems. There are hundreds of Computer Users Groups around the world, supported by IT global enterprises such as Google, Xerox, HP, Oracle, IBM, Microsoft, Cisco, and Red Hat. These groups are informal associations for technical discussion where people feel relaxed and able to exchange knowledge with their peers, in a free and informal way. Working as learning spaces, UGs are helping millions of developers to seek all sorts of information [5]. As an example, Oracle stated (May 2012) that the Java community is composed of nine million Java developers around the world. Every major city has local groups of these corporate social networks, such as the 175 Java User Groups - JUG. Peers are all collaboratively teaching and learning, on a non-formal basis but, how does this learning happen? We aim to investigate this aspect of the work of User's Group, and to base our work in ideas from "Computer-Supported Collaborative Learning" - CSCL, "Communities of Practice" and "Weak Ties".

## 3. BACKGROUND & RELATED WORK

Granovetter (1973, 1983) proposed the idea that weak ties in networks connecting between various groups, breaks the cluster configuration (strong ties), and function as bridges through which circulate innovations. [1] "In strong ties networks, there is a common identity, the dynamics generated in these interactions do not extend beyond the clusters, for this reason, in those networks one seek people with strong references for decision-making. Weak ties are fundamental to spread innovation because they connect us with several other groups, breaking the setting of "isolated islands of clusters" and assuming the configuration of social network. In the same way Zhu (2013) showed that members overlapping participation in other groups are an important factor in the survival of Online Communities. [2] Wenger (1998) defines Communities of Practice - CoP as "[...] a group of people who share a concern, a set of problems or a passion about a topic, deepening their knowledge and expertise in this area by interacting on an ongoing basis." [3] CoP are composed by the Core group (leader, guru, coordinator, moderator, mentor, facilitator), Active members (user, agitator, volunteer, participant) and people doing silent Peripheral participation (lurker). When the space becomes the Internet, a CoP is transformed into a learning Social Network - SN and becomes a mediated knowledge community (as the case of computer corporate UG), because it broadens its scope. Mediated by the Web, the scale of a CoP transformed into a SN can reach millions of members [4]. In "Communities of Practice: a study of Brazilian Java User Groups" Oliveira (2005) showed the relationship between the CoP and the UG, strengthened the role of the leader of these groups and concluded that developers came to UG because they want to learn. These UG are spaces where people feel empowered to search and share knowledge freely with their peers [5]

ICER'14, August 11–13, 2014, Glasgow, Scotland, UK.
ACM 978-1-4503-2755-8/14/08.
http://dx.doi.org/10.1145/2632320.2632334

## 4. STATEMENT OF THESIS/PROBLEM

We understand that, within the scope of learning supported by computers, CSCL covers four areas (or facets) which are of interest of this research, Communities of Practice, Discussion Lists, Social Networks and User Groups. The data obtained so far suggest that the participation model created by Wenger in 2002, for the CoP (where the goal of the group is the practice), is essentially also valid for UGs (where the goal of the group is the community). We have identified four groups that seem to form the structural body of the UG: the Core Group, Active Member, the Peripheral Group and Innovation Vectors (IV) who embody the Weak Ties. The first three are founded in the work of Wenger to the extent that they represent participation in CoP and the concept of IV was a contribution derived from the work of Granovetter (1983) on the transfer of innovation in SN (whose focus is to facilitate people to make contact) and in Discussion Lists (whose purpose is to help people to interact around a topic). These Information Vectors (Weak Ties) are responsible, we suggest, for the dissemination of knowledge within communities, and are a key to understanding the process of learning within the UG.

Our hypothesis is that the external visitors (often company-funded "evangelists" and/or other UG leaders) coming in as technical speakers to community events are responsible for the process of information shared inside the group. Also, peripheral members of one group, when moving between different communities often bring new information, a hot topic discussed in another groups, in a process of cross pollination, making the role of "Bees" to the this UG. Therefore, visitors or members moving freely between UG, without strong relations with the community are the weak ties that bring innovation to the groups, the Innovation Vectors, and consequently improve the process of teaching / learning of their members.

The objectives of the proposed thesis are: (General) - A proposal for modelling computer learning on the Social Networks created/supported by computer corporations, from requirements that have been previously established for the design, planning, implementation and management of User's Group. (OB1) - Identify the learning patterns in these Social Networks; (OB2) - Propose a theoretical framework for characterizing the learning phenomena of these Social Networks; (OB3) - Validate and apply the bases defined previously in computing Users Group.

## 5. RESEARCH GOALS & METHODS

To reach the objective of this research, which is "learning happens in a collaborative environment because the Innovation Vectors bring knowledge to the community", two instruments need to be developed, a questionnaire and a small scale diary, to UG developers who accept support this study. The methodology proposed is a mix of quantitative analysis of data collected from the questionnaire that will inform a qualitative analysis over selective variables identified.

An ethnographic study of the participation in theses communities will be performed, - among the global UG leaders to determine the size of the Core and IV components of their groups, and – among the group members to determine the collaborative process they use to obtain solutions to their technical problems in the UG. Learning is very hard to measure because people participating in any UG have different personal agendas. A very individualized learning process happen however we can measure their behaviour based on their personal declarations. The individual learning behaviour of a UG member can show us that there is a bridge between participation and learning. To address these two points we will need to examine the learning behaviour of members of these communities. Developers around the world who self-identify as UG members will be asked to record their learning experiences in a diary, during three months. The goal is to have them record every learning interaction they had in the previous week which was the result of an interaction with the UG organization (for example, participation in a community meeting, watching a group presentation or interacting with a UG Discussion List) AND/OR a personal social/technical contact with a group member (physical or virtual). Additional interviews by Skype will be conducted for clarification.

## 6. DISSERTATION STATUS

During the first year of this research a number of activities were undertaken. Two questionnaires and interview-based studies have been conducted and a number of other activities undertaken: 1 - the term User Group was defined, 2 - a video presenting the professional and academic motivations of the author related to this work was produced, 3 - a text about the history of the Brazilian Java community was written, 4 - a text analysing the peculiar characteristics of the process of leadership in a UG, 5 - the external entities that influence the structure and the dynamic of the community was identified, 6 - the perceptions and understanding of the UG leaders of the notion of Collaboration were evaluated. A model of the structure and dynamics of UG was created and now need to be validated.

For the second year a study about collaborative learning in an UG, based on the narrative of their members is proposed. To accomplished this task it is necessary to develop and deploy instruments to validate these models; these activities should take next twelve months.

At this stage of the research, only the literature review can be considered reasonably complete; all the work of modelling and conducting the field research still needs to be developed.

## 7. EXPECTED CONTRIBUTIONS

This work will contribute to studies in the CSCL knowledge area, assist User Groups in their mission to better support professional developers in their lifelong learning and enhance the employability of their members in the IT market.

## 8. REFERENCES

[1] Granovetter, M. (1983). The strength of Weak Ties: A network theory revisited. Sociological theory, 1(1), pp. 201-233.

[2] Zhu, H., Kraut, R. and Kittur, A. (2013). The impact of membership overlap on the survival of online communities. In Proceedings of CHI, pp. 281–290.

[3] Wenger, E. (1998). Communities of Practice: Learning, meaning, and identity. Cambridge University Press.

[4] Wenger, E., White, N. and Smith, J. D. (2009). Digital habitats: Stewarding technology for communities. Cpsquare.

[5] Oliveira, D. (2005). Comunidades de Prática: um estudo dos Grupos de Usuários Java brasileiros. Master's thesis, Universidade Católica de Brasília.

# Evaluating Diversity Initiatives in Computer Science: Do They Have Unintended Side-Effects?

Elizabeth Patitsas
University of Toronto
Department of Computer Science
Toronto, Ontario, Canada
patitsas@cs.toronto.edu

## ABSTRACT

In the past three decades, a great deal of effort has been put into trying to improve female participation in computer science. Yet, the numbers in North America haven't budged: women continue to make up 18% of CS majors [3]. Could it be that these well-intentioned efforts to increase diversity are not having the effects we want – or worse, are having subtle, counterproductive effects? Sociologists and social psychologists have documented several ways in which diversity initiatives can be undermined – or even have counterproductive effects. Are these phenomena present in women-in-CS initiatives? In my research, I am interested in evaluating *how* we as a community are working to increase diversity in CS.

## Categories and Subject Descriptors

K.3.2 [**Computers and Education**]: Computers and Information Science Education—*Computer Science Education*.

## Keywords

Diversity, women in computer science

## 1. RESEARCH SITUATION

I am 16 months into my PhD programme in Computer Science at the University of Toronto. I anticipate achieving candidacy next summer (2015), proposing my thesis the summer after (2016) and then defending the summer of 2017. At this point in the programme I am completing the coursework requirement and planning my research.

I have completed two of the seven milestones in my programme: forming my thesis committee, and presenting to them a broad topic on which I wish to do my research. By the time I present at ICER this summer I expect to be done a third milestone, presenting an in-depth literature review of the research in my area.

## 2. CONTEXT AND MOTIVATION

Improving diversity in CS is an important goal; we know that as a community we produce better results when we work in diverse teams, and incorporate many different viewpoints [8]. Many CS departments, companies and other institutions are already working to improve the rates at which women join and remain in the field. Other initiatives exist for underrepresented minorities (URMs).

But despite diversity initiatives existing throughout the field, the numbers haven't been getting much better over time. The intent is there, but not the results. In contrast, scientific fields like biology and medicine were, only a few decades ago, more male-dominated than CS. Yet despite having relatively few diversity initiatives, these fields now include a large number of women.

For my PhD, I will investigate the effects of diversity initiatives in CS. Could it be the case that these initiatives are inadvertently triggering stereotype threat in minorities, or otherwise having counterproductive effects? By giving extra assistance to women and URMs, are we unintentionally reinforcing their otherness, and causing them to feel more out of place?

We know from the social psychology literature that affirmative action programmes can have negative, counterproductive effects [4, 5, 7, 9]. Identifying any negative effects of women-in-CS initiatives, and how they can be mitigated, is important in improving diversity in the field.

## 3. BACKGROUND & RELATED WORK

In my research, I have found it helpful to distinguish between two types of interventions:

- *Explicit interventions* target female students and is explicit in their purpose; examples include societies for women in STEM, events for women, women-only mentorship programmes, and awards for women.

- *Implicit interventions*, which are "stealthy" [10], do not acknowledge the purpose of supporting women and are open to more than women. Examples of implicit interventions include having all students write "self-affirming" essays about their personal values, holding sessions telling all students that intelligence is not fixed, and providing gender-neutral mentoring [10]. These interventions target underlying reasons that women do not major in or stay in STEM, such as stereotype threat, lower self-efficacy, lack of mentorship, and unwelcoming environments. These interventions disproportionately help women, and often also help men.

The research on implicit interventions has been very positive, and has been documented to also help students of colour and students of low socio-economic backgrounds [10]. Benefits have been documented for explicit interventions: students of colour receiving awards for students of colour have higher self-efficacy [6], and women in CS clubs have provided many women with a sense of community in the field.

However, explicit interventions also come with baggage. As a form of preferential selection, the minority group that is targeted is reminded of their minority status. Social psychologists have observed that this can cause stereotype threat [2] as well as decreased self-efficacy [4].

Stigmatization can also be a problem: female professors who receive grants for women in STEM are more likely to have lower self-esteem for only being good enough for the "women's grant" [9], and audit studies of female programmers have found that women associated with affirmative action are viewed as less competent than women not associated with affirmative action [5].

Also of note is a series of studies by Kaiser et al [7]. They described fictional companies to study participants, varying whether the company had a diversity office (or in other studies, had received an award for diversity, or a diversity policy, etc). They then described a fictional individual in the company who had been the victim of discrimination, and asked participants questions about their impressions of the individual and of the company. Through six studies, they consistently found that when a company had a diversity structure, the individual was was viewed as less competent, and their discrimination claim was viewed less seriously.

While we know there *can* be counterproductive effects to explicit interventions, it is not always clear that they will occur in the computer science context. Furthermore, there can be mixed evidence: as noted, awards for students of colour, which may trigger stereotype threat – but they can boost self-esteem, an effect which may dominate.

## 4. PROBLEM, GOALS AND METHODS

Three common explicit interventions in computer science are Women in CS clubs, awards/scholarships for female undergraduates, and mentorship programmes for female undergraduates. I am interested in investigating:

1. Whether these three types of interventions trigger stereotype threat – and for how long. To test this, I plan to expose students to either a women-in-CS mentorship advertisement, a gender-neutral mentorship advertisement, or nothing, before they complete a computer science test. Unlike other stereotype threat studies, I would also like to follow-up with the participants to see how long the effect persists.

2. Whether access to these interventions leads women who are discriminated against to be viewed more harshly. To this end, I plan to perform a replication of Kaiser's studies with an academic computer science context.

3. Whether these interventions reinforce subtyping (a "female computer scientist" is a different mental category than a "computer scientist"). I have yet to design a study to test this.

## 5. DISSERTATION STATUS

At this point in my programme I have been focusing on the theoretical grounding for my research. I've conducted literature reviews of how sociologists evaluate diversity initiatives, the social psychology of preferential selection, and the issues facing women and racial minorities in computer science. A current project of mine is applying a Systems Thinking approach to analysing the different "leverage points" in the educational system for improving the numbers of women in CS.

The next step in my research is to begin collecting data. I have put together two study designs so far. At the consortium, I would like feedback study design, and on the ethical implementation of my stereotype threat study.

## 6. EXPECTED CONTRIBUTIONS

I expect to contribute to the research community a better understanding of why diversity initiatives in CS work (or don't work), and how to improve them.

## 7. REFERENCES

[1] C. Alvarado, Z. Dodds, and R. Libeskind-Hadas. Increasing women's participation in computing at Harvey Mudd College. *ACM Inroads*, 3(4):55–64, Dec. 2012.

[2] R. P. Brown, T. Charnsangavej, K. A. Keough, M. L. Newman, and P. J. Rentfrow. Putting the" affirm" into affirmative action: preferential selection and academic performance. *Journal of personality and social psychology*, 79(5):736, 2000.

[3] N. C. for Women and I. Technology. By the numbers, 2013.

[4] M. E. Heilman and V. B. Alcott. What I think you think of me: Women's reactions to being viewed as beneficiaries of preferential selection. *J. of App. Psych.*, 86(4):574, 2001.

[5] M. E. Heilman, C. J. Block, and P. Stathatos. The affirmative action stigma of incompetence: Effects of performance information ambiguity. *Acad. of Mgmnt. J.*, 40(3):603–625, 1997.

[6] S. Hu. Scholarship awards, student engagement, and leadership capacity of high-achieving low-income students of color. *The Journal of Higher Education*, 82(5):511–534, 2011.

[7] C. R. Kaiser, B. Major, I. Jurcevic, T. L. Dover, L. M. Brady, and J. R. Shapiro. Presumed fair: Ironic effects of organizational diversity structures. 2012.

[8] K. V. Siakas and E. Georgiadou. Empirical measurement of the effects of cultural diversity on software quality management. *Software Quality Journal*, 10(2):169–180, 2002.

[9] M. Van den Brink and L. Stobbe. The support paradox: Overcoming dilemmas in gender equality programs. *Scand. J. of Mgmnt.*, 2013.

[10] D. S. Yeager and G. M. Walton. Social-psychological interventions in education. *Rev. of Ed. Research*, 81(2):267–301, 2011.

# Physical Computing in Computer Science Education

Mareen Przybylla
Department of Didactics of Informatics, University of Potsdam
August-Bebel-Str. 89
14482 Potsdam, Germany
przybyll@cs.uni-potsdam.de

## ABSTRACT

Physical computing covers the design and realization of interactive objects and installations and allows students to develop concrete, tangible products of the real world, which arise from the
learners' imagination. This can be used in computer science education to provide students with interesting and motivating access
to the different topic areas of the subject in constructionist and
creative learning environments. The aim of the doctoral thesis is
to analyze the phenomenon of physical computing in order to
situate possible new contents within the field of computer science
education. It will be analyzed what effects physical computing has
on student's motivation, creativity, learning success, growth in
competences and their understanding of computer science and
computing systems.

## Categories and Subject Descriptors

K.3.2 [**Computers and Education**]: Computer and Information
Science Education – *computer science education.*

## General Terms

Design, Experimentation

## Keywords

Physical Computing, Constructionism, Interactive Objects, Motivation, Creativity, Curriculum

## 1. RESEARCH SITUATION

I am a doctoral student at the University of Potsdam with Prof. Dr.
Andreas Schwill as my advisor. I am designing my own schedule
and am not involved in a larger project or program. I enrolled as a
PhD student in spring 2013 and intend to complete my degree
within three to four years. Until now, I have worked on the theoretical framework of my research. A pre-study for the main research is scheduled for the school year starting in late summer
2014, the main study will be conducted in 2015/16.

## 2. CONTEXT AND MOTIVATION

Physical computing has become increasingly popular in extracur-
ricular computer science education contexts, such as afternoon
workshops or summer camps. In recent years several approaches
have even focused on involving programmable tangible media
into regular computer science classes; England for instance has
even anchored the control or simulation of physical systems in

*ICER'14*, August 11–13, 2014, Glasgow, Scotland, UK.
ACM 978-1-4503-2755-8/14/08.
http://dx.doi.org/10.1145/2632320.2632336

their national curriculum. With physical computing, constructionist learning and typical processes of computer science education
can be brought together in a creative and practical fashion. Students are provided with opportunities to make their own interactive objects and thus to develop concrete, tangible products of the
real world, which arise from their own imagination and that can
be learnt with in many ways. Different physical computing project
ideas are frequently presented at conferences, but they only rarely
reach teachers, even though they regularly express their interest
when introduced to physical computing in teacher training workshops. Thus it is the aim of my work to analyze the phenomenon
of physical computing in the context of computer science education and thereby make it accessible for teachers.

## 3. BACKGROUND & RELATED WORK

Physical computing has received a lot of attention throughout the
last years, especially by non-computer scientists. Among makers
(hobbyists, artists, designers) who use Arduino, the most popular
platform for physical computing at the time, physical computing
is considered as an activity that involves „...prototyping with electronics, turning sensors, actuators and microcontrollers into materials for designers and artists." [1] The term 'physical computing'
was initially used by [2] who wanted to strengthen the role of the
physical body in computing. Others, often in educational settings,
have adapted the term and use it in a wider meaning: they see
physical computing as connecting computers to the physical
world. (e.g. [3]) In English-speaking contexts, more and more
scientific publications devote themselves to the topic. Blikstein
for instance has investigated physical computing kits for their
underlying design principles. [4] In the context of computer science education, only few publications exist that usually focus on a
particular topic area, mostly programming. (e.g. [5])

## 4. STATEMENT OF THESIS/PROBLEM

Despite its potentials for constructionist learning environments,
until now physical computing has not been suitable for classroom
use for many teachers. My work is guided by the hypothesis that
there exists a computer science curriculum based on physical
computing that can be used in two ways: to teach computer science with physical computing or to selectively use physical computing as an entry point to different topic areas of computer science. This curriculum consists of contents to which physical computing can add value, can be used as a tool or can be used as reference. There will also be contents where physical computing
cannot be used to teach computer science. Therefore, it is my aim
to provide the community with a constructionist computer science
curriculum based on physical computing as well as settings, activities and examples for classroom use. To do so, it is necessary to
address the following problems:

- Define physical computing in the context of computer
  science education and situate it content wise

- Identify competences and areas of computer science that are accessible or become irrelevant with physical computing and describe intended mechanisms
- Develop suitable instruments to measure the effects of physical computing in comparison to other approaches

## 5. RESEARCH GOALS & METHODS

In order to achieve the goal of developing a computer science curriculum based on physical computing, the research is guided by the following research questions:

1. How is *physical computing* to be understood in terms of computer science education and classroom teaching?
2. Which new *competences* and *areas of computer science* are accessible and which become irrelevant?
3. Are there *changes in value* (benefits or challenges) to teaching approaches with physical computing as opposed to teaching approaches where non-physical systems are designed?

While initially the first question was pursued mainly by literature review, the findings were influenced by the results of a pilot project and will be further evaluated in school settings. Similarly, for the second question earlier research, university programs, programs by other institutions, textbooks on the wider topic of physical computing and computer science curricula were analyzed and the results are to be verified in practical settings. The third question entails the hypothesis that there are differences to other approaches of teaching and that with physical computing particular intended mechanisms will take place. Those mechanisms (e.g. 'Students will automatically have questions about analog/digital data') need to be validated or falsified with observations, interviews or questionnaires. The main study of the dissertation will explore what benefits physical computing can bring to the classroom by investigating the following research question:

4. Which *effects* does physical computing in computer science education have on students concerning success in learning, growth in competences, motivation, being creative, perception of computer science and computing systems?

This will be the central question of my thesis. To find answers to this question, a study will be conducted in a partner school where physical computing activities will be developed together with teachers according to their particular lesson plans. Instruments to measure success in learning may include tests, quizzes and retrospect interviews. Instruments to measure the development of competences will be competence-oriented tasks. In order to find out about possible changes in students' motivation and creativity, standardized test items will be used in pre-/post-questionnaires, which will also contain test items for qualitative data that give an impression of students' perception of computer science and computing systems.

## 6. DISSERTATION STATUS

Until now I have worked on the theoretical framework of my research. This included a definition of physical computing in the context of computer science education in public schools, the description of typical processes, products and tools and the identification of key competences to be gained with physical computing. [6] Further, I have theoretically developed a syllabus of topics suitable for a constructionist computer science curriculum based on physical computing. In a next step it needs to be investigated, how the powerful ideas that underlie the contents and concepts mentioned in the syllabus can be taught. Technical competences to be gained in this field and competence levels depending on learners' age and grade can then be defined and illustrated with exemplary physical computing activities. In order to later investigate the effects of physical computing activities on learners and how learners are influenced by physical computing activities, a pre-study questionnaire was developed to investigate students' current understanding of informatics devices and their perception of computer science classes. This study was conducted with 115 students in secondary schools in Berlin and Brandenburg who had no physical computing experience with the aim of getting an overall impression of the current situation and of the applicability of the questionnaire. [7] This questionnaire partly needs to be reworked for the pre-study to be conducted during the school year 2014/15. Until then, additional learning scenarios will be developed for different topic areas. Additionally, measurement methods need to be developed in order to investigate the effects physical computing has on students. I hope that during the Consortium I can discuss those measurement instruments and get methodological assistance. The lessons learnt in the preliminary study will then be used to design and conduct the main study during the school year of 2015/16.

## 7. EXPECTED CONTRIBUTIONS

Until now, physical computing has not been suitable for classroom use for many teachers. The further development of the existing construction kit "My Interactive Garden" [8] is supposed to help changing the situation. Curriculum projects will be developed, implemented and evaluated in school, so that in the end the community will be provided with a constructionist computer science curriculum based on physical computing as well as settings, activities and examples for classroom use.

## 8. REFERENCES

[1] M. Banzi, *Getting Started with Arduino*, 2nd Editio. Sebastopol, CA: O'Reilly Media / Make, 2011.

[2] D. O'Sullivan and T. Igoe, *Physical Computing: Sensing and Controlling the Physical World with Computers*. Boston,: Thomson Course Technology PTR, 2004.

[3] S. Libow Martinez and G. Stager, *Invent to Learn - Making, Tinkering, and Engineering in the Classroom*. Torrance, CA: Constructing Modern Knowledge Press., 2013.

[4] P. Blikstein, "Gears of Our Childhood: Constructionist Toolkits, Robotics, and Physical Computing, Past and Future," 2013, pp. 173–182.

[5] K. Qiu, L. Buechley, E. Baafi, and W. Dubow, "A curriculum for teaching computer science through computational textiles," *Proc. 12th Int. Conf. Interact. Des. Child. - IDC '13*, pp. 20–27, 2013.

[6] M. Przybylla and R. Romeike, "Key Competences with Physical Computing," in *Proceedings of Key Competencies in Informatics and ICT 2014*, 2014.

[7] M. Przybylla and R. Romeike, "Overcoming Issues with Students' Perceptions of Informatics in Everyday Life and Education with Physical Computing Suggestions for the Enrichment of Computer Science Classes," in *ISSEP 2014 - 7th Conference on Informatics in Schools: Situation, Evolution and Perspectives*, 2014.

[8] M. Przybylla and R. Romeike, "My Interactive Garden – A Constructionist Approach to Creative Learning with Interactive Installations in Computing Education," 2012, pp. 395–404.

# User Models of Reasoning and Understanding in App Inventor

Mark Sherman
University of Massachusetts Lowell
1 University Avenue
Lowell, Massachusetts, 01854, United States
msherman@cs.uml.edu

## ABSTRACT

Development of instrumentation into MIT App Inventor will allow me to extract patterns of usage, or "trajectories" including working around problems, that programmers employ while working on their projects. These trajectories will be analyzed to develop user models of reasoning and understanding in App Inventor. A comparison study will explore the cognitive differences between blocks-based programming and an equivalent text-based language with identical available high-level abstractions. This work will conclude with a new model of blocks-based cognition, and likely create many recommendations for language development, both visual and textual, and improvements to App Inventor technology and pedagogy.

## Categories and Subject Descriptors

K.3.2 [**Computers and Education**]: Computers and Information Science Education—*Computer Science Education*.

## General Terms

Measurement, Experimentation

## Keywords

Mobile, App Inventor, Instrumentation, Events, CS0, CS1

## 1. RESEARCH SITUATION

I am near completion in the doctoral program at UMass Lowell. I earned my MS here with a research thesis in 2010. I continued immediately into the PhD program, and have qualified as a candidate, so all that remains is my dissertation. My department has strict requirements to propose a dissertation, with a full literature review and the majority of data collection already done. A dissertation proposal is often just 3-4 months before the final defense. I intend to defend a proposal within 6-9 months. I have a breadth of work from the past four years that I am applying to my dissertation, which I will explain below.

*ICER'14*, August 11–11, 2014, Glasgow, Scotland.
ACM http://dx.doi.org/10.1145/2632320.2632340.

My masters research was about how novices (7th and 8th graders) use testing and iteration in engineering problem solving. This was an in-lab experiment on a small cohort of human subjects [6]. But that's a story for another day.

Since my masters, I have worked on a variety of projects. I have taught courses, including our university's CS 1, as a lecturer. I created the material, delivered the lectures, managed the TA's, everything. I have worked on auto-assessment systems for grading coursework, and used that data to do research on their effectiveness [5]. I have built hardware devices, from micro controllers to robotic systems.

Most recently I have been heavily involved with MIT App Inventor, where I work with a multi-institution grant developing and disseminating App Inventor pedagogy. I have put extensive effort into the development of a rubric to assess computational thinking in App Inventor.

## 2. CONTEXT AND MOTIVATION

There exists research on various language for learnability, use in beginning courses, effects on future programming habits, and more. But there is rarely a comparison against graphical programming, specifically blocks. Block programming has grown considerably in recent years, powered by popular beginner languages like Scratch, and more recently, the versatile Blockly library, but there remains little research on their true cognitive benefits, or lack thereof.

Visual languages are well-known for their high degrees of discoverability and reduced syntax, which are arguably beneficial to accessibility for beginners, but there has been little work into the cognitive differences that emerge from learning and working with such languages. The closest such work is [3], that compared Scratch and Logo, which are similar, but do not offer similar interfaces, tools, nor resultant programs.

MIT App inventor is entirely events-based [8]. The strictly event-driven nature of App Inventor changes the way many canonical CS behaviors and concepts are used, and this is also interesting to me.

## 3. BACKGROUND & RELATED WORK

Building instrumentation into a student's programming environment is becoming common, with influences such as [4]. These instruments can snapshot the program as the student writes it, capturing the state and changes, which can expose how the student dealt with various issues they encountered. This sort of instrument is becoming so important, some have developed interfaces to visualize code trajectory data [2].

App Inventor is purely and ruthlessly events-based [8], and very few languages, none of them for beginners, share that property. Events-based programming for beginners has been studied in depth [1, 7], but that work was done without a language that made events as easy and as necessary as App Inventor. Mobile computing provided an impetus to further develop events-based languages, making now the appropriate time to revisit and further the study of events-based programming on learning and programming cognition.

## 4. PROBLEM, GOALS, METHODS

Are there different cognitive processes involved in programming with blocks than text? Are there indicators to the programming and programming learning process that are exposed by working with blocks languages?

More generally, how does a person reason with blocks? Is it different than reasoning with text? Are there advantages or deficits?

To explore this, I will implement instrumentation into MIT App Inventor that will capture the process a person goes through while programming, exposing their "trajectory" through the project.

With this tool, I will be able to develop a grounded-theory code set, apply those codes to the behaviors of a test cohort, and begin to develop models of cognitive interaction with blocks.

I will, in a separate experiment, compare blocks to text directly. A Wellesley College student has developed a text language that is isomorphic to the App Inventor blocks language. This language has full access to the high-level feature abstractions of App Inventor. With equally powerful tools and libraries, a study comparing this text language and this blocks language will be the best and closest isolation of the visual factor yet attempted.

Does the event-based nature of App Inventor have an impact on the user's learning to program? This goal will be treated as part of the programming trajectory analysis.

## 5. DISSERTATION STATUS

I am at the beginning of my dissertation. In this formative stage, I know that the technology I will build is tractable, the science is desirable, and the literature supports my line of inquiry. This is why I feel the doctoral consortium is perfect for me— it is at a time when I will have my foundation complete, but early enough that I can grow and pivot my big ideas.

I will develop the core instrument over this summer, and have the first cohort for experimental data collection participate during this fall semester. (Institutional compliance for human subjects research will be prepared this summer, for fall-semester approval.)

The Fall 2014 cohort will be select sections of college courses using App Inventor, where the instructor will use a research-specific instance of App Inventor with their students which houses my instrumentation. From this data, I will develop the coding protocol, and prepare for subsequent human testing over the winter and spring.

In total, I will have human testing data and analysis complete and analyzed for this time next year, providing for a late summer or autumn defense in 2015.

## 6. EXPECTED CONTRIBUTIONS

Expected contributions include a validation of blocks-based programming, and recommendations for learning with App Inventor. Models of learning for blocks-based programming will be identified, as will the relationship with it and events-based programming.

As a side effect, the instrument will be the core part of an automated, dynamic feedback system for App Inventor. The instrument may also be included in the global deployment of App Inventor, allowing for collection of trajectories of thousands of users, which could then be analyzed using machine learning techniques [4].

## 7. REFERENCES

[1] K. B. Bruce, A. P. Danyluk, and T. P. Murtagh. Event-driven programming is simple enough for cs1. In *Proceedings of the 6th Annual Conference on Innovation and Technology in Computer Science Education*, ITiCSE '01, pages 1–4, 2001. URL: http://doi.acm.org/10.1145/377435.377440.

[2] K. Heinonen, K. Hirvikoski, M. Luukkainen, and A. Vihavainen. Using codebrowser to seek differences between novice programmers. In *Proceedings of the 45th ACM Technical Symposium on Computer Science Education*, SIGCSE '14, pages 229–234, 2014. URL: http://doi.acm.org/10.1145/2538862.2538981.

[3] C. M. Lewis. How programming environment shapes perception, learning and goals: Logo vs. scratch. In *Proceedings of the 41st ACM Technical Symposium on Computer Science Education*, SIGCSE '10, pages 346–350, 2010. URL: http://doi.acm.org/10.1145/1734263.1734383.

[4] C. Piech, M. Sahami, D. Koller, S. Cooper, and P. Blikstein. Modeling how students learn to program. In *Proceedings of the 43rd ACM Technical Symposium on Computer Science Education*, SIGCSE '12, pages 153–160, 2012. URL: http://doi.acm.org/10.1145/2157136.2157182.

[5] M. Sherman, S. Bassil, D. Lipman, N. Tuck, and F. Martin. Impact of auto-grading on an introductory computing course. *J. Comput. Sci. Coll. (CCSCNE)*, 28(6):69–75, June 2013. URL: http://dl.acm.org/citation.cfm?id=2460156.2460171.

[6] M. Sherman, F. Martin, and M. Scribner-MacLean. The role of iteration in the design processes of middle school students. In *Proceedings of the 8th ACM Conference on Creativity and Cognition*, C&#38;C '11, pages 391–392, 2011. URL: http://doi.acm.org/10.1145/2069618.2069711.

[7] L. A. Stein. Beyond objects. In *Educator's Symposium, Conference on Object Oriented Programming Systems, Languages, and Applications, Atlanta, Georgia*, 1997.

[8] F. Turbak, M. Sherman, F. Martin, D. Wolber, and S. C. Pokress. Events-first programming in app inventor. *J. Comput. Sci. Coll.*, 29(6):81–89, June 2014. URL: http://dl.acm.org/citation.cfm?id=2602724.2602739.

# How Can We Improve Notational Expertise?

Alistair Stead
The University of Cambridge
The Computer Laboratory
Cambridge, UK
ags46@cam.ac.uk

## ABSTRACT

The increasing popularity of educational programming languages and renewed emphasis on learning to program in school has led to a situation where students are finding it difficult to make the transition to novice-friendly visual notation to text-based notation. In my work, I investigate the ways in which concepts can be transferred between notations, and how novice programming environments can support users in the acquisition of the necessary notational expertise to competently use text-based notation.

## Categories and Subject Descriptors

K.3.2 [**Computers and Education**]: Computers and Information Science Education—*Computer Science Education*.

## General Terms

Novice Programming, Syntax, Visual Languages, Text Languages

## Keywords

D.2.6 [Programming Environments]: Interactive environments
D.3.1 [Programming]: Languages - Syntax

## 1. RESEARCH SITUATION

I am beginning the third year of a Ph.D. at The University of Cambridge's Computer Laboratory. My background is in Computer Science and Human-Computer Interaction. The areas of my current research are the psychology of programming and computer science education.

I gained confirmation of candidacy by submitting a written proposal and completing an oral defence of my work with internal examiners at the end of my first year and anticipate completing work on my thesis in Spring 2015. In order to graduate, I am required to provide a thesis and complete an oral defence with both an internal and external examiner.

Thus far, I have completed interviews with teachers, developed an novice programming tool called "DrawBridge" to

*ICER'14,* August 11-13, 2014, Glasgow, Scotland, UK.
ACM 978-1-4503-2755-8/14/08.
http://dx.doi.org/10.1145/2632320.2632341.

facilitate my research, and carried out two studies based on the tool. I plan to complete further studies based on an improved iteration of the tool that will include improved assessment methods.

## 2. CONTEXT AND MOTIVATION

Over the past several years there has been a surge in interest and support of learning to program. Programming, or coding, has been lauded as a valuable asset in ones career, a fun hobby, and even an essential of modern-day living. As a result, school curricula are changing emphasis from developing skill with software applications, to focusing on algorithms and programming concepts.

The growing popularity of visual programming environments such as Scratch and Alice, and their use at progressively earlier ages has resulted in a problem faced both in and out of the classroom:- how can novice programmers acquire understanding and expertise of text notation without being obstructed by common barriers to textual programming.

## 3. BACKGROUND & RELATED WORK

In mathematics, as in programming, problems can often be viewed, manipulated, solved and even assessed using more than one suitable representation [6] (for example fractions and decimals). Symbolic manipulation is so commonly used in mathematics that some learners may find it difficult to decouple the manipulation from underlying mathematical concepts. The Computational Thinking (CT) agenda [10], like the "new maths" agenda of the 1960s focuses on the underlying concepts such as problem decomposition and pattern recognition [3], rather than any individual language syntax. Teachers are encouraged to use modelling and simulation to equip students with CT techniques. Resnick argues that in addition to these techniques, to truly think computationally, one must be able to express oneself in a computational medium [9] (p68).

In the psychology of programming field, it is understood that the type of symbolic representation used has implications for its usability [4] and therefore is more or less appropriate depending on the goal of the programmer [7]. Visual notation, such as the block notations used in Scratch and Alice, provide many usability benefits that are suited to novice programmers (for example low levels of error proneness and premature commitment). This is recognised in teaching practice as the "syntax-free" approach [2]. However, the benefits are reduced when transitioning to more conventional text notation where the environment is typically not targeted at novices, and syntax knowledge is required [1] [5]. We think that novices may benefit from the development of notational expertise, which would allow them to master more than one notation, recognise concepts in notation, and translate between notations.

## 4. STATEMENT OF THESIS/PROBLEM

My research question is: To what extent can novice programmers acquire notational expertise by using a multi-representation development environment.

DrawBridge was developed to address this research question. It is a novice programming environment that scaffolds the learning process by allowing users to first interact with concrete representations such as paper and direct-manipulation, before moving to more abstract, symbolic, visual and text representations. DrawBridge moves between representations from left to right, and displays two representations on screen at once, allowing novices to see correspondences between representations, which work bi-directionally.

Current sub-research questions are as follows:

- Does visual notation as a scaffolding mechanism affect students' ability to acquire notational expertise?

- Does the inclusion of concrete representations affect students' ability to acquire notational expertise?

- Does the inclusion of concrete representations affect scaffolding using visual notation?

- Does highlighting correspondences between multiple representations affect acquisition of notational expertise?

## 5. RESEARCH GOALS & STATUS

In my first year, I completed eight semi-structured interviews with teachers from secondary schools in Cambridgeshire. The interviews focused on current teaching practices, tools and assessment in ICT and Computer Science lessons. Each teacher gave suggested feedback and improvements on an early prototype of DrawBridge, which was used to inform subsequent design.

After completion of the DrawBridge implementation, I carried out a between-participants classroom study with 21 Year 7 participants, split into four groups. The study used pre- and post-test assessment and focused on the research sub-questions mentioned previously, including the effect of the order of representations within DrawBridge, and whether the inclusion of concrete representations improved students' ability to understand text syntax. The results of the study were mixed, showing no significant difference between groups with and without concrete representations, and slight improvement between groups using visual representations as scaffolding. As a result, I carried out a second, more focused think-aloud study with three Year 7 participants in a non-classroom setting, the results of which are currently being analysed.

My research goals are to investigate reliable assessment methods for notational expertise with novice programmers. The assessment should be integrated into DrawBridge itself. In order to investigate the most effective assessment method for notational expertise, I plan to carry out a comparative study using several candidate assessment methods, such as Parsons problems. I also plan to carry out a further development iteration of DrawBridge to add an interactive "on-boarding" introduction, the chosen assessment method, and a more complete animation API to give users more incentive to transition from direct manipulation to symbolic representations. With the improved version, I plan to carry out a longer, multi-lesson, classroom-based study to investigate remaining research questions.

I have a work-in-progress paper describing the origins of my work [8], and a paper in review that describes the classroom study.

By participating in the Doctoral Consortium, I hope to gain valuable feedback on work completed thus far, and receive advice on assessment methods targeting syntax understanding and notation translation ability.

## 6. EXPECTED CONTRIBUTIONS

I anticipate that the results of my work will contribute to the computer science education community by providing guidance for notational expertise assessment methods, and by presenting results on these tools in classroom environments. The design of DrawBridge was based on theoretical foundations from psychology of programming research. Features were improved and grounded by teacher feedback. As well as my significant research contributions, I also hope to give guidance to researchers developing new novice tools.

## 7. REFERENCES

[1] Paul Denny, Andrew Luxton-Reilly, Ewan Tempero, and Jacob Hendrickx. Understanding the Syntax Barrier for Novices. *Proceedings of the 16th annual joint conference on Innovation and technology in computer science education - ITiCSE '11*, page 208, 2011.

[2] Sally Fincher. What are We Doing When We Teach Programming? *Frontiers in Education Conference*, 1:8–12, 1999.

[3] Google. What is Computational Thinking, 2013.

[4] T.R.G. Green and M Petre. Usability Analysis of Visual Programming Environments: A 'Cognitive Dimensions' Framework. In *Journal of Visual Languages and Computing*, number January, pages 1–51, 1996.

[5] Sarah K Kummerfeld and Judy Kay. The Neglected Battle Fields of Syntax Errors. *Proceedings of the fifth Australasian conference on Computing education*, pages 105–111, 2006.

[6] David Niemi. Assessing in Mathematics : Problem and Conceptual Understanding Representations, Solutions, Justifications, and Explanations. *The Journal of Educational Research*, 89(6):351–363, 1996.

[7] John F. Pane and Brad A. Myers. Usability Issues in the Design of Novice Programming Systems. (August), 1996.

[8] Alistair G Stead and Alan F Blackwell. Representational Formality in Computational Thinking. In *Psychology of Programming Work in Progress*, number July, 2013.

[9] The National Academy of Sciences. Report of a Workshop of Pedagogical Aspects of Computational Thinking Committee for the Workshops on Computational Thinking. Technical report, 2011.

[10] Jeannette M. Wing. Computational Thinking. *Communications of the ACM*, 49(3):33, March 2006.

# Author Index